# URBAN ECONOMETRICS:
## MODEL DEVELOPMENTS AND
## EMPIRICAL RESULTS

**RESEARCH IN URBAN ECONOMICS, Volume 6**

*Editor:* Robert D. Ebel, *Director, Economics & Finance, Corporate Competitive Strategies, Northwestern Bell, Minneapolis*

# URBAN ECONOMETRICS:
## MODEL DEVELOPMENTS AND
## EMPIRICAL RESULTS

*by*  JAMES B. KAU
*Department of Real Estate and*
*Legal Studies*
*University of Georgia*

C. F. LEE
*Department of Finance*
*University of Illinois*

C. F. SIRMANS
*Department of Finance*
*Louisiana State University*

 JAI PRESS INC.

*Greenwich, Connecticut*                    *London, England*

# CONTENTS

v

## PART III.   URBAN HOUSING PRODUCTION

### PART IV.   URBAN LAND MARKET

## PART V.   URBAN POPULATION DENSITY

## PART VI.   SUMMARY

# List of Figures

# List of Tables

# PREFACE

Urban economics has become a major area of interest in recent years. Economic theory and econometric methods are required for students of urban economics to command the field. The main purposes of this book are to theoretically derive some key urban economics models, to show how these models can be empirically tested using advanced techniques, and to discuss how the theoretical models and empirical results can be used for urban policy decisions.

The book contains sixteen chapters and is divided into six parts. Part I discusses the purposes and structure of the book. Part II investigates the economic theory and econometric methods necessary to understand the theoretical and empirical issues in urban economics. Part III examines the urban housing production process using alternative production functions. Part IV discusses how land values are determined and how spatial variation affects the land market. Part V explores urban population density and structure. Urban policy decisions are also discussed in detail. Part VI summarizes the urban economic models and related empirical results presented in this book. Implications for future research are also indicated. Finally, some of the data used in the empirical results are presented in the Appendices.

There are three possible alternative uses for this book: (i) as a supplemental textbook for urban economics courses, (ii) as a reference book for applied econometrics, or (iii) as a reference book in urban economic research.

This book represents the culmination of research efforts over several years. Many colleagues provided helpful comments. These include: Richard Arnott, Jan Brueckner, John Clapp, Peter Colwell, Douglas Diamond, James Henderson, Carter Hill, John McDonald, Edwin Mills, Richard Muth, N. S. Revankar, and Paul Rubin. Articles based on some of these results appeared in the *Journal of Urban Economics*, *Urban Studies*, *Journal of Regional Science* and *Regional*

*Science and Urban Economics*. Chapter 15 was written in collaboration with S. R. Johnson and Chapter 14 with C. S. Chen. We are grateful to Ms. Harriette Scott for skillfully typing the final draft of the book. We are also grateful to our families for their support.

*James B. Kau*, Athens, GA
*C.F. Sirmans*, Baton Rouge, LA
*C.F. Lee*, Champaign, IL

PART I


INTRODUCTION
_____

Chapter 1

AN OVERVIEW

## 1.1  Introduction

During the past decade there has been an increasing aware-
ness of the importance and implications of changes in urban
spatial structure.  Urban areas are places where market
activities produce much higher employment and residential
densities.  Changes in these densities lead to dramatic
fluctuations in urban land values and structures.  Understanding the source of these changes provides insights that
will lead to a better understanding of the nature of urban
areas.

In the United States land is mainly allocated among
alternative uses by the private market with some government
regulation.  The main focus of this study is to understand
the process of the market place in structuring urban areas.
The market is composed of a large number of producers and
consumers acting in their self-interest making decisions
that in the aggregate determine the size and shape of cities.

Urban areas seem to be characterized by tall closely
spaced buildings that gradually decrease in height from the
urban center.  As one examines the urban area more closely
it becomes clear that the change in structure is not so
smooth.  This variation in structure is as diverse and varied as one could possibly imagine.  Age and height variations are commonly in evidence and outlying areas often become additional concentrations of population.

One of the primary goals of this book is to develop models which help explain urban spatial structure. Essentially one can start with the basic concepts of supply and demand. The demand represents the consumers of housing services. Using the accepted techniques or urban economics to take account of space this study concentrates on changes in the specification of supply. Current models are often unable to explain the variations in urban structure or land values. It is the goal of this study to provide additional techniques and insights that might help explain urban structure.

Much of the unexplained variation in residential development can be explained by using more sophisticated production functions. The standard urban models use the Cobb-Douglas function which has a number of restrictions. All of these restrictions mean less information concerning the reasons for urban change. The major components added by using more complicated production functions are variability in factor substitution and technological change.

The importance of the substitution assumption can be demonstrated in various urban economic problems. For example, the land-rent gradient of a city hinges not only on transportation costs and income but on the shape of the production function within the city. Assuming unitary elasticities of substitution (Cobb-Douglas) for all firms leads to restrictive conclusions on the shape and variability of the rent and population gradients. Also unit elasticity of substitution results in constant relative shares of income received by the factor. The relative shares of income received by capital and land vary within cities which again reflects the inappropriateness of the Cobb-Douglas production function when dealing with the complexities of urban areas.

The major purpose of this book is to present various modifications to the theoretical models or urban spatial structure and to use these new models to develop more reliable measures of changes in population densities, rental values and the elasticity of substitution within and between urban areas. All of which presents a unified description of the determinants of urban land use.

The book is divided into four major sections. Part II has four chapters on theory and methodology. Part III has three chapters on estimating the elasticity of substitution between land and capital and one chapter on the effects of technological change. In Part IV there are three chapters on the urban land markets. Finally, Part V explains population density patterns.

## 1.2  Theory and Methodology

The purpose of this section is to lay the foundation necessary for the determination of urban spatial structure. The foundation of urban spatial structure is mainly determined by the supply and demand of building services and the ease of substitution between land and non-land factors. The models presented in this section are concerned with the urban residential sector. Both production and demand theory are used to derive the conditions for equilibrium in the urban housing market. The production and demand theory used in the analysis of urban structure is similar but not identical to classical economic theory. Therefore, it is important to discuss and compare modern urban economics with the standard economic model.

In Chapter 2 we investigate the theoretical foundation of urban spatial structure by using a Cobb–Douglas production function. The results indicate under what conditions the exponential density gradient is the true specification. These conditions are that the compensated price elasticity of demand for housing must be equal to negative one and the elasticity of substitution between capital and land is unity. Problems related to these necessary restrictive assumptions of the Cobb–Douglas function are presented.

In Chapter 3 the Cobb-Douglas production function will be generalized to allow the elasticity of substitution $(\sigma)$ to be any constant instead of taking on a value of unity. The constant elasticity of substitution (CES) production function allows the elasticity to vary and is used in this chapter. This production function assumes that the elasticity of substitution is constant but is not restricted a priori to any value. It is assumed that changes in relative factor inputs and prices do not alter the elasticity. The value of the elasticity is determined by the underlying technology. The constancy of the elasticity refers to its invariance with respect to changes in relative factor supplies and not to transformations of the underlying technology. These properties of the CES relative to the Cobb-Douglas are as important for studying the production of housing service as for studying the production of other commodities by firms.

Chapter 3 develops a general functional form for explaining the behavior of land rent and population density and examines the effect on this form of assuming the price elasticity for housing equal to minus one and the elasticity of substitution equal to one. Also the supply and demand functions for housing services are derived in detail. It is shown that land rent is negatively related to the elasticity of substitution, whereas population density has a positive relationship.

The results of Chapter 3 suggest that if a Cobb-Douglas instead of CES production function is employed the impact of capital-land substitution is restricted a priori. In addition the impact of the capital-land ratio on the output of housing services is entirely neglected. Therefore, the study of urban land use based upon a Cobb-Douglas is subject to specification bias.

Chapter 4 specifies a variable elasticity of substitution (VES) production function and explores the relationship between the VES and CES production function. The VES function allows the elasticity of substitution, $\sigma$ , to be variable. The elasticity is allowed to change with either output or factor ratios. Since the capital-land ratios within a city significantly change with distance, it may well be important to use a variable elasticity of substitution to inquire into the determination of urban spatial structure. The results suggest that urban planning cannot entirely rely upon the distance variable. The theory indicates that other parameters may play an important part in determining urban structure.

The last chapter in this section presents the econometric techniques necessary for empirically analyzing urban structure. The techniques vary from simple regression to varying coefficient models. First, basic concepts of regression are analyzed. Second, multiple regression is also reviewed in accordance with the concepts of a single regression model. The usefulness of determining the best functional form is examined. Next, by comparing simple and multiple regression, it is shown that using a random coefficient instead of the fixed coefficient of estimating urban structure. Generalized least square models and then possible applications to spatial analysis were discussed along with two alternative switching regression techniques.

## 1.3   The Elasticity of Substitution

Production theory recognizes that the elasticity of substitution between factor inputs can vary depending on the factor input ratio and/or output. Since the ratio of land to non-land inputs varies significantly within urban areas, the a priori restriction of a constant elasticity will lead to specification bias. Chapters 6-9 will provide empirical evidence that using the Cobb-Douglas or CES production function is inappropriate for an urban area.

Chapter 6 examines the elasticity of substitution between land and capital in urban housing production using Revankar's variable elasticity of substitution production function a methodology to select between the CES and VES functional forms is developed. For the CES, the elasticity may be estimated by a long-linear equation with the value of capital-land ratio a function of land rent. The VES is a linear function of the relationship between the intensity of land use and the factor price ratio. A functional form analysis is used to solve the problem of selecting between the VES and CES production functions. The results implied that a more correct specification of this relationship would be through the use of a VES production function. Using the VES function, a range from 0.95 to 0.66 was indicated for the elasticity of substitution.

In Chapter 7 the variable elasticity of substitution (VES production function is expanded upon to derive an urban land use model and to investigate the impact on urban structure of a changing elasticity of substitution of land for capital. This chapter also estimates the elasticity of substitution for multi-family housing. The results indicate again that the elasticity varies with distance and that using a Cobb-Douglas or CES to derive a density gradient will result in biased estimates. A VES production function produces a density-gradient function which decreases at a numerically faster rate with respect to distance. The evidence also suggests that city planning cannot entirely rely upon the distance variable. The evidence suggests that other parameters may play an important part in determining urban spatial structure. The variation of the elasticity of substitution indicates that these constraints affect the variation of population density with respect to distance. The results conform other evidence that the capital-land ratio can be taken as a proxy for measuring the impact of technological change and the effect of past development on future land use.

Both Chapters 6 and 7 demonstrated the usefulness of the VES production function for the study of urban spatial structure. The VES was used to obtain estimates of the elasticity. In all cases these elasticity estimates were for a particular region and were aggregated for that region. The purpose of Chapter 8 is to provide evidence on exactly how the elasticity of substitution varies over time and space. There are a number of reasons for the elasticity of substitution to vary. The capital-land ratios are clearly not the same for each region. Firms producing urban structure may have significantly different production functions relative to output. Furthermore, technological limitations due to differing institutional or informational constraints will alter the elasticity of substitution. The results are conclusive, the elasticity varies significantly over time and space. To indicate that a single estimate exists is to fail to understand the economic adjustment mechanism of production to variations in technology and relative prices.

Chapter 9 using the procedures developed by Revankar measured the presence of technical change in single-family housing production. Using the VES function, tests were performed on the elasticity of substitution and on neutral and non-neutral technical change. The evidence indicates that the cities examined experienced significant neutral and non-neutral technical progress. The results indicate that productivity changes have occurred in the housing sector at a greater rate than in other sectors of the economy. This suggests that rising prices in housing are due to changes in factor prices not to the lack of productivity.

## 1.4 The Urban Land Market

This section studies the determinants and patterns of urban land values. Using historical data for Chicago a thorough analysis of the functional forms, the price elasticity and the rate of return is conducted.

Chapter 10 provides evidence on the functional form of the relationship between land values and distance from the city center. Statistical transformation procedures developed by Box and Cox are used to help determine the price elasticity of demand for housing services. A functional form parameter is introduced to test whether the negative exponential function provides an accurate description of land value patterns. The functional form parameter can also be used to determine the price elasticity of housing demand. The result of Chapter 10 indicates that the price elasticity for housing shifted from elastic to unitary elasticity of demand. The negative exponential form proved to be incorrect in four of the six years tested. The generalized rent gradient derived in this paper indicates that the elasticity of rent with respect to distance is a function not only of distance but also of rent. Such a result may have important implications for analyzing the impact of historical rental patterns on current rates.

Chapter 11 examines the price elasticity of demand for residential site for 31 urban areas in the United States

over the time period 1966 to 1978. Such an examination allows an understanding of how the price elasticity has
changed over time in these areas. Using the interurban estimates of the elasticity of substitution from Chapter 8,
the relative share of land, and assuming that the elasticity of demand for housing services and the elasticity of
supply of capital inputs are constant across housing areas,
estimates of the demand price elasticity for land were made
for 31 FHA housing market areas over the period 1966 to
1978. These estimates indicate an inelastic demand for residential sites in all housing areas for all time periods.
In general, the demand for land was less inelastic in the
later time period.

Chapter 12 is concerned with the rate of return on
land. There has been a significant movement toward tangible assets such as land in recent years. The model uses a
generalized least squares (GLS) estimator to obtain a mean
and the best linear unbiased predictor of the rate of return. Overall, the results indicate no risk premium for
land relative to bonds. The insignificant risk-premium and
the significant net revenue of holding land would indicate
that land is not a risk premium asset relative to bonds.
The evidence presented in this chapter indicates that the
efficient market hypothesis might well apply to real estate
investments. The same data is also used to examine the variations in the rate of return over space. There was significant variation in the rate of return over space.

## 1.5  Urban Population Density

This last major section of the book concentrates on population densities. The spatial pattern of population densities is important in urban economic analysis. Changing
population densities influence the intensity of demand for
municipal services and the design of transport systems.

The main purpose of Chapter 13 is to examine the functional relationship between the population density and distance. A functional form parameter is used to test whether
the negative exponential function accurately describes the
density-distance relationship. In addition the functional

form parameter can be used to test whether the price elasticity of demand for housing services is minus one. The data show that the exponential function is in 50% of the cases not the appropriate specification. Evidence also suggests that where the exponential function is inappropriate and the functional form parameter positive, the price elasticity of demand for housing is greater than minus one. The results also indicate that functional forms other than exponential should be considered.

One of the implications of Chapter 13 is the rejection of the negative-exponential function. The main purpose of Chapter 14 is to investigate the stability urban structure thus providing insights into the stability of the density gradient. Three econometric techniques are used. First a Goldfeld and Quandt F-statistic is used to detect the possibility of heterstochastic behavior of the residuals. Second a shifting regression technique is used to detect the possibility of structural changes in the density gradient within an urban area. Third two random coefficient methods are used to detect the stochastic behavior and structural changes in the density gradient. This procedure would capture any changes due to population shifts as transportation routes. Using all three techniques one finds significant structural shifts in all cases. In general, the ordinary least squares density gradient estimates have overestimated the impacts of transportation cost on the population density of an urban area and understated the importance of other urban factors.

Chapter 15 uses a varying coefficient model (VCM) to expand the usefulness of the exponential density gradient. The VCM is a method for introducing city and inter-city specific variables into the study of urban structure. A major advantage of the VCM is that it permits the introduction of such variables while retaining an interpretation which can be reconciled with the body of theory justifying the use of the exponential functional form. This facilitates comparisons of results obtained by applying the VCM with the massive empirical literature on urban density functions. In fact, most estimated density functions are but special costs of the VCM with a polynomial structure relating the density function coefficients to the socioeconomic conditioning variables.

Application of the VCM provided a number of results. First, the apparent questions about the appropriateness of the exponential functional form and specification errors associated with the omission of city and inter-city variables can be handled within the context of the VCM framework. Second, the results show that the conditioning variables reflecting transport mode, age of city, household income, and population can be used to provide explanations of structural differences between cities and inter-cities areas. Of these the most interesting relate to income, transport mode and density trade-offs.

The most important results from the application of VCM concern the use of the urban density function as a tool for policy analysis and projection. In the past, empirical work on urban density functions has been largely descriptive. The VCM expands the application for the density function.

PART II


THEORY AND METHODOLOGY

## Introduction

The purpose of this section is to lay the foundation necessary for the determination of urban spatial structure. Chapter 2 presents a simple Cobb-Douglas demand and supply model of urban residential land used developed by Mills. The model provides the theoretical foundations necessary in the understanding of urban spatial structure. Besides providing the general framework the model gives insights into such problems as what conditions are required to obtain an exponential density gradient. Chapters 3 and 4 expand the Mills' model by changing the supply side of the model. Chapter 3 analyzes the benefits of using constant elasticity of substitution (CES) production functions whereas Chapter 4 explores the implicatins of a variable elasticity of substitution (VES). Both Chapters 3 and 4 provide the groundwork for future empirical studies presented later in the book. Chapter 5 presents a brief review of the types of econometric techniques used through-out the book. It is not intended as a self-contained study of econometrics but instead will provide information into the types of techniques useful for urban studies and the sources where additional material can be found.

Chapter 2

THE FOUNDATIONS OF URBAN SPATIAL STRUCTURE

## 2.1  Introduction

Urban areas are places where large amounts of labor and capital are combined with small amounts of land in producing goods and services.  Intensive development of central cities is another way of saying that the ratio of non-land to land inputs is greater relative to other areas.

The foundation of urban spatial structure is mainly determined by the supply and demand of building services, the ease of substitution between land and non-land factors, and the determination of optimal city size.  The model presented in this chapter is concerned with the urban residential sector.  Both production and demand theories are used to derive the conditions for equilibrium in the urban housing market.  The production and demand theory used in the analysis of urban structure is similar but not identical to classical economic theory.  Therefore, it is important to discuss and compare modern urban economics with the standard economic model.  It is well-known that Muth (1969) and Mills (1981) have derived the basic theoretical foundations for urban economics.  Hence, this chapter will draw upon both Muth and Mills' work with discussion on Arnott (1980), Brueckner (1980, 1982) and Wheaton's (1982) dynamic urban model.

This chapter is divided into six sections. Spatial equilibrium will be explored in Section 2.2. The production function used in the urban economic theory will be discussed in Section 2.3. In Section 2.3 explicit and implicit production functions and the elasticity of substitution between land and non-land factors are covered. Section 2.4 will present Mills' simplified mathematical model of urban structure and its solutions. Also the limitations of Mills' model will be discussed. Possible extensions of Mills' model will be explored in Section 2.5. Section 2.6, the intertemporal models or urban development derived by Arnott, Brueckner and Wheaton are discussed and reviewed. Section 2.7 will present the summary and concluding remarks.

## 2.2 Determinants of Locational Equilibrium

If commuting cost depends only on the distance between place of residence and the city center, it follows that land rent and the intensity of land use also depend on distance. The implication is that all the land u miles from the center commands the same rent and is used with the same capital-land ratio. Thus, distance becomes a very important variable in the study of urban structure.

It is assumed that housing services are produced with land $[L(u)]$ and capital $[K(u)]$, u distance from the city center. The implicit production function can be defined as $Xs(u) = f(K(u),L(u))$. Examples of explicit production functions are Cobb-Douglas, constant elasticity of substitution (CES), variable elasticity of substitution (VES), and transcendental logarithmic. The Cobb-Douglas production function is explored in this chapter. The other three production functions are used in Chapter 3, 4, and 5. One of the major differences among these production functions is the behavior of the elasticity of substitution. This elasticity is examined for each of the production functions.

One of the unique features of urban economics relative to nonspatial consumer behavior theory is the choice of location. The most general way to introduce location into the model would be to include distance (u) in the utility function. It could then represent all the subjective costs of commuting, such as time forgone from their activities, fatigue, strain, and boredom. Therefore the distance variable u is an additional dimension in urban spatial structure analysis. This unique feature of urban analysis means that urban spatial analysis is a relatively more involved application of micro-economic analyses.

Finally, city size is the other unique factor in the determination of locational equilibrium. Henderson (1974) has using the Cobb-Douglas production function, determined optimal city size. Upton (1981) has derived a general equilibrium model of city size. However, Upton does not introduce the site-specific factors into locational equilibrium.

## 2.3  The Elasticity of Substitution for Factor Inputs

One of the important parameters for a production function is the elasticity of substitution. In urban economics, the main factor inputs for producing housing service are the capital ($K(u)$) and land ($L(u)$), u distance from the center. The implicit form of the production function for housing services Xs, can be defined as Xs = $f(K(u), L(u))$. In this section the basic definition of the elasticity of substitution for urban factor inputs is explored. When the ratio of prices of two inputs changes, the cheaper input will be substituted for the more expensive input. The extent to which one input will be substituted for the other can be measured by the concept of the elasticity of substitution. The elasticity of substitution, $\sigma$ , may be defined as the ratio of the relative change in the least-cost input combination to the relative change in the price ratio while total production remains constant. If the least-cost combination of two input factors is capital K and land L, and their price ratio is n/r, then the elasticity of substitution can be defined as

$$\sigma = \frac{\text{relative change in K/L}}{\text{relative change in n/r}}$$

$$= \frac{\dfrac{d(\frac{K}{L})}{K/L}}{\dfrac{d(\frac{n}{r})}{n/r}} = d\left(\frac{K/L}{n/r}\right) \cdot \frac{n/r}{K/L} \qquad (2.1)$$

The elasticity of substitution coefficient will lay on an interval $0 \leq \sigma \leq \infty$.

The elasticity of substitution ($\sigma$) for the Cobb-Douglas function is unity, the $\sigma$ for the constant elasticity of substitution (CES) function, is a constant, and the $\sigma$ for the variable elasticity of substitution (VES) function is a function of the capital/land ratio.

### 2.4 The Cobb-Douglas Model of Urban Structure

Application of Cobb-Douglas production in the analysis of urban structure is discussed in this section. Applications of the CES and the VES production function in urban economics will be explored in Chapter 3 and 4 respectively.

#### 2.4.1. The Theoretical Foundation of Urban Structure: The Mills Model

Using the Cobb-Douglas production function, the output of housing services Xs(u), depends on the inputs of land and capital employed at u distant from the city center in the following way:

$$Xs(u) = AL(u)^{\alpha} K(u)^{1-\alpha} \qquad (2.2)$$

where A and $\alpha$ are constants, A is a scale parameter and is the distribution parameter. In addition, Equation (2.2) assumes constant returns to scale.

If both input and output markets are perfectly competitive, the firms will use the amount of inputs that equate the value of marginal product to input rental rates at each u. If the market for housing capital is national, the rental rate on capital is independent of both distance, u, and the amount used in the entire urban area. Land rent r(u) and the price for housing services p(u) are determined by the model. Both depend on u.

Following Mills (1981), other equations required to define a simplified mathematical model of urban structure are developed in this section.

If Equation (2.2) is differentiated, it is seen that the marginal products of land and capital are

$$MP_{L(u)} = \alpha AL(u)^{\alpha-1}K(u)^{1-\alpha} = \alpha Xs(u)/L(u)$$

and

$$MP_{K(u)} = (1-\alpha)AL(u)^{\alpha}K(u)^{-\alpha} = (1-\alpha)Xs(u)/K(u)$$

Therefore the equations relating the value of the marginal product (VMP) of each factor to their rental rates are

$$\frac{\alpha p(u)Xs(u)}{L(u)} = r(u) \tag{2.3}$$

and

$$\frac{(1 - \alpha)p(u)Xs(u)}{K(u)} = n \tag{2.4}$$

If Equations (2.3) and (2.4) are multiplied by their respective input amounts and divided by p(u)Xs(u), they show that the ratio of each input's renumeration to total revenue equals the input's exponent in Equation (2.2). These ratios are the shares of the factors in housing rental revenues; hence, $\alpha$ is called the distribution parameter. The value of $\alpha$ determines the distribution of housing rental revenues between the two inputs. Since the exponents in Equation (2.2) add to one, competitive renumeration of land and capital exhausts total revenue, thus verifying the Wicksteed-Wicksell theorem. A typical house may be worth four times the land it occupies, which suggests that $\alpha$ might be about 0.2.

Equation (2.2) can be generalized to allow a nonconstant return to scale case as

$$Xs(u) = A \ L(u)^{\alpha} K(u)^{\overline{\beta}} \qquad (2.5)$$

Equation (2.5) will not be a constant return type of production function unless $\alpha + \overline{\beta} = 1$. If $\alpha + \overline{\beta} > 1$, then it is an increasing return to scale type of production function; if $\alpha + \overline{\beta} < 1$, then it is a decreasing return to scale type of production function. If, for example both input and output markets are perfect and returns to scale are constant, optimal city size cannot be obtained.

It is assumed that all workers receive the same income w, determined outside the model, and that all have the same tastes. The demand function for housing services per worker living at u, xd(u), is assumed to be

$$xd(u) = Bw^{\theta_1} p(u)^{\theta_2} \qquad (2.6)$$

where B is a scale parameter, and depends on the units in which housing services are measured. The terms $\theta_1$ and $\theta_2$ are the income and price elasticities of demand for housing, as can be verified by computing the elasticities from Equation (2.6). Unlike other demand functions, Equation (2.6) assumes the elasticities to be constant, and has been used in many applied studies of demand theory. Housing per worker depends on u, as Equation (2.6) indicates. Housing is not an inferior good; hence, $\theta_1 > 0$. The housing demand function slopes downward, hence $\theta_2 < 0$. Xd(u), total housing demand at u, is housing demand per worker multiplied by N(u), the number of workers living at u:

$$Xd(u) = Xd(u)N(u) \qquad (2.7)$$

In equilibrium, housing demand and supply must be equal at each u:

$$Xd(u) = Xs(u) \qquad (2.8)$$

In addition, it is assumed that thet impact of commuting cost can be expressed in an equation written as

$$P'(u)xd(u) + T = 0 \qquad (2.9)$$

Here $p'(u)$ is the slope of $p(u)$, and T is the cost of commuting. Equation (2.9) says that families are unable to increase utility by moving their households if the change in the cost of housing from a move is just offset by the change in commuting cost.

In discussing the sufficient conditions for negative exponential population densities, Brueckner (1982) argued that the definition of w defined by Mills (1981) is not exactly correct. Based upon Muth (1969, chapter 4), Brueckner suggested that a disposable income (w-T) instead of w should be used. Then the price elasticity $\theta_2$ as defined in Equation (2.6) should be redefined as the income compensated price elasticity. Finally Equation (2.9) has implicitly assumed that the cost of commuting is linearly related to the distance from the central of business district (CBD). This assumption is not necessarily applicable to every SMSA. For example, in a multi-centered city, the commuting cost will not necessarily be linearly related to distance from the CBD. Griffith (1981) has carefully discussed the issues relating to a model of urban population density in a multi-centered city. In addition, both Richardson (1977) and White (1977) have questioned the specification of the negative exponential density gradient model which will be discussed in the next section.

It has been assumed that $\phi$ radians of land are available for housing at each u, so that $\phi u$ is the length of the semicircle available for housing u miles from the city center. Land used for housing cannot exceed what is available, and no available land can be left unused out to the edge of the urban area. Thus

$$L(u) = u\phi \qquad (2.10)$$

It is assumed that nonurban uses of land command a rent $\bar{r}$. Therefore, the urban area can extend only as far as households can bid land away from nonurban uses. Thus, the distance from the center to the edge of the urban area is $\bar{u}$ miles, where

$$\bar{r(u)} = \bar{r} \qquad (2.11)$$

Finally, the land available for housing must house all N workers in the urban area. If N(u) workers live u miles from the center, the total number of workers in the urban area is the sum or integral of N(u) for values of u from $\underline{u}$ to $\bar{u}$, that is

$$\int_{\underline{u}}^{\bar{u}} N(u)du = N \qquad (2.12)$$

The model is now complete. The first eight equations relate the eight variables Xs(u), L(u), K(u), p(u), r(u), xd(u), Xd(u), and N(u) at each value of u. Their solution provides the value of each variable at each u between $\underline{u}$ and $\bar{u}$. Equation (2.9) contains a derivative of p(u) with respect to u, a differential equation, its solution requires a predetermined value of the variable at some u. It is shown below how Equation (2.9) can be expressed as a differential equation in r(u). Equation (2.10) then provides the required value of r(u) at $\bar{u}$, known as an initial condition for the differential equation. Finally, Equation (2.12) can be solved for the variable $\bar{u}$.

Once the model is solved, it shows a complete picture of the housing sector of the urban area. For each value of u, it gives land rent and the rental rate of housing services. From the solution for K(u) and L(u), it is easy to compute the capital land ratio at each u. From the solution of N(u), population density can be computed at each u.

## 2.4.2. Solution of the Model

The land-rent function is the key to the foregoing model. Once it has been found, all the other variables can be calculated easily. The first step in solving r(u) is to derive a well-known relationship between input and output prices for the Cobb-Douglas production function. Solving Equations (2.3) and (2.4) for $L(u)$ and $K(u)$ gives

$$L(u) = \frac{\alpha p(u)Xs(u)}{r} \qquad K(u) = \frac{(1 - \alpha)p(u)Xs(u)}{n}$$

Substituting these expressions for $L(u)$ and $K(u)$ in Equation 2.2 and rearranging terms gives

$$p(u) = [A\alpha^{\alpha}(1 - \alpha)^{1-\alpha}]^{-1}n^{1-\alpha}r(u)^{\alpha} \qquad (2.13)$$

Equation (2.13) indicates that $p(u)$ is proportionate to $r(u)$ raised to a power between zero and 1. Thus, housing prices are high wherever land rents are high, but housing prices rise less than proportionately with land rents because of factor substitution. If $\alpha$ is 0.2, then a 10 percent rise in land rent will lead to a two percent rise in housing prices.

The derivative of Equation (2.13) with respect to $u$ is

$$p'(u) = A^{-1}\left(\frac{\alpha n}{1 - \alpha}\right)^{1-\alpha}r(u)^{-(1-\alpha)}r'(u) \qquad (2.14)$$

where $r'(u)$ is the slope of $r(u)$. Now, substitute Equation (2.6) for $xd(u)$ in Equation (2.9), substitute Equation (2.13) for $p(u)$ and Equation (2.14) for $p'(u)$ and collect terms. We obtain

$$E^{-1}r(u)^{\beta-1}r'(u) + T = 0 \qquad (2.15)$$

where $E$ and $\beta$ stand for collections of constants,

$$E^{-1} = \alpha Bw^{\theta_1}[A\alpha^{\alpha}(1 - \alpha)^{1-\alpha}]^{-(1+\theta_2)}n^{(1-\alpha)(1+\theta_2)}$$

and

$$\beta = \alpha(1 + \theta_2)$$

Equation (2.15) expresses the differential Equation (2.9) in terms of $r(u)$. Using the initial condition of Equation (2.11), the solution is

$$r(u) = [\bar{r}^{\beta} + \beta TE(\bar{u} - u)]^{1/\beta} \qquad \text{if } \beta \neq 0 \qquad (2.16)$$

and

$$r(u) = re^{TE(\bar{u}-u)} \qquad \text{if } \beta = 0 \qquad (2.17)$$

In Equation (2.17), the term e is the base of the natural logarithm. This equation therefore indicates that, when $\beta$ is zero, land rent decreases exponentially as u increases. Both equations indicate that r(u) equals $\bar{r}$ when u equals $\bar{u}$. It can be seen from the definition of $\beta$ that, $\beta$ equal zero, and Equation (2.17) applies, when $\theta_2$ is equal to -1. Empirically, if $\theta_2$, the price elasticity of demand for housing, is approximately -1, the exponential function [Equation (217)] should therefore be a good approximation of urban land-rent functions. The term $\beta$ is positive if $\theta_2 > 1$, that is, if housing demand is price-inelastic. Regardless of the sign of $\beta$, r(u) is steep at small value of u and flat at large values of u.

Equations (2.16) and (2.17) contain the variable u, representing the radius of the urban area. So far, Equation (2.12) has not been used and u has not been computed. Using the equilibrium condition of Equation (2.8), Equation (2.7) can be written:

$$N(u) = \frac{Xs(u)}{xd(u)} \qquad (2.18)$$

Taking the ratio of Equation (2.3) to Equation (2.4), K(u) can be expressed in terms of L(u):

$$K(u) = \frac{1-\alpha}{\alpha n} r(u)L(u) \qquad (2.19)$$

Now substitute this expression for K(u) in Equation (2.1). The result is

$$Xs(u) = A\left(\frac{1-\alpha}{\alpha n}\right)^{1-\alpha} r(u)^{1-\alpha} L(u) \qquad (2.20)$$

Substitute Equation (2.13) for p(u) in Equation (2.6). Then, in Equation (2.7) substitute Equation (2.6) for xd(u) and Equation (2.20) for Xs(u). Rearranging terms gives

$$\frac{N(u)}{L(u)} = Er(u)^{1-\beta} \qquad (2.21)$$

If both sides of this equation are multiplied by $L(u)$, Equation (2.10) is substituted for $L(u)$, and the result is integrated from $\underline{u}$ to $u$, an expression for the left-hand side of Equation (2.12) results. Equating it to N provides the equation from which $\underline{u}$ can be calculated. The result, however is cumbersome and so is not presented here.

Equation (2.21) shows how the number of resident workers per square mile varies with u. Except for a multiplicative factor equal to the reciprocal of the labor force participation rate, it is the same as population density, and so will be referred to as "population density" from here on. Equation (2.21) expresses a remarkable result; population density is proportionate to land rent raised to the power $1 - \beta$. The term $1 - \beta$ must be positive, since $\theta_2$ is negative. Thus, as would be expected, population density is high wherever land rent is high. More important, if $\beta = 0$, so that Equation (2.17) applies, population density is proportionate to land rent and therefore declines exponentially with u just as land rent does. Exponential functions have been used in many applied studies of urban population density and have been found to fit the data very well. Thus, Equation (2.21) provides a link between theory and observation.

A universal conclusion of urban population-density studies is that density functions become flatter through time. Many writers have hypothesized that increasing incomes and falling commuting costs have caused the density function to flatten. The mathematical model here shows that this hypothesis is correct. The population density function of Equation (2.21) will be flatter, the larger is the coefficient of u in Equation (2.16) or (2.17; that is, the closer is the coefficient to zero. Both increases in w and decreases in T flatten the density function by increasing the coefficients of u in Equations (2.16) and (2.17).

It is easy to see that finding r(u) is the key to solving the mathematical model. Many of the other variables have already been expressed as functions of r(u); the term p(u) can be calculated from Equation (2.13); the term L(u) is given by Equation (2.10); the term Xs(u) can be calculated from Equation (2.20); and the term N(u) can be calculated from Equation (2.21).

## 2.5  Generalizations of the Mills Model

The basic urban structure model developed in Section 2.4 was taken from Mills (1981). Throughout our book the Mills model is expanded upon both theoretically and empirically. Using the basic relationships developed by Mills (1981), the implications of the CES and VES functions are explored. Also a number of generalized empirical studies are developed to investigate urban structure. In this section we will briefly review two of these generalizations.

### 2.5.1  Derivation of the Generalized Functional Form

Kau and Lee (1976b,c) demonstrated that Equation (2.16) can be rewritten as,

$$\frac{D(u)^{\frac{\beta}{1-\beta}}-1}{\frac{\beta}{1-\beta}} = \frac{(Er^{-\frac{1}{1-\beta}})^{\frac{\beta}{1-\beta}}-1}{\frac{\beta}{1-\beta}} + (1-\beta)TE^{\frac{\beta}{1-\beta}}(\bar{u}-u) \qquad (2.22)$$

It can be shown that Equation (2.22) will become Equation (2.17) when $\beta$ approach zero. Let $\beta/1-\beta$ be equal to $\lambda$, then Equation (2.22) will reduce to,

$$\frac{D\lambda(u)-1}{\lambda} = \frac{[(C^{\lambda}-1)}{\lambda} + \gamma\bar{u}] - \gamma u \qquad (2.23)$$

where $C = Er^{-\frac{1}{1-\beta}}$, $\gamma = (1-\beta)TE^{\frac{1}{1-\beta}}$. Since there exist only two observable variables, D(u) and u in Equation (2.23), it can be written as

$$\frac{D\lambda(u)-1}{\lambda} = D_0 - \gamma u \qquad (2.24)$$

where $D_0 = [\dfrac{(C^{\lambda}-1)}{\lambda} + \gamma\bar{u}]$.

Equation (2.24) belongs to one of the cases that Box and Cox (1964) have derived for determining the true function form. If $\lambda$ approaches zero, then Equation (2.24) will become

$$\log D(u) = \acute{D_0} - \gamma u \qquad (2.25)$$

where $\acute{D_0} = \log C + TE\bar{u}$

This implies that the negative exponential function is only a special case of Equation (2.24); therefore Equation (2.24) can be regarded as a generalized functional form to be used to determine the true relationship between population density and distance in a SMSA.

Theory and empirical results of housing demand functions have been subject to significant research in the last two decades. Mayo (1981) has reviewed theoretical and empirical results related to Equation (2.6). He concluded that the price elasticity of demand for both renters and owners is generally larger than $-1.9$. This implies that the generalized functional form as indicated in Equation (2.24) is an important specification in estimating the density gradient.

### 2.5.2  Problems with the Model

There are two implications associated with the results developed in this section and the previous section; (1) if the demand elasticity for the housing service is not equal to negative one, then the relationship between population and distance is no longer a negative exponential. Therefore, the normal OLS regression technique is no longer suitable for estimating the density gradient for a SMSA. The Box and Cox's (1964) functional form technique, which will be used to estimate the density gradient associated with Equation (2.24) will be explored in Chapter 5; (2) distance is essentially used as a proxy of transportation costs, and some other important characteristic variables such as income and race have not been used to describe the population

density distribution of a SMSA. Therefore, using such models as developed in Section 2.4 to empirically determine
urban structure may well be subject to the problems of measurement and specification errors. These issues will be
explored in Chapter 5.

### 2.5.3. Problems of Using Cobb-Douglas Production

It is well-known that the Cobb-Douglas production
function assumes that the elasticity of substitution between capital and land is unity. This kind of restrictive
assumption can bias the results. Theoretical problems of
using Cobb-Douglas production function instead of other
more general production function are discussed in Chapter
3.

Essentially Chapter 3 demonstrates in a theoretical
fashion that variations in the elasticity of substitution
will have significant impact on the shape of the
production-isoquant and thus affect urban structure. The
solution to this bias, that is a solution to the problem of
using a Cobb-Douglas, is to use the CES and VES production
functions. This is demonstrated later.

### 2.6 Growth Models: A Brief Review

The Muth and Mills' models discussed in the previous
sections are based upon static theory of residential urban
location and land use. This approach assumes perfect
molleability of capital and ignores growth and the durability of housing and urban infrastructure. To reduce
these weaknesses, Arnott (1980), Brueckner (1980), Wheaton
(1982) and others have developed urban growth models.

Wheaton (1982) argued that the static, long-run equilibrium portrayed by the Muth and Mill's model is never, in
fact, achieved. He also argued that the weaknesses of Anas
(1978) and Harrison and Kain's (1974) dynamic model are the
assumptions that: (i) residential capital is perfectly
durable, and (ii) the development of each zone proceeds under myopic foresight. Overall, Anas and Harrison and Kain
have found that the declining density gradients so widely

found empirically, are not due to an equilibrium tradeoff between transportation costs and land consumption but rather to a widespread historical trend of rising incomes and/or falling construction cost.

Based upon the theory of rent maximization, (or competitive locational bidding) and the intertemporal model specification, Wheaton demonstrated that the maximized present value of rental payments will vary through the future, depending on such market parameters as: Income, transportation costs, and population. Wheaton's solution reveals several interesting features about the nature of development under perfect foresight. The main results are: (i) The present value of rents (or price of land) instead of the density of development declines continuously with greater distance. (ii) The density gradient depends exclusively on the historical trends in various market parameters. Rising income, falling travel costs and faster population growth all help to create a decreasing density gradient, while the opposite trends can lead to density gradients that increase with commuting distance. (iii) The pattern of growth can occur from the edge of the city inward.

One of the important implications of the intertemporal urban model in urban structure analysis is that there might exist structural shifts or urban density gradients. Recently, Brueckner (1980, 1981) has theoretically and empirically developed a vintage model of urban growth. His theoretical results indicate this a growing city may exhibit a saw tooth-shaped spatial contour of building ages, a feature which in turn yields striking discontinuous contours for structural and population density. The empirical issue of dynamic urban growth model is discussed in Chapters 5 and 14 in further detail.

## 2.7    Concluding Remarks

In this chapter we investigated the theoretical foundation of static urban spatial structure by using a Cobb-Douglas production function. The results indicated under what conditions the exponential density gradient is the true specification. Problems that relate to the necessary restrictive assumption of the Cobb-Douglas function were discussed. The dynamic urban models derived by Arnott, Brueckner and Wheaton are also briefly reviewed. In future chapters the implications and impact of developing a more generalized model will be explored.

Chapter 3

# CES PRODUCTION FUNCTION

## 3.1.  Introduction

In Chapter 2 the Cobb-Douglas production function was discussed.  The strength and weakness of using the Cobb-
Douglas production function in investigating the urban
structure was also explored.  In this chapter the Cobb-
Douglas production function will be generalized to allow
the elasticity of substitution ($\sigma$) to be any constant instead of taking on a value of unity.  The constant elasticity of substitution (CES) production function allows the
elasticity to vary in accordance with the empirical re-
quirement under consideration.  This production function
assumes that the degree of substitution is constant but is
not restricted a priori to any value.  It is only assumed
that changes in relative factor inputs and prices do not
alter the elasticity.  The value of elasticity is determined by the underlying technology.  Changes in the underlying technology affects the elasticity for every level of
the factor inputs and prices.  Hence, the constancy of the
elasticity refers to its invariance with respect to changes
in relative factor supplies and not to transformations of
the underlying technology.  The characteristic of an abstract technology are identified by the CES production
function.  That is to say, it permits us to measure changes
in the efficiency of a technology, in the technologically
determined returns to scale, in the capital intensity of a

33

technology and in the ease of substitution of land for capital. These properties of the CES relative to the Cobb-Douglas are as important for studying the production of housing services as for studying the production of commodities by industrial firms.

The CES production was derived independently by two groups: (1) Arrow, Cheney, Minhas and Solow (1961) [ACMS] and (2) Brown and de Cani (1963) [BD]. ACMS using a regression technique and BD using a differential equation technique to drive the CES production function. BD's method of deriving the CES production function is summarized in the appendix. Following Brown (1968), the form of CES production function and its neoclassical properties will be discussed in detail. Using the CES production function, urban structured relationships will be presented in accordance with the paper by Kau and Lee (1976a).

### 3.2. The CES Production Function: The General Theory

Since understanding the mathematical derivation of the CES production function is not essential to its use, the derivation is relegated to an appendix to this chapter. The CES production function may be stated as

$$Xs = A[\alpha \ L^{-\rho} + (1-\alpha)K^{-\rho}]^{-v/\rho} \qquad (3.1)$$

where

$Xs$ = output

$L$ = utilized amount of input L

$K$ = utilized amount of input K

where each variable is measured in index terms with a standard base period. The four parameters, A, $\alpha$, $\rho$, and v, represent the four characteristics of technology. The parameter A is a scale parameter indicating technological efficiency. The parameter $\alpha$ indicates the degree of capital intensity with $0 < \alpha < 1$. The parameter v represents returns to scale. The parameter $\rho$ is used to define the elasticity of substitution of input factor K for factor L. The elasticity of substitution is defined as

$$\sigma = \frac{1}{1+\rho} \tag{3.2}$$

### 3.2.1. Properties of the CES Production Function

It is desirable for a production function to exhibit three characteristics:

1. Marginal products for the inputs should be positive.

2. Marginal products should decrease with increasing output.

3. The production function should be capable of indicating any degree of returns to scale.

This section, following closely the presentation by Brown (1968), illustrates the fact that the CES production function exhibits these characteristics.

The marginal product of factor K is

$$\frac{\partial Xs}{\partial K} = h1Xs^{1+(\rho/v)}L^{-\rho-1} \tag{3.3}$$

where $h_1 = (1 - \alpha)vA^{-\rho/v}$. Since constant returns to scale $(v = 1)$ will be assumed in the following sections, the marginal product of factor K with constant returns to scale may be stated as

$$\frac{\partial Xs}{\partial K} = (1-\alpha)Xs^{1+\rho/}A^{\rho}K^{1+\rho} \tag{3.4}$$

It is apparent that the marginal product of factor K depends only on production Xs and the utilization of factor K and is positive. The marginal product of factor L is

$$\frac{\partial Xs}{\partial K} = h_2 Xs^{1+(\rho/v)}L^{-\rho-1} \tag{3.5}$$

where $h_2 = \alpha v A^{-\rho/v}$ and for constant returns to scale

$$\frac{\partial Xs}{\partial L} = \alpha Xs^{1+\rho} / A^\rho L^{1+\rho}$$

which is again positive. Thus both marginal products for factor inputs are positive.

If marginal products decrease with increasing output, then

$$\frac{\partial^2 Xs}{\partial K^2} < 0$$

$$\frac{\partial^2 Xs}{\partial K^2} = \left(\frac{J}{K}\right)\left(\frac{\partial Xs}{\partial K} - \frac{Xs}{k}\right) \qquad (3.6)$$

where

$$J = \left(\frac{1}{A}\right)^\rho \left(\frac{1-\alpha}{\sigma}\right)\left(\frac{Xs}{K}\right)^\rho$$

or

$$\frac{\partial^2 Xs}{\partial K^2} = \frac{JXs}{L^2}\left[\frac{1}{[\alpha/(1-\alpha)](z)^{\rho+1}} - 1\right] \qquad (3.7)$$

where $z = \frac{K}{L}$. The marginal product function will be downward sloping $\frac{\partial^2 Xs}{\partial K_2} < 0$ if $\dfrac{1}{[\alpha/(1-\alpha)]z^\rho + 1} < 1$.

Since $o < \alpha < 1$, $\dfrac{\alpha}{(1-\alpha)}(z)^\rho$ is positive and $\dfrac{1}{[\alpha/(1-\alpha)]z^\rho + 1}$

$< 1$, the marginal product of factor K declines with increasing output.

When economies or diseconomies of scale are introduced, (that is, $v \neq 1$), the marginal products may not decline with increasing output. To see this, take the second partial with respect to factor K permitting v to have a value other than 1

$$\frac{\partial^2 Xs}{\partial K^2} = \frac{1}{\sigma} h_1 Xs^{1+\rho/v} K^{-\rho-2} \left[ \frac{\sigma(v + \rho)}{\alpha/(1-\alpha)u^\rho + 1} - 1 \right] \qquad (3.8)$$

when v $<$ 1, the second derivative becomes more negative so that the marginal product curve is even more steeply negatively sloped than with constant returns to scale. When v $>$ 1, a sufficiently large value of v may result in a positive second derivative. In this case, the marginal product curve would not be downward sloping but rather upward sloping. However, this case is not disturbing since, with sufficiently large economies of scale, one would not expect the marginal product of factor K to decline. Hence, the CES production function is consistent with theoretical expectations.

The final characteristic that the production function should be capable of indicating any degree of returns to scale is, of course, met by permitting v to assume various values with v = 1 denoting constant returns to scale.

### 3.2.2. The Marginal Rate of Substitution

Having demonstrated that the CES production function has the three desirable characteristics postulated in the previous section, the marginal rate of substitution of factor K for factor L will be derived by taking the ratios of the marginal products:

$$R = \frac{\partial Xs}{\partial K} \frac{\partial Xs}{\partial L} = \frac{\alpha}{1-\alpha} \left( z \right)^{1/\sigma} = \alpha' z^{1/\sigma} \qquad (3.9)$$

where $\alpha' = \frac{\alpha}{1-\alpha}$ and $z = \frac{K}{L}$. In one sense $\alpha$ may be consi-

dered a measure of the intensiveness of factor L in the technology. If $\alpha$ is small implying a production process that is highly K intensive, a one unit reduction in the factor K rate must be compensated for by a larger increase in the rate of factor L than if the process were less factor K intensive.

Note that the marginal rate of substitution is a function of $\sigma$, the elasticity of substitution. If the elasticity of substitution is high then factor K is easily substituted for factor L and when factor K is reduced factor L must be increased but not by as many units as when the elasticity of substitution is low and the inputs are not easily substitutable for one another. This is a result of the elasticity of substitution being low, factors are dissimilar and the law of diminishing returns takes hold more rapidly for increasing ratios of the marginal products than when $\sigma$ is high.

In equilibrium the marginal rate of substitution of factor K for factor L is equal to the ratio of the rent per unit of factor L and the rent per unit of factor K:

$$\frac{\partial Xs}{\partial K} \frac{\partial Xs}{\partial L} = \frac{r}{n} = \bar{\delta} \qquad (3.10)$$

r = real rental of a unit of factor L

n = real rental of a unit of factor K.

For constant returns to scale, $v = 1$,

$$\bar{\delta} = \alpha' z^{1/\sigma} \quad \text{or} \qquad (3.11)$$

$$\bar{\delta}/z = \alpha' z^{(1/\sigma)-1} = \alpha' z^{\rho}. \qquad (3.12)$$

The CES production function has no limit when $\sigma > 1$ but does have a finite limit when $\sigma < 1$. Rewriting the CES function as

$$Xs = A \left[ \alpha L^{1-(1/\sigma)} + (1-\alpha) K^{1-(1/\sigma)} \right]^{\frac{\sigma v}{\sigma-1}} \qquad (3.13)$$

and holding factor L constant while varying factor K, the limit may be taken as factor K gets infinitely large given $\sigma > 1$:

$$\lim_{\substack{K \to \infty}} Xs \Bigg|_{\sigma > 1} = \lim_{K \to \infty} A \left[ L^{1-(1/\sigma)} + (1-\alpha)K^{1-(1/\sigma)} \right]^{\frac{\sigma v}{\sigma-1}} \Bigg|_{\sigma > 1} = \infty$$

$$\qquad (3.14)$$

Now consider the case when $\sigma < 1$. Rewrite the CES function as

$$Xs = \frac{A}{\left[\dfrac{\alpha}{L^{(1/\sigma)-1}} + \dfrac{1-\alpha}{K^{(1/\sigma)-1}}\right]^{\frac{\sigma\,v}{1-\sigma}}} \tag{3.15}$$

Take the limit:

$$\lim_{K\to\infty} X \Big|_{\sigma<1} = \lim_{K\to\infty} \frac{A}{\left[\dfrac{\alpha}{L^{(1/\sigma)-1}} + \dfrac{1\ \alpha}{K^{(1/\sigma)-1}}\right]^{\frac{\sigma\,v}{1-\sigma}}} \Bigg|_{\sigma<1} \tag{3.16}$$

$$= BL^{v}$$

where

$$B = A\alpha - [\sigma v/(1-\sigma)]. \tag{3.17}$$

Thus when $\sigma > 1$, the CES production function has no limit; however, when $\sigma < 1$, the CES production has a finite limit; the function reaches a maximum when one factor is increased as the other is held constant. When $\sigma > 1$, the factors are similar and substitute easily for one another. As one factor increases infinitely, the technology permits the increasing factor to be substituted relatively easily for the constant factor so that the output increases infinitely. On the other hand, when $\sigma < 1$, the factors do not substitute easily for one another and, adding increasing amounts of one factor to a constant amount of the other factor, output eventually reaches a limit.

### 3.3. Capital-Land Substitution, Urban Land Use and the CES

The purpose of this section is to present a new model that will explain the patterns of urban land use. Much of the variation in residential development and structure that occurs in cities is explained by the properties of production functions. The major components of production variations for any set of outputs in an urban area are factor substitution and technological efficiency. Relative factor prices vary over a wide range wthin a city resulting in capital-land ratios exemplified by the comparison of highrise apartments to single family dwellings. To understand the effects of changing factor prices and the corresponding change in factor ratios, it is necessary to make assumptions about capital-land substitutions. The assumption most used originates from a Cobb-Douglas function, which implies a unitary elasticity of substitution between capital and land. From a mathematical point of view the Cobb-Douglas function is very convenient, but economic analysis based on unitary elasticity may lead to restrictive conclusions about land-use patterns of urban areas.

The importance of the substitution assumption can be demonstrated in various urban economic problems. For example, the land-rent gradient of a city hinges not only on transportation cost and income but also on the shape of production functions within the city. Unitary elasticities of substitution for all firms lead to restrictive conclusions on the shape and variability of rent gradients. Also, unit elasticity of substitution leads to the assumption of constant relative shares of income received by the factors. The relative shares of income received by capital and land vary within cities which again reflects the inappropriateness of the Cobb-Douglas production function when dealing with the complexities of urban areas.

This section derives determinants of land-use patterns in accordance with an aggregated constant elasticity of substitution (CES) production function. CES production functions assume the degree of substitution to be constant but not restricted a priori to any specified value. The constant elasticity implies invariance of $\sigma$, the elasticity of substitution, relative to changing factor supplies and not to changing technology. Brown (1968), has pointed out that variations in the elasticity of substitution between factors of production, $\sigma$ , result in nonneutral technological change. In a Cobb-Douglas function $\sigma$ is unity and unchanging; therefore, it is difficult to determine a priori how nonneutral technological change associated with $\sigma$ affects output. Both the Cobb-Douglas and Leontief production functions are special cases of the CES function.

The next section provides an aggregate model of land-use patterns. Because of the complexity of CES functions, the model is at times cumbersome; however, the additional insights into land-use patterns gained from the CES outweigh these costs. In Section 3.3.2, the effects of assuming alternative values of price elasticities and    on the estimation of the density gradient are investigated. Section 3.3.3 will determine the effects of technological change on the supply and demand of housing services, the rental of land, and population densities. Section 3.3.4 will summarize and state the conclusions.

### 3.3.1. Derivation of the Model

Both Mills (1967, 1972b, 1981) and Muth (1969) used a Cobb-Douglas production function which assumes the elasticity of substitution to be one. This retriction is relaxed using a CES production function defined as

$$Xs(u) = A[\alpha L(u)^{-\rho} + (1 - \alpha)K(u)^{-\rho}]^{(-1/\rho)} \qquad (3.18)$$

where $K(u)$ and $L(u)$ represent inputs of capital and land in the production of housing services [$Xs(u)$] u miles from the city center. A and $\alpha$ are scale and distribution parameters, respectively, and $\rho$ is a transformation of the elasticity of substitution, $\sigma$, and will be referred to as the substitution parameter.

The elasticity of substitution $\sigma = 1/(1 + \rho)$. Values of $\rho$ vary from $-1$ to $\infty$, which allows $\sigma$ to range from $\infty$ to 0. As $\rho \to \infty$, the elasticity of substitution tends to zero which gives us Leontief production functions with fixed proportions between land and capital. $\rho = -1$ is the case of straight-line isoquants and $\rho > -1$ implies isoquants convex to the origin. As $\rho \to 0$ then $\sigma \to 1$, which is the Cobb-Douglas case.

A demand function for housing services per worker at u, xd(u) is defined as

$$xd(u) = Bw^{\theta_1} p(u)^{\theta_2} \qquad (3.19)$$

where B is a scale parameter and depends upon the units in

which housing services are measured, w is income for workers, $p(u)$ is the price of housing services at distance u, $\theta_1$ is income elasticity and $\theta_2$ is price elasticity.

From Equation (3.18) the relationship between the value of the marginal product and its rental for both land and capital can be written as

$$r(u) = p(u)\alpha Xs(u)^{1+\rho} / A^\rho L(u)^{1+\rho} \qquad (3.20)$$

$$n = p(u)(1-\alpha)Xs(u)^{1+\rho}/A^\rho K(u)^{1+\rho} \qquad (3.21)$$

Solving (3.20) and (3.21) for $L(u)$ and $K(u)$ and substituting into (3.18), we have

$$p(u) = A^{-1}[\alpha^{1/(1+\rho)}r(u)^{\rho/(1+\rho)}$$

$$+ (1-\alpha)^{1/(1+\rho)}n^{\rho/(1+\rho)}]^{(1+\rho)/\rho} \qquad (3.22)$$

From Equation (3.22), the price elasticity of housing with respect to n and $r(u)$ can be rewritten as

$$\frac{\partial p(u)}{\partial n}\frac{n}{P(u)} = \left[\frac{p(u)(1-\alpha)^{-1/\rho}}{A^{-1}n}\right]^{-\rho/(1+\rho)} \qquad (3.23)$$

$$\frac{\partial p(u)}{\partial r(u)}\frac{r(u)}{p(u)} = \left[\frac{p(u)\alpha^{-1/\rho}}{A^{-1}r(u)}\right]^{-\rho/(1+\rho)} \qquad (3.24)$$

Equations (3.23) and (3.24) allows the elasticities of housing services with respect to n and $r(u)$ to vary with changes in n and $r(u)$. These elasticities will reduce to $(1-\alpha)$ and $\alpha$ when the elasticity of substitution between land and capital is unity. This is the case obtained with the Cobb-Douglas function. When the elasticity of substitution is infinite, then both Equations (3.23) and (3.24) will approach zero; when the elasticity of substitution approaches zero, Equations (3.23) and (3.24) will approach

$A^{-1}n/p(u)$ and $A^{-1}r(u)/p(u)$, respectively.[1]

Muth (1969) and Mills (1981), using constrained utility maximization, have derived a differential equation to describe the relationship between the change in the cost of housing and the change in commuting cost as

$$P'(u)xd(u) + T = 0 \tag{3.25}$$

where $p'(u)$ is the slope of $p(u)$ and T is the cost of commuting. Substituting Equation (3.19) into Equation (3.25) we have

$$p'(u)Bw^{\theta_1}p(u)^{\theta_2} + T = 0 \tag{3.26}$$

Using the initial condition of Equation (5), the solution[2] of the differential equation (3.26) can be written as

$$p(u) = [\bar{p}^{-(\theta_2+1)} + T(\bar{u} - u)(\theta_2 + 1)/Bw^{\theta_1}]^{1/(\theta_2+1)(1+\rho)} \tag{3.27}$$

where $\bar{u}$ is the distance from the city center to the edge of the urban area, and $\bar{p} = p(\bar{u})$. Substituting Equation (3.22) into Equation (3.29) and with some rearrangement, we have

$$r(u) = \{\alpha^{-1/(1+\rho)}A^{\rho/(1+\rho)}[\bar{p}^{-(\theta_2+1)} +$$

$$T(\bar{u} - u)(\theta_2 + 1)Bw^{\theta_1}]^{\rho/(\theta_2+1)(1+\rho)}$$

$$- [1 - \alpha)/\alpha]^{1/(1+\rho)}n^{\rho/(1+\rho)}]^{(1+\rho)/\rho} \tag{3.28}$$

where $\bar{p} = A^{-1}[\alpha^{1/(1+\rho)}\bar{r}^{-\rho/(1+\rho)} +$

$$(1 - \alpha)^{1/(1+\rho)}n^{(\rho/(1+\rho)}]^{(1+\rho)/\rho}$$

Equation (3.28) states that the rental rate of land is a function of distance and the rental rate of capital. It can also be shown that the partials of $r(u)$ with respect to u and n are negative.

By applying the mathematical theorem that the mean value of order zero is the geometric mean (see Hardy, Littlewood, and Polya (1934), and L'Hopital's Rule, Equation (3.28) can be reduced to three limiting forms, (1) $\theta_2 \rightarrow -1$; (2) $\rho \rightarrow 0$; (3) $\theta_2 \rightarrow -1$ and $\rho \rightarrow 0$.

(1) As $\theta_2$, the price elasticity approaches minus one,

Equation (3.28) can be rewritten as [3]

$$r(u) = \{\alpha^{-1/(1+\rho}_A{}^{\rho/(1+\rho)}[_p^{-\rho/(1+\rho)}e^{\rho(1+\rho)t(\bar{u}-u)/Bw\theta}_1]$$

$$- \{(1-\alpha)/\alpha]^{1/(1+\rho)}_n{}^{\rho/(1+\rho)}\}^{(1+\rho)/\rho} \quad (3.29)$$

Equation (3.29) states that the rental rate of land is negatively related to distance and the rental rate of capital.

(2) As $\rho$ approaches zero, Equation (3.28) can be rewritten as

$$r(u) = \{A\alpha^{\alpha}(1-\alpha)^{1-\alpha}]^{1/\alpha}_n{}^{(\alpha-1)/\alpha}[_p^{-(\theta_2+1)} +$$

$$t(\bar{u}-u)(\theta_2 + 1)/Bw^{\theta_1}]^{1/\alpha(\theta_2+1)} \quad (3.30)$$

where $\bar{p} = \{A\alpha^{\alpha}(1-\alpha)^{1-\alpha}]^{-1}r^{\alpha}n^{1-\alpha}$ and $\bar{r} = r(\bar{u})$. Equation (3.30) states that land rent is inversely related to distance. This reduces to the general case presented by Mills [1981, p. 227, Eq. A-14a].

(3) As $\rho$ approaches zero and $\theta_2$ approaches minus one, Equation (3.28) can be rewritten as

$$r(u) = \bar{r}e^{T(\bar{u}-u)/\alpha Bw^{\theta_1}} \quad (3.31)$$

which gives us a negative exponential function. Equation (3.31) reduces to the specific case presented by Mills [1981, p. 227, Equation A.14b]. The three cases above demonstrate the importance and implication of assuming $\theta_2 = -1$ and $\rho = 0$.

To derive the relationship between the population density and the rental of land, r(u), Mills, [1981, p. 228] has defined

$$N(u) = Xs(u)/xd(u) \quad (3.32)$$

where N(u) = the number of workers living at u,

Xs(u) = output of housing services, and

Xd(u) = housing demand per worker at u.

From Equations (3.20) and (3.21) it can be shown that

$$K(u) = \left[\frac{(1-\alpha)r(u)}{\alpha n}\right]^{1/(1+\rho)} L(u) \tag{3.33}$$

Substituting Equation (3.33) into Equation (3.18) we have

$$Xs(u) = AL(u)\left\{\alpha + \left[\frac{(1-\alpha)\ r(u)}{\alpha n}\right]^{-\rho/(1+\rho)} (1-\alpha)\right\}^{-1/\rho}$$

From Equation (3.19) and Equation (3.22), we also have

$$xd(u) = Bw^{\theta_1} A^{-\theta_2} [\alpha^{1/(1+\rho)} r(u)^{\rho/(1+\rho)} +$$
$$(1-\alpha)^{1/(1+\rho)} n^{/(1+\rho)}]^{\theta_2(1+\rho)/\rho/\rho} \tag{3.35}$$

Substituting (3.34) and (3.35) and (3.32), we have

$$D(u) = \frac{N(u)}{L(u)} = \frac{B^{-1}w^{-\theta_1}A^{\theta_2+1}\left[\alpha + \left(\frac{r(u)}{\alpha r}\right)^{-\rho/(1+\rho)}(1-\alpha)^{1/(1+\rho)}\right]^{-1/\rho}}{[\alpha^{1/(1+\rho)}r(u)^{\rho/(1+\rho)} + (1-\alpha)^{1(1+\rho)}n^{\rho/(1+\rho)}]^{\theta_2(1+\rho)/\rho}} \tag{3.36}$$

Equation (3.36) is the density function for any given urban area and it can be shown that D(u) is a positive function of r(u) and decreases with increasing distance and n.

Similar to the limiting cases of Equation (3.28), three limiting cases for Equation (3.36) can be written as follows:

(1)  As $\theta_2$ approaches negatives one, Equation (3.36) can be rewritten as

$D(u) =$

$$\frac{1}{Bw\theta^1} \frac{\left[\alpha + \left(\frac{r(u)}{\alpha n}\right)^{-\rho/(1+\rho)} (1-\alpha)^{1/(1+\rho)}\right]^{-1/\rho}}{[\alpha^{1/(1+\rho)} r(u)^{\rho/(1+\rho)} + (1-\alpha)^{1/(1+\rho)} n^{\rho/(1+\rho)}]^{-(1+\rho)\rho}}$$

$$(3.37)$$

In Equation (3.37) the partials of $D(u)$ with respect to $r(u)$ and $n$ are the same sign as in Equation (3.36)

(2) As $\rho$ approaches zero, Equation (3.36) reduces to

$$D(u) = (1/Bw^{\theta_1})A^{\theta_2+1}\alpha^{-(1-\alpha)} + \alpha\theta_2 n^{-(1-\alpha)(\theta_2+1)}$$

$$x \ r(u)^{1-\alpha(\theta_2+1)}(1 - \alpha)^{-(\theta_2+1)} \qquad (3.38)$$

This also reduces to the general case presented by Mills [1981, p. 227, Eq. A.14a] when Equation (3.30) is substituted into Equation (3.38).

(3) As $\rho$ approaches zero and $\theta_2$ approaches negative one, then Equation (3.36) reduces to

$$D(u) = (1/B\alpha w^{\theta_1})r(u) \qquad (3.39)$$

This reduces to Mill's equation [1981, p. 227, Eq. A.14b] when Equation (3.31) is substituted into Equation (3.39). In the next section, the above model is used to analyze the effects of assuming alternative values of $\theta_2$ and $\rho$ on the estimation of the density gradient.

### 3.3.2.  CES and the Functional Form of the Density Gradient

Section 3.31 derived various functional forms depending on the assumptions concerning the limiting values of $\theta_2$, the price elasticity of demand and $\rho$, and the elasticity of substitution parameter. In this section, the effects of assuming alternative values of $\theta_2$ and $\rho$ on the estimation of the density gradient are investigated.

If the elasticity of substitution is unity, then the functional form of the density gradient depends upon the values of $\theta_2$. From Equation (3.30), (3.31), (3.38) and

(3.39), we have[4]

$$D(u) = E[\bar{r}^{-\beta} + \beta TE(\bar{u} - u)]^{(1-\beta)/\beta} \text{ if } \beta \neq 0 \qquad (3.40)$$

and

$$D(u) = E(\bar{r}e^{TEu})e^{-TEu} \text{ if } \beta = 0 \qquad (3.41)$$

where

$D(u)$ = population density at distance $u$,

$\beta = \alpha(1 + \theta_2)$

$$E = \alpha Bw^{\theta_1}[A\alpha^{\alpha}(1 - \alpha)^{1-\alpha}]^{-(\theta_2 + 1)} n^{(1-\alpha)(\theta_2 + 1)} \qquad (3.42)$$

$n$ = rental rate of housing capital, which is assumed independent of $u$,

$T$ = commuting cost per mile,

$\bar{u}$ = the distance from the city center to the edge of the urban area,

$\bar{r}$ = rent on nonurban uses of land and

$r(\bar{u}) = \bar{r}.$

If $\theta_2 = -1$, then $\beta = 0$, the density function is described by Equation (3.41).

Muth (1969) and Mills (1972b) have employed the semi-log functional form,

$$\log D(u) = \gamma_0 - \gamma u \qquad (3.43)$$

where $\gamma_0$ and $\gamma$ are regression coefficients, to estimate the density gradient for Equation (3.41). Kau and Lee (1976b, c) have successfully derived the functional form used in estimating Equation (3.40). It is defined as

$$[D(u)^{\lambda} - 1]/\lambda = \gamma'_0 - \gamma' u \qquad (3.44)$$

where $\lambda$ is the functional form parameter and $\gamma'_0$ and $\gamma'$ are the regression coefficients. If $\lambda$ approaches zero then Equation (3.44) reduces to Equation (3.43). Since $\beta = \lambda/(1 + \lambda)$ $\beta$ will be significantly different from zero if $\lambda$ is significantly different from zero. Since $\beta = (1 + \theta_2)$ and if $\beta$ is different from zero then $\theta_2$ is not equal to minus one. A Box and Cox (1964) transformation technique can be used to estimate $\lambda$, $\gamma'_0$ and $\gamma'$. Also, in accordance with Taylor's Series, Equation (3.44) can be expanded as

$$\log D(u) = Do - \gamma u - \nabla[\text{Log } D(u)]^2 \qquad (3.45)$$

where $\nabla = 1/2\lambda$, $\lambda < 1$ and $\gamma$ = unbiased density gradient. This implies that the estimated density gradient obtained from Equation (3.43) will be biased unless $\lambda$ is not significantly different from zero. Thus it is clear from Equations (3.44) and (3.45) that the density gradient estimated from the semilog Equation (3.43) is subject to specification error unless the price elasticity of demand is negative unity.

The bias in estimating the density gradient may also be affected by the elasticity of substitution. From Equations (3.28) and (3.36) the density function can be approximately written as

$$D(u) = E[\bar{r}\beta + \beta T(E(\bar{u} - u)]^{(1-\beta)/\beta} \qquad (3.46)$$

$$+ \text{ omitted terms associated with the}$$
$$\text{elasticity of substitution.}$$

In sum, the density gradient obtained by Equation (3.43) is subject to two possible bias: (1) the bias associated with the elasticity of substitution parameter $\rho$ and (2) the bias associated with the price elasticity. The density gradient obtained from Equation (3.44) is subject to only one possible bias – that associated with $\rho$.

The bias related to $\rho$ and $\theta_2$ affects both cross-section and time-series estimates. Harrison and Kain (1974) and Mills (1972b) have attempted to estimate changes in the density gradient over time using a negative exponential functional form. Their conclusions, reached by making comparisons among cross-sectional estimates for different time periods, was that the density gradient has declined over time. This procedure does not correct for changes in $\rho$ and $\theta_2$. Thus, the estimated results may not be a reliable source of information concerning changes in the density gradient. For example, assume that the density gradient has actually increased over time. It would then be possible, using either the Harrison and Kain (1974) or Mills 1972b) exponential estimation procedure, to derive erroneous results indicating a decline in the gradient because of the implicit bias of excluding information on $\rho$ and $\theta_2$. Bias due to changes in $\theta_2$ can be corrected by using Equation (3.44) for estimating the density gradient.

A completely specified density function can be obtained by substituting Equation (3.28) into (3.36). A direct method of estimating the density gradient for this complete form is still an open question. However, if the elasticity of substitution parameter[5], $\rho$ , and the price elasticity, $\theta_2$ , are estimated independently, then these estimated values could be used in the complete form along with numerical analysis techniques to estimate the density gradient.

## 3.4. Urban Growth, Technological Change and Urban Land Use

Urban growth analysis is centered on two approaches. First is Losch's central place theory which states that scale and other agglomeration economies result in concentrated production in central places. Second, regional comparative advantage· produces specialized production and trade which seeks out areas of relatively lower interregional transportation cost.

This section is concerned with the unexplored effects of technological change on urban growth and land use. It is assumed that urban growth takes place either through the growth of capital or land. The effect of technological change on growth depends critically on the assumptions concerning relative factor growth. Different relative rates of growth for capital and land will be examined and compared. The large number of separate urban areas makes possible the existence of different relative growth rates of land and capital. In some areas, growth may be reduced by

restrictive land-use zoning such as limiting housing development to single family dwellings of a certain size or by
limits on structural heights of buildings. For other cities the restrictions may come about due to geographical
phenomena such as rivers, lakes, or mountainous areas.
Both limits on capital and land growth will be explored.

There are two general types of technological change -
neutral and nonneutral. A neutral change produces variation in production but does not affect the marginal rate of
substitution of land for capital. Thus, variations in the
efficiency of a technology and economies of scale produce
neutral technological change. Nonneutral change alters the
production function and is either land or capital saving.
If the marginal product of capital rise relative to the
marginal product of land for each factor combination, there
is a land-saving technological change. As shown in previous studies (Brown [1968, p. 56]) when the capital is
growing faster relative to land, technological progress,
which eases the substitution of capital for land, will be
capital using.

The implications of urban growth and land use will be
discussed with respect to the impacts of the variation of $\rho$
on the supply and the demand for housing services. Brown
(1968) has shown that when $\sigma$ increases, i.e., when it becomes easier to substitute factors of production, output
will increase for a given set of factors of production.
Thus, there is a positive relationship between the elasticity of substitution and the supply of housing services,
i.e., $\partial Xs(u)/\partial\rho < 0$.

To investigate the relationship between the elasticity
of substitution and the demand for housing services, we
differentiate p(u) with respect to $\rho$. From Equation (3.22)
it can be shown that

$$\frac{\partial p(u)}{\partial \rho} = A^{-1}(1/\rho X^{w-1}[1/(1+\rho)] \ \alpha^{1/(1+\rho)} \ r(u)^{(1+\rho)} \log\left(\frac{r(u)}{\alpha}\right)$$

$$+ (1-\alpha)^{1/(1+\rho)} n^{\rho/(1+\rho)} \log\left(\frac{n}{1-\alpha}\right) - \frac{(\log G) \ (G)}{\rho}$$

$$(3.47)$$

where $G = \alpha^{1/(1+\rho)} r(u)^{\rho/(1+\rho)} (1 - \alpha)^{1/(1+\rho)} n^{\rho/(1+\rho)}$,

and $\quad w = (1 + \rho)/\rho$

It is difficult to determine the sign of Equation (3.47) directly. However, the sign of all the limits can be determined.

By L'Hopital's rule, it can be shown that

$$\lim_{\alpha \to 1} \frac{\partial p(u)}{\partial \rho} = \lim_{r \to 0} \frac{\partial p(u)}{\partial \rho} = 0 \qquad (3.48)$$

and

$$\lim_{\alpha \to 1} \frac{\partial p(u)}{\partial \rho} = \lim_{n \to 0} \frac{\partial p(u)}{\partial \rho} = 0 \qquad (3.49)$$

Equation (3.48) and (3.49) indicate no relationship between the price of housing services and the elasticity of substitution. If we integrate this result with the demand equation, we can conclude that an increase in the elasicity of substitution will have no effect on the demand for housing services, i.e., $\partial xd(u)/\partial \rho = 0$.[6]

If locational choice is assumed independent of the total demand for housing services then from Equation (3.28), we have the reduced form

$$r(u) = \alpha/(1 - \alpha)[K(u)/L(u)]^{1+\rho} n \qquad (3.50)$$

The derivative of $r(u)$ with respect to $\rho$ is

$$\frac{\partial r(u)}{\partial \rho} = n[\alpha/(1 - \alpha)[K(u)/L(u)]^{1+\rho} \log [K(u)/L(u)] \qquad (3.51)$$

To investigate the sign of Equation (3.51), we assume $K/L = 1$ for any base year; then, $\partial r(u)/\partial \rho$ is less (greater) than zero when land is growing faster (slower) than capital. Given that capital is expanding faster than land, then the relationship between the elasticity of substitution, $\sigma$, and $r(u)$ is negative, i.e., $\partial r(u)/\partial \rho > 0$.[7]

Finally, the relationship between the population density and the elasticity of substitution is analyzed by assuming that total population $N(u)$ is defined as

Xs(u)/xd(u). The derivative of N(u) with respect to $\rho$ can be determined by the sign of $\partial xd/\partial\rho$ and $\partial Xs/\partial\rho$. From Equations (3.48) and (3.49) we have shown that $\partial xd/\partial\rho$ is zero. From Brown (1968, p. 57), it can also be shown that $\partial xd/\partial\rho$ is negative. Therefore, it can be concluded that $\partial N(u)\partial\rho$ is negative. This implies that an increase in the elasticity of substitution between land and capital will increase the total population of an urban area.

The impact of the elasticity of substitution on population density, N(u)/L(u), can be determined by $\partial N(u)/\partial\rho$ and $\partial L(u)/\partial\rho$. Assuming $L(u)/\partial\rho$ is insignificant,[8] we can conclude that an increase in the elasticity of substitution will increase the population density of an urban area. Hence, if technology is improving the substitutability of capital for land and if public policies through zoning ordinances are restricting the use of land, then urban growth would lead to greater density. This may result in more congestion, higher rents, and more pollution. Thus, if the desired goal is a better urban environment, policies which restrict the available land supply may not be successful. Since population movements cannot be restricted within the United States, urban growth can be controlled only with policies that limit both the growth of capital and land. Limits on capital expansion would only produce urban sprawl. A combination of building codes, tenant restrictions, and zoning would reduce density and urban sprawl by limiting population growth.

A combination of land-use zoning and limits on capital expansion, such as restricting high-rise apartments, may produce a non-polluted and less dense urban environment for current residents at the expense of those who are denied the option of moving to a more crowded environment at a lower money cost. Also some current residents who do not value less crowding but choose to remain may be forced to pay for it through higher rents. Restricting factors of production such as land and capital results in a different urban environment but not necessarily a better environment for all concerned. In fact the net benefit even after compensation may be negative.

## 3.5. Summary and Conclusion

This chapter has employed the CES production function instead of the Cobb-Douglas function to investigate the impact of capital-land substitution on urban land use. First, a general functional form for explaining the behavior of land rent and population density is derived. The effect on the general form of assuming the price elasticity for housing equal to minus one and the elasticity of substitution equal to one is investigated. Second, the impact of the elasticity of substitution on the price of housing services, the supply of, and the demand for housing services is derived in detail. From these results it is shown that land rent is negatively related to the elasticity of substitution, whereas population density has a positive relationship.

If a Cobb-Douglas instead of CES production function is employed to investigate urban land use, the impact of capital-land substitution is restricted a priori. In addition, the impact of the capital-land ratio on the output of housing services is entirely neglected.[9] Therefore, the study of urban land use based upon Cobb-Douglas production functions is subject to specification bias.

Based upon the CES production function, it has been shown that Equations (3.36) through (3.39) the negative exponential functional relationship between density and distance can be ascertained only when the price elasticity of housing services is negative unity and the elasticity of substitution is unity.

Finally, CES production function, the Cobb-Douglas production function, and the Leontief function are derived in this chapter. All three assume a constant elasticity of substitution between capital and land. Their derivation proceeds directly from the definition of the elasticity of substitution. In the next chapter the implications of a variable elasticity-of-substitution are explored.

## NOTES

1. Since $\lim_{\rho \to \infty} (1/\rho) = 0$ and $\lim \rho/(1+\rho) = \lim_{\rho \to \infty} 1/[1 + (1/\rho)] = 1$.

2. Equation (3.26) can be rewritten as $dp(u)Bw^{\theta_1}p^{\theta_2} + Tdu = 0$. Integrating and determining the initial value, we have $Bw^{\theta_1}p^{\theta_2+1}/(\theta_2 + 1) + Tu = Bw^{\theta_1}\bar{p}^{\theta_2+1}/(\theta_2 +1) + T\bar{u}$. After some rearrangement, we obtain Equation (3.27).

3. Since $[\bar{p}^{-(\theta_2+1)} + T(\bar{u}-u)(\theta_2 +1)/Bw^{\theta_1}]^{\rho/(\theta_2+1)(1+\rho)} = \exp\{\rho/(1+\theta_2)(1+\rho) \log[\bar{p}^{-(\theta_2+1)} + T(\bar{u}-u)(\theta_2 +1)/Bw^{\theta_1}]\}$ by L'Hopital's rule, it can be shown that this reduces to $\bar{p}^{-\rho/(1+\rho)} e^{\rho+(u-u)/(1+\rho)Bw^{\theta_1}}$ as $\theta_2$ approaches $-1$.

4. This equation is obtained by substituting Mills (1981) Equation A.14a, p. 227 into Equation A.17, p. 228.

5. For an example of previous empirical estimates of the elasticity of substitution see Kau, Lee and Sirmans (1979), Koenker (1972), Sirmans, Kau and Lee (1979) and McDonald (1981).

6. It can be shown that all relevant limits are zero and therefore concluded that a rise in $\rho$ does not change the demand for housing. However, this proof does not assure that $\partial p(u)/\partial\rho = 0$ for all values of $\alpha$, $r(u)$, and $n$.

7. The justification of this technique can be found in Brown (1968, pp. 59-60).

8. Since land is relatively restricted in supply it is assumed that $\partial L(u)/\partial\rho$ approaches zero. Therefore

$$\partial D(u)/\partial\rho = \{L(u)[\partial N(u)/\partial\rho] - N(u)[\partial L(u)/\partial\rho]\}/[L(u)]^2 < 0.$$

9. Following Kmenta (1967) and McCarthy (1967), the CES function can be approximated as

$$Xs = AL^{\alpha}K^{1-\alpha}[K/L]^{-\frac{1}{2}\rho(\alpha)(1-\alpha)\ln(K/L)},$$

where $\rho < 1$.

From this relationship it is clear that the K/L ratio can not be neglected except when $\rho$ is equal to zero or when K/L is equal to one. Since K/L is subject to changes in units of measurement, a numeraire should be used to normalize K/L over distance. In general, K/L is not the same over distance and the impact of K/L on Xs should not be neglected in an urban land-use study.

Chapter 4


A VES PRODUCTION FUNCTION


### 4.1. Introduction

In the last two chapters, the Cobb-Douglas (CD) and constant elasticity of substitution (CES) production functions
were analyzed. The types of urban spatial structure implied by such functions were determined. The Cobb-Douglas
production function assumes that the elasticity of substitution, $\sigma$, is unity whereas the CES production function
allows the value of $\sigma$ to be determined by data. In principle, however, the elasticity of substitution can be a variable depending upon output and/or the factor combination
[See Hicks (1948) and Allen (1956)], so that the assumption
of a constant $\sigma$ may lead to specification bias. Since the
capital-land ratios within a city significantly change with
distance, it may well be important to use a variable elasticity of substitution to inquire into the determination of
an urban spatial structure.

In this chapter, a specific variable elasticity of
substitution (VES) prduction function is investigated and
the relationship between the VES and the CES production
function is explored. Implications of the VES production
function for urban structure study are discussed as well as
the functional form and the properties of the VES production function. In addition, a weak disposability input
(WDI) production function which integrates CD, CES and VES
will be explored.

## 4.2. Properties of a VES Production Function

One way to allow the elasticity of substitution, $\sigma$ , to be a variable, is either to generalize the CD production function or generalize the CES production function. The Cobb-Douglas production function can be generalized as [see Liu and Hildebrand (1965)]

$$Xs = A\exp[\bar{a}K/L]K^{\alpha-1}L^{\alpha} \tag{4.1}$$

where Xs, K and L are as before and A, $\bar{a}$, and $\alpha$ are parameters. This function reduces to the CD function when $\bar{a}$ = 0, given by

$$Xs = AK^{1-\alpha}L^{\alpha} \tag{4.2}$$

The elasticity of substitution, $\sigma$ for (4.1) can be defined as,

$$\sigma = \frac{(\bar{a}z+1-\alpha)(\alpha-\bar{a}z)}{(\bar{a}z+1-\alpha)(\alpha-\bar{a}z)-\bar{a}z} \tag{4.3}$$

where z = K/L. The behavior of $\sigma$ in (4.3) is complex.

Other CD generalizations can be found in Revankar (1971a). Note that the Revanker type of VES production function, which will be discussed later in this section, is also a CD type of generalization.

There are two kinds of CES generalizations to be discussed here. Sato (1975, 241-246) has followed Kmenta's (1967) CES approximation and defined a VES production function as[1]

$$\ln Xs/AL = \delta\ln K/L - \rho\delta(1-\delta)(\ln K/L)^2 \tag{4.4}$$

where Xs is the output, K is capital, L is land, A, $\delta$ and $\rho$ are parameter as defined in Chapter 3. Sato has also shown that the elasticity of substitution ($\sigma$) for Equation (4.4) can be defined as

$$\sigma = 1-1/[1+\{(\bar{\bar{a}}+2\bar{\bar{b}}\ln K/L)^2 - (\bar{\bar{a}}+2\bar{\bar{b}}\ln K/L)\}/2\bar{\bar{b}}] \qquad (4.5)$$

where $\bar{\bar{a}} = \delta$ and $\bar{\bar{b}} = \rho\delta(1-\delta)$.

Another generalized CES production function developed by Liu and Hildebrand (1965) is defined as[2]

$$Xs = \{(1-\alpha)K^\rho + \alpha K^{\delta\rho}L(1-\delta)\rho]^{1/\rho} \qquad (4.6)$$

where Xs, K and L are as before and A, $\alpha$, $\delta$, and $\rho$ are parameters. If $\delta = 0$, then Equation (4.6) reduces to the CES production function,

$$Xs = A[(1-\alpha)\bar{K}^\rho + \bar{L}^\rho]^{-1/\rho} \qquad (4.7)$$

The elasticity of substitution for (4.6) is defined as

$$\sigma = \frac{1}{1-\rho+\dfrac{\delta\rho}{S_k}} \qquad (4.8)$$

where $S_k$ is the capital's share.

Although Equation (4.6) is known to have important economic implications [see Liu and Hildebrand (1965)] it has nonlinearities which make econometric methods of estimation difficult. In addition, the behavior of $\sigma$ in (4.8), is not easily comprehensible.

Revankar (1971a) has derived a VES production function, as follows,

$$Xs = AK^{(1-\delta\rho)}[L+(\rho-1)K]^{\nu\delta\rho} \qquad (4.9)$$

$$A>0, \nu>0$$

$$0<\delta<1, \qquad 0\leq\delta\rho\leq1.$$

$$\frac{L}{K} > (\frac{1-\rho}{1-\delta\rho})$$

Where Xs is output, K is capital, and L is land; $\nu, \delta, \rho$ and $\gamma$ are production function parameters. The elasticity of substitution $\sigma$ for Equation (4.9) can be defined as

$$\sigma = \sigma(K,L) = 1 + \frac{\rho-1}{1-\delta\rho} \cdot \frac{K}{L} \tag{4.10}$$

This implies that the $\sigma$ for the VES varies linearly with the capital-land ratio around the intercept term of unity. We assume that $\sigma > 0$ in the empirically relevant range of $K/L$. This requires that $L/K > (1-\rho)/(1-\delta\rho)$ as indicated in (4.9). Also the elasticity of substitution ranges from zero to infinity.[3]

Some properties of the VES production function are now discussed. First the VES satisfies the requirements of a neo-classifical production function:

$\dfrac{\partial Xs}{\partial L}$ = marginal product of land

$$= v\delta\rho \ \frac{Xs}{L+(\rho-1)K} > 0 \tag{4.11}$$

$\dfrac{\partial Xs}{\partial K}$ = marginal product of capital

$$= v(1-\delta\rho)\frac{Xs}{K} + v\delta\rho(\rho-1) \ \frac{Xs}{L+(\rho-1)} > 0 \tag{4.12}$$

$$\frac{\partial\left[\dfrac{\partial Xs}{\partial K}\dfrac{\partial Xs}{\partial L}\right]}{\partial(K/L)} \leqq 0$$

$$\tag{4.13}$$

where $(\partial Xs/\partial K)/(\partial Xs/\partial L)$ = the marginal rate of substitution of capital for land

$$= ((\rho-1)/(1-\delta\rho))+((1-\delta\rho)/\delta\rho)/(L/K) \tag{4.14}$$

Second, the VES includes the Cobb-Douglas function ( $\rho = 1$ ) and the linear production function ( $\rho = 1/\delta$ ) as a special case.

Third, the VES differs from the CES in one important respect. The CES requires that the elasticity of substitution be the same as all points of an isoquant, independent of the level of output, hence at all points of the isoquant map. The VES on the other hand, requires that the substitution parameter should be the same only along a ray (like OP in Figure 4.1); the substitution parameter can vary along an isoquant.

## 4.3. Relationship between the VES and CES Function

Both CES and VES production functions are generalized cases of Cobb-Douglas production, however, the VES is not the generalized case of the CES production function. But, the indirect relationship between the CES and the Cobb-Douglas can be derived by first-order optimization conditions.

Given constant returns to scale in both CES and VES production function, competitive conditions in the factor and the production markets, and profit-maximization, the marginal conditions are obtained by equating the marginal physical products of lands and capital to their prices. Thus, for the VES, we have

$$\delta\rho \, \frac{Xs}{L_1} = n \tag{4.15}$$

$$(1-\delta\rho)\frac{Xs}{K} + \delta\rho(\rho-1)\frac{Xs}{L_1} = n \tag{4.16}$$

where r is the price of land and n is the price of capital. Dividing (4.16) by (4.15) and using $L_1 = L+(\rho-1)K$, we obtain

$$\frac{L}{K} = G_0 + G_1\frac{n}{r} \tag{4.17}$$

where $G_0 = (1-\rho)/(1-\delta\rho)$ and $G_1 = \delta\rho/(1-\delta\rho)$.

For the CES, it can be shown

$$\log (L/K) = G_0' + G_1'\log(n/r) \tag{4.18}$$

where $G_0' = (1/1-\rho)\log(\delta/(1-\delta)$ and $G_1' = 1/1-\rho = \sigma$. By comparing Equation (4.17) with Equation (4.18) it is found that the land-capital ratio is a linear function of the relative price, $n/r$ in the VES function and the land-capital ratio is a log-linear function of $n/r$, in the CES production function.

The linear versus log-linear relationship, implied by the VES versus the CES function, also appears in the behavior of the relative income shares of land and capital, i.e.,

$$\frac{rL}{nK} = G_1 + G_0\frac{r}{n} \tag{4.19}$$

for the VES production function and

$$\log(\frac{rL}{nK}) = G_0' + (1-G_1')\log\frac{r}{n} \tag{4.20}$$

for the CES prodution function. Thus the VES subscribes to the view of a linear model while the CES sees it as a log-linear model. The choice between the linear and the log-linear function can be empirically determined by the generalized transformation technique developed by Box and Cox (1964). This technique will be discussed in the next chapter in detail, and applied in Chapters 6, 10, and 13.

Fare and Jansson (1975) derived a weak disposability input (WDI) production function. The WDI production function can be directly integrated with the CES and VES production functions.

Fare and Jansson's WDI production function can be defined as

$$Xs = A[(1-\delta)(K-b_1L)^{-\rho} + \delta(L-b_k:K)^{-\rho}]^{-1/\rho} \tag{4.21}$$

if $(K-b_1\cdot L)$ and $(L-b_k\cdot K) \geqq 0$

= 0 otherwise

$Xs$, $A$, $K$ and $L$ are defined before, and $\delta$, $\rho$, $\gamma$, $b_1$ and $b_k$ are parameters. If both $b_1$ and $b_k$ are equal to zero, then

Equation (4.21) reduces to the CES production function as defined in Chapter 3. If $b_1 = 0$ and $\rho \to 0$, then Equation (4.21) reduces to Revankar's VES production function. If $b_1 = 0$, $b_k = 0$ and $\rho \to 0$ then Equation (4.21) reduces to CD function as defined in Chapter 2.

## 4.4. A VES Approach to Determine Urban Spatial Structure

In the last two chapters, we have used both the Cobb-Douglas and CES production function to derive urban structure. Now, the VES production function will be used to derive urban structure.

Using the production Equation (4.9) and the elasticity of substitution Equation (4.10) a general model for explaining urban spatial structure can be developed. To do this a demand function for housing services at u[as in Chapter 2] is defined as

$$xd(u) = Bw^{\theta_1}p(u)^{\theta_2}, \qquad (4.22)$$

where:

> B  = a scale parameter and depends upon the units in which housing services are measured,

> w  = the income for workers,

> p(u) = the price of housing services at distance u,

> $\theta_1$ = income elasticity, and

> $\theta_2$ = price elasticity of demand for housing services.

From equation (4.9) the relationships between the value of the marginal product and its rental rates for land and capital, r(u) and n respectively, can be written as

$$\frac{\partial Xs(u)}{\partial L(u)} = v\delta\rho \frac{Xs(u)}{L(u)+(\rho-1)K(u)} = \frac{r(u)}{p(u)} \qquad (4.23)$$

and

$$\frac{\partial Xs(u)}{\partial K(u)} = (1-\delta\rho)\frac{Xs(u)}{K(u)} + v\delta\rho(\rho-1)\frac{Xs(u)}{L(u)+(\rho-1)K(u)}$$

$$= \frac{n_t}{p(u)} \ . \tag{4.24}$$

From Equations (4.23) and (4.24), the marginal rate of substitution of capital for land, S, is

$$S = \frac{(\rho-1)}{\delta\rho} + \frac{1-\delta\rho}{\delta\rho}\frac{L(u)}{K(u)} \ . \tag{4.25}$$

Note that S changes linearly with capital intensity.

From Equations (4.23) and (4.24) we have

$$L(u) = vp(u)Xs(u)[\frac{\delta\rho}{r(u)} - \frac{(1-\delta\rho)(\rho-1)}{n - r(u)(\rho-1)} \tag{4.26}$$

and

$$K(u) = p(u)Xs(u)\ \frac{v\ (1-\delta\rho)}{n-r(u)(\rho-1)} \ . \tag{4.27}$$

As $v = 1$, substituting Equations (4.26) and (4.27) into Equation (4.9) we have

$$p(u) = A^{-1}[n-r(u)(\rho-1)]^{1-\delta\rho}(1-\delta\rho)^{\delta\rho-1}\ [r(u)]^{\delta\rho}(\delta\rho)^{-\delta\rho}. \tag{4.28}$$

From Equation (4.28) the price elasticities of housing with respect to n and r(u) can be written as

$$\frac{\partial p(u)}{\partial n}\ \frac{n}{p(u)} = \frac{n(1-\delta\rho)}{n-r(u)(\rho-1)} \tag{4.29}$$

and

$$\frac{\partial p(u)}{\partial r(u)}\ \frac{r(u)}{p(u)} = \frac{\delta\rho n-r(\rho-1)}{n-r(\rho-1)} \ . \tag{4.30}$$

Equations (4.29) and (4.30) allow the elasticities of housing services with respect to n and r(u) to vary with changes in n and r(u). These elasticities will reduce to $1-\alpha$ and $\alpha$ respectively when the elasticity of substitution between land and capital is unity. This is the case obtained with the Cobb-Douglas function.

Mills (1981) and Muth (1969), using constrained utility maximization, have derived a differential equation to describe the relationship between the change in the cost of housing and change in commuting cost as

$$p'(u)xd(u)+T = 0, \tag{4.31}$$

where

p'(u) is the slope of p(u) and
T        is the cost of commuting.

Substituting Equation (4.22) into Equation (4.31) we have

$$p'(u)Bw^{\theta_1}[p(u)]^{\theta_2} + T = 0. \tag{4.32}$$

By use of the initial condition of Equation (4.32), obtained from Equation (4.31), the solution of the differential Equation (4.32) can be written as

$$p(u) = \left[ \bar{p}^{\theta_2+1} + \frac{T(\bar{u}-u)(\theta_2+1)}{Bw^{\theta_1}} \right]^{1/(\theta_2+1)}, \tag{4.33}$$

where

$\underline{u}$ is the distance from the city center to the edge of the urban area, and

$$\bar{p} = p(\bar{u}). \tag{4.34}$$

Substituting Equation (4.28) into Equation (4.33) we have

$$\left[\bar{p}^{-\theta_2} + 1 + \frac{T(\bar{u}-u)(\theta_2+1)}{Bw\,\theta_1}\right]^{1/(1+\theta_2)}$$

$$= A^{-1}[n-r(u)(\rho-1)]^{1-\delta\rho}(1-\delta\rho)^{\delta\rho-1}[r(u)]^{\delta\rho}(\delta\rho)^{-\delta\rho} \quad (4.35)$$

Equation (4.35) can be rewritten as

$$r(u) = [A(\delta\rho)^{\delta\rho}(1-\delta\rho)^{1-\delta\rho}]^{1/\delta\rho}n^{(\delta\rho-1)/\delta\rho}$$

$$x\left[1 - \frac{r(u)}{n}(\rho-1)\right]^{(\delta\rho-1)/\delta\rho}\left[\bar{p}^{-\theta_2+1} + \frac{T(\bar{u}-u)(\theta_2+1)}{Bw^{\theta_1}}\right]^{1/\delta\rho(\theta_2+1)} \quad (4.36)$$

This implies that the explicit relationship between r(u) and u cannot be derived unless $\rho$ is equal to unity. If $\rho$ = 1 then Equation (4.36) reduces to

$$r(u) = [A\delta(1-\delta)^{1-\delta}]^{1/\delta}n^{(\delta-1)/\delta}$$

$$x\left[\bar{p}^{-\theta_2+1} + \frac{T(\bar{u}-u)(\theta_2+1)}{Bw^{\theta_1}}\right]^{1/\delta(\theta_2+1)} , \quad (4.37)$$

where

$$\bar{P} = A^{-1}(1-\delta)^{\delta-1}\delta^{-\delta}\bar{r}^{-\delta}n^{1-\delta} \quad (4.38)$$

and

$$\bar{r} = r(\bar{u}). \quad (4.39)$$

Equations (4.37), (4.38), and (4.39) are identical to the general case presented by Mills (1981).

To derive the relationship between the population density and the rental of land, r(u), Mills (1981, page 228) has defined

$$N(u) = \frac{Xs(u)}{xd(u)} , \quad (4.40)$$

where

N(u) is the number of workers living u miles from the urban center,

Xs(u) is the output of housing services u miles from the urban center, and

xd(u) is the housing demand per worker living u miles from the urban center.

From Equations (4.26) and (4.27) it can be shown that

$$K(u) = \left\{ \frac{1-\delta\rho}{n-r(u)(\rho-1)} \Big/ \left[ \frac{\delta\rho}{r(u)} - \frac{(1-\delta\rho)(\rho-1)}{n-r(u)(\rho-1)} \right] \right\} L(u) \qquad (4.41)$$

Substitution of Equation (4.41) into Equation (4.9) gives

$$Xs(u) = AL(u) \left[ \frac{\delta\rho}{r(u)} - \frac{(\rho-1)(1-\delta\rho)}{n-r(u)(\rho-1)} \right]^{-1}$$

$$\times \left[ \frac{1-\delta\rho}{n-r(u)(\rho-1)} \right]^{1-\delta\rho} \left[ \frac{\delta\rho}{r(u)} \right]^{\delta\rho}. \qquad (4.42)$$

From Equations (4.22) and (4.28).

$$xd(u) = Bw^{\theta_1} A^{-\theta_2} [n-r(u)(\rho-1)]^{\theta_2(1-\delta\rho)}$$

$$\times (1-\delta\rho)^{\theta_2(\delta\rho-1)} [r(u)]^{\delta\rho\theta_2} (\delta\rho)^{-\delta\rho\theta_2}. \qquad (4.43)$$

Substitution of Equations (4.42) and (4.43) into Equation (4.36) gives

$$D(u) = \frac{N(u)}{L(u)} = B^{-1} w^{-\theta_1} A^{\theta_2+1}$$

$$\times [n-r(u)(\rho-1)]^{(\theta_2+1)(\delta\rho-1)} (1-\delta\rho)^{(\theta_2+1)(1-\delta\rho)}$$

$$\times \left[ \frac{\delta\rho}{r(u)} - \frac{(\rho-1)(1-\delta\rho)}{n-r(u)(\rho-1)} \right]^{-1}$$

$$\times \left[ \frac{\delta\rho}{r(u)} \right]^{\delta\rho} [r(u)]^{-\delta\rho\theta_2} (\delta\rho)^{\delta\rho\theta_2}. \qquad (4.44)$$

This is the population density in terms of n, r(u), $\rho$, and other parameters.

4.5. Summary and Conclusion

This chapter has shown that urban planning cannot entirely rely upon the distance variable. The theory suggests that other parameters may play an important part in determining urban spatial structure. The variation of the elasticity of substitution indicates that institutional or production constraints exist and that these constraints effect the variation of population density with distance. Future chapters will concentrate on empirically testing the VES model.

Figure 4.1. Isoquants of the VES Production Function for different Values of $\rho$ *.

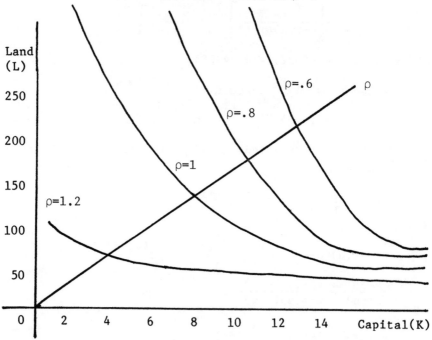

*
Note: Graph from Revankar (1971a).

## NOTES

1.    Sato (1979) pointed out that this approximation was recently generalized to n factors by Christensen et al. (1973), "Who named it the "transcendental logarithmic function." The usefulness of applying a transcendental logarithmic function to urban economics is still an open question.

2.    Liu and Hildebrand (1965) have shown that the main economic implication of Equation (4.6) is that $\ln(Xs/L) = f(\text{Land rate, } K/L \text{ ratio})$.

3.    The Revankar VES varies linearly with the capital-land ratio, around the intercept term of unity. More specifically when $\rho < 1$ ($>1$), it decreases (increases) steadily with the capital-land ratio and stays below (above unity over the entire range. A crossover can be secured in the VES function in a time-series context where the VES is modified to incorporate biased technical change [see Chapter 9].

Chapter 5

ECONOMETRIC TECHNIQUES IN SPATIAL ANALYSIS

## 5.1. Introduction

Econometric techniques have developed rapidly in the last two decades. Applications of alternative econometric methods in spatial analysis has provided increased insight into urban structure. Applications of econometrics can be classified into static and dynamic urban model estimation. The static urban model does not take growth and durability of housing and urban infrastructure into account, hence, the key variable used to describe urban structure is distance. The dynamic urban model has explicitly considered the growth pattern and the durability of housing. It is found that market parameters such as income, transportation cost, and population are also important variables for describing the urban structure. In this chapter we will discuss econometric methods for the study of both static and dynamic urban structure models. There are seven alternative econometric techniques to be briefly present in this chapter. They are:

1. Simple regression,

2. multiple regression,

3. generalized functional form,

4. random coefficient regression,

5. generalized least squares,

6. switching regressions, and

7. a varying coefficient model.

Methods (1) through (5) can be used to investigate alternative static urban structure models; method (6) can be used to test the existence of dynamic urban structure models; method (7) can be used to investigate the implications of the urban growth model in estimating density gradients.

## 5.2. Simple Regression

Simple regression is used to investigate the relationship between two variables when one of the variables is the explained (dependent) variable and the other variable is the explanatory variable (independent variable). In Chapter 2, a theoretical relationship between the population density and distance is defined as

$$D(u) = D(o) \, e^{-\gamma u + e(u)} \tag{5.1}$$

where $D(u)$ is the population density $u$ distance from the city center, $D(o)$ is the density at the city center, $\gamma$ the density gradient, and $e(u)$ the error term. To estimate the population density gradient, $\gamma$, we take the natural logarithm transformation, of Equation (5.1),

$$\log D(u) = \log D(o) - \gamma u + e(u), \tag{5.2}$$

Data on population density, $D(u)$, and distance, $u$, within a SMSA can be used to fit the ordinary least square regression (OLS) of Equation (5.2) and to obtain the parameter, $\gamma$. To simplify the notations, we let

$y_i = \log D(u)$ and $x_i = u$ and rewrite (5.2) as

$$y(u)_i = \alpha_i + \beta_i x_i + e(u)_i \tag{5.3}$$

where $\alpha_i = \log D_0 i$, $\beta_i = -\gamma$ and i equals the number of observations.

Statistical techniques related to estimating Equation (5.3) can be summarized as:

A.  Calculation of Estimators

    (1)  $\hat{\alpha}$, the intercept,

    (2)  $\hat{\beta}$, the slope,

    (3)  $\bar{R}^2$, adjusted coefficient of determination,

    (4)  $\hat{e}(u)$, the estimated error term,

    (5)  $\hat{y}(u)$, the estimate log density,

    (6)  SSE, the sum of square errors, and

    (7)  ESS, the explained sum of square errors.

B.  Properties and Tests of Estimators

    (1)  assumptions required,

    (2)  properties of blue estimators,

    (3)  $\sigma_\alpha^2$, standard error of $\hat{\alpha}$,

    (4)  $\sigma_{\hat{\beta}}^2$, standard error of $\hat{\beta}$,

    (5)  $\hat{S}^2$, estimate of population variance for the dependent variable,

    (6)  t-test,

    (7)  F-test,

    (8)  nonlinearity, and

    (9)  error bounds when forecasting.

It is important to understand that $\alpha$ and $\beta$ in Equation

(5.3) are true population parameters. The parameters are generally estimated by sample data. In most studies of urban structure, a set of pairwise data, i.e., population density and distance within a SASA, are used to estimate these parameters. To do sample estimation, an error term, e(u), is included (see Johnson, 1972) for these reasons:

1. to capture an imperfect specification, such as either using a linear model where a non-linear one may be more meaningful or unwillingly ignoring factors which relate to the dependent variable,

2. to capture the factors which are hard to be quantified,

3. to capture some measurement errors associated with a particular variable that is not measured with precision.

In sum, there is always an element of unknowns in the behavior of any system and the insertion of an errors term is appropriate. Incidentally, it should be noted that the independent variable $(x(u)_i$ is assumed to be exogenous supplied, i.e., $x_i$ is assumed non-random or fixed.

The simple estimated regression line of (5.3) can be defined as

$$\hat{y}(u)_i = \hat{\alpha} + \hat{\beta} x_i, \qquad (5.4)$$

Where $\hat{a}$ and $\hat{\beta}$ are point estimates of unknown population parameters $\alpha$ and $\beta$ respectively. $\hat{y}(u)$ is the estimated value coresponding to a given value of $x_i$. $\bar{y}(u)$ is the conditional mean, i.e., the mean given the information $x_i$. Using this conditional mean, the total sum of squared errors [SSE] of $y(u)_i$ can be decomposed into (dropping u for convenience),

$$\sum_{i=1}^{n} (y_i - \bar{y})^2 = \sum_{i=1}^{n} (\hat{y}_i - \bar{y})^2 + \sum_{i=1}^{n} (y_i - \hat{y}_i)^2 \qquad (5.5)$$

The first items of right hand side (RHS) is explained sum

of squared errors (ESS) and the second item is the unexplained sum of squared errors (UESS). The method used to derive the estimated regression line is the ordinary least squares (OLS) method, i.e.,

$$\min \sum_{i=1}^{n} e_i^2 = \sum_{i=1}^{n} (y_i - \hat{y}_i)^2 = \sum_{i=1}^{n} (y_i - \hat{a} - \hat{\beta})^2 \qquad (5.6)$$

Taking the derivative of Equation (5.6) with respect to $\hat{\alpha}$ and $\hat{\beta}$ we can obtain a two-equation system for estimating $\hat{\alpha}$ and $\hat{\beta}$. It can easily be shown that

(A)  $\hat{\beta} = Cov(y_i, x_i)/Var(x_i)$           (5.7)

(b)  $\hat{\alpha} = \bar{y} - \beta\bar{x}$

To measure how much the variation of $y_i$ can be explained by the variation of $x_i$, the coefficient of determination ($R^2$) can be derived from Equation (5.5) as

$$R^2 = \frac{\sum_{i=1}^{n} (\hat{y}_i - \bar{y})^2}{\sum_{i=1}^{n} (y_i - \bar{y})^2} = - \frac{\sum_{i=1}^{n} (y_i - \hat{y}_i)^2}{\sum_{i=1}^{n} (y_i - \bar{y})^2} \qquad (5.8)$$

$$= \frac{\text{explained variation}}{\text{total variation}}$$

The coefficient of determination, $R^2$ can be used to determine how much variation of log $D(u)$ can be explained by the distance variable, $u_i$.

Standard tests of simple linear regression of Equation (5.3) require several assumptions about the error term, $e_i$:

(i)  $e_i$ has a mean (expectation) of zero; $E(e_i) = 0$

(ii)  all $e_i$'s have a common constant and finite variance for all i; $Var(u_i) = \sigma_i^2$. This property known as 'homoscedasticity'.

(iii)   error terms are independent of the explanatory

variable, i.e., $E(xi, e_i) = 0$ for all.  This

assumption is upheld if all $x_i$s are treated

as non-random.  Since $Cov(x_i, e_i) = E(x_i, e_i) -$

$E(x_i)E(e_i) = 0$ from assumption (i), we also

know the $E(e_i) = 0$.  Therefore, $E(x_i, e_i) = 0$.

(v)   For the sake of completeness, one of the

other implicit assumptions is, $E(e_{j_i}, e_{p_i}) = 0$,

where j and p are two different cities.  Stated

verbally, this implies that the error term of

"our" simple regression model for $j^{th}$ city is

not correlated with that of another regression

of city p.

    Under assumptions (i) – (v), it can be proved that $\hat{\alpha}$
and $\beta$ are the best linear unbiased estimators (BLUE) of the
parameter $\alpha$ and $\beta$ respectively.  BLUE indicates the
presence of three properties i.e., linearity, unbiasedness,
and efficiency.  If the errors, $e_i$, follow a normal distribution, then $\hat{\alpha}$ and $\hat{\beta}$ also follow a normal distributions,
i.e.,

(A)   $\hat{\alpha} \sim N(\alpha, \hat{s}^2_{\hat{\alpha}})$,                                    (5.9)

(B)   $\hat{\beta} \sim N(\beta, \hat{s}^2_{\hat{\beta}})$,

where

(A)   $\hat{s}^2_{\hat{\beta}} = (SEE)^2 / \Sigma(y_i - \bar{y})^2$,

(B) $\quad \hat{S}^2_{\hat{\alpha}} = (SEE)^2 / \dfrac{\Sigma y_i^2}{N\Sigma(y_i - y)2}$ $\qquad$ (5.10)

(C) $\qquad SEE = \dfrac{\Sigma e_i^2}{n-2}$

SEE is the standard errors of estimation for the linear regression $\hat{S}_{\hat{\beta}}$ and $\hat{S}_{\hat{\alpha}}$ are standard errors for the estimated $\beta$ and the estimated $\beta$ respectively. SEE can be used to determine the goodness of fit for the regression. $\hat{S}^{\wedge}$ and $\hat{S}^{\wedge}$ can be used to test whether the estimated $\beta$ and the estimated $\alpha$ are significantly different from zero.

## 5.3. Multiple Regression

Besides the distance variable, some other urban characteristics, e.g., income, age, geographic restrictions and variations of transportation modes can be used to improve the explanatory power of the simple regression model as defined in Equation (5.3). Following Theil (1971), a multiple regression urban spatial model can be defined as

$$Y_i = \alpha_i + \beta_1 x_{1_i} + \beta_2 x_{2_i} + \beta_3 x_{3_i} + \ldots \beta_k x_{k_i} + e_i \qquad (5.11)$$

where $y_i$ is the defined as population density as in Equation (5.3), $x_{1i}$ = the distance from its center, $u_i$, and $x_2$, $x_{3_i}$ ... and $x_k$ are other urban characteristics.

The model defined in Equation (5.11) is a multiple regression with k explanatory variables. In the matrix form Equation (5.11) can be written as

$$y = \chi\hat{\beta} + e'$$

where $\hat{\beta} = (\hat{\beta}_1, \hat{\beta}_2, \ldots \hat{\beta}_k)$, $e' = (e_1, e_2 \ldots e_k)$, and

$$\chi = (x_2 \ldots x_k). \qquad (5.12)$$

Before discussing how to estimate the regression coefficients, $\beta_1$, $\beta_2$, $\beta_2$, ... and $\beta_k$, two additional assumptions are necessary for multiple regression. The first assumption states that the explanatory variables are independent of each other; this is necessary for obtaining efficient estimates of $\beta_1$, $\beta_2$ ... and $\beta_m$. The second assumption is that the number of observations, n, will be greater than the number of explanatory variables k(i.e., that the rank of $\chi = k$).

Estimating the coefficients is straight forward. The $\hat{\beta}$ coefficient as indicated in Equation (5.12) can be obtained by using the familiar least-squares procedure. Minimizing the sum of squared errors (SSE) with respect to we get

$$\hat{\beta} = (\chi'\chi)^{-1}\chi'Y \qquad (5.13)$$

The variance-covariance matrix of $\hat{\beta}$ is

$$\text{Var} (\hat{\beta}) = \sigma_e^2 (\chi'\chi)^{-1} \qquad (5.14)$$

and the standard errors of $\hat{\beta}_1$, $\hat{\beta}_2$, ... and $\hat{\beta}_k$ can be used to calculate the t statistics for testing the null hypothesis

$$H_0: \quad \hat{\beta}_k \neq 0. \qquad (5.15)$$

Finally, the coefficient of determination ($R^2$) can be used to test the goodness of fit for a multiple regression $R^2$ is defined as

$$R^2 = \sum_{t=1}^{n} (\hat{y}_t - \bar{y})^2 / \sum_{t=1}^{n} (y_t - \bar{y})^2 \qquad (5.16)$$

In a multiple regression the $R^2$ is not the most appropriate indicator for measuring the goodness of fit since the SEE is always decreased if the number of explanatory variables

is increased, regardless of the significance of the addi
tional variables. Therefore, an adjusted $R^2$ as defined in
Equation (5.17) is always used to determine the goodness of
fit for a multiple regression

$$\bar{R}^2 = 1 - \frac{n-1}{n-k} (1-R^2) \tag{5.17}$$

Clearly, if $(1-R^2)$ decreases at a slower rate than $(n-k)$

due to the addition of more variables, $\bar{R}^2$ will actually decline, indicating that the extra variables do not provide
any further information. Applications of multiple regression to spatial analysis will be discussed through-out the
book.

### 5.4. Generalized Functional Form and Urban Structure

In Chapers 2, 3, and 4, it has been shown that the functional forms of urban structure analysis are essentially
determined by the specification of (i) demand function of
housing services and (ii) the production function of housing services. The applications of generalized functional
form, developed by Box and Cox (1964) and Zarembka (1968),
to urban density analysis are due to Kau and Lee (1976a,
1976b). Based upon Kau and Lee, the procedure is now discussed.

Two generalized functional forms for describing the
relationship between the population density (D) and distance (u) are defined as

$$(D_i^{\lambda} - 1)/\lambda = \gamma_0 - \gamma_1 u_i + \varepsilon_i \tag{5.18}$$

and

$$D^{\lambda'} - 1)/\lambda' = \gamma_0' - \gamma_1' (U_i^{\lambda'} - 1)/\lambda' + \varepsilon_i' , \tag{5.19}$$

where $\gamma_0$, $\gamma_1$, $\gamma_0'$, and $\gamma_1'$ are regression parameters $\lambda$ and

$\lambda'$ are functional form parameters, and the disturbance
terms ($\varepsilon_i$ and $\varepsilon_i'$ ) are normally distributed with zero means

and variances of $\sigma^2$ and $\sigma'^2$, respectively.

For (5.18), if $\lambda = 1$, linear density is regressed on distance. If $\lambda$ approaches zero, the dependent variable is the natural logarithm of density. Similarly, (5.19) will reduce to the linear form when $\lambda'$ is equal to one and to a double logarithmic form when $\lambda'$ approaches zero. Following the Taylor's theorem, (5.19) can be approximated as

$$\log D = \gamma_0 - \gamma u_i + \gamma' u_i^2, \tag{5.20}$$

where $\gamma' = 1/2\lambda\gamma$ and $\lambda < 1$.

This demonstrates that the negative quadratic exponential form used by [Latham and Yeates (1970)] is a special case of (5.18). Using maximum likelihood techniques developed by [Box and Cox (1964)] and $\lambda$ and $\lambda'$, the regression coefficients are estimated from the data.

Under the assumption of normality, the probability density function for $\varepsilon_i$ in (5.18) is written as

$$f(\varepsilon_i) = (2\pi\sigma^2)^{-1/2} \exp(-1/2(\varepsilon_i/\sigma^2)). \tag{5.21}$$

If the $\varepsilon$'s are identically and independently distributed, the log likelihood function for (5.21) can be written as

$$\log L = 0 \; \underline{n} \; \log 2\pi\sigma^2 + (\lambda - 1) \sum_{i=1}^{n} \log D_i$$

$$\frac{1}{2\sigma^2} \sum_{i=1}^{n} \left[ \frac{D_i^{\lambda} - 1}{\lambda} - \gamma_0 + \gamma u_i \right]^2 \tag{5.22}$$

The logarithmic likelihood is maximized with respect to $\sigma^2$, $\gamma_0$ and $\gamma_1$, given $\lambda$. The maximum likelihood estimate of $\sigma^2$ for the given $\lambda$, $\hat{\sigma}^2(\lambda)$, is then the estimated variance of the disturbances of regressing $(D_i^{\lambda} - 1)/\lambda$ on $u_i$.

Replacing $\sigma^2$ by $\hat{\sigma}^2$ $(\lambda)$, the maximum log likelihood $[L_{max}(\lambda)]$ for (5.18) is

$$L_{max}(\lambda) = -\frac{n}{2} \log 2\pi\hat{\sigma}^2(\lambda) - \frac{n}{2} + (\lambda - 1) \sum_{i=1}^{n} \log D_i \qquad (5.23)$$

Box and Cox [1984, p. 216) indicate that an approximate 95 percent confidence region for   is obtained from

$$L_{max}(\hat{\lambda}) - L_{max}(\lambda) < \frac{1}{2}\chi^2(.05) = 1.92) \qquad (5.24)$$

Equations (5.23) and (5.24) with $\lambda'$ can also be derived for (5.19) by a similar procedure. Equation (5.23) is used to test whether the functional form parameters, $\lambda$ and $\lambda'$, are significantly different from zero and/or one.

To test the importance of the quadratic term of distance in explaining the population density, the log likelihood for (5.25) and (5.26) are estimated.

$$D_i = \beta_0 - \beta_1 u_i + \beta_2 u_i^2 + e_i, \text{ and} \qquad (5.25)$$

$$\log D_i = \beta_0' - \beta_1' u_i + \beta_2' u_i^2 + e_i', \qquad (5.26)$$

where $e_i$ and $e_i'$ = the disturbance terms, $\beta_0$, $\beta_1$, $\beta_2$, $\beta_0'$, $\beta_1'$

and $\beta_2'$ are regression parameters.

## 5.4.1. An Example of Functional Form Procedure

The data for this example consist of a random sample of 45 census tract densities measured  u miles from the Central Business District for each of 50 U.S. cities in 1970.

The appropriate power transformations for (5.18) and (5.19) is determined by iterating $\lambda$ and $\lambda'$ between $-.50$ and 1.50 at intervals of 0.1. The maximum likelihood estimates of these iterations for each of 50 cities indicate that the functional form parameters ( $\lambda$ and $\lambda'$ ) for 45 cities in this study are significantly different from one, and approximately 50 percent of them are significantly different from zero at the .05 level.

| Estimated $\lambda$ values | Number of Cities | Estimated $\lambda'$ values | Number of cities |
|---|---|---|---|
| $\hat{\lambda} \neq 0$ | 23 | $\hat{\lambda}' \neq 0$ | 29 |
| $\hat{\lambda} \neq 1$ | 45 | $\hat{\lambda}' \neq 1$ | 45 |

In most cases it is preferred to use simple transformations to facilitate interpretation of the empirical results. Five alternative specifications are examined - they are linear (5.18) with $\lambda = 1$), semi-log (5.18) with $\lambda \to 0$), double-log (5.18) with $\lambda' \to 0$), quadratic (5.25), semi-log quadratic (5.26). The log likelihood for each specification is calculated using (5.24). These formulations encompass the Clark and Muth exponential models (5.18) with $\lambda \to 0$) and the Latham and Yeates model (5.26) with the addition of other alternative specifications for comparison.

Using the critical value of 1.92 from (5.24), the results indicate that the logarithmic specifications dominate the linear specifications. But it is difficult to differentiate the semi-log from the double-log functional forms, since their log likelihood values are similar. Also, there exist some cities in which the optimal functional form is either linear or linear quadratic.

The results would suggest that the functional form varies among cities. For both the semi-log and the double-log functional forms, there is no statistical justification for preferring a priori one specification over another. The variation among all functional forms for all cities is of enough significance to warrant empirical investigation for each particular case [further explanation is provided in Chaper 13].

Box and Cox (1964) have ascertained that after suitable transformation of the dependent variable, (a) the expected values of the transformed observations are described by a model of simple structure, (b) the error variance is constant and (c) the observations are normally distributed. In addition, Box and Tidwell (1962) have shown that the main purpose of transforming the independent variable is to reduce the function in these transformed variables to as simple a form as possible. From the implications of these transformations and the empirical results, it is concluded that both semi-log and double-log relationships are not always a sufficient functional form to be used to describe the relationship between the population density and distance within a SMSA.

The study leaves unexplained the variation of $\lambda$ among cities. Further research is necessary to explain the possible effects of central city densities, age, geographic restrictions and variation in transportation modes on the functional form.

## 5.5. Random Coefficient Models

The density gradient model in Equation (5.2) is a fixed regression model. Kau and Lee (1977) developed a random coefficient model for estimating the density gradient. Following Kau and Lee (1977), the application of random coefficient regression model to spatial analysis is discussed.

In accordance with Muth (1969), the fixed coefficient models of estimating the density gradient can be defined as

$$\log D_i = \log D_0 - \gamma u_i + e_i, \qquad (5.27)$$

and

$$\log D_i = \log D_0 - \gamma u_i + cX_i + dP_i + mZ_i + e_i', \qquad (5.28)$$

where $D_i$ is the population density; $u_i$ the distance from the central business district (CBD); $\gamma$ the fixed coefficient density gradient; $D_0$ the density of the central area of the city; $e_i$ and $e_i'$ are the error terms with zero mean and variance $\sigma_0^2$ and $\sigma'^2_0$; b, c, d and m regression coeffi-cients; and $X_i$, $P_i$ and $Z_i$ represent various explanatory va riables.

Equations (5.27) and (5.28) imply that the regression coefficient of u in responsiveness to log $D_i$ is fixed in-stead of stochastic. However, it is clear that distance u is only one of the important factors determining the density gradient of a city. It is obvious that Equation (5.27) is a misspecified equation unless c, d and m are not significantly different from zero. In principal, $X_i$, $P_i$ and $Z_i$ should be explicitly included in an empirical study.

However because of collection cost, measurement error and multicollinearity specification (5.27) is still used. If X, P and Z are omitted from the equation then it seems much more reasonable to regard $\lambda$ as only a mean value of a ran-dom response of population density to distance.

Hildreth and Houck (1968) have employed two examples to justify the necessity to random coefficient models, i.e., (a) response of a plant to nitrogen fertilizer, and (b) response of a household to the level of income. For case (a) the random coefficient assumption can be used to take care of the variation of the regression coefficients associated with the omitted factors, e.g., temperature and rainfall. For case (b) the random coefficient assumption can be used to take care of the variation of the coeffi-cient associated with the omitted demographic factors. A random coefficient model is proposed to substitute for the fixed coefficient model as described by Equation (5.27) to estimate the mean value and variance of the stochastic den-sity gradient.

In accordance with Theil's (1971) random coefficient model, Equation (5.27) is rewritten as

$$\log D_i = \log D_0 - \bar{\bar{\gamma}}_i u_i + e_i, \qquad (5.30)$$

where $\overline{\overline{\gamma}}_i$ is a random coefficient estimate of the density gradient and is normally distributed with mean $\overline{\gamma}$ and variance $\sigma_1^2$. In addition, it is assumed that $e_i$ is independent of $(\gamma_i - \overline{\gamma})$. Under this circumstance, the negative exponential functional relationship is defined as

$$D_i = D_0 \exp(-\gamma u_i - (\gamma_i - \overline{\gamma}) u_i - e_i), \qquad (5.31)$$

where $\exp(-(\gamma_i - \overline{\gamma}) k_i + e_i)$ is log-normally distributed with mean $\exp(\sigma_0^2 + u_i^2 \sigma_1^2)$ and variance $\exp(\sigma_0^2 + u_i^2 \sigma_1^2 (\exp(\sigma_0^2 + u_i^2 \sigma_1^2) - 1)$. However, $\log[\exp(-\gamma_i - \overline{\gamma}) u_i + \sigma_1)]$ is normally distributed with mean zero and variance $\sigma_0^2 + u_i^2 \sigma_1^2$. This is an important property which allows us to apply regression technique to the logarithmic transformation of (5.31).

Equation (5.30) is a linear regression model with random slope $\overline{\gamma}_i$. It can be rewritten into a fixed coefficient model as

$$\log D_i = \log D_0 - \gamma u_i + \varepsilon_i^*, \qquad (5.32)$$

where $\gamma$ is the fixed coefficient density gradient with

$$\varepsilon_i^* = \varepsilon_i + (\gamma_i - \overline{\gamma}) u_i \sim N(0, \sigma_0^2 + u_i^2 \sigma_1^2). \qquad (5.33)$$

This is a fixed coefficient regression model with a heteroscedastic error term, therefore the generalized least squares method (G.L.S.) instead of the ordinary least squares method (O.L.S.) should be employed to estimate $\gamma$ to improve its efficiency. Note that the point estimate of $\gamma$ from Equation (5.27) will not be significantly different from the estimated $\gamma$ in Equation (5.32), but the estimated $\gamma$ from Equation (5.32) permits a derivation of the population interval-estimate (variance) for the density gradient.

Theil has shown that Equation (5.34) below can be used

to estimate both $\sigma_0^2$, the residual variance of the dependent variable density, and $\sigma_1^2$ , the population variance of the density gradient, simultaneously:

$$e_i^2 = \sigma_0^2 P_i + \sigma_1^2 Q_1 + f_i , \tag{5.34}$$

where

$e_i$ = 0.L.S. residual,

$$P_i = 1 - u_i^2/\Sigma u_i^2 , \tag{5.35}$$

$$Q_i = u_i^2 \cdot (1 - 2(u_i^2/\Sigma u_i^2) + \Sigma u_i^4/(\Sigma u_i^2)^2), \tag{5.36}$$

$$f_i \sim N(0, 2(\sigma_0^2 P_i + \sigma_1^2 Q_1)^2). \tag{5.37}$$

Chapter 14 provides empirical estimates of the fixed and random coefficient of the density gradients and of $\sigma_0$ and $\sigma_1^2$.

## 5.6.  Generalized Least Squares (GLS)

This section is concerned with violations of two assumptions required by the error term and independence of explanatory variables from the error term. Homoscedasticity is lost when the error term variance changes across distance or across time. Independence of the explanatory variables from the error term may not exist for several reasons, but we will be interested in the situation of errors-in-variables, i.e., the regressors of a regression are measured with errors. The errors-in-variables problem will be explored in the next section.

In urban economics, there are two possible cases that should use the GLS estimators, i.e. (i) single equation and (ii) multiple equation case. First, the single equation is discussed. The residual variance of Equation (5.3) might change with distance, i.e.,

$$Var[e(u)] = u_i^2 \sigma_e^2 \qquad (5.38)$$

Kau, Lee and Chen (1983) [see Chapter 14] have empirically demonstrated this kind of heteroscedasticity in estimating the density gradient. Actually the random coefficient model as defined in the previous section is also one of the heteroscedasticity cases. The GLS estimator can be used to improve the efficiency of the density gradient for these two cases.

Now the multiple regression GLS case for urban economics application is explored. Following Kau, Lee and Sirmans (1980) [KLS], a two-equation system can be used to estimate the elasticity of substitution for the CES and the VES production functions. Zellner's (1962) seemingly unrelated regression (SUR) has been used to improve the efficiency of the estimators. The two-equation system used by KLS can be defined as

$$\text{(A)} \quad Y_1 = b_{10} + b_{11}x_{11} + b_{12}x_{12} + e_1 \qquad (5.39)$$

$$\text{(B)} \quad Y_2 = b_{20} + b_{21}x_{21} + b_{22}x_{22} + e_2 \qquad (5.40)$$

where $Y_1$ and $Y_2$ represent output/capital and land/capital ratios, $x_{11}$, $x_{12}$, $x_{21}$, $x_{22}$ represent capital rent, land rent and their combinations.

In a marix notation Equation (5.39) and (5.40) can be defined as

$$Y = \chi\beta + E, \qquad (5.41)$$

where $y' = [Y_1, Y_2]$, $\chi = \begin{bmatrix} x_{11} & x_{12} \\ x_{21} & x_{22} \end{bmatrix}$,

$$\beta' = \begin{bmatrix} b_{10} & b_{20} \\ b_{11} & b_{21} \\ b_{12} & b_{22} \end{bmatrix} \quad \text{and } E' = [e_1, e_2].$$

What is essentially done, is to pool the data for the two different equations, and define a variance matrix for disturbance terms as

$$\Omega = \begin{bmatrix} \sigma_1^2 & \sigma_{12} \\ \sigma_{21} & \sigma_2^2 \end{bmatrix} \tag{5.42}$$

If $\sigma_{12} = \sigma_{21} \neq 0$, then a GLS estimator is defined in Equation (5.43) and can be used to define the estimated $\beta$ as

$$\hat{\beta} = (\chi'\Omega^{-1}\chi)^{-1}(\chi'\Omega^{-1}y). \tag{5.43}$$

## 5.7.  Switching Regression

The standard problem of switching regimes in regression theory consists of (1) testing the null hyotheses, that no switch in regimes took place against the alternative that the observations were generated by two (or possibly more) distinct regression equations and (2) estimating the two (or more) regimes that gives rise to data.

Following Quandt (1972), given n observations and k independent variables, the null hypothesis is expressed by

$$Y = \chi\beta + e \tag{5.44}$$

where Y is the nx1 vector of observations on the dependent variable, $\chi$ the nxk matrix of observations on independent variables, e the nx1 vector of unobservable error terms distributed as $N(0,\sigma^2 I)$ and $\beta$ is the kx1 vector of coefficients to be estimated.

The alternative hypothesis is expressed by asserting that there exists some permutation of the rows of Y and X so that they may be partitioned

$$Y = \begin{vmatrix} Y_1 \\ Y_2 \end{vmatrix} \ , \ X = \begin{vmatrix} x_1 \\ x_2 \end{vmatrix} \tag{5.45}$$

and that

$$Y_1 = X_1 \beta_1 + e_1 \tag{5.46}$$

and

$$Y_2 = X_2 \beta_2 + e_2 \tag{5.47}$$

where $e_1$ and $e_2$ are distributed as $N(0, \sigma_1^2 I)$ and $N(0, \sigma_2^2 I)$ respectively, and where $(\beta_1, \sigma_1^2) \neq (\beta_2, \sigma_2^2)$.

If under the alternative hypothesis, the subsets of observations corresponding to (5.46) and (5.47), respectively, are identified on a priori grounds, the problem of testing the null hypothesis is solved exactly by the Chow test (1960). The corresponding estimation problem is solved by estimating Equations (5.46) and (5.47) separately by least squares.

Other approaches to the problem deal with the more difficult circumstances in which it is known which, if any, observations were generated by regime 1 and which by regime 2. There are two alternative methods, used by urban economists to detect the existence of dynamic structure of urban space that will be discussed in this section.

## 5.7.1. Quandt's Two Regime Method

Following Quandt (1958, 1960), the likelihood ratio used to test the two regime switching point can be defined as

$$\bar{\lambda} = -2[(t)\log \hat{\sigma}_1 + (T-t)\log \hat{\sigma}_2^{T-t} - T\log \hat{\sigma}]$$

where t and T represent a number of observations for first regime and over-all regime respectively. $\hat{\sigma}_1$ and $\hat{\sigma}_2$ represent the standard error of estimate for over-all regime, first regime, and second regime respectively. $\bar{\lambda}$ is a Chi-square distribution with four degrees of freedom. Hence the estimated $\bar{\lambda}$ can be used to determine the switching point. Brueckner (1981) has used this technique to investigate the vintage model of urban growth.

### 5.7.2. FHM Model

Farley and Hinich (1970) assume that all possible switching points are equally likely and derive a likelihood ratio test for the null hypothesis. Farley, Hinich and McGuire (1975) [FHM] have shown that Farley and Hinich method can be simplified as a multiple regression model can be defined as

$$Y_t = a + \beta X_t + \gamma Z_t + e_t$$

where $Z_t = tXt$ and $t = \frac{1}{n}, \frac{2}{n}, \ldots, 1$. $a$, $\beta$ and $\gamma$ are regression parameters and $e_t$ is the error term.

The estimated t statistics associated with estimated $\gamma$ can be used to test whether there exist some shifts of the structure of a regression. Kau, Lee and Chen (1983) have used this technique to investigate the stability or the urban spatial structure [see Chapter 14].

### 5.8. Varying Coefficient Model [VCM]

To let both the intercept and slope of Equation (5.2) become function of tract specific and citywide conditioning variables ($x_1$, $x_2$, $x_3$ and $x_4$). Johnson and Kau (1980) specify a two variable coefficient equation as

$$\text{(A)} \quad \log D_0 = \beta_0^0 + \beta_1^0 x_1 + \beta_2^0 x_2 + \beta_3^0 x_3 + \beta_4^0 x_4 \qquad (5.50)$$

$$\text{(B)} \quad = \beta_0^1 + \beta_1^1 x_1^2 + \beta_2^1 x_1^2 + \beta_3^1 x_2^2 + \beta_4^1 x_2^2 + \beta_5^1 x_3^2 +$$
$$\beta_6^1 x_3^2 + \beta_6^1 x_4^2 + \beta_7^1 x_4^2 + \beta_8^1 x_4^2 \qquad (5.51)$$

where $x_1$, $x_2$, $x_3$ and $x_4$ represent selected income, public/private transportation, age and population variables.

By combining Equations (5.2), (5.50) and (5.41), Johnson and Kau (1980) have derived the varying $\log D_o$ and $\gamma$

estimators.    This VCM will be discussed in Chaper 15 in detail.

## 5.9. Summary

In this chapter, econometric techniques necessary to do spatial analysis are explored in accordance with recent research papers.    First, basic concepts of regression are analyzed.    Second, multiple regression is also reviewed in accordance with the concepts of single regression. The usefulness of determining the best functional form is examined.    Next, by comparing simple multiple regression, it is shown that using a random coefficient instead of the fixed coefficient for estimating the density gradient of a SMSA may be necessary.    The procedure of random coefficient is also discussed in some detail.    Generalized least square models and their possible applications to spatial analysis were also discussed.    Finally two alternative switching regression techniques were also explored.

PART III


URBAN HOUSING PRODUCTION
_____

## Introduction

Part III examines empirically the elasticity of substitution. The Cobb-Douglas function assumes that the elasticity is one. Chapter 6 estimates the elasticity using both a CES and VES production function. The results indicate that the Cobb-Douglas is not the appropriate functional form and that the VES provides more information concerning variations in the elasticity. Since the evidence in Chapter 6 suggests using the VES, Chapter 7 expands on the impliations of a variable elasticity of substitution. Specifically, in what way does different values of the elasticity effect residential land use. Chapter 8 provides estimates of the elasticity of substitution over time and for different cities. Finally, Chapter 9 examines, first the existence and extent of technological change in housing and second determines its impacts on the elasticity. Overall this section provides strong evidence that the elasticity of substitution does vary within an urban area and that the determinants of this variation have significant impact on urban structure.

Chapter 6

THE ELASTICITY OF SUBSTITUTION:

A COMPARISON OF THE CES AND VES APPROACH

## 6.1. Introduction

The literature on urban economies has expanded rapidly in recent years.[1]  Recent studies by Mills (1967, 1972), Schuler (1974), and Smith (1976) have investigated the problems associated with urban spatial structure.  Many of the models which have been developed to explain urban land-use patterns rest on the properties of production functions,[2] [See Chapters 2, 3, 4].  Differing factor price ratios within urban areas, particularly land prices, result in differing capital-land ratios exemplified by high-rise apartments and single family dwellings.  To treat the effect of changing factor prices on factor ratios, it is necessary to make an assumption about the elasticity of substitution between capital and land.  This has been done in the literature by assuming a unitary elasticity parameter (Cobb-Douglas) or by obtaining direct estimates of the substitution parameter based on the assumption that it is constant over the range of observed data (CES production function).[3]

Production theory, however, recognizes that the elasticity of substitution between factor inputs can vary depending on the factor input ratios and/or output [Hicks (1948) and Allen (1956)].  Since the ratio of land to nonland (capital) inputs varies significantly within urban areas, the a priori restriction of a constant elasticity will lead to specification bias. The next four chapters will provide evidence that using the Cobb-Douglas or CES production function is inappropriate for an urban area. Papers that continue to use the CES format [See Clapp (1979, 1981)] are invarantly producing biased estimates. Revankar (1966, 1971a) has recently developed a production function which allows the elasticity of substitution to vary depending on the factor ratio. The purpose of this chapter is to examine the elasticity of substitution between land and capital in urban housing production using Revankar's variable elasticity of substitution (VES) production function. A methodology to select between the CES and VES functional forms is proposed and some preliminary empirical evidence is presented. The chapter can be outlined as follows: Section 2 reviews the model of urban housing production; Section 3 contains some preliminary empirical estimates of both the constant elasticity of substitution (CES) and the variable elasticity of substitution (VES) production functions; Section 4 examines the functional form using the Box and Cox transformation procedures presented in Chapter 5; summary and conclusions are in the final section.

## 6.2. The CES and VES Model

The model in this paper is similar to that used by Muth (1971) and Koenker (1972). For a representative firm in the competitive housing industry, the following can be written:

$$Xs = F(L, K) \tag{6.1}$$

$$pF_L = r \tag{6.2}$$

$$pF_K = n \tag{6.3}$$

$$pXs = rL + nK \tag{6.4}$$

Equation (6.1) is the production function; Equation (6.2) and (6.3) are the profit maximizing conditions, and Equation (6.4) is a condition of competitive equilibrium for the industry. The physical quantities of output, land, and a composite factor, capital, are represented by Xs, L, and K; p, r, and n are the respective prices of output and input factors and the subscripts denote marginal products.[4]

## 6.2.1 The CES

The functional relationship between the observed magnitudes of pXs, L and r that will accurately estimate the elasticity of substitution between land and capital is of interest in this paper. Assuming that Equation (6.1) is linearly homogeneous and has a constant elasticity, say $\sigma$, over the data, the well known CES function [see Arrow et al. (1961)] result is as follows:

$$Xs = A[\alpha L^{-\rho} + (1 - \alpha)\bar{K}^{\rho}]^{(-1/\rho)} \qquad (6.5)$$

where K and L represent inputs of capital and land in the production of housing; A and $\alpha$ are scale and distribution parameter and $\sigma = 1/(1 + \rho)$. As $\rho$ approaches zero, Equation (6.5) becomes a Cobb-Douglas production function and the elasticity of substitution $\sigma$ becomes unity.

A profit maximizing firm under the assumption of competitive factor markets will set the ratio of the marginal products, $F_L/F_K$, equal to the ratio of factor price ratio, r/n. Hence, the elasticity of substitution, $\sigma$, may be expressed as the slope parameter in the log-linear equation,

$$\ln(nK/L) = \beta_0 + \sigma(\ln\bar{r}). \qquad (6.6)$$

Equation (6.6) expresses the functional relationship between the intensity of land use, measured in the dollar value of physical structure per square foot of site, nK/L, and the prices of the land and non-land factors. The price of the non-land factor input is assumed to be invariant with respect to location [Muth (1969), pp. 52-53].

## 6.2.2. The VES

As indicated by Hicks (1948) and Allen (1956) and discussed by Revankar (1971), the elasticity of substitution can be variable depending upon output and/or factor combinations. Hence, the a priori constraint implicit in the CES that the value of $\bar{\sigma}$ is invariant with L/K can lead to specification bias. It is thus important to determine the most appropriate functional form of the relationship between the factor input ratio and factor price ratio. Several recent articles by Lovell (1973a, 1973b), Lu and Fletcher (1968), and Revankar (1971a) have suggested the use of variable elasticity of substitution (VES) production functions which are designed to capture the relationship between the elasticity of substitution and output and/or factor combinations.

Revankar (1971a) has recently proposed the following variable elasticity of substitution production function:[5]

$$Xs = AL^{v(1 - \delta\rho)} [K + (\rho - 1) L]^{v\delta\rho} \qquad (6.7)$$

where Xs is output, K is capital, L is land; and $\delta$, $\rho$, and v are parameters with the following constraints:

$$v > 0 \qquad (6.8)$$

$$A > 0 \qquad (6.9)$$

$$0 < \delta < 1 \qquad (6.10)$$

$$0 \leq \delta\rho \leq 1 \qquad (6.11)$$

and

$$K/L > \frac{1 - \rho}{1 - \delta\rho} \qquad (6.12)$$

Revankar (1971a, p. 65) shows that the elasticity of substitution for this VES function is [6]

$$\sigma = 1 + \frac{\rho - 1}{1 - \delta\rho} \frac{L}{K} \qquad (6.13)$$

Thus, $\sigma$ varies with the land-capital ratio around the intercept of unity.

Assuming constant returns to scale, i.e., v = 1 in Equation (6.7), competitive conditions in factor and product markets and profit-maximizing, the marginal conditions for the VES are

$$nK/L = \beta_0' + \beta_1(r) \qquad (6.14)$$

where $\beta_0' = (1 - \rho)/(1 - \delta\rho)$ and $\beta_1 = \delta\rho/(1 - \delta\rho)$. As can be seen by comparing the VES case, Equation (6.14) with the CES case, Equation (6.6), the latter postulates a log-linear function, whereas the former is a linear function of the relationship between the intensity of land use and the factor price ratio.[7]


## 6.3. Empirical Estimates: CES and VES Functions


Equation (6.6) can be estimated in the following stochastic form under the assumption of a constant elasticity of substitution by,

$$\ln(nK/L) = \beta_0 + \sigma(\ln r) + u_i \qquad (6.15)$$

where $\sigma$ is the elasticity of substitution and $u_i$ is a randomly distributed error term with mean of zero and constant variance.[8] A percentage change in the intensity of land use with respect to a percentage change in the price of land is represented by $\sigma$. A test of the model is based on a sample of single-family housing data for Santa Clara County, California.[9] These data were used in the study of land values by Wendt and Goldner (1966). The data, containing 98 observations and based on FHA new applications, included the average lot value, average selling price of properties, and the average size of the lot of the various Census tracts.

### 6.3.1. The Estimated CES

Estimating equation (6.15) yields):

$$\ln(nK/L) = 1.022 + .766(\ln r) \qquad (6.16)$$
$$\qquad\quad (.004) \quad (.069)$$

where the standard errors are shown in parentheses below the coefficients. The variation in land prices explains 60 percent of the variation in the intensity of land use. This result indicates that a one percent increase in the land price induces a .77 percent increase in the intensity of land use. A 95 percent confidence interval for the elasticity of substitution is (.628, .904). The estimated elasticity is less than and significantly different from one indicating the inappropriateness of assuming a Cobb-Douglas production function. This result suggests that the CES function model developed in Chapter 3 is superior to the Cobb-Douglas.

### 6.3.2. The Estimated VES

Equation (6.14), and VES case, was estimated, by adding a disturbance term of the ordinary sort, with the following results:

$$nK/L = .323 + 2.650(r) \qquad (6.17)$$
$$(.123) \quad (.206)$$

where the standard errors are in parentheses. Equation (6.17) had an adjusted coefficient of determination of .63. Since $\beta_0' \neq 0$ at the 95 percent level of confidence, the Cobb-Douglas production function can be rejected using Equation (6.13). The elasticity of substitution for the VES production function can be calculated using Equation (6.13) and the mean L/nK ratio:

$$\sigma = 1 - .323(.537) = .827 \qquad (6.18)$$

The VES estimate of the elasticity at the mean factor input ratio is larger than the CES estimate. The range in the L/nK ratio was from .23 to 1.04. Using this range and Equation (6.13), the elasticity of substitution varies from .925 to .664. While the results should be interpreted with caution, the methodology of applying the variable elasticity of production function to urban housing output has important implications for the analysis of urban spatial structure. The next section provides an empirical test to discriminate between the CES and VES functional forms.

### 6.4. Functional Form Analysis

The problem of selecting between the VES and CES production functions can be viewed as one of discriminating between two specifications of a postulated relationship between intensity and land-use and factor-price ratios, where the price of capital is invariant. The CES specification is log-linear; the VES is linear. Discrimination of goodness-of-fit criteria is inappropriate since the dependent variables are not the same.

As discussed in Chapter 5, Box and Cox (1964) have provided a technique to discriminate between linear and log-linear functional forms.[10] Consider the following relation between intensity of land-use and the factor price ratio:

$$(nK/L)^{\lambda} = a_0 + a_1 (r)^{\lambda} \tag{6.19}$$

where   is the parameter of the power transformation on the variables.

Using the Box-Cox procedure, Equation (6.19) can be written as

$$\frac{(nK/L)^{\lambda} - 1}{\lambda} = a_0' + a_1' \frac{(r)^{\lambda} - 1)}{\lambda} + u_i \tag{6.20}$$

where $u_i$ is the disturbance term that is normally distributed with zero mean and constant variance. Equation (6.20) can be estimated using maximum likelihood techniques. As noted by Lovell (1973a), the differential Equation (6.20) defines a whole class of production functions, two of which are the CES and the VES. When $\lambda \to 0$, then Equation (6.20) approaches Equation (6.6), the CES case, and if $\lambda \to 1$, then (6.20) reduces to (6.14), the VES form.

The logarithm of the likelihood function is maximized with respect to $a_0'$, $a_1'$ and the variance of the residual given $\lambda$. For the given $\lambda$, the maximum likelihood estimate of the variance of the disturbances is given by the regression of $\underset{L}{nK^{\lambda}}$ on $(r)^{\lambda}$ as transformed according to Equation (6.20). Box and Cox (1964) have derived a maximum logarithmic likelihood for determining the functional form parameter, except for a constant, as

$$\text{Lmax}(\lambda) = -\frac{N}{2} \ln\hat{\sigma}^2 (\lambda) + (\lambda - 1) \sum_{i-1}^{N} \ln \frac{nK}{L} \qquad (6.21)$$

where N is the sample size. Equation (6.21) may be calculated for different values of $\lambda$ to find the maximized log likelihood over the entire parameter space. An approximate 95 percent confidence region for $\lambda$ can be obtained from

$$2[\text{Lmax}(\hat{\lambda}) \text{ Lmax}(\lambda)] < \chi_1^2(\alpha) = 1.92) \qquad (6.22)$$

where $\chi_1^2$ denotes the $\chi^2$ statistics with one degree of freedom.

Using this approach, Equation (6.20) was estimated using values between -.5 and 1.5, at intervals of .1 to transform the variables. This results in twenty-one equations for which the Lmax($\lambda$)'s are plotted in Figure 1.

### 6.4.1. The Optimal Functional Forms

The results for Equation (6.20) indicate that the log maximum (see Figure 6.1) of the likelihood function is 119.1 at $\lambda$ = .7. Using Equation (6.22), a 95 percent confidence interval around $\lambda$ is (.2, 1.1). Thus it includes the VES function. The hypotheses that the CES is the appropriate function cannot be accepted. This result tends to indicate that the elasticity of substitution is not constant within this sample of a single-family housing market. The result also demonstrates the need for analyzing the elasticity of substitution between land and non-land input by using a production function which would allow the elasticity to vary with output and/or factor proportions.

### 6.5. Summary and Conclusions

The elasticity of substitution between land and non-land factors in the production of urban housing is an important aspect of urban spatial structure analysis. This chapter has introduced the variable elasticity of substitution (VES) production function for the analysis of urban housing

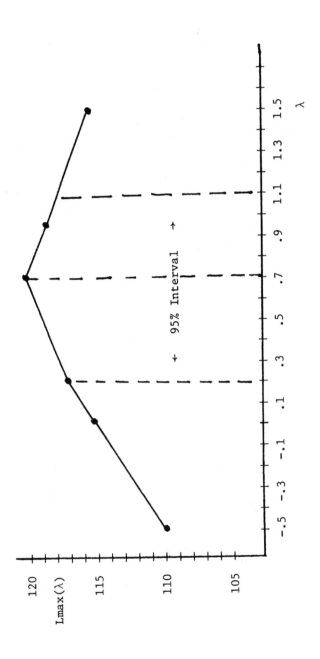

Figure 6.1

production. The authors developed in Chapter 3 a model of urban land-use based on the CES production function, which extended the urban models introduced by Mills (1967, 1972) and Muth (1969). This chapter has indicated that urban models should also be developed which rest on the properties of the VES production function, developed in Chapter 4.

Some illustrative empirical estimates using both the CES and VES specifications were provided to demonstrate the methodology introduced in this chapter. The results for the CES production function indicated that a one percent increase in the factor-price ratio would lead to a .77 percent increase in the intensity of land use as measured by the dollar value of physical structure per square foot of site. Using the VES function, a range from .95 to .66 was indicated for the elasticity of substitution. A test of the functional form of the relationship between the intensity of land use and the relative factor prices indicated that the CES form is possibly not the correct specification. The results implied that a more correct specification of this relationship would be through the use of a VES production function. This result will be explored in greater detail in the next chapter on urban spatial structure. In particular since the production function reflects technology, and if technology varies across space, then the production relationships may be different by region [see Chapter 8]. Likewise, the methodology should be applied to different types of "capital" inputs, i.e., multi-family housing, single-family housing, commercial properties, and industrial properties, [see Chapter 7], since all compete for land in an urban area.

(Notes follow)

NOTES

1. See, for example, Goldstein and Moses (1973) and Mills (1981, 1972b).

2. See, for example, the urban models by Muth (1969), Mills (1972b), Kau and Lee (1976a,b), and Fallis (1975). Atkinson (1975) has recently provided a discussion of the empirical estimates of the elasticity of factor substitution. It is interesting to note that he fails to consider the importance of this parameter in models of urban structure.

3. See, for example, Koenker (1972), Muth (1969, 1971), Fallis (1975), Clapp (1979, 1981), and Smith (1976).

4. The value of output and factor shares are in terms of stocks. This differs from the conventional procedure in manufacturing studies using flows.

5. It should be noted that this VES function is the inverse case of the one in Revankar (1971a). Revankar's footnote 19 has indicated the existence of the inversed VES production function.

6. Equation (6.13) has been derived in Revankar (1966). If $\rho$ approaches zero, then $\sigma$ reduces to unity and Equation (6.7) becomes a Cobb-Douglas function.

7. Both the CES and VES production functions are generalized cases of Cobb-Douglas production function. However, it cannot be shown that VES function is a generalized case of CES productin function [see Revankar (1971a)]. Hence the linear vs. the log-linear relationship explored in section 6.4 will be the key concept for discriminating the CES from the VES production function.

8. Preliminary test indicated no serious heteroscedasticity problems.

9. See Wendt and Goldner (1966) for a more complete discussion of the data. While the empirical results have

limitations, these data are sufficient to demonstrate the methodology proposed for examining the housing production function. The model should be tested on different cities, different types of housing and using larger samples.

10. This technique has been used by Zarembka (1968), White (1972), Heckman and Polachek (1974) and others.

Chapter 7

A VES PRODUCTION FUNCTION:

SOME THEORETICAL AND EMPIRICAL EXTENSIONS

## 7.1.  Introduction

The previous chapters introduced the variable elasticity-of-substitution (VES) production function and compared it to the CES function.  Also the Box and Cox (1964) functional form technique was introduced to test whether the VES or CES was the appropriate format.  The results clearly indicate that the VES is the form to use.  Thus both the theory of Chapter 4 and the initial empirical estimates of Chapter 6 indicate that further exploration of the VES would prove rewarding.

In this chapter the variable-elasticity-of-substitution (VES) production function developed by Revankar (1971a) is expanded upon to derive an urban land-use model and to investigate the impact on urban structure of a changing elasticity of substitution of land for capital.[1]  Many urban problems such as decentralization, the impact of higher gasoline prices on urban structure, and population growth, cannot be completely understood without knowledge about the elasticity of substitution.

Empirical studies on urban structure have often assumed a fixed value for the elasticity of substitution ($\sigma$) between capital and land.  Initially urban models assumed very simple types of production functions, such as the fixed-coefficient and linear-coefficient models, with $\sigma$ equal to zero and infinity respectively.  Muth (1969), using a Cobb-Douglas production function with $\sigma$ equal to unity, derived the conditions for a negative-exponential function between density and distance. Mills (1981), also using Cobb-Douglas functions, developed additional insights into urban structure. The basic concept of the Mills and Muth models is the trade-off between lower housing prices and greater transportation costs as the commuting distance to the job increases. As various parameters affecting this trade-off change, the urban spatial structure alters shape. Recent criticisms of these models by Wheaton (1977) and Diamond (1978) indicate that more attention must be paid to the impact of amenities and to locational choice. Although realistic urban-location patterns are complex, the Mills and Muth models can be used to understand certain important characteristics of urban areas. Examples would include the benefits and affects of transport improvements such as a rapid-transit system, or the effects of population-density restrictions or large-lot zoning on urban spatial structure.

The value of $\sigma$ can range between zero and infinity; thus any empirical study using production functions which assumes any specific constant value of $\sigma$ can lead to specification bias. Specification bias means that the impact of changes in the model's parameters, such as income and transportation costs, are incorrectly measured, which could lead to false conclusions [see Clapp 1977, 1981) for an example of such bias]. This study will test whether the Mills, Muth and other models are incorrectly specified because of their assumption of a fixed elasticity of substitution.

Recently Fallis (1975), Kau and Lee (1976a), Clapp (1979, 1981) and Muth (1975) have used a constant-elasticity-of-substitution (CES production function to investigate the structure of a city [see Chapter 3]. The CES production function arbitrarily constrains $\sigma$ to be a constant and does not allow it to vary with a change in the price of land or capital (that is, with changes in the factor-input ratio). However, as demonstrated by Hicks (1948) and Allen (1956), $\sigma$ can vary depending on the factor combinations and output. Relative factor prices vary over a wide range within an urban area, and result in a variety of capital-land ratios (K/L) whose range is exemplified by the difference between high-rise apartments and single-family dwellings. Thus a CES production function with a

constant $\sigma$ within a specified urban area will lead to specification bias. Revankar's VES production function incorporates the impact of the elasticity of substitution ($\sigma$)
and the K/L ratio, and thus eliminates any specification
bias associated with changes in $\sigma$ and the factor ratio.

In Section 7.2 the importance of allowing changes in
the elasticity of substitution within an urban area is discussed. Also the bias in the density gradient resulting
from omitting changes in $\sigma$ is investigated. In Section 7.3
empirical estimates are presented for the elasticity of
substitution associated with CES and VES production functions. It is also shown that the VES method can be used to
take the change of $\sigma$ into account. Finally, in Section
7.4, the results of this chapter are summarized.

### 7.2. Impact of the Elasticity of Substitution on the Density-Distance Function

The VES production function differs from the CES production
function in its isoquant mapping. [An isoquant mapping is
a set of curves showing all possible (efficient) combinations of inputs capable of producing a corresponding set of
outputs.] The elasticity of substitution (the percent
change in the capital-land ratio divided by the percent
change in their price ratio) for the CES production function is the same at all points on the isoquant mapping, and
is thus independent of output and the K/L ratio. The VES
production function does not require that the elasticity of
substitution by the same. Thus $\sigma$ can vary with output and
with changes in the K/L ratio; it can increase steadily
from zero to infinity. In terms of the isoquants, this is
demonstrated by their becoming more flattened with increased output. Also it is shown later in this study that
the isoquant becomes flatter with a decrease in the K/L ratio for the same output.

The properties of the VES function are especially important for studies of urban structure. First, studies by
Kau and Lee (1976c), Mills (1971b), and Muth (1969) have
demonstrated the existence of a downward sloping land-rent

gradient; therefore the K/L ratio will decrease with increasing distance from the urban center.[2] Thus firms producing urban structures will become more capital-intensive near the urban center.

Second, firms producing urban structure may have significantly different production functions relative to output. For example, firms producing high-rise condominiums near the urban center may have significantly different iso-quant mappings than firms producing single-family dwellings on the outskirts of an urban area.[3]

Third, because of natural and technological limitations, the ability to substitute capital for land decreases with increasing capital intensity. For example, the heights of buildings are limited by space requirements for elevators and the size of the foundation. Therefore the decrease in land rents with distance from the urban center and the corresponding decrease in the K/L ratio result in the elasticity of substitution increasing with distance.

Technological limitations, changes in K/L ratios, and different production functions make the Cobb-Douglas and CES production functions inefficient tools for analyzing urban structure. Hence, the statistical studies on urban structure which use Cobb-Douglas (Mills, 1981; Muth, 1969) or CES (Fallis, 1975; Koenker, 1972; Muth, 1975; Tooze, 1976) production functions have biased empirical estimates.

### 7.2.1. Adaptation of the Muth Model

The effect of variation in rentals and in the elasticity of substitution on the intensity of residential land use can be investigated by use of the theoretical framework developed by Muth (1969). The essence of the Muth model necessary for this paper is contained in the derivation of the locational equilibrium of producers. Producers of housing combine land and capital in production to maximize profits. Therefore

$$\pi = p(L, K)Xs(L, K) - rL - nK, \tag{7.1}$$

where

$\pi$  is profit,
p  is the price of a unit of housing (dependent on L and K),
Xs  is the output of housing (dependent on L and K),
L  is the input of land,
K  is the input of capital,
r  is the price of a unit of land, and
n  is the price of a unit of capital.

If it is assumed that housing and land prices vary only with distance, u, from the central business district (CBD) and that there are similar production functions for each unique location, then differentiation of Equation (7.1), with rearrangement of terms, and the assumption that in equilibrium $d\pi = 0$ gives

$$\frac{1}{r} \cdot \frac{\partial r}{\partial u} = \frac{1}{\rho_L}\left(\frac{1}{p} \cdot \frac{\partial P}{\partial u}\right) - \frac{\rho_K}{\rho_L}\left(\frac{1}{n} \cdot \frac{\partial n}{\partial u}\right), \qquad (7.2)$$

where

$$\rho_L = \frac{rL}{PXs} \quad \text{and} \quad \rho_K = \frac{nK}{PXs}. \qquad (7.3)$$

Equation (7.2) implies that the rents on land will be bid up by firms in locations where the product price is high owing to favorable location.

The effects of variation in land rents and in the elasticity of substitution on land use can be derived by assuming that factor payments exhaust receipts. Thus

$$pXs = rL + nK. \qquad (7.4)$$

Dividing both sides by L, differentiating with respect to u, using the definition of the elasticity of substitution and Equation (7.2), and assuming no variation in capital costs, one derives the following equation:

$$\frac{\partial}{\partial u}\left(\ln \frac{pXs}{L}\right) = \left(1 + \frac{\rho_k}{\rho_L}\sigma(u)\right)\frac{1}{p} \cdot \frac{\partial p}{\partial u} < 0. \qquad (7.5)$$

pXs/L is a measure of the intensity of residential land use in terms of the value of housing produced per unit of land. The negative sign of Equation (7.5) indicates the slope of the specified density function. The slope varies inversely with the relative importance of land and directly with the elasticity of substitution, and $\partial P/\partial u$.

The variations in the slope of the curve which relates the logarithm of the value of housing per square mile to distance from the CBD is obtained by differentiating Equation (7.5) with respect to u. It is assumed that $\sigma$, the elasticity of substitution, is a function of distance u. The result is

$$\frac{\partial^2}{\partial u^2}\left(\ln\frac{pXs}{L}\right) = \left(1 + \frac{\rho_K}{\rho_L}\sigma(u)\right)\frac{\partial}{\partial u}\left(\frac{1}{p}\frac{\partial p}{\partial u}\right) + \frac{1}{p}\cdot\frac{\partial p}{\partial u}\left\{\sigma(u)[\sigma(u)-1]\right.$$

$$\left.\frac{\rho_K}{\rho_L}\frac{1}{r}\frac{\partial r}{\partial u}\right\} + \frac{1}{p}\cdot\frac{\partial p}{\partial u}\frac{\rho_K}{\rho_L}\cdot\frac{\partial\sigma(u)}{\partial u}\quad . \tag{7.6}$$

It has been shown by Muth (1969) that the slope of the log price–distance function tends to decline numerically with distance from the CBD. Thus

$$\frac{\partial}{\partial u}\left(\frac{1}{P}\cdot\frac{\partial P}{\partial u}\right) > 0 \quad . \tag{7.7}$$

The second term on the right-hand side of Equation (7.6) represents the bias associated with assuming a Cobb-Douglas function. Empirically (demonstrated later in the paper) $\sigma$ ranges from 0.09 to 0.93. The theoretical model indicates that $(\partial P/\partial u)/p < 0$ and $\partial r/\partial u < 0$. Also $\rho_K/\rho_L$ increases with distance [4] when $\sigma < 1$. Thus the second term on the right-hand side of Equation (7.6) is negative or zero.

The third term on the right-hand side of Equation (7.6) represents the bias associated with assuming a constant elasticity of substitution and provides the impact of changing elasticity of substitution on density. Since empirically it will be shown that $\sigma$ increases with distance and since $\sigma < 1$, $\rho_K/\rho_L$ increases with distance. Thus, since $(\partial P/\partial u)P < 0$, the third term on the right-hand side is negative or zero.

The second and third terms both indicate a density function concave to the origin, whereas the first term would produce a convex curve. The negative curvature of the second two terms tends to offset the positive curvature imparted to Equation (7.6) by the log price-distance function. Hence, the density gradient may be approximately constant even though the price gradient declines with distance from the CBD. If the impact of variations in the elasticity of substitution is greater than the convexity imposed by the price-distance function, then the density gradient may have a negative curvature, so that population densities would decline less rapidly than negative-exponentially with distance from the CBD. In this case, if the price gradient is held constant, an increase in demand for housing would increase the output of housing and population more rapidly in the outer parts of the city.

Urban models using Cobb-Douglas, CES production functions or the generalized Muth (1969) model, as represented by Equation (7.2) and (7.5) and the first two terms on the right-hand side of Equation (7.6), will be biased in their prediction of structural changes. Transformation procedures and statistical techniques have been developed by the authors, [see Chaper 5], to reduce the extent of this bias.

The purpose of this section has been to demonstrate the bias associated with restricting the elasticity of substitution to unity as well as with assuming a constant elasticity of substitution throughout an urban area. In the following section the CES and VES production functions are estimated using multi-family housing. This provides additional tests on the suitability of the Cobb-Douglas or CES production function. The results again indicate that the elasticity of substitution does vary within an urban area.

7.3. Multi-family Housing and the CES and VES Production Functions

The VES and CES production functions relate the output-capital ratio to factor prices. The major difference lies in the fact that the VES function is linear while the VES is log-linear. A stochastic model of the VES function may be written (Revankar, 1967) as:

$$\ln pXs = b_0 + b_1 X^* + \varepsilon_1, \tag{7.8}$$

where

$$X^* = (1 - \delta\rho)\ln K + \delta\rho\ln[L + (\rho - 1)K], \tag{7.9}$$

$$b_0 = \ln A, \tag{7.10}$$

and

$$b_1 = v; \tag{7.11}$$

and

$$\frac{pXs}{K} = F_1 n + F_2 r + \varepsilon_2, \tag{7.12}$$

where

$$F_1 = \frac{1}{q(1 - \delta\rho)}, \tag{7.13}$$

$$F_2 = \frac{1 - \rho}{q(1 - \delta\rho)} \tag{7.14}$$

$$q = \exp \frac{\sigma}{2}, \tag{7.15}$$

n is the price per unit of capital, and r is the price per unit of land;

and

$$\frac{L}{K} = G_0 + G_1 \frac{n}{r} + \varepsilon_3, \tag{7.16}$$

where

$$= \frac{1 - \rho}{1 - \delta\rho} \tag{7.17}$$

and

$$G_1 = \frac{\delta\rho}{1 - \delta\rho} \qquad (7.18)$$

Thus the estimation of the VES function results in the empirical determination of the parameters A, v, $\delta$, and $\rho$. These parameters are estimated by use of Zellner's (1962) seemingly unrelated regression (SUR) technique. The simultaneous estimation of Equation (7.12) and (7.16) results in efficient estimates for $F_1$, $F_2$, $G_0$, and $G_1$. With these estimates, $\rho$ and $\delta$ can be determined from

$$\rho = 1 - \frac{G_0}{1 + G_1} \quad , \qquad (7.19)$$

and

$$\delta = \frac{G_1}{1 + G_1 - G_0}$$

These estimates can in turn be used to estimate Equation (7.8).

The elasticity of substitution, $\sigma$, is obtained from

$$\sigma = 1 + \frac{\rho - 1}{1 - \delta\rho} \frac{K}{L} = 1 - G_0 \frac{K}{L}. \qquad (7.21)$$

The VES and CES functions are generalizations of the Cobb-Douglas function. Thus a test is necessary to determine the relevance of using a VES or CES function. The relationship between the VES and Cobb-Douglas functions can be tested by use of Equation (7.21) with $G_0 \neq 0$ the elasticity of substitution is thus not equal to one, as implied by the Cobb-Douglas specification. This same test is provided for in the CES function by testing if the slope coefficient is equal to unity in Equation (7.28) and (7.31).

The data used in this paper, from Koenker (1972), is based on the tax-assessment records for all private multi-family housing constructed in Ann Arbor, Michigan, from 1964 through 1966. The sample consistent of 122 observations. It was assumed that there is no systematic bias in the assessment estimates of actual market values of the properties and of the sites. The prices of land and capital were determined as the prices per square foot. The size of the building site and the number of units were contained in the data set.

The seemingly unrelated regression estimates of Equation (7.12) and (7.16) are (with standard errors in parentheses)

$$\frac{pXs}{K} = \frac{0.717 + 0.678n + 1.023r}{(0.144)(0.032) \quad (0.011)} \tag{7.22}$$

and

$$\frac{L}{K} = \frac{0.681 + 0.086 \, n}{(0.098) \, (0.008)\overline{r}} \tag{7.23}$$

Thus

$$\rho = 1 - \frac{G_0}{1 + G_1} = 0.373 \tag{7.24}$$

and, at the mean K/L ratio,

$$\sigma = 1 - G_0 \frac{K}{L} = 0.514. \tag{7.25}$$

The capital-land ratio in the sample ranged from 1.336 to 0.104. Thus the elasticity of substitution, derived from Equation (7.22), varies from 0.090 to 0.929. These empirical results tend to support the use of a VES function and lend significant insight into the range of the elasticity of substitution in an urban area.

The factor intensity parameter, $\delta$ , is equal to

$$\delta = \frac{G_1}{1 + G_1 - G_0} = 0.212. \tag{7.26}$$

The estimate of the production function in Equation (7.8), without restricting the returns-to-scale parameter, v, to unity, is

$$lnpXs = 0.270 + 0.930X*, \quad \text{with } \overline{R}^2 = 0.962. \tag{7.27}$$
$$(0.176) \, (0.017)$$

Thus $\ln A = 0.270$ and $v = 0.930$.

The marginal conditions for the CES production function are:

$$\ln \frac{pXs}{K} = F_1' + F_2' \ln(n), \tag{7.28}$$

where

$$F_1' = -\frac{\rho}{1-\rho} \cdot \ln\delta - \frac{1}{1-e} \ln(1-\delta) \tag{7.29}$$

and

$$F_2' = \frac{1}{1-\rho} = \sigma \; ; \tag{7.30}$$

and

$$\ln\frac{L}{K} = G_0' + G_1' \ln \frac{n}{r}, \tag{7.31}$$

where

$$G_0' = \frac{1}{1-\rho} \ln \frac{\delta}{1-\delta} \tag{7.32}$$

and

$$G_1' = \frac{1}{1-\rho} = \sigma. \tag{7.33}$$

Equations (7.28) and (7.31) were estimated with Zellner's efficient technique by restricting $F_2' = G_1' = \sigma$. These results are (with standard errors in parentheses)

$$\ln^{pXs} = 1.148 + 0.619\ln(n) \tag{7.34}$$
$$(0.066) \; (0.026)$$

and

$$\ln \frac{L}{K} = -0.925 + 0.619\ln\frac{n}{r}. \tag{7.35}$$
$$(0.053) \; (0.026)$$

Thus, the elasticity of substitution is 0.619 in the CES case.

## 7.4.  Summary and Conclusion Remarks

Based upon the VES production function, a land-use model has been derived to show that neither the Cobb-Douglas nor the CES production functions can take into account a changing elasticity of substitution of capital for land. It has also been shown that the ratio between the rental rates of land and capital may be an additional exploratory variable for the density-gradient function.

The results for multi-family housing indicate that the elasticity of substitution does change with distance in an urban area and that the use of a Cobb-Douglas or CES production function to derive a density gradient will result in biased estimates. A VES production function produces a density-gradient function which decreases at a numerically faster rate with respect to distance. In sum, this study has not only found a most useful application for the VES production function but has also shown that city planning (or urban-structure determination) cannot entirely rely upon the distance variable. The evidence suggests that other parameters may play an important part in determining urban spatial structure. The variation of the elasticity of substitution indicates that institutional or technological constraints exist and that these constraints affect the variation of population density with respect to distance. The results confirm other evidence [see Chapter 12, 13 and 14] that the capital-land ratio can be taken as a proxy for measuring the impact of technological change and the effect of past development on future land use.

(Notes follow)

## NOTES

1.  Other forms of VES production functions have been developed (see Bruno, 1968; Liu and Hilderbrand, 1965; Sato, 1975).  Revankar's VES production function was selected since it is a generalized case of the Cobb-Douglas production function and it also allows us to discriminate between the VES and the CES (constant-elasticity-of-substitution) production functions on statistical grounds.

2.  The relationship estimated, by using data from Ann Arbor, Michigan (see Section 7.3) is

$$\ln \frac{K}{L} = 0.237 - 0.122\ln(u), \qquad \text{with } \bar{R}^2 = 0.75,$$
$$\quad\;\; (0.032)\;(0.007)$$

where u is the distance from the urban center and the numbers in parentheses are the standard errors.  The price of capital (n) relative to the price of land (r) increased with distance, as indicated by

$$\ln \frac{n}{r} = 0.969 + 9.953 \ln(u), \qquad \text{with } \bar{R}^2 = 0.82.$$
$$\quad\;\; (0.053)\;(0.041)$$

3.  Data in this study are for multifamily dwellings only.  Therefore it is assumed for the empirical estimates that the production function is the same for different outputs and firms.

4.  The total value of capital relative to total land varied with respect to distance according to

$$\ln\frac{nK}{rL} = 1.379 + 0.392 \ln(u), \text{ with } \bar{R}^2 = 0.42.$$
$$\quad\;\; (0.053)\;(0.042)$$

This is to be expected since the elasticity ($\sigma$) is less than one.

Chapter 8


THE ELASTICITY OF SUBSTITUTION OVER TIME AND SPACE


## 8.1. Introduction


Both Chapters 6 and 7 demonstrated the usefulness of the VES production function for the study of urban spatial structure. Chapter 6 introduced the VES for the analysis of single-family housing. Using the VES, a range from 0.66 to 0.95 was indicated for the elasticity-of-substitution. Chapter 7 developed a detailed analysis of the VES production function and provided some estimates for multi-family dwellings. In all cases these elasticity estimates were for a particular region and were aggregated for that region.

There are a number of reasons for the elasticity-of-substitution to vary over time and space. The capital-land ratios are clearly not the same for each region, and the firms producing urban structure may have significantly different production functions relative to output. Furthermore, technological limitations due to differing institutional or informational constraints will alter the elasticity of substitution, [see Chapter 7, pages 3-10].

The purpose of this chapter is to provide evidence on exactly how the elasticity of substitution varies over time and space. The time period is 1966 to 1978 and the space is 31 different U.S. cities.[1]

## 8.2. The Model and Empirical Results

In Chapters 4, 6, and 7 we analyzed and reviewed Revankar's (1971a) variable elasticity of substitution production function:

$$Xs = AK^{v(1-\delta\rho)}[L + (\rho-1)K]^{v \delta\rho} \qquad (8.1)$$

when Xs is output, K is the non-land (capital, L is land; and v, $\sigma$, $\rho$, and A are parameters with the following constraints:

$$A > 0 \qquad (8.2)$$

$$v > 0 \qquad (8.3)$$

$$0 < \delta < 1 \qquad (8.4)$$

$$0 \leq \delta\rho \leq 1 \qquad (8.5)$$

and

$$L/K > (\frac{1-\rho}{1-\delta\rho}). \qquad (8.6)$$

Revankar (1971a) shows that the elasticity of substitution for the VES function is

$$\sigma = 1 + (\frac{\rho-1}{1-\delta\rho}) K/L \qquad (8.7)$$

Thus, $\sigma$ varies with the capital-land ratio around the intercept of unity. Table 8.1 contains the capital-land ratios for 31 cities over the 1966-1978 time period. Significant variation does exist across time and space, thus indicating either technological or relative price differences.

Assuming constant returns to scale, i.e., v = 1 in (8.1), competitive factor and product markets, and profit-maximizing, the elasticity of substitution, $\sigma$, between land and structures for the 31 FHA housing area was estimated by regressing the factor input ratios on the relative factor prices. Thus,

Table 8.1.  Capital-Land Ratio For
Various Cities:  1966-1978*

| City | 1966 | 1967 | 1968 | 1969 | 1970 | 1971 | 1972 | 1973 | 1974 | 1975 | 1976 | 1977 | 1978 |
|---|---|---|---|---|---|---|---|---|---|---|---|---|---|
| | | | | | | | | | | | **YEAR** | | |
| Albuquerque | .174 | .184 | .181 | .178 | .184 | .175 | .118 | .181 | .158 | .175 | .173 | .177 | .184 |
| Charlotte | .100 | .092 | .078 | .086 | .095 | .095 | .107 | .105 | .091 | .101 | .088 | .079 | .093 |
| Columbus, OH | .116 | .115 | .134 | .131 | .144 | .141 | .144 | .153 | .140 | .148 | .136 | .153 | .149 |
| Dallas | .157 | .143 | .151 | .153 | .163 | .165 | .185 | .122 | .190 | .194 | .191 | .188 | .197 |
| Dayton | .106 | .108 | .121 | .118 | .118 | .135 | .124 | .120 | .132 | .127 | .108 | .129 | .133 |
| Denver | .127 | .150 | .156 | .152 | .139 | .130 | .133 | .145 | .206 | .147 | .134 | .143 | .152 |
| El Paso | .181 | .158 | .149 | .167 | .180 | .177 | .183 | .197 | .211 | .191 | .187 | .194 | .195 |
| Fresno | .193 | .209 | .188 | .185 | .214 | .198 | .194 | .213 | .181 | .202 | .210 | .191 | .185 |
| Greensboro, NC | .090 | .094 | .105 | .103 | .105 | .108 | .104 | .099 | .130 | .1171 | .106 | .091 | .089 |
| Houston | .171 | .177 | .179 | .185 | .206 | .203 | .191 | .183 | .206 | .212 | .202 | .201 | .210 |
| Jacksonville | .132 | .150 | .141 | .143 | .146 | .139 | .136 | .149 | .147 | .139 | .152 | .135 | .130 |
| Las Vegas | .187 | .187 | .197 | .206 | .222 | .184 | .235 | .214 | .207 | .194 | .194 | .215 | .209 |
| Los Angeles | .204 | .230 | .246 | .217 | .233 | .235 | .248 | .219 | .231 | .237 | .216 | .207 | .226 |
| Louisville | .114 | .115 | .108 | .116 | .123 | .120 | .114 | .123 | .123 | .126 | .133 | .114 | .122 |
| Memphis | .120 | .119 | .102 | .122 | .134 | .136 | .151 | .142 | .120 | .136 | .139 | .143 | .140 |
| Miami | .140 | .133 | .148 | .146 | .152 | .175 | .166 | .138 | .151 | .170 | .225 | .210 | .212 |
| Nashville | .072 | .073 | .079 | .087 | .086 | .086 | .089 | .092 | .098 | .079 | .087 | .086 | .077 |
| Oklahoma City | .130 | .129 | .133 | .135 | .137 | .135 | .143 | .145 | .159 | .165 | .162 | .167 | .172 |
| Orlando | .155 | .133 | .138 | .139 | .140 | .140 | .134 | .150 | .151 | .147 | .133 | .142 | .153 |
| Phoenix | .201 | .207 | .174 | .182 | .190 | .195 | .247 | .188 | .192 | .157 | .170 | .177 | .209 |
| Sacramento | .171 | .186 | .177 | .178 | .194 | .170 | .190 | .195 | .189 | .194 | .182 | .181 | .195 |
| San Diego | .164 | .189 | .151 | .170 | .175 | .186 | .205 | .193 | .188 | .186 | .216 | .217 | .219 |
| San Francisco | .198 | .199 | .206 | .206 | .228 | .283 | .278 | .291 | .317 | .247 | .240 | .175 | .186 |
| San Jose | .231 | .233 | .228 | .218 | .253 | .251 | .266 | .248 | .233 | .228 | .225 | .217 | .225 |
| Seattle | .143 | .117 | .120 | .122 | .132 | .131 | .127 | .143 | .129 | .143 | .138 | .146 | .143 |
| Shreveport | .094 | .118 | .084 | .092 | .146 | .135 | .169 | .159 | .166 | .133 | .129 | .165 | .144 |
| Spokane | .092 | .125 | .122 | .089 | .106 | .092 | .103 | .107 | .106 | .093 | .091 | .084 | .087 |
| Stockton | .191 | .196 | .162 | .177 | .205 | .198 | .189 | .207 | .214 | .200 | .191 | .199 | .207 |
| Tampa | .146 | .139 | .142 | .145 | .152 | .139 | .149 | .141 | .157 | .171 | .154 | .179 | .174 |
| Tulsa | .138 | .123 | .125 | .128 | .131 | .133 | .146 | .145 | .148 | .162 | .161 | .159 | .154 |
| Vallejo | .207 | .179 | .180 | .198 | .199 | .204 | .247 | .214 | .210 | .214 | .199 | .193 | .185 |

*Source:  Federal Housing Administration, FHA Homes, Washington, D.C., various years.
See Appendix A for a detailed listing of the data.

$$L/K = \gamma_0 + \gamma_1 (n/r) \tag{8.8}$$

where K is the structures input (square feet of improved living area), L is the land input (square feet of land), r is the price of land per square foot and n is the price of the structure (non-land) per unit of living area, and $\gamma_0 = (1-\rho)/(1-\delta\rho)$ and $\gamma_1 = \delta\rho/(1-\delta\rho)$.

Equation (8.8) was estimated using the cross-section data for each year. These estimates are given in Table 8.2. The elasticity of substitution can be calculated using Equation (8.7) and the estimates from (8.8) as,[2]

$$\sigma = 1 - \gamma_0 (K/L) \tag{8.9}$$

Using Equation (8.9), the elasticity of substitution was calculated for each city for every year. The estimates of Equation (8.9) are given in Table 8.3 for every city and time period.

Table 8.3 provides clear evidence that the elasticity-of-substitution varies over time and space. In the next section an analysis of such variation is conducted.

### 8.3. Variations in $\sigma$ over Time and City

The elasticity of substitution ($\sigma$) estimates in Table 8.3 were analyzed for trends over time, across regions, and by city size. In general, the elasticity of substitution increased over time, with 23 of the 31 cities having significant coefficients when regressed on a time variable. Regional differences were examined using a dummy variable for cities in the east or west.[3] The elasticity of substitution was significantly lower in the western cities. City size was examined using three dummy variables for cities with population of less than one-half million, between one-half and one million, and greater than one million. There were significant differences in the elasticity of substitution by city size with the elasticity being lower in large cities.

Table 8.2. Estimates of Relative Factor
Inputs as a Function of Factor Prices:
1966-1978*

**Dependent Variable = L/K**

| | Year | | | | | | | | | | | | |
|---|---|---|---|---|---|---|---|---|---|---|---|---|---|
| | 1966 | 1967 | 1968 | 1969 | 1970 | 1971 | 1972 | 1973 | 1974 | 1975 | 1976 | 1977 | 1978 |
| Constant | 3.026 (.472) | 3.576 (.514) | 3.635 (.489) | 3.641 (.429) | 3.356 (.410) | 3.350 (.350) | 3.154 (.403) | 3.211 (.397) | 3.003 (.433) | 3.009 (.433) | 2.805 (.418) | 2.420 (.366) | 2.228 (.359) |
| n/r | .122 (.012) | .104 (.013) | .103 (.012) | .096 (.010) | .096 (.011) | .101 (.009) | .103 (.011) | .100 (.011) | .107 (.013) | .105 (.012) | .117 (.012) | .134 (.210) | .141 (.022) |
| $\bar{R}^2$(OLS) | .766 | .661 | .675 | .723 | .724 | .761 | .734 | .719 | .694 | .718 | .783 | .849 | .857 |

Note: Standard errors of the regression coefficients are in parenthesis. All coefficients are significant at the 5% level.

Table 8.3.  VES Estimates of Elasticity of
Substitution For Various Cities:  1966–1978*

| City | 1966 | 1967 | 1968 | 1969 | 1970 | 1971 | 1972 | 1973 | 1974 | 1975 | 1976 | 1977 | 1978 |
|---|---|---|---|---|---|---|---|---|---|---|---|---|---|
| Albuquerque | .4735 | .3420 | .3410 | .3530 | .3825 | .4138 | .6278 | .4188 | .5225 | .4434 | .5147 | .5717 | .5900 |
| Charlotte | .6974 | .6710 | .7160 | .6874 | .6812 | .6818 | .6625 | .6628 | .7267 | .6961 | .7532 | .8088 | .7928 |
| Columbus, OH | .6450 | .5888 | .5121 | .5238 | .5167 | .5277 | .5458 | .5087 | .5796 | .5547 | .6185 | .6297 | .6680 |
| Dallas | .5249 | .4886 | .4502 | .4438 | .4530 | .4475 | .4165 | .4156 | .4294 | .4163 | .4642 | .5450 | .5611 |
| Dayton | .6792 | .6138 | .5594 | .5711 | .6040 | .5478 | .6089 | .6147 | .6036 | .6179 | .6971 | .6878 | .7037 |
| Denver | .6147 | .4636 | .4320 | .4475 | .5335 | .5645 | .5805 | .5344 | .3814 | .5577 | .6241 | .6559 | .6613 |
| El Paso | .4523 | .4350 | .4575 | .3930 | .3959 | .4071 | .4228 | .3674 | .3664 | .4253 | .4755 | .5305 | .5655 |
| Fresno | .4160 | .2326 | .3255 | .3275 | .2818 | .3367 | .3881 | .3161 | .4565 | .3922 | .4110 | .5378 | .5878 |
| Greensboro, NC | .7277 | .6639 | .6250 | .6256 | .6476 | .7382 | .6720 | .6821 | .6096 | .6479 | .7027 | .7798 | .8017 |
| Houston | .4826 | .3670 | .3483 | .3275 | .3087 | .3200 | .3976 | .4124 | .3814 | .3621 | .4334 | .5138 | .5321 |
| Jacksonville | .6006 | .4636 | .4866 | .4802 | .5100 | .5344 | .5711 | .5216 | .5586 | .5817 | .5736 | .6733 | .7104 |
| Las Vegas | .4341 | .3313 | .2827 | .2512 | .2550 | .3836 | .2588 | .3128 | .3784 | .4163 | .4558 | .4797 | .5343 |
| Los Angeles | .3827 | .1773 | .1043 | .2112 | .2182 | .2128 | .2178 | .2968 | .3063 | .2869 | .3941 | .4991 | .4965 |
| Louisville | .6550 | .5888 | .6068 | .5783 | .5872 | .5980 | .6404 | .6050 | .6306 | .6209 | .6269 | .7241 | .7782 |
| Memphis | .6369 | .5745 | .6286 | .5565 | .5503 | .5444 | .5237 | .5440 | .6396 | .5908 | .6101 | .6539 | .6881 |
| Miami | .5764 | .5244 | .4611 | .5693 | .4899 | .4138 | .4764 | .5569 | .5465 | .4885 | .3689 | .4918 | .5277 |
| Nashville | .7821 | .7390 | .7124 | .6838 | .7114 | .7119 | .7193 | .7046 | .7057 | .7623 | .7560 | .7919 | .8284 |
| Oklahoma | .6066 | .5387 | .5147 | .5093 | .5402 | .5478 | .5490 | .5344 | .5225 | .5035 | .5456 | .5959 | .6168 |
| Orlando | .5310 | .5244 | .4975 | .4947 | .5302 | .5310 | .5774 | .5484 | .5465 | .5577 | .6269 | .6564 | .6591 |
| Phoenix | .3918 | .2594 | .2936 | .3384 | .3625 | .3468 | .2210 | .3763 | .4234 | .3276 | .5232 | .3717 | .5343 |
| Sacramento | .4826 | .3349 | .3555 | .3530 | .3489 | .4305 | .4007 | .3739 | .4324 | .4163 | .5895 | .5620 | .5655 |
| San Diego | .5037 | .3241 | .4502 | .3821 | .4127 | .3769 | .3534 | .3803 | .4354 | .4403 | .3941 | .4749 | .5121 |
| San Francisco | .4009 | .2884 | .2500 | .2512 | .2348 | .0520 | .1232 | .0656 | .0480 | .2568 | .3268 | .5765 | .5856 |
| San Jose | .3010 | .1668 | .1699 | .2076 | .1309 | .1592 | .1610 | .2037 | .3003 | .3139 | .3689 | .4749 | .4987 |
| Seattle | .5673 | .5816 | .5631 | .5565 | .5570 | .3612 | .5994 | .5408 | .6126 | .5697 | .6129 | .6467 | .6814 |
| Shreveport | .7156 | .5780 | .6942 | .6656 | .5100 | .5478 | .4670 | .1894 | .5015 | .5998 | .6382 | .6007 | .6792 |
| Spokane | .7215 | .5530 | .5558 | .6765 | .6443 | .6918 | .6751 | .6564 | .6817 | .7202 | .7447 | .7967 | .8062 |
| Stockton | .4220 | .2991 | .4102 | .3566 | .3120 | .3367 | .4039 | .3353 | .3574 | .3982 | .4642 | .5184 | .5388 |
| Tampa | .5582 | .5029 | .4830 | .4729 | .4899 | .5344 | .5301 | .5472 | .5285 | .4855 | .5680 | .5668 | .6123 |
| Tulsa | .5824 | .5602 | .3449 | .5347 | .5604 | .5545 | .5394 | .5344 | .5556 | .5125 | .5484 | .6152 | .6569 |
| Vallejo | .3736 | .3599 | .3446 | .2803 | .3322 | .3166 | .2210 | .3128 | .3694 | .3561 | .4418 | .5329 | .5878 |

Note: Calculated using equation 8.9 in text and the results in
Table 8.2 and the K/L ratio in Table 8.1.

The pooled time series cross-sectional estimates for variations in elasticity of substitution and the price elasticity was as follows:

$$\sigma_{it} = .4772 + .0097(\text{Time}) + .0415(\text{Size1}) + .0930(\text{Size2}) -$$
$$\phantom{\sigma_{it} =} (.0166) \; (.0015) \qquad\quad (.0138) \qquad\qquad (.0140)$$

$$.1447(\text{West})$$
$$(.0123)$$

where:

$\sigma_{it}$ = the elasticity of substitution in the $i^{th}$ city for $t^{th}$ time period ($i = 1, \ldots, 31$ and $t = 1, \ldots, 13$),

Time = the time variable with 1966 equal to 1,

Size1 = dummy variable for cities of population less than one-half million,

Size2 = dummy variable for cities of population between one half and one million, and

West = dummy variable for cities in the west.

The standard errors are in parentheses below the coefficients. The total sample size was 403 (thirty-one cities for thirteen time periods). The adjusted $R^2$ for the elasticity of substitution equation was .45. These pooled results follow the same general pattern as the individual city and time period results. All coefficients are significant at traditional levels.

Table 8.4 provides the empirical estimates for each of the cross-sections of $\sigma$.

### 8.4. Summary and Conclusions

Many recent papers [see Smith (1976) and Clapp (1979, 1981)] have sought to establish a single unbiased estimate of the elasticity-of-substitution. It is clear from this

Table 8.4. Cross-Sectional Estimates of Variation
in Elasticity of Substitution: 1966–1978a

| | | | | | | | Year | | | | | | |
|---|---|---|---|---|---|---|---|---|---|---|---|---|---|
| Variable | 1966 | 1967 | 1968 | 1969 | 1970 | 1971 | 1972 | 1973 | 1974 | 1975 | 1976 | 1977 | 1978 |
| Constant | .6125* (.0386) | .5425* (.0463) | .5134* (.0469) | .5093* (.0452) | .5059* (.0465) | .4818* (.0518) | .5169* (.0579) | .5207* (.0467) | .5211* (.0451) | .5259* (.0383) | .5542* (.0392) | .6097* (.0321) | .6652 (.0372) |
| Size 1 | .0065 (.0415) | .0111 (.0498) | .0582 (.0504) | .0399 (.0486) | .0159 (.0500) | .0686 (.0557) | .0571 (.0623) | .0165 (.0502) | .0587 (.0485) | .0586* (.0412) | .0658* (.0421) | .0324 (.0345) | .0474* (.0368) |
| Size | .0631* (.0416) | .0716* (.0498) | .1008* (.0505) | .0882* (.0487) | .1036* (.0501) | .1274* (.0558) | .0967* (.0623) | .0962* (.0503) | .1152* (.0485) | .1108* (.0412) | .1083* (.0422) | .0968* (.0346) | .0460 (.0426) |
| West | -.1474* (.0368) | -.1867* (.0441) | -.1779* (.0447) | -.1636* (.0431) | -.1504* (.0444) | -.1413* (.0494) | -.1606* (.0552) | -.1582* (.0446) | -.1478* (.0430) | -.1316 (.0365) | -.1153* (.0374) | -.0792* (.0306) | -.1200* (.0369) |
| $\bar{R}^2$ | .449 | .465 | .459 | .430 | .425 | .361 | .296 | .428 | .433 | .474 | .410 | .399 | .347 |

Notes: a Standard errors in parentheses

t = significant at 10% level.

chapter that this is not possible. The elasticity varies for a number of reasons, both across time and space. To indicate that a single estimate exists is to fail to understand the economic adjustment mechanism of production to variations in technology and relative prices.

## NOTES

1. The data for this study are the average values for FHA new houses. While the data have some limitations [see Muth (1971) for a discussion], they are the most comprehensive data available. The data were taken from FHA Homes (various years) [1975] published by the Department of Housing and Urban Development. The structure input (K) is the average improved living area for new houses, L is the average lot size, r is the estimated land price per square foot, and n is the estimated construction cost per square foot of living area.

2. To illustrate, the estimates in Table 8.3 were calculated as follows using Equation (8.9) and the estimates of Equation (8.8) in Table 2. The estimate of $\gamma_0$ (Equation 8.8, Table 2) is 3.026 for 1966. The K/L ratio for Albuquerque in 1966 was .1740. Using Equation (8.9),

$$\sigma = 1 - 3.026 \ [.1740]$$

$$\sigma = .4735$$

as shown in Table 8.3. This process was then repeated using the K/L ratio for each city for each year and the estimates in Table 8.2 for the various years.

3. The excluded category was cities with population greater than one million.

Chapter 9


TECHNOLOGICAL CHANGE AND SPATIAL ANALYSIS


9.1.  Introduction


In previous chapters the VES production function was used to generate estimates of the elasticity of substitution and to indicate the variability of the elasticity within an urban area.  Thus the VES allowed us to achieve additional insights into the dynamics of urban spatial structure. This chapter will demonstrate the usefulness of the VES function in estimating technological change and economic growth in housing.

Housing cost has risen dramatically in recent years; some evidence suggests that one reason is poor productivity,.  Studies on growth are generally for the economy as a whole with construction being one of the sectors.  The traditional belief is that the housing sector lags in growth behind all other sectors of the economy [see Schultz (1962), Alterman and Jacobs (1961), Amano (1964), Kendrick (1963), Johnson (1968), Nelson, et al. (1967), Harber and Levinson (1976), and Domar (1962).]  Dacy (1965), with a simple modification of the input cost index, measured price and productivity in construction over the period 1947-69. The results indicated that productivity in construction advanced in line with the economy as a whole.

Many studies have investigated the importance of technological change as a determinant of growth for the U.S. economy [see David and DeKlundert (1965), Denison (1962), Domar (1962) and Grilches (1963)].  Studies using a Cobb-

Douglas production function with an elasticity of substitution, $\sigma$ , equal to unity cannot distinguish Hicksian neutral and non-neutral components of technical change [see Nelson (1967)]. Some studies of growth have used the constant elasticity of substitution (CES) production function [see David and DeKlundant (1965)]. The CES function constrains $\sigma$ to be a constant and does not allow it to vary with economic variables in the production function. Previous chapters (6, 7 and 8) have examined the variation in $\sigma$ for housing production with time, distance, and the capital-land ratio.

This chapter will investigate the importance of neutral and non-neutral technological change and elasticity of substitution ($\sigma$ ) on urban housing growth and population density. This is accomplished by using a variable elasticity of substitution (VES) production function developed by Revankar (1967, 1971a). This VES function allows for several novel features.[1] The neutral and non-neutral components of technical change are measured and their contribution to economic growth in housing determined. There is a link between $\sigma$ and time which is useful since changes in $\sigma$ are evidence of biased technical change. The rate of change of bias depends upon the stock of capital per unit of land. A sudden change in the growth of capital resulting in a higher capital-land ratio would induce landsaving innovations to absorb the increased capital.

The results of this chapter indicate that both neutral and non-neutral technical change has occurred in housing production for the 1966-1978 period with neutral change being the dominate force. On average 5 to 7 percent of growth in housing is due to technological change, with the elasticity of substitution of capital for land varying with time and the capital-land ratio. The dominance of neutral change would suggest that efficiency and economics of scale play the major role in growth [see Brown (1966)] with capital intensity and the elasticity of substitution, representing (non-neutral) biased technical change, providing only a minor contribution.

9.2. Technological Change, Density Gradient and the VES: A Theoretical Model

A production function which incorporates the impact of changing elasticities of substitution, capital-land ratio, and technologies in the VES function presented by Revankar (1971b),

$$Xs_t = A\exp(ht)[k_t]^{v(1-\delta\rho)}[L_t+(\rho-1)(1+bt)K_t]^{v\,\delta\rho}, \qquad (9.1)$$

where

$Xs_t$ is the output of housing services u miles from the urban center at time t,

$K_t$ is the input of capital u miles from the urban center at time t,

$L_t$ is the input of land u miles from urban center at time t, and

A, h, v, $\delta$, $\rho$, b are parameters such that

$$A > 0, \qquad v > 0, \qquad (9.2)$$

$$0 < \delta < 1, \qquad 0 \leq \delta\rho \leq 1, \qquad (9.3)$$

and

$$\frac{L_t}{K_t} > \frac{(1-\rho)(1+bt)}{1 - \delta\rho} \qquad (9.4)$$

The distance from (u) has been made implicit as a matter of convenience. Neutral technical change is represented by exp(ht), with h referred to as the neutrality parameter. Nonneutral technical change is reflected by the term 1 + bt, which is linear in time, with b referred to as the nonneutrality parameter.

A neutral technological change does not alter the marginal productivity ratio, whereas a nonneutral technical change is capital-using (land-using) if it increases the marginal product of capital (land) relative to land (capital), while holding the capital-land ratio constant.

The elasticity of substitution for the VES function (9.1) is

$$\sigma_t = 1 + \frac{(\rho-1)(1+bt)}{1 - \delta\rho} \frac{K_t}{L_t} \qquad (9.5)$$

In this formulation $\sigma$, varies linearly with time at each capital-land ratio. The presence of b measures the effect of bias in technical change in terms of its effect on the elasticity of substitution. Also $\sigma_t$ varies with the capital-land ratio in each time period. Thus, as was astutely demonstrated by Revankar (1971b), the elasticity of substitution has a two-way linear dependence: (1) on t for a given capital-land ratio and (2) on the capital-land ratio for a given t. The VES function reduces to the Cobb-Douglas function when $\rho = 1$, for all t.

A demand function for housing services for a given time t, $xd_t$, is defined as

$$Xd_t = Bw_t^{\theta_1} p_t^{\theta_2}, \qquad (9.6)$$

where

B       is a scale parameter and depends upon the units in which housing services are measured,

$w_t$      is the income for workers for a given time period t,

$P_t$      is the price of housing services at distance u for a given time period t,

$\theta_1$      is income elasticity, and

$\theta_2$      is price elasticity.

From Equation (9.1) the relationships between the value of the marginal product and its rental rates for land and capital, $r_t$ and $n_t$ respectively, can be written as

$$\frac{Xs_t}{L_t} = v\delta\rho \left[ \frac{Xs_t}{L_t + (\rho - 1)(1 + bt)K_t} \right] = \frac{r_t}{P_t}$$

and

$$\frac{\partial Xs_t}{\partial K_t} = v(1 - \delta\rho)\frac{Xs_t}{K_t} + v\delta\rho(\rho - 1)(1 + bt) \left[ \frac{Xs_t}{L_t + (\rho-1)(1+bt)K_t} \right]$$

$$= \frac{n_t}{P_t} \tag{9.8}$$

From Equations (9.7) and (9.8) the marginal rate of substitution of capital for land, $S_t$, is

$$S_t = \frac{(\rho-1)(1+bt_t)}{\delta\rho} + \frac{(1-\delta\rho)L_t}{\delta\rho K_t} \tag{9.9}$$

Note that $S_t$ changes linearly with time, and capital intensity remains constant. If the technical bias is capital-using then the time rate of increase is $S_t$, at a fixed capital intensity is

$$\frac{dS_t}{dt} = \frac{(\rho-1)b}{\delta\rho} > 0. \tag{9.10}$$

The time elasticity of $S_t$ is

$$E_t = (\rho-1)b(\rho-1)(1+bt)+1-\delta\rho)\frac{L_t}{K_t} . \tag{9.11}$$

The elasticity is higher at greater capital-land ratios; that is, higher $K_t L_t$ ratios lead to a greater rate of capital-using inventions.

From Equations (9.7) and (9.8) we have

$$L_t = vp_t Xs_t \left[ \frac{\delta\rho}{r_t} - \frac{(1-\delta\rho)(\rho-1)(1+bt)}{n_t - r_t(\rho-1)(1+bt)} \right] \tag{9.12}$$

and

$$K_t = p_t Xs_t \left[ \frac{v(1-\delta\rho)}{n_t - r_t(\rho-1)(1+bt)} \right] \tag{9.13}$$

As $v = 1$, substituting Equations (9.12) and (9.13) into Equation (9.1) we have

$$P_t = A^{-1}\exp(-ht)[n_t - r_t(\rho-1)(1+bt)]^{1-\delta\rho}(1-\delta\rho)^{\delta\rho-1} \qquad (9.14)$$

$$\times [r_t]^{\delta\rho}(\delta\rho)^{-\delta\rho}.$$

From Equation (9.14) the price elasticities of housing with respect to $n_t$ and $r$ can be rewritten as

$$\frac{\partial P_t}{\partial n_t}\frac{n_t}{P_t} = \frac{n_t(1-\delta\rho)}{n_t - r_t(\rho-1)(1+bt)} \qquad (9.15)$$

and

$$\frac{\partial P_t}{\partial r_t}\frac{r_t}{P_t} = \frac{\delta\rho n_t - r_t(\rho-1)(1+bt)}{n_t - r_t(\rho-1)(1+bt)}. \qquad (9.16)$$

Equations (9.15) and (9.16) allow the elasticity of housing services with respect to $n_t$, and $r_t$ to vary with changes in $n_t$ and $r_t$. These elasticities will reduce to $1-\alpha$ and $\alpha$ respectively when the elasticity of substitution between land and capital is unity. This is the case obtained with the Cobb-Douglas function.

Mills (1981), using constrained utility maximization, has derived a differential equation to describe the relationship between the change in the cost of housing and the change in commuting cost as

$$p_t' x_d + T = 0, \qquad (9.17)$$

where

$p_t'$ is the slope of $p_t$ and

$T$ is the cost of commuting.

Substituting Equation (9.6) into Equation (9.17) we have

$$p_t' B w_t^{\theta_1}[p_t]^{\theta_2} + T = 0. \qquad (9.18)$$

By use of the initial condition of Equation (9.18), obtained from Equation (9.17), the solution of the differential Equation (9.18) can be written as

$$P_t = \left[ p_t^{-\theta_2+1} + \frac{T(\bar{u}-u)(\theta_2+1)}{Bw\theta_{1t}} \right]^{1/(\theta_2+1)} \tag{9.19}$$

where

$\bar{u}$ is the distance from the city center to the edge of the urban area, and

$$\bar{p}_t = p_t(\bar{u}). \tag{9.20}$$

Substituting Equation (9.14) into Equation (9.19) we have

$$\left[ p_t^{-\theta_2+1} + \frac{T(\bar{u}-u)(\theta_2+1)}{Bw\theta_t^1} \right]^{1/(1+\theta_2)} \tag{9.21}$$

$$=A^{-1}exp(-ht)[n_t - r_t(\rho-1)(1+bt)]^{1-\delta\rho}(1-\delta\rho)^{\delta\rho-1}[r_t]^{\delta\rho}(\delta\rho)^{-\delta\rho}$$

Equation (9.21) can be rewritten as

$$r_t = [Aexp(ht)(\delta\rho)^{\delta\rho}(1-\delta\rho)^{1-\delta\rho}]^{1/\delta\rho}n_t^{(\delta\rho-1)/\delta\rho}$$

$$x\left[1 - \frac{r_t}{n_t}(\rho-1)(1+bt)\right]^{(\delta\rho-1)/\delta\rho}\left[p_t^{-\theta_2+1}+\frac{T(\bar{u}-u)(\theta_2+1)}{Bw\theta_{1t}}\right]^{1/\delta\rho(\theta_2+1)} \tag{9.22}$$

This implies that the explicit relationship between $r_t$ and u cannot be derived unless $\rho$ is equal to unity. If $\rho = 1$ then Equation (9.22) reduces to

$$r_t = [A\ exp(ht)\delta^\delta(1-\delta)^{1-\delta}]^{1/\delta}n_t^{(\delta-1)/\delta}$$

$$x\left[p_t^{-\theta_2+1} + \frac{T(\bar{u}-u)(\theta_2+1)}{Bw\theta_{1t}}\right]^{1/\delta(\theta_2+1)} \tag{9.23}$$

where

$$\bar{p}_t = A^{-1}exp(-ht)(1-\delta)^{\delta-1} - \bar{r}^\delta n_t^{1-\delta} \tag{9.24}$$

and

$$\bar{r}_t = r_t(\bar{u}). \tag{9.25}$$

This is identical to the general case presented by Mills (1981a) except for the time variable.

To derive the relationship between the population density and the rental of land, $r_t$, Mills (1981, page 228) has defined

$$N_t = \frac{Xs_t}{Xd_t} \quad , \tag{9.26}$$

where $N_t$ is the number of workers living u miles from the urban center at time t,

$Xs_t$ is the output of ousing services u miles from the urban center at time t, and

$xd_t$ is the housing demand per worker living u miles from the urban center at time t.

From Equations (9.12) and (9.13) it can be shown that

$$K_t = \left\{ \frac{1-\delta\rho}{n_t - r_t(\rho-1)(1+bt)} \Bigg/ \left[ \frac{\delta\rho}{r_t} - \frac{(1-\delta\rho)(\rho-1)(1+bt)}{n_t-r_t(\rho-1)(1+bt)} \right] \right\} L_t. \tag{9.27}$$

Substitution of Equation (9.27) into Equation (9.1) gives

$$Xs_t = A \exp(ht)L_t \cdot \left[ \frac{\delta\rho}{r_t} - \frac{(\rho-1)(1-\delta\rho)}{n_t-r_t(\rho-1)(1+bt)} \right]^{-1} \tag{9.28}$$

$$x \left[ \frac{1-\delta\rho}{n_t-r_t(\rho-1)(1+bt)} \right]^{1-\delta\rho} \left[ \frac{\delta\rho}{r_t} \right]^{\delta\rho}$$

From Equations (9.6) and (9.14).

$$xd_t = Bw^{\theta_1}A^{-\theta_2}(\exp(-h\theta_2 t)[n_t-r_t(\rho-1)(1+bt)]^{\theta_2(1-\delta\rho)}$$

$$x(1-\delta\rho)^{\theta_2(\delta\rho-1)}[r_t]^{\delta\rho\theta_2}(\delta\rho)^{-\delta\rho\theta_2}. \tag{9.29}$$

Substitution of Equations (9.28) and (9.29) into Equation (9.26) gives

$$D_t = \frac{N_t}{L_t} = B^{-1}w_t^{-\theta_1}A^{\theta_2+1} \exp[ht(\theta_2+1)]$$

$$[n_t-r_t(\rho-1)(1+bt)]^{(\theta_2+1)(\delta\rho-1)}(1-\delta\rho)^{(\theta_2+1)(1-\delta\rho)}$$

$$x \left[ \frac{\delta\rho}{r_t} - \frac{(\rho-1)(1-\delta\rho)}{n_t - r_t^{(\rho-1)(1+bt)}} \right]^{-1}$$

$$x \left( \frac{\delta\rho}{r_t} \right)^{\delta\rho} [r_t]^{-\delta\rho\theta_2} (\delta\rho)^{\delta\rho\theta_2} \quad .$$

This is the population density in terms of $n_t$, $r_t$, b, t, and other parameters.

To compare this density function with those derived from the Cobb-Douglas production function, a static population-density model is derived from Equation (9.30) by removing the time variable (see Chapter 4). With time removed and $\rho = 1$, Equation (9.30) reduces to Mill's (1981) generalized results. If $\rho$ is not equal to zero then n and r are additional variables needed to explain the change of population density within a city. This essentially is due to the VES production function having explicitly taken the K/L ratio into account. The argument can be shown explicitly by rewriting the static version of the VES function for within a city as

$$Xs = A[K]^{v(1-\delta\rho)}[L]^{v\delta\rho}[1 + (\rho - 1) \frac{K}{L}]^{\alpha\delta\rho} \qquad (9.31)$$

The K/L ratio changes over distance, and therefore K/L becomes an important factor in explaining the supply of housing services unless the value of $1-\rho$ is trivial. In sum, the density gradient estimated by using the negative-exponential function is generally biased.

In the following section a regression model is derived for estimating the variation of the elasticity of substitution within an urban area and the impact of technical change on housing. Some empirical results are estimated to demonstrate the importance of the possible impact of changes in technology on economic growth.


9.3. Technological Change and the VES: An Empirical Model


Using Equation (9.1) and the equation for the elasticity of substitution (9.5) the empirically estimable relationships are derived by assuming competitive equilibrium in the factor markets and equating the marginal products of capital and land to the respective factor prices. From these equations[2] we have

$$\frac{Xs_t}{K_t} = \frac{n_t}{1-\delta\rho} + \frac{1-\rho}{1-\delta\rho}(r_t) t) + \frac{(1-\rho)b}{1-\delta\rho}(t)(r_t) \qquad (9.32)$$

$$\frac{L_t}{K_t} = \frac{1-\rho}{1-\delta\rho} + \frac{(1-\rho)b}{1-\delta\rho}(t) + \frac{\delta\rho}{1-\delta\rho}\frac{(n_t)}{(r_t)} \qquad (9.33)$$

In the empirical section Xs equals the value of output (pXs) since a pure physical measure of output is not available. Equation (9.32) states that the output-capital ratio depends on n and r. Furthermore, depending on (1 + bt), the influence of land price on the output-capital ratio may become more pronounced or weakened with time. If b < 0 and (1 + bt) > 0, the price of land will have gradually less effect on the average product of capital. Equation 9.33 states that the land-capital ratio depends on relative factor prices ($n_t/r_t$) and biased technical change. If $\rho < 1$ and b < 0 (land-saving bias), the land-capital ratio falls unless offset by a rise in the price of capital. This encourages land-saving technology and the growth of capital in housing production. Also using the VES function (9.1), the marginal rate of substitution of capital for land ($MCL_t$) is

$$MCL_t = \frac{(\rho-1)(1+bt)}{\delta\rho} + \frac{1-\delta\rho}{\delta\rho}\frac{L_t}{K_t} . \qquad (9.34)$$

$MCL_t$ depends on non-neutral change but not on neutral change. Thus $MCL_t$ moves linearly with time holding capital intensity constant. For example, if $\rho < 1$ and b < 0, it is clear from (9.34) that the non-neutral change is land-saving.[3]

Equation (9.33) can be modified to provide implications for the behavior of factor income shares. Multiplying both sides by $r_t/n_t$, we have

Where $r_t L_t$ equals land's share and $n_t K_t$ equals capital's share. The assumption of constant return to scale implies that $Xs_t = r_t L_t + n_t K_t$.

## 9.3.1. Estimating Equations

The estimation procedure is a simultaneous system with a production function and two behavioral equations. The production function is the natural log of Equation (9.1) divided by $K_t$ and assuming $v = 1$,

$$\ln \frac{Xs_t}{K_t} = \ln A + ht + \delta\rho\ln \frac{L_t}{K_t} + (\rho - 1)(1 + bt) + \varepsilon_{0t} \quad (9.36)$$

The behavioral Equations (9.32) and (9.33) are presented in a stochastic version assuming the private construction sector is profit-maximizing and that the deviations of desired and actual inputs are uncorrelated with the disturbance term $\varepsilon_{0t}$. The lack of correlation between the deviations of desired and actual inputs insures no correlation of $(\varepsilon_{1t}, \varepsilon_{2t})$ with $\varepsilon_0$ [see Zellner, Kmenta and Dreze (1966) and Revankar (1971a, 1971b)]. The equations are

$$\frac{Xs_t}{K_t} = gF_0 n_t + gF_1 r_t + gF_2 tr_t + \varepsilon_{1t} \quad (9.37)$$

where $F = \frac{1}{1-\delta\rho}$, $F = \frac{1-\rho}{1-\delta\rho}$, $F = \frac{(1-\rho)b}{1-\delta\rho}$,

$g^{-1} = E(e^{\varepsilon_0})$ and $\varepsilon_{1t}$ is the disturbance term,

and

$$\frac{L_t}{K_t} = G_0 + G_1 t + G_2(n_t/r_t) + \varepsilon_2 t \quad (9.38)$$

where $G = \frac{1-\rho}{1-\delta\rho}$, $G = \frac{(1-\rho)b}{1-\delta\rho}$, $G = \frac{\delta\rho}{1-\delta\rho}$ and $\varepsilon_{2t}$ is

the disturbance term.

We estimate Equations (9.37) and (9.38) simultaneously according to Zellner's (1962) efficient regression method. Estimates of $G_0$, $G_1$ and $G_2$ yield $\rho$, b and $\delta\rho$ since

$1-\hat{\rho} = \hat{G}_0/(1 + \hat{G}_2)$, $\hat{b} = \hat{G}_1/\hat{G}_0$ and $\hat{\delta\rho} = \hat{G}_2/(1 + \hat{G}_2)$.

Next $\hat{\rho}$ and $\hat{b}$ are used to construct the series

$$L_t^* = L_t/K_t + (\hat{\rho} - 1)(1 + \hat{b}t), \text{ and} \tag{9.39}$$

$\hat{\delta\rho}$ is used to construct

$$Z_t = \ln(V_t/K_t) - \hat{\delta\rho}\ln L_t^* . \tag{9.40}$$

We estimate A and h by regressing $Z_t$ on t, we have[4]

$$Z_t = \ln A + ht + \varepsilon_{0t} \tag{9.41}$$

Finally the average elasticity of substitution, $\bar{\sigma}$ over the sample is estimated as

$$\hat{\bar{\sigma}} = 1/T \sum_{t=1}^{T} \hat{\sigma}_t = 1 - \hat{G}_0 \frac{1}{T} \sum_{t=1}^{T} \frac{K_t}{L_t} - \hat{G}_0 \hat{b} \frac{1}{T} \sum_{t=1}^{T} t \cdot \frac{K_t}{L_t} \tag{9.42}$$

Several hypotheses can now be tested. The Cobb-Douglas versus the VES is tested by examining whether $\sigma = 1$. This is done by testing $\rho = 1$, that is, whether

$G_0 = \dfrac{1-\rho}{1-\delta\rho}$ is equal to zero. This is based on whether $\hat{G}_0$

is significantly different from zero. The existence of non-neutral technical change is tested by $\hat{b} = 0$, i.e.,

$G_1 = \dfrac{(1-\rho)b}{1-\delta\rho} = 0.$ Neutral technical change is examined by

testing whether the coefficient of t in Equation (9.41) is significantly different from zero.

### 9.3.2.  The Empirical Results

The data are FHA single-family new housing for the time period 1966 to 1978. While the data have some limitations [see Muth (1971) for a detailed discussion], this is the most comprehensive data set available for empirical testing of the model. These data contain the value (selling price), the estimated land value, improved living area, lot size, price of land per square foot, and the estimated replacement cost per square foot of improved living area. All data are averages for new housing for the various housing areas, essentially standard metropolitan statistical areas. The data are in real terms. The first step is to determine the adequacy of Cobb-Douglas function. The SUR estimation of Question (9.38)[5] is shown in Table 9.1 for various cities over the period 1966-1978.

In addition to the four cities shown in Table 9.1, the model was tested on data for thirty-one cities. The qualitative results for the majority of these cities were the same as those in Table 9.1. As shown in Table 1, $G_0$ is significantly different from zero. This indicates that the Cobb-Douglas function is inappropriate. Given the acceptability of the VES, we can now test for neutral and non-neutral technical change.

The coefficient of $t(\hat{G}_1)$ from the estimation of Equation (9.38) is significantly different from zero, therefore the construction of single-family housing for the cities over the period has experienced a significant component of biased (non-neutral) technical change. Note

that $(\hat{G}_1 = \hat{G}_0\hat{b} < 0$ so that $\hat{b} < 0$ since $\hat{G}_0 > 0$. Also $\hat{\rho} < 1$

given $\hat{G}_0/1+G_1 > 0$. With $\hat{b} < 0$ and $\hat{\rho} < 1$ the non-neutral

change is land-saving.

The significance of neutral technical change is determined from Equation (9.41) based on whether the coefficient of t is different from zero. The estimation of Equation (9.41) is shown in Table 9.1.

The coefficient of t is positive and significant. This indicates that U.S. single family construction over the period of 1966 to 1978 has been characterized by the technology of a VES production function and has experienced neutral and land-saving technical change.

Table 9.1. Production Function Estimates
for Various Cities: 1966-1978[a]

| Independent Variable | City | | | | | | | |
|---|---|---|---|---|---|---|---|---|
| | Dallas | | Dayton | | Louisville | | Stockton | |
| | L/K | $z_t$ | L/K | $z_t$ | L/K | $z_t$ | L/K | $z_t$ |
| (Equation No.) | (9.38) | (9.41) | (9.38) | (9.41) | (9.38) | (9.41) | (9.38) | (9.41) |
| Constant | 5.1530 (.654)* | 2.4336 (.03525)* | 2.3862 (1.1038)* | 2.1729 (.0197)* | 5.0916 (1.3069)* | 2.3575 (.0311)* | 3.0642 (.6920)* | 2.3188 (.0468)* |
| Time (t) | -.09556 (.02599)* | .05072 (.00444)* | -.2166 (.0292)* | .06716 (.00248)* | -.0743 (.0286)* | .0749 (.0039)* | -.09797 (.02278)* | .0709 (.0059)* |
| n/r | .04538 (.01692)* | | .2126 (.0352)* | | .1047 (.0355)* | | .11656 (.0321)* | |
| $\bar{R}^2$ (O.L.S.) | .903 | .915 | .851 | .984 | .627 | .968 | .662 | .923 |
| D-W (O.L.S.) | 1.700 | 1.052 | 1.402 | 1.350 | 1.846 | 1.454 | 1.992 | .8748 |

Note: [a]Standard errors are in parentheses, with * representing significance at the .05% level.

### 9.4. Technical Change and the Elasticity of Substitution In Housing

The elasticity of substitution, $\sigma_t$, depends on time and the $K_t/L_t$ ratio. Thus for each point in time for the observed $K_t/L_t$ ratio there is a $\hat{\sigma}_t = 1 - (G_0)(1 + bt)K_t/L_t$. Replacing $G_0$ and by by their estimates, and starting from t=1 note that (1 + bt) remains positive over the sample period implying that $\sigma$ is less than unity in most cities (see Table 9.2). This result supports the estimates in Chapter 7 and others and is in disagreement with Smith (1976) and Clapp (1979). Two other effects are occurring with respect to $\hat{\sigma}_t$. First, $\sigma_t$ continuously increases over time for a given capital-land ratio. This is the consequence of land-saving bias in housing ($\hat{b} < 0$, $\hat{\rho} < 1$). Second, $\sigma_t$ falls with increasing capital-land ratios, at a given point in time. Thus $\sigma_t$ is governed by two forces: land-saving technical change increases it and rising capital-land ratios lower it. Table 9.2 presents the $\hat{\sigma}_t$ series for the sample period. Changes in the $K_t/L_t$ always lead to inverse changes in $\sigma_t$. The average $\bar{\sigma}_t$ over the time period for each city is shown in Table 9.2, all less than unity.[6] The general impression is that the capital-land ratio has not been the dominating factor as compared to the land-saving bias, in influencing the movement of $\sigma_t$.

### 9.5. Technical Change and Economic Growth in Housing

The rates of growth of the inputs of land and capital explain between 93% to 95% of the observed rate of growth of housing output. Land has been obtaining a decreasing share over time while capital's share has been increasing. The residual portion, that part of the output growth not explained by the growth of the inputs, is treated as determined by the technological change. The technological change is treated as an additional input [see David and DeKlundert (1965) and Revankar (1971b)] and the production function is written as

Table 9.2. Estimates of the Elasticity of Substitution ($\sigma_t$), the Marginal Rate of Substitution (MCL$_t$) and the Contribution of Biased Component of Technical Change for Various Cities, 1966-1978.

| | Dallas | | | | Dayton | | | |
|---|---|---|---|---|---|---|---|---|
| | Variable | | | | Variable | | | |
| Year | $K_t/L_t$ | $\hat{\sigma}_t$ | $\widehat{MCL}_t$ | %Bias | $K_t/L_t$ | $\hat{\sigma}_t$ | $\widehat{MCL}_t$ | %Bias |
| 1966 | .157 | .205 | 28.66 | .261 | .106 | .771 | 34.29 | .408 |
| 1967 | .146 | .293 | 45.30 | .175 | .108 | .789 | 34.35 | .410 |
| 1968 | .151 | .264 | 38.50 | .203 | .121 | .790 | 30.57 | .460 |
| 1969 | .153 | .269 | 38.72 | .202 | .1111 | .821 | 32.85 | .432 |
| 1970 | .163 | .236 | 31.88 | .241 | .118 | .847 | 33.83 | .422 |
| 1971 | .165 | .246 | 32.94 | .234 | .135 | .853 | 29.68 | .482 |
| 1972 | .185 | .172 | 20.53 | .352 | .124 | .892 | 33.95 | .425 |
| 1973 | .182 | .200 | 24.10 | .309 | .120 | .921 | 36.05 | .403 |
| 1974 | .189 | .190 | 22.16 | .333 | .132 | .943 | 33.70 | .432 |
| 1975 | .194 | .188 | 21.37 | .345 | .127 | .972 | 36.00 | .407 |
| 1976 | .191 | .216 | 24.87 | .304 | .108 | 1.000 | 43.52 | .338 |
| 1977 | .188 | .248 | 29.14 | .265 | .129 | 1.028 | 37.39 | .396 |
| 1978 | .197 | .231 | 25.87 | .295 | .133 | 1.057 | 37.47 | .397 |
| Mean Value | .174 | .227 | 29.54 | .271 | .112 | .899 | 34.90 | .416 |

City

| | Louisville | | | | Stockton | | | |
|---|---|---|---|---|---|---|---|---|
| 1966 | .144 | .430 | 36.14 | .150 | .191 | .433 | 19.45 | .355 |
| 1967 | .115 | .431 | 35.74 | .151 | .196 | .439 | 19.24 | .360 |
| 1968 | .108 | .476 | 42.15 | .131 | .162 | .552 | 29.29 | .247 |
| 1969 | .116 | .442 | 36.25 | .150 | .177 | .528 | 25.67 | .280 |
| 1970 | .123 | .421 | 32.72 | .165 | .205 | .472 | 19.78 | .356 |
| 1971 | .120 | .442 | 36.20 | .154 | .198 | .510 | 22.08 | .323 |
| 1972 | .114 | .447 | 39.80 | .139 | .189 | .550 | 24.99 | .290 |
| 1973 | .123 | .447 | 34.75 | .157 | .208 | .527 | 21.76 | .330 |
| 1974 | .123 | .445 | 35.29 | .155 | .214 | .532 | 21.28 | .338 |
| 1975 | .126 | .451 | 34.17 | .160 | .200 | .583 | 24.99 | .293 |
| 1976 | .133 | .431 | 30.98 | .175 | .191 | .622 | 27.99 | .264 |
| 1977 | .114 | .520 | 43.46 | .129 | .199 | .624 | 26.85 | .275 |
| 1978 | .122 | .496 | 38.72 | .143 | .207 | .629 | 26.08 | .284 |
| Mean Value | .119 | .455 | 36.57 | .151 | .195 | .539 | 23.80 | .307 |

$$Xs_t = f(K_t, L_t, t)e^{at} \tag{9.43}$$

where the function f has the third input t representing technological progress, with $e^{at}$ the disturbance term. Differentiating (9.43) with respect to t and rearranging terms, the growth rate of the residual ($R_t$) is

$$\frac{\dot{R}_t}{R_t} = \frac{\dot{Xs}_t}{Xs_t} - \frac{(n_t K_t)}{Xs_t} \frac{\dot{K}_t}{K_t} - \frac{(r_t L_t)}{Xs_t} \frac{\dot{L}_t}{L_t} \tag{9.44}$$

$$= \frac{\partial f}{\partial t}/f + \dot{a}t \tag{9.45}$$

The dot (.) denotes the time derivative of the variables. The firm term of (9.45) represents technical change and the second term represents the omitted inputs from the production function. In the VES case, Equation (9.45) reduces to Revankar (1971b),

$$\frac{\dot{R}_t}{R} = h + \frac{\delta\rho(\rho - 1)bK_t}{L_t + (\rho - 1)(1 + bt)K_t} + a_t \tag{9.46}$$

The residual growth rate ($\dot{R}_t/R$) is composed of three terms: First h, the contribution of neutral change, second, b, the non-neutral change, and third, the unexplained residual. The second term is zero when b = 0. The value of h is the coefficient of t from Equation (9.41), Table 9.1. The average growth rate of the residual and biased technical change is computed by regressing logarithms of variables $Xs_t$, $K_t$ and $L_t$ on time and calculating the growth rate by evaluating the average land share at each point in time.

As shown in Table 9.3, the average value of the residual growth rate is approximately 7% over the period 1966-1978. The value of h, the contribution of neutral technical change to the residual growth rate, implies that the neutral technical change contributes approximately 95% of the residual growth rate. The value of the second term in Equation (9.46) represents the non-neutral technical progress to the growth rate. Its share averages about 4.0% which is much smaller than the neutral change.[7] Neutral and non-neutral change represents an average 99.9% of the growth rate of the residual; the remainder is insignificant

Table 9.3. Summary of Residual Growth, Neutral and Non-Neutral Contribution
for Various Cities

|  | City | | | |
|  | Dallas | Dayton | Louisville | Stockton |
| --- | --- | --- | --- | --- |
| Residual Growth Rate | 5.36% | 7.13% | 7.64% | 7.39% |
| Neutral Contribution to Residual Growth | 5.07% | 6.72% | 7.49% | 7.09% |
| Non-Neutral Contribution to Residual Growth | .271% | .416% | .151% | .286% |
| Neutral Share | 94.6% | 94.2% | 98.0% | 95.9% |
| Non-Neutral Share | 5.1% | 5.8% | 2.0% | 3.9% |
| Total Factor Productivity | 5.34% | 7.13% | 7.64% | 7.38% |
| % of Residual Growth Rate Unexplained | 0.001% | 0.00% | 0.00% | 0.001% |

suggesting minor problems with omitted variables. The total factor productivity index had a growth rate of between 5 and 7%.

Neutral technical change accounts for about 95% of total factor productivity and is fairly constant across cities. The non-neutral change varied through time thus causing changes in the total index. The biased component is presented in Table 9.2. The pattern indicates that the elasticity of substitution movements are the same as the variations in the capital-land ratio. This, along with the fact that capital-land ratio and the non-neutral change move together, implies that the non-neutral change becomes more important in periods of rising capital-land ratios. Given that the elasticity of substitution rises with the capital-land ratio, we can conclude that housing construction has had rising capital intensities at higher elasticities of substitution due to the role of non-neutral land-saving technical change.[8]

The marginal product of capital to land ($MCL_t$) forms the bases for any comparison of biased technical change. Table 9.2 presents estimates of this ratio using Equations (9.34). It has the same determinant as $\hat{\sigma}_t$, i.e., the ratio declines with rising capital-land ratios and increases with land-saving innovations. Neither the capital-land ratio nor land-saving innovations seems to dominate.[9]

## 9.6. Summary and Conclusion

Following the procedures developed by Revankar (1967, 1971b), time-series data on single-family housing was used to measure the presence of technical change in housing production. Using a VES production function, tests were performed on the elasticity of substitution and on neutral and non-neutral technical change. The results indicate that the cities examined experienced significant neutral and non-neutral technical progress.

The elasticity of substitution varies with the capital-land ratio and with time. It increases over time with each capital-land ratio due to land-saving bias in technical change. It decreases with the capital-land ratio at each point in time. With significant land-saving technical change over the period, the $\hat{\sigma}_t$, has been steadily increasing over time. Furthermore, $\hat{\sigma}$ is in general less than unity which is consistent with other findings. The neutral technical change has proceeded at a rate of about 7% with the land-saving bias changing at about .3%. The neutral component has contributed approximately 95% of the residual growth rate whereas the bias change about 4%.

These results indicate that productivity changes have occurred in the housing sector at a greater rate than in other sectors of the economy. This suggests that rising prices in housing are due to changes in fator prices not to the lack of productivity. Dacy (1965) and Oster and Quigley (1977) have offered some explanations of productivity increase which include increases in capital per land, shift in construction product mix, geographical distribution, increase in corporate share, and a decrease in regulatory barriers such as building codes. This study demonstrates that positive productivity changes have occurred. Future research should investigate the sources of productivity changes and the corresponding implications for housing policy.


## NOTES


1. A number of VES functions have been introduced in the literature. Revankar's function has several useful properties relative to the Liu and Hildebrand (1965) and Sato and Hoffman (1968), VES functions. The Revankar VES is simple with an uncomplicated elasticity-of-substitution function. The Revankar function is estimated in a simultaneous equation framework and the average elasticity of substitution is easily obtained. Also this function is general enough to cover special cases of the CES, the Cobb-Douglas, the fixed coefficient and straight-line isoquant models.

2. The equations are

$$(1 - \delta\rho) \frac{Xs_t}{K_t} + \delta\rho(\rho-1)(1+bt) \frac{Xs_t}{L_{1t}} = n_t \qquad (9.1a)$$

$$\frac{\delta\rho Xs_t}{L_{1t}} = r_t \qquad (9.2a)$$

Where $L_{1t} = L_t + ( - 1)(1+bt)K$. Substituting (9.2a) in (9.1a) and rearranging we obtain (9.32). Dividing (9.1a) by (9.2a) and rearranging we obtain (9.33).

3. The time rate of increase in $MCL_t$ at a given capital-land ratio is

$$\frac{d(MCL_t)}{d(t)} = \frac{(\rho - 1)b}{\delta\rho} > 0. \qquad (9.3a)$$

4. The regression of Equation (9.41) indicated no significant serial correlation among the disturbances. If serial correlation is present then the estimated A and h are taken from the following regression.

$$Z_t - \rho_1 Z_{t-1} = \ln A(1 - \rho_1) + \rho_1 A + (1 - \rho_1)A t + \varepsilon_{1t}^1 \qquad (9.4a)$$

Where $\rho_1$ equals the estimated serial correlation coefficient.

5. We have tested the model ($\rho = 1$ and $b = 0$) using the coefficient of Equation (9.37). The same test could be based on the coefficient of Equation (9.38). This alternative procedure leads to the same conclusions.

6. Other studies dealing with the economy as a whole found the elasticity of substitution to be less than unity. Kendrick and Sato (1963) estimated $\hat{\sigma} = 0.58$, Brown and DeCani (1963) obtained $\hat{\sigma} = 0.47$, Ferguson (10) estimate is 0.67, David and DeKlundert (1965) obtained 0.32, Kravis (1959) and $\hat{\sigma} = 0.58$, and Sato (1967) estimated $\hat{\sigma} = 0.53$. Sato and Hoffman (1963) using a CES function and setting $\sigma_t = a+bt$ found $\sigma_t$ decreasing with time. In a recent study by

Takayama (1974) $\hat{\sigma}$ is equal to 0.65. Takayama (1974) also found evidence of bias technical change. None of these studies deal with capital-land substitution.

7. The results in this study indicate more technological change in housing than for the economy as a whole. Revankar (1971b) and David and DeKlundert (1965) estimates for neutral change were 2.4% and 2.3%, respectively. Revankar's (1971b) non-neutral change was an average 0.11 and increased at an increasing rate whereas David and DeKlundert (1965) was -.72%, increasing at a decreasing rate. Our study had non-neutral increasing at an increasing rate of approximately 5%.

8. The time profile of bias technical change indicates that the capital-land ratio and biased technical change move together suggesting that the biased component in periods is marked by rapidly rising capital-land ratios.

9. The warranted time-rate of decline in the land-capital ratio for example, in Stockton is $(1 - \rho)b/(1 - \delta\rho)$ = -.0980. The average time-rate of decline over the whole period has been -0.0510 which is two times slower. Thus over time with the relative slow rate of capital growth the capital using innovations are not significant enough to always increase the rate of return of capital.

PART IV


URBAN LAND MARKET
_____

## Introduction

This section studies the determinants and patterns of urban land values. Chapter 10 uses historical data for Chicago and the Box and Cox transformation technique to test alternative forms of the land value gradient. The results indicate that the price elasticity for housing has shifted over time from elastic to unitary. Also it was shown that the elasticity of rent with respect to distance is a function not only of distance but also of rent. Chapter 11 provides a detailed break-down of the price elasticity of demand for urban residential land over the time period 1966 - 1978 and for 31 different cities. In most cases the elasticity was less than one. Chapter 12 presents an application of the land value data in terms of measuring the rate of change of land values over time. The results indicate that rates of land returns appear comparable to that of high grade bonds.

Chapter 10


URBAN LAND VALUE FUNCTIONS



10.1.   Introduction


The spatial pattern of land influences the structural characteristics of an urban area.   Changes in income, transportation cost and migration affect land values which in
turn alter production factor ratios and the corresponding
urban structural patterns.   Hence, it is important to develop urban land value functions which accurately describe
changes in spatial structure.   Muth (1969) and Mills
(1981), using Cobb-Douglas demand and supply functions for
housing, derived conditions for the existence of an exponential function between land values and distance.   One
condition for an exponential function is a price elasticity
of demand for housing equal to minus one.

    This chapter provides evidence on the functional form
of the relationship between land values and distance from
the city center and re-evaluates the results obtained by
Mills (1971b) in his study or urban land values.   Statistical transformation procedures developed by Box and Cox
(1964) and techniques developed by Kau and Lee (1976b,c)
for determining the price elasticity of demand for housing
services are used.   The Box and Cox transformation technique introduces a functional form parameter to generalize
the land value function.[1]   This parameter can be used to
test whether the negative exponential function provides an
accurate description of land value patterns.   The functional form parameter can also be used to determine price
elasticity of housing demand.

This chapter is divided into five sections. In the second section, Mills' derivation of the negative exponential function is reviewed. The third section provides a discussion of the relationship between urban land values and distance. In the fourth and fifth section, two data sets are used to test both the negative exponential and generalized functional relationships discussed in the third session. Finally the sixth section summarizes the results.

## 10.2. The Exponential Land Value Function

Following Mills (19781) (see Chaper 2), the production function for housing services at distance u, Xs(u) is

$$Xs(u) = AL(u)^{\alpha}K(u)^{1-\alpha} \qquad (10.1)$$

where $K(u)$ and $L(u)$ represent inputs of capital and land in the production of housing services u miles from the center and A and $\alpha$ are scale and distribution parameters, respectively, for a Cobb-Douglas production function.

In deriving a negative exponential function to describe the relationship between the land rent $r(u)$ and the distance u, Mills has also defined a demand function for housing services at u, xd(u), as

$$Xd(u) = Bw^{\theta_1}p(u)^{\theta_2} \qquad (10.2)$$

where:

    B = a scale parameter which depends upon the units
        in which housing services are measured;

    w = income of residents;

    p(u) = price of housing services at distance u;

    $\theta_1$ = income elasticity; and

    $\theta_2$ = price elasticity.

Using the first order conditions for profit maximization in producing housing services, the aggregate demand derived from 10.12 and other equilibrium conditions [see Chapter 2], Mills (1981) derived the following relationship between land rents r(u) and distance.

$$r(u) = [\bar{r}^\beta + \beta TE(\bar{u}-u)]^{\frac{1}{\beta}} \quad \text{if } \beta \neq 0 \tag{10.3}$$

and

$$r(u) = \bar{r}e^{TE(\bar{u}-u)} \quad \text{if } \beta = 0 \tag{10.4}$$

where:

r(u) = land rents at distance u,

$$\beta = \alpha(1+\theta_2), \tag{10.5}$$

$$E^{-1} = \alpha Bw^{\theta_1}[A\alpha^\alpha(1-\alpha)^{1-\alpha}]^{-1+\theta_2}n^{(1-\alpha)(1+\theta_2)},$$

n = rental rate for housing capital,

T = the commuting cost per mile,

$\bar{u}$ = the distance from the center to the edge of the urban area,

$\bar{r}$ = rent on non-urban uses of land, and

$r(\bar{u}) = \bar{r}.$

Equation (10.4) demonstrates that rents decline exponentially with distance if and only if $\beta$ is equal to zero. This result also implies that the population density declines exponentially with distance if and only if the price elasticity, $\theta_2$, is minus one.

## 10.3. The Generalized Rent Function

Following the procedure developed by Kau and Lee (1976b,c) and after some rearrangements, Equation (10.3) can be rewritten as

$$\frac{r(u)^{\beta}-1}{\beta} = \frac{\bar{r}^{\beta}-1}{\beta} + TE(\bar{u}-u) \tag{10.6}$$

It can be shown that (10.6) becomes (10.4) when approaches zero. Since there are only two observable variables, r(u) and u in (10.6), it can be written

$$\frac{r^{\lambda}(u)-1}{\lambda} = r_0 - \gamma u \tag{10.7}$$

where:

$$\lambda = \beta, \ r_0 = \frac{\bar{r}^{\beta}-1}{\beta} = \gamma\bar{u} \text{ and } \gamma = TE$$

(10.7) belongs to one of the cases that Box and Cox (1964) have derived for determining the true functional form. If $\lambda$ approaches zero, then (10.7) becomes

$$\log r(u) = r_0 - \gamma u \tag{10.8}$$

This implies that the negative exponential function is a special case of (10.7); therefore, (10.7) can be regarded as a generalized functional form to determine the true relationship between rent and distance in an urban area. An additive stochastic term can be introduced into (10.7) and the relationship defined as,

$$\frac{r^{\lambda}(u)-1}{\lambda} = r_0 - \gamma u + \varepsilon_i \tag{10.9}$$

where $\varepsilon_i$ is normally distributed with zero mean and variance $\sigma^2$ and $r_0$ and $\gamma$ are regression parameters with $\lambda$ a functional form parameter.

An alternative functional form, with less theoretical foundation than (10.7), can be used to incorporate the double-log function used by Mills (1981). The generalized functional form is

$$\frac{r(u)^{\lambda'}-1}{\lambda'} = \gamma_0' - \gamma_1' \frac{(u_i^{\lambda'}-1)}{\lambda'} + \varepsilon_i \tag{10.10}$$

where $\gamma_0'$ , $\gamma_1'$ are regression parameters, $\lambda'$ is a functional form parameter and the disturbance term $\varepsilon_i'$ is normally distributed with zero mean and variance $\sigma^2$.

If $\lambda = 1$ in (10.9), linear rent is regressed on distance; if $\lambda$ approaches zero the natural logarithm of rent becomes the dependent variable. Similarly, (10.10) reduces to the linear form when $\lambda'$ equals one and to a double logarithmic form when $\lambda'$ approaches zero.

Under the assumption of normality, the probability function for $\varepsilon_i$ in (10.9) is

$$f(\varepsilon_i) = (2\pi\sigma^2)^{-\frac{1}{2}} \exp(-\tfrac{1}{2}(\varepsilon_i^2/\sigma^2)) \qquad (10.11)$$

If the $\varepsilon_i$'s are identically and independently distributed, the log likelihood function for (10.11) is written as

$$\text{Log } L = -\frac{N}{2}\log 2\pi\sigma^2 + (\lambda-1)\sum_{i=1}^{N} \log r(u) - \frac{1}{2\sigma^2}\sum_{i=1}^{N}$$

$$\left(\frac{r^\lambda(u)-1}{\lambda} - r_0 + \gamma u_i\right)^2 \qquad (10.12)$$

where N = sample size.

The logarithmic likelihood is maximized with respect to $\sigma^2$, $r_0$ and $\gamma$, given $\lambda$. The maximum likelihood estimate of $\sigma^2$ for the given $\lambda$, $\hat{\sigma}^2(\lambda)$, is then the estimated variance of the disturbances of regressing $(r_i^\lambda-1)/\lambda$ on $u_i$. Replacing $\sigma^2$ by $\hat{\sigma}^2(\lambda)$, the maximum log likelihood $[L_{MAX}(\lambda)]$ for (10.9) is, except for a constant,

$$L_{MAX}(\lambda) = \frac{-n}{2}\log\hat{\sigma}^2(\lambda) + (\lambda-1)\sum_{i=1}^{N} \log r_i(u) \qquad (10.13)$$

Box and Cox (1964) indicate that an approximate 95 percent confidence region for $\lambda$ is obtained from

$$L_{MAX}(\hat{\lambda}) - L_{MAX}(\lambda) < 1/2\chi^2 \ (.05) = 1.92) \qquad (10.14)$$

(10.13) and (10.14) with $\lambda'$ can be derived for 10-10 by a similar procedure. Equation (10.14) is used to test whether the functional form paramters $\lambda$ and $\lambda'$ are significantly different from zero and/or one. Note that the optimum point estimate, $\hat{\lambda}$, provides an estimate of $\beta$. From the relationship between $\beta$ and $\theta_2$ defined in (10.5), the assumption of unitary price elatsicity can also be tested statistically.

## 10.4. Empirical Results

Initially three regressions were estimated for each year representing the linear, exponential and double logged functional forms, with land values as the dependent variable and distance as the independent variable.

The data for this analysis are land values[2] for the Chicago metropolitan area for 1836, 1857, 1873, 1892, 1910 and 1928 from a study by Homer Hoyt (1932). This sample was selected so that comparison could be made with the Mills study[3] and because there is no other comparable historical series that allows comparing land value patterns over long periods of time. Land values are dollars per acre and distance is airline miles from the intersection of State and Madison Streets.

The functional form parameter is determined by transforming $r(u)$ and $\varepsilon_i$ in accordance with Equations (10.9) and (10.10) using $\lambda$ s between $-0.50$ and $1.50$ at intervals of $0.1$. Twenty-one regressions were run for each year. The $L_{MAX}$ $(\lambda)$s of the six time periods are calculated by Equation (10.13). The maximum likelihood estimates of (10.9) are presented in Table 10.1. The results for the exponential equation are also pesented so that comparisons can be made to Mills' original estimates.[4] This will be discussed later.

The maximum likelihood estimates of $\lambda$ for the six years for Chicago using the Hoyt are listed in Table 10.2. In general $L_{MAX}(\lambda)$ is not symmetrically distributed with respect to its maximum likelihood value; therefore, the lower and upper bond are calculated respectively. Using

Table 10.1.  Chicago Land Value Gradients:
1836–1928[a]

| Year | Regression | Constant | Distance | Elasticity[b] | $\bar{R}$ | N |
|------|-----------|----------|----------|-----------|-----|---|
| 1836 | Exponential | 5.632<br>(44.832) | -.403<br>(27.168) | -3.12 | 781 | 208 |
| | Maximum<br>Likelihood[c] | 3.247<br>(62.550) | -.197<br>(36.800) | -4.53 | .834 | 208 |
| 1857 | Exponential | 8.748<br>(70.886) | -.513<br>(35.742) | -4.04 | .858 | 211 |
| | Maximum<br>Likelihood | 6.791<br>(79.751) | -.365<br>(36.800) | -4.69 | .866 | 211 |
| 1873 | Exponential | 9.980<br>(71.655) | -.344<br>(21.011) | -2.66 | .682 | 206 |
| | Maximum<br>Likelihood | 6.386<br>(98.374) | -.161<br>(21.105) | -2.97 | .684 | 206 |
| 1892 | Exponential | 10.043<br>(52.558) | -.246<br>(11.169) | -1.97 | .418 | 173 |
| | Maximum<br>Likelihood | 6.611<br>(72.400) | -.134<br>(12.678) | -2.42 | .401 | 173 |
| 1910 | Exponential[d] | 10.584<br>(52.018) | -.319<br>(12.678) | -2.35 | .566 | 123 |
| 1928 | Exponential | 11.736<br>(72.390) | -.220<br>(11.735) | -1.74 | .497 | 139 |

Notes:

[a] t–values are in parentheses.

[b] This is the elasticity of land value with respect to distance.
See (10.17) in the text.

[c] See (10.9) in text.

[d] The exponential equation is the maximum likelihood estimate for
1910 and 1928.

Table 10.2.  The Price Elasticity of Demand for Housing
Chicago, 1936–1928

| Year | $\beta$-Value[a] | | Price Elasticity of Demand[b] |
|------|------------|------|----------------------|
| 1836 | −.25 (−.30 ~ −.20) | Elastic | −2.25 (−1.67 ~ −3.00) |
| 1857 | −.07 (−.08 ~ −.05) | Elastic | −1.35 (−1.17 ~ −1.53) |
| 1873 | −.10 (−.16 ~ −.05) | Elastic | −1.50 (−1.17 ~ −2.07) |
| 1892 | −.09 (−.15 ~ −.02) | Elastic | −1.40 (−1.07 ~ −2.00) |
| 1910 | 0.00 (−.15 ~ + .05) | Unitary | −1.00 (− .83 ~ −2.00) |
| 1928 | 0.00 (−.12 ~ + .05) | Unitary | −1.00 (− .83 ~ −1.80) |

Notes:  [a]95% confidence internal in parentheses

[b]The point estimate of the elasticity of demand for
housing is based on $\alpha = .20$.  The earliest estimate
of $\alpha$ from Hoyt (1933) indicated $\alpha = .27$.  The elasticities in parentheses are based on estimates of
$\alpha$ of .30 and .15, using the largest and smallest
estimates of $\beta$, respectively.

10.14, the point estimate and the 95 percent confidence region for $\lambda$ are calculated and listed in Table 10.2.

The functional form analysis as presented in Table 10.2 indicates that for 4 out of the 6 years the estimated $\lambda$ is significantly different from zero at the 5 percent level. Since $\lambda = \beta$ and because $\beta = \alpha(1 + \theta_2)$, it can be concluded that the price elasticity of demand for housing services is significantly different from minus one when $\beta$ is significantly different from zero. Given downward sloping demand curves for housing, then $\alpha > \beta$ when $\beta > 0$. Thus when $\beta > 0$ demand is inelastic. When $\beta < 0$ and since $\alpha > 0$, the demand for housing services is elastic.

In all significant cases for 10.7, $\beta$ is less than zero implying an elastic demand for housing services in the earlier years. For 1910 and 1928, $\beta$ was not signficantly different from zero thus implying unit elasticity.[5] Thus over time, there appears to be a shift away from elastic to unitary and inelastic demands for housing services. This is demonstrated in Figure 10.1 where $L_{MAX}(\hat{\lambda})$ for 1836, 1892 and 1928 is plotted and reveals a movement of $\lambda$ towards zero. Note that the cases provided are significantly different from each other.[6]

The generalized rent gradient is derived by rewriting (10.7) as

$$r(u) = [\lambda r_0 - 1 - \lambda \gamma u]^{1/\gamma} \qquad (10.15)$$

and taking the derivative of (10.15) with respect to u, and rearranging terms, the generalized rent gradient is

$$\frac{\partial r}{\partial u} = -\gamma \frac{r}{r^\lambda} \qquad (10.16)$$

The elasticity of rent with respect to distance is

$$E_r = \frac{\partial r}{\partial u} \cdot \frac{u}{r} = \frac{-\gamma u}{r^\lambda} \qquad (10.17)$$

If $\lambda = 0$, then $E_r = -\gamma u$ which is the elasticity for the exponential rent gradient. The generalized rent gradient and its elasticity are a function not only of a u but also of

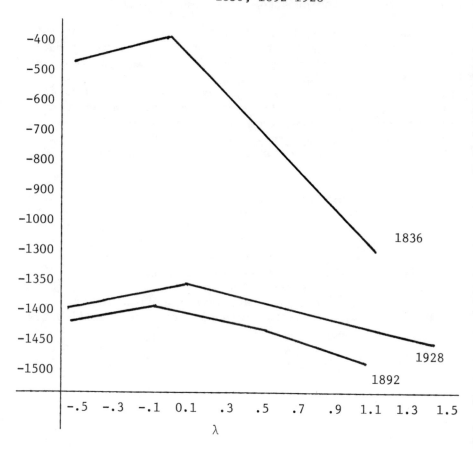

Figure 10.1. Log Maximum Values:
1836, 1892 1928

r(u). The time trend of increasing $\beta$ provides an explanation in addition to increasing u and decreasing $\gamma$ for the observed "flattening" of the function over time.

The effect of this additional term, r(u) is to reduce or increase the elasticity relative to the exponential gradient as $\lambda$ is greater or less than zero, respectively. Thus the conclusion for Chicago is that between 1830 and 1930 the elasticity of the rent gradient has been decreasing over time. If past historical rental patterns affect current rents, then (10.1) may allow measurement of the impact of past development on current rental gradients by taking account of historical rental patterns.[7]

Using (10.17) the elasticity of rent with respect to distance was calculated with the results presented in Table 10.1. The elasticity increases over time, with the exception of a slight rise in 1857, from a low of -4.53 in 1836 to -1.74 in 1928, using the maximum likelihood estimates. The maximum likelihood estimates have a higher absolute elasticity than those presented by Mills using the exponential equation as shown in Table.1. This result further demonstrates the necessity of using the generalized elasticity equation when analyzing the urban land value gradient.

## 10.5. Some Further Land Value Estimates

Using the Olcott data (see Appendix C) for Chicago for 1910, 1920, 1930, 1940, 1950 and 1970, the various forms of the land value of gradient were estimated. The results for the linear, double-log, and exponential estimates are in Tables 10.3, 10.4 and 10.5, respectively.

These estimates follow the same general pattern as the Hoyt data estimates. Land values decline with distance from the city center: In general, the gradient becomes flattened over time.

Table 10.3.

Land Value Gradients: Chicago, 1910–1970[a]
Unlogged OLS Estimates

| INDEPENDENT VARIABLE | YEAR | | | | | | |
|---|---|---|---|---|---|---|---|
| | 1910 | 1920 | 1930 | 1940 | 1950 | 1960 | 1970 |
| CONSTANT | 312.99 (4.40) | 594.5640 (3.91) | 641.854 (4.95) | 248.194 (4.08) | 279.0472 (3.92) | 330.762 (4.58) | 747.301 (5.33) |
| DISTANCE | -35.5736 (3.69) | -68.0396 (3.30) | -62.1954 (3.35) | -24.9194 (3.02) | -27.9460 (2.89) | -26.8206 (2.74) | -67.7609 (-3.56) |
| $\bar{R}^2$ | .05 | .04 | .04 | .03 | .03 | .03 | .04 |

Note: [a] t-value are in parentheses

170

Table 10.4.

Land Value Gradients: Chicago, 1910-1970[a]
Double Logged OLS Estimates

| INDEPENDENT VARIABLE | YEAR | | | | | | |
|---|---|---|---|---|---|---|---|
| | 1910 | 1920 | 1930 | 1940 | 1950 | 1960 | 1970 |
| CONSTANT | 5.3723 (36.75) | 5.5398 (37.90) | 5.7420 (35.69) | 4.6734 (36.11) | 4.6646 (37.99) | 5.0079 (43.36) | 5.8867 (52.00) |
| DISTANCE | -1.3006 (-16.85) | -1.1037 (-14.30) | -.6545 (-7.70) | -.5658 (-8.28) | -.4755 (-7.33) | -.2447 (-4.01) | -.4135 (-6.92) |
| $\bar{R}^2$ | .50 | .42 | .18 | .20 | .16 | .05 | .15 |

Note: [a] t-value are in parentheses

171

Table 10.5.

Land Value Gradients: Chicago, 1910–1970[a]
Exponential OLS Estimates

| INDEPENDENT VARIABLE | YEAR | | | | | | |
|---|---|---|---|---|---|---|---|
| | 1910 | 1920 | 1930 | 1940 | 1950 | 1960 | 1970 |
| CONSTANT | 4.8414 | 4.9645 | 5.3031 | 4.2423 | 4.1764 | 4.5361 | 5.4676 |
| | (35.29) | (35.49) | (36.33) | (35.55) | (36.72) | (44.11) | (52.54) |
| DISTANCE | -.2631 | -.2049 | -.1071 | -.0850 | -.0528 | -.0053* | -.0467 |
| | (-14.15) | (10.81) | (-5.41) | (-5.25) | (-3.42) | (.38) | (-3.31) |
| $\bar{R}^2$ | .42 | .29 | .09 | .09 | .04 | .0005 | .04 |

Note: [a] t-value are in parentheses

## 10.6. Summary and Conclusions

The purpose of this chapter was to provide evidence on the functional form of the relationship between land values and distance from the city center. Using historical data for Chicago, the Box and Cox transformations technique was used to test alernative forms of the land value gradient. These estimates help to clarify the previous work by Mills (1971b).

The results indicated that the price elasticity for housing shifted from elastic to unitary elasticity of demand. The negative exponential form derived in the theoretical model by Muth (1969) and Mills (1981) proved to be the correct form in only two of the six years tested. The generalized rent gradient derived in this paper indicates that the elasticity of rent with respect to distance is a function not only of distance but also of rent. This result may have important implications for analyzing the impact of historical rental patterns on current rates. Future research is necessary to establish the importance of this relationship between past and current rents.

### NOTES

1. This technique has been used to test the functional form of the population density gradient [Kau and Lee (1976b,c)], the money demand function (Zarembka (1968)], and the earning-schooling relationship (Heckman and Polacheck (1974)].

2. Following Mills (1971b), the data are on urban land values. It is assumed that the capitalization rate, at any given time differs little from one place to another in an urban area. Hence values and rents will be a constant ratio.

3. Mills (1971b) did not include the land value data for 1892 in his study.

4.    The slight variations in the estimated parameters as compared to Mills (1971b) are probably due to inexact methods of measuring distance to the CBD.

5.    Kau and Lee's study (1976c) of density gradient functional forms indicates a minus one price elasticity for housing in 1970 for Chicago.  Their study also indicated that for the 50 cities analyzed no cases resulted in a significant elastic demand for housing and approximately 50% of the cities had inelastic demands.

6.    The results for (10.10) indicate that the   values are significantly different from zero for the three earlier time periods.  Given the previous result with (10.9), this is not unexpected but confirms the necessity to use a generalized functional form when analyzing urban spatial structure.

7.    See Harrison and Kain (1974, 1977) and White (1977) for a discussion of the cumulative impact of time on the spatial structure of an urban area.

Chapter 11

THE PRICE ELASTICITY OF DEMAND

FOR URBAN RESIDENTIAL LAND

## 11.1. Introduction

Numerous studies have investigated the determinants of urban land values.[1] These studies may be divided into those analyzing intraurban and interurban variations.[2] Marginal productivity theory, which forms the basis of factor price determination, has received recent application to the theory of land rent and land use.[3] If land is viewed as an input into the production of goods and services, for example housing services, the demand for land as a factor is a derived demand.[4] Neoclassical theory of factor price determination tells us that firms and industries will employ the level of factors only insofar as their employment contributes to the goods and services valued by consumers. Another question of importance, which has received little attention in the literature, concerns the determinants, not of the level of factor demand, but of its elasticity, i.e., its responsiveness to changes in factor prices.[5] Knowledge of this price elasticity provides important insights into understanding the housing problems of urban areas.

The purpose of this chapter is to examine the price elasticity of demand for residential sites for 31 urban areas in the United States over the time period 1966 to 1978. Such an examination allows an understanding of how the price elasticity has changed over time in these areas. This chapter extends the preliminary work of Sirmans and Redman (1979) and Kau and Sirmans (1981) and can be outlined as follows: Section 11.2 outlines the methodology

175

for estimating the price elasticity of an input factor, in this case land; Section 11.3 provides some estimates for 31 urban areas for the 1966 to 1978 time period; summary and conclusions of this chapter are in the final section.

## 11.2. The Theory of Derived Demand

The theory of derived demand links distribution theory and the supply conditions of productive factors.[6]   The elasticity of derived demand for land as an input factor has received little attention in land economics literature. The forces influencing the elasticity of demand for a productive factor, such as land, are:   (i) the elasticity of demand for the final product, (ii) the elasticity of substitution in production, (iii) the elasticity of supply of other input factors, and (iv) the relative importance of the factor.

Marshall's well-known four rules of derived demand, under the special case of fixed factor proportions as applied to land, are:

1.  The demand for land is likely to be more elastic, the more elastic is the demand for the output it contributes to produce, in this case housing services.

2.  The demand for land is likely to be more elastic, the more readily substitutes for land in the production process can be obtained.

3.  The demand for land is likely to be more elastic, the more elastic is the supply of its cooperate agents of production.

4.  The demand for land is likely to be less elastic, the less important is the part played by the cost of land in the total cost of the production of housing.

Hicks (1932) confirmed these rules for the general case where the elasticity of substitution is not necessarily equal to zero, with the exception of the fourth

rule. Only if the elasticity of demand for the final product is greater than the elasticity of substitution between
factors of production is the fourth rule true. If the demand for the final product, housing services, is fairly
elastic, while substitution is difficult, the condition
will hold for the fourth rule. This "importance of being
unimportant" condition is true only when the consumer can
substitute more easily than the housing producer.

In a model of housing production, the price elasticity
of derived demand may be written formally using the following definitions. Assume a production function for housing which may be written,

$$Xs = f(L, K) \tag{11.1}$$

where Xs is output of housing services, L is land input,
and K is capital (structure) input. The production function is assumed to be a continuous, twice differentiable
homogeneous function of the first degree. The elasticity
of demand for housing services is

$$\eta = - \frac{dXs}{dp} \cdot \frac{p}{Xs} \tag{11.2}$$

where p is the price of housing services. The price elasticity of derived demand for land is

$$\Omega = \frac{dL}{dr} \cdot \frac{r}{L} \tag{11.3}$$

where r is the unit price of the land input. The elasticity of supply of capital input is

$$E_K = \frac{dK}{dn} \cdot \frac{n}{K} \tag{11.4}$$

where n is the unit price of the non-land input. The relative shares of the land and capital factor inputs are

$$\alpha_L = \frac{rL}{pXs} , \quad \text{and} \tag{11.5}$$

$$\alpha_K = \frac{nK}{pXs} \tag{11.6}$$

where $\alpha_L + \alpha_K = 1$. The elasticity of substitution between land and capital is

$$\sigma = [d(K/L)/(K/L)]/[d(r/n)/(r/n)]. \tag{11.7}$$

Under the assumptions of competition in both factor and product markets and constant returns to scale in the production function [Equation (11.1)], the price elasticity of derived demand can be expressed as

$$\Omega = \frac{\eta\sigma + E_k(\alpha_L + \alpha_K\sigma)}{\alpha_L\sigma + \alpha_K\eta + E_k} \tag{11.8}$$

Equation (11.8) is the same as Hicks' formulation and requires that the price elasticity of demand for housing services be treated as a positive number of calculation purposes.[7,8]

In the typical model of housing production, the price elasticity of supply of other factors ($E_K$) is assumed to be infinity. Using the assumption, Equation (11.8) reduces to,

$$\Omega = \alpha_L\eta + \alpha_K\sigma \tag{11.9}$$

The next section uses Equation (11.9) to estimate the price elasticity of demand for urban residential land in 31 FHA housing areas over the time period 1966 to 1978.

## 11.3. Estimates of Demand Price Elasticity for Land

In order to estimate the price elasticity of derived demand for land, $\Omega$ , estimates are required for the price elasticity of demand for housing services, $\eta$ , the elasticity of substitution, $\sigma$ , the elasticity of supply of non-land input, $E_K$, and the relative factor share of land, $\alpha_L$. Since any or all of these may vary across urban areas, we will first discuss the estimates of these parameters to be used in this paper. Following this discussion, the price elasticity of land will be presented and discussed.

Numerous studies have examined the price elasticity of demand for housing, $\eta$. Kau and Lee (1976c) have recently provided a comprehensive study of elasticity of demand for housing in 50 SMSA's in 1970. Of the 50 cities included in the Kau and Lee study, approximately 50 percent indicated a price elasticity of demand for housing services which was significantly less than unity in absolute value.[9] For the other 50 percent the hypothesis that the price elasticity was equal to minus one could not be rejected. One of the interesting findings of their study was that no city exhibited a significant elastic demand for housing. These results tend to imply that the price elasticity of demand for housing services is greater than minus one.

Other studies which have examined the demand price elasticity for housing services include Muth (1972), Reid (1962) Lee (1964), and Gerking and Boyes (1980). These estimates for all types of housing services indicate a price elasticity of unity or slightly higher in absolute value. While the literature lacks a comprehensive study of interurban variation in the price elasticity, the above estimates, particularly the Kau and Lee study, provide a strong case for demand elasticity of one or less in absolute value.

In Chapter 8 we presented estimates of the elasticity of subsdtitution between land and nonland for various FHA housing areas over the 1966 to 1978 time period. We will use the estimates from Table 8.3 to calculate the price elasticity of demand for land for the same housing areas.[10]

There is no empirical evidence available for the elasticity of supply of other inputs, $E_K$, in the production of housing. The literature which does exist, Muth (1972, 1969) and Clawson (1971), makes a strong case that there probably exists a highly elastic supply. These arguments are based on the relative ease with which builders move in and out of the construction industry. No literature exists on the interurban variation in the elasticity of supply. The assumption used in this paper is, as discussed previously, that the elasticity of supply of other inputs is infinity and that the elasticity of supply of other inputs is constant across housing areas.

The final factor necessary for estimating the price elasticity of derived demand for land is the relative share of site value, $\alpha_L$, in total costs. The relative share for each city for each year was taken from the FHA data and as shown in Table 11.1.[11]

The price elasticity of demand for residential sites, $\Omega$, for single family housing for the 31 housing areas for the 1966-1978 period was estimated using Equation (11.9) and the estimates of $\eta$, $\sigma$ and $\alpha_L$. The estimates, in absolute values, are shown in Table 11.2. These estimates indicate that in no city was there an elastic demand for residential land.

## 11.3.1.  Sensitivity Analysis

In this section, we examine the sensitivity of the price elasticity of demand for land in the 31 areas using various assumptions concerning the price elasticity of demand for housing. The previous estimates assumed that $\eta$ was equal to $-1.0$. The empirical evidence on $\eta$ suggests, however, that the price elasticity of demand for housing is between $-.5$ and $-2.0$.

Tables 11.3, 11.4, and 11.5 contain the estimates of using assumptions for  of $-.5$, $-1.5$, and $-2.0$, respectively. As the results indicate, the price elasticity of demand for land is fairly insensitive to assumptions about the price elasticity of demand for housing. The results follow Marshall's first rule.

## 11.3.2.  Price Elasticity Over Time

The price elasticity ($\Omega$) estimates in Table 11.2 were examined for trends over time, across regions, and by city size. In general, the price elasticity of demand for land increased (in absolute value) over time, was significantly lower in the western cities, and was significantly lower the greater the city size.

The pooled time series cross-sectional estimates for variations in the price elasticity were as follows:

Table 11.1. Land's Share in Total Sale
Price of New Single Family Houses for
Various Cities: 1966-1978*

| City | 1966 | 1967 | 1968 | 1969 | 1970 | 1971 | 1972 | 1973 | 1974 | 1975 | 1976 | 1977 | 1978 |
|---|---|---|---|---|---|---|---|---|---|---|---|---|---|
| Albuquerque | .1544 | .1559 | .1488 | .1507 | .1484 | .1507 | .1444 | .1436 | .1407 | .1357 | .1502 | .1541 | .1568 |
| Charlotte | .1868 | .1750 | .1667 | .1623 | .1447 | .1556 | .1620 | .1609 | .1612 | .1663 | .1717 | .1517 | .1557 |
| Columbus, OH | .2004 | .2078 | .2064 | .2031 | .1833 | .1852 | .1847 | .1904 | .1886 | .1771 | .1858 | .1941 | .1855 |
| Dallas | .1484 | .1498 | .1552 | .1602 | .1726 | .1924 | .1919 | .1928 | .1952 | .1601 | .1729 | .1722 | .1761 |
| Dayton | .2127 | .2338 | .2331 | .2279 | .2267 | .2029 | .1935 | .1968 | .2021 | .1885 | .1957 | .1911 | .1813 |
| Denver | .1751 | .1684 | .1630 | .1644 | .1587 | .1690 | .1600 | .1559 | .1476 | .1363 | .1366 | .1419 | .1362 |
| El Paso | .1558 | .1514 | .1432 | .1348 | .1408 | .1463 | .1448 | .1418 | .1472 | .1365 | .1423 | .1400 | .1384 |
| Fresno | .1824 | .1893 | .1891 | .1903 | .1902 | .1969 | .1955 | .1977 | .1811 | .1881 | .2179 | .2203 | .2211 |
| Greensboro, NC | .1601 | .1489 | .1621 | .1593 | .1511 | .1564 | .1674 | .1496 | .1598 | .1703 | .1580 | .1699 | .1725 |
| Houston | .1588 | .1563 | .1549 | .1561 | .1548 | .1521 | .1408 | .1446 | .1372 | .1448 | .1605 | .1794 | .2032 |
| Jacksonville | .1554 | .1386 | .1399 | .1300 | .1277 | .1306 | .1394 | .1322 | .2332 | .1631 | .1684 | .1917 | .1580 |
| Las Vegas | .1815 | .1834 | .1871 | .1751 | .1961 | .2284 | .2283 | .2134 | .2006 | .1818 | .2022 | .2024 | .2063 |
| Los Angeles | .2713 | .2939 | .3120 | .3439 | .3186 | .3379 | .3281 | .3068 | .2683 | .2799 | .3820 | .2952 | .1901 |
| Louisville | .2025 | .1948 | .1905 | .1909 | .1746 | .1934 | .1939 | .1862 | .1853 | .1775 | .1835 | .1781 | .1742 |
| Memphis | .1622 | .1597 | .1632 | .1976 | .1503 | .1573 | .1577 | .1693 | .1645 | .1518 | .1696 | .1734 | .1644 |
| Miami | .2131 | .2046 | .2028 | .2448 | .1799 | .1622 | .1875 | .2205 | .2473 | .2499 | .2481 | .2520 | .2554 |
| Nashville | .1798 | .1784 | .1750 | .1929 | .1625 | .1757 | .1734 | .1699 | .1747 | .1733 | .1811 | .1861 | .1813 |
| Oklahoma City | .1547 | .1525 | .1464 | .1721 | .9262 | .1435 | .1427 | .1428 | .1367 | .1249 | .1284 | .1295 | .1358 |
| Orlando | .1251 | .1744 | .1674 | .2007 | .1613 | .1569 | .1552 | .1466 | .2005 | .2176 | .2130 | .1903 | .1838 |
| Phoenix | .1920 | .1905 | .1874 | .2332 | .1897 | .1874 | .1725 | .1693 | .1747 | .1921 | .1866 | .1844 | .1762 |
| Sacramento | .2359 | .2333 | .2244 | .2731 | .2104 | .2005 | .2006 | .1967 | .1808 | .1656 | .1753 | .1838 | .1802 |
| San Diego | .2601 | .2613 | .2667 | .2969 | .2385 | .2375 | .2335 | .2604 | .2711 | .2575 | .2797 | .2924 | .3149 |
| San Francisco | .2252 | .2617 | .2546 | .3141 | .2539 | .2495 | .2671 | .2667 | .2735 | .2672 | .2525 | .2654 | .2986 |
| San Jose | .2520 | .2507 | .2678 | .2957 | .2557 | .2573 | .2630 | .2754 | .2775 | .2918 | .2795 | .3078 | .3850 |
| Seattle | .1818 | .1847 | .1962 | .2127 | .2019 | .2055 | .1980 | .1881 | .1806 | .1680 | .1714 | .1784 | .1911 |
| Shreveport | .1574 | .1560 | .1595 | .1830 | .1420 | .1549 | .1532 | .1446 | .1585 | .1538 | .1677 | .1872 | .1796 |
| Spokane | .1171 | .1034 | .1051 | .1494 | .1031 | .1100 | .1082 | .1079 | .1096 | .1100 | .1162 | .1390 | .1592 |
| Stockton | .2006 | .2085 | .2009 | .2132 | .1871 | .2117 | .1947 | .1939 | .1774 | .1684 | .1739 | .1676 | .1820 |
| Tampa | .1830 | .1688 | .1749 | .2085 | .1482 | .1529 | .1568 | .1533 | .1498 | .1675 | .1881 | .1758 | .1755 |
| Tulsa | .1698 | .1693 | .1782 | .1887 | .1748 | .1662 | .1553 | .1642 | .1511 | .1457 | .1454 | .1601 | .1542 |
| Vallejo | .2395 | .2429 | .2445 | .2956 | .2330 | .2395 | .2241 | .2362 | .2030 | .2159 | .1947 | .1833 | .2369 |

*Source: Federal Housing Administration, FHA Homes, Washington, D.C., various years.

Table 11.2. Price Elasticity of Derived Demand
for Residential Land for Various Cities:
1966-1978*

Assuming $\eta = -1.0$

| City | 1966 | 1967 | 1968 | 1969 | 1970 | 1971 | 1972 | 1973 | 1974 | 1975 | 1976 | 1977 | 1978 |
|---|---|---|---|---|---|---|---|---|---|---|---|---|---|
| Albuquerque | .5548 | .4446 | .4391 | .4505 | .4741 | .5024 | .6815 | .5023 | .5926 | .5449 | .5876 | .6377 | .6543 |
| Charlotte | .7539 | .7286 | .7633 | .7381 | .7273 | .7313 | .7172 | .7171 | .7708 | .7466 | .7956 | .8378 | .8951 |
| Columbus, OH | .7161 | .6743 | .6128 | .6205 | .6053 | .6152 | .6297 | .6022 | .6589 | .6336 | .6894 | .7016 | .7296 |
| Dallas | .5954 | .5653 | .5355 | .4329 | .5474 | .5536 | .5285 | .5283 | .5408 | .5098 | .5568 | .6234 | .6384 |
| Dayton | .7474 | .7041 | .6621 | .6688 | .6938 | .6396 | .6845 | .6905 | .6837 | .6899 | .7564 | .7475 | .7575 |
| Denver | .6830 | .5539 | .5246 | .5383 | .6075 | .6381 | .6477 | .6070 | .4727 | .6180 | .6754 | .7031 | .7075 |
| El Paso | .5376 | .5205 | .5352 | .4748 | .4810 | .4938 | .5064 | .4571 | .4597 | .5037 | .5301 | .5962 | .6254 |
| Fresno | .5525 | .3941 | .4449 | .4555 | .4184 | .4673 | .5077 | .4513 | .5549 | .5065 | .5393 | .6397 | .6789 |
| Greensboro, NC | .7670 | .7139 | .6858 | .6852 | .7008 | .6948 | .7269 | .7297 | .6720 | .7079 | .7497 | .8172 | .8360 |
| Houston | .5648 | .4659 | .4492 | .4325 | .4157 | .4234 | .4824 | .4974 | .4663 | .4545 | .5243 | .6010 | .6272 |
| Jacksonville | .6627 | .5379 | .5568 | .5478 | .5726 | .5952 | .6309 | .5848 | .6615 | .6499 | .6454 | .7359 | .7562 |
| Las Vegas | .5368 | .4539 | .4169 | .3823 | .4011 | .5244 | .4280 | .4594 | .5031 | .5224 | .5658 | .5850 | .6340 |
| Los Angeles | .5502 | .4192 | .3838 | .4825 | .4672 | .4788 | .4744 | .5L25 | .4925 | .4865 | .5650 | .6470 | .5922 |
| Louisville | .7249 | .6689 | .6817 | .6588 | .6593 | .6754 | .7101 | .6785 | .6990 | .6882 | .6954 | .7732 | .7755 |
| Memphis | .6958 | .6425 | .6893 | .6441 | .6179 | .6161 | .5988 | .6212 | .6989 | .6529 | .6762 | .7139 | .7394 |
| Miami | .6667 | .6217 | .5704 | .5992 | .5817 | .5089 | .5746 | .6546 | .6587 | .6163 | .5235 | .6199 | .6483 |
| Nashville | .8213 | .7856 | .7627 | .7448 | .7583 | .7625 | .7680 | .7548 | .7571 | .8036 | .8002 | .8306 | .8595 |
| Oklahoma City | .6675 | .6090 | .5866 | .5937 | .6043 | .6127 | .6134 | .6009 | .5878 | .5655 | .6039 | .6482 | .6688 |
| Orlando | .5897 | .6073 | .5816 | .5961 | .6060 | .6046 | .6430 | .5890 | .6374 | .6539 | .7064 | .7218 | .7218 |
| Phoenix | .5086 | .6150 | .4260 | .4927 | .4834 | .4692 | .3554 | .4985 | .5241 | .6183 | .6122 | .6507 | .6164 |
| Sacramento | .6047 | .4901 | .5001 | .5297 | .4859 | .5447 | .5210 | .4971 | .5350 | .5130 | .5790 | .6425 | .6438 |
| San Diego | .6329 | .5007 | .5968 | .5656 | .5528 | .5249 | .5044 | .5417 | .5885 | .5845 | .5636 | .6284 | .6657 |
| San Francisco | .5538 | .4746 | .4410 | .4864 | .4291 | .2885 | .3574 | .3143 | .3084 | .4554 | .4968 | .6889 | .7093 |
| San Diego | .4771 | .3757 | .3922 | .4419 | .3595 | .3755 | .3817 | .4230 | .4945 | .5141 | .5453 | .6365 | .6917 |
| Seattle | .6460 | .6589 | .6488 | .6508 | .6464 | .6514 | .6787 | .6272 | .6826 | .6420 | .6792 | .7097 | .7423 |
| Shreveport | .7604 | .6438 | .7430 | .7268 | .5796 | .6179 | .5487 | .5633 | .5806 | .6614 | .6989 | .6754 | .7368 |
| Spokane | .7542 | .5992 | .6025 | .7249 | .6810 | .7257 | .7103 | .6935 | .7166 | .7511 | .7744 | .8250 | .8371 |
| Stockton | .5378 | .4452 | .5287 | .4938 | .4407 | .4771 | .5200 | .4642 | .4714 | .4995 | .5574 | .5992 | .6228 |
| Tampa | .6390 | .5863 | .5734 | .5828 | .5655 | .6056 | .6038 | .6166 | .5991 | .5716 | .6493 | .6430 | .6803 |
| Tulsa | .6533 | .6347 | .6260 | .6225 | .6372 | .6285 | .6110 | .6109 | .6227 | .5835 | .6141 | .6768 | .7098 |
| Vallejo | .5237 | .5154 | .5048 | .4930 | .4878 | .4803 | .3956 | .4751 | .4974 | .4951 | .5505 | .6185 | .6855 |

Note: *Calculated using Equation (11.9) in text and assuming  = -1.0, using the estimates of  from
Table 8.3 and land's share from Table 11.1.

Table 11.3. Price Elasticity of Derived Demand
for Residential Land for Various Cities:
1966-1978*

Assuming $\eta = -.5$

| City | 1966 | 1967 | 1968 | 1969 | 1970 | 1971 | 1972 | 1973 | 1974 | 1975 | 1976 | 1977 | 1978 |
|---|---|---|---|---|---|---|---|---|---|---|---|---|---|
| Albuquerque | .4776 | .3667 | .3647 | .3652 | .3999 | .4269 | .6093 | .4305 | .5221 | .4771 | .5125 | .5607 | .5759 |
| Charlotte | .6605 | .6411 | .6770 | .6570 | .6550 | .6535 | .6362 | .6367 | .6902 | .6635 | .7098 | .6420 | .7473 |
| Columbus, OH | .6149 | .5704 | .5096 | .5190 | .5137 | .5226 | .5374 | .5070 | .9892 | .5451 | .5965 | .6046 | .6369 |
| Dallas | .5212 | .4904 | .4579 | .4528 | .4611 | .4574 | .4326 | .4319 | .4432 | .4298 | .4704 | .5375 | .5504 |
| Dayton | .6411 | .5872 | .5456 | .5549 | .5805 | .5382 | .5878 | .5921 | .5827 | .5957 | .6586 | .6520 | .6669 |
| Denver | .5955 | .4697 | .4431 | .4561 | .5282 | .5536 | .5677 | .5291 | .3989 | .5499 | .6071 | .6322 | .6394 |
| El Paso | .4597 | .4448 | .4636 | .4074 | .4106 | .3107 | .4340 | .3862 | .3861 | .4355 | .4790 | .5262 | .5564 |
| Fresno | .4313 | .2995 | .3504 | .3604 | .3233 | .3689 | .4100 | .3525 | .4644 | .4125 | .4304 | .5296 | .5684 |
| Greensboro, NC | .6870 | .6395 | .6048 | .6056 | .6253 | .6166 | .6432 | .6749 | .5921 | .6228 | .6707 | .7323 | .7498 |
| Houston | .4854 | .3878 | .3718 | .3545 | .3383 | .3474 | .4120 | .4251 | .3977 | .3821 | .3821 | .4441 | .5256 |
| Jacksonville | .5850 | .4686 | .4885 | .4828 | .5088 | .5299 | .5612 | .5187 | .5449 | .5687 | .5612 | .6401 | .6772 |
| Las Vegas | .4461 | .3622 | .3234 | .2948 | .3031 | .4102 | .3139 | .3527 | .4028 | .4315 | .4647 | .4838 | .5273 |
| Los Angeles | .4146 | .2723 | .2278 | .3106 | .3079 | .3099 | .3104 | .3591 | .3584 | .3466 | .4240 | .4994 | .4972 |
| Louisville | .6237 | .5715 | .5865 | .5634 | .5720 | .5790 | .6132 | .5854 | .6064 | .5995 | .6037 | .6842 | .6884 |
| Memphis | .6147 | .5627 | .6077 | .5453 | .5428 | .5375 | .5200 | .5366 | .6167 | .5770 | .5914 | .6272 | .6572 |
| Miami | .5602 | .5194 | .4690 | .4768 | .4918 | .4278 | .4809 | .5444 | .5351 | .4914 | .4015 | .4939 | .5206 |
| Nashville | .7314 | .6964 | .6752 | .6484 | .6771 | .6747 | .6813 | .6699 | .6698 | .7170 | .7097 | .7376 | .7689 |
| Oklahoma City | .5902 | .5239 | .5134 | .5077 | .5346 | .5410 | .5421 | .5295 | .5195 | .5031 | .5397 | .5835 | .6009 |
| Orlando | .5272 | .5201 | .4979 | .4958 | .5254 | .5262 | .5654 | .5157 | .5372 | .5451 | .5999 | .6267 | .6299 |
| Phoenix | .4126 | .5198 | .3323 | .3761 | .3885 | .3755 | .2692 | .4139 | .4368 | .5223 | .5189 | .5585 | .5283 |
| Sacramento | .4868 | .3735 | .3879 | .3932 | .3807 | .4445 | .4207 | .3988 | .4446 | .4302 | .4914 | .5506 | .5537 |
| San Diego | .5029 | .3701 | .4635 | .4172 | .4336 | .4061 | .3877 | .4115 | .5430 | .4558 | .4238 | .4622 | .5083 |
| San Francisco | .4262 | .3438 | .3137 | .3294 | .3022 | .1638 | .2239 | .1812 | .1717 | .3218 | .3706 | .5562 | .5600 |
| San Jose | .3511 | .2504 | .2583 | .2941 | .2367 | .2469 | .2502 | .2853 | .3558 | .3682 | .4056 | .4826 | .4992 |
| Seattle | .5551 | .5666 | .5507 | .5445 | .5455 | .5487 | .5797 | .5332 | .5923 | .5580 | .5935 | .6205 | .6468 |
| Shreveport | .6817 | .5659 | .6635 | .6353 | .5086 | .5405 | .4721 | .4910 | .5014 | .5845 | .6151 | .5818 | .6470 |
| Spokane | .6957 | .5475 | .5500 | .6502 | .6295 | .5707 | .6562 | .6396 | .6618 | .6961 | .7163 | .7555 | .7575 |
| Stockton | .6375 | .3410 | .4283 | .3863 | .3472 | .3713 | .4227 | .3673 | .3827 | .4153 | .4705 | .5151 | .5318 |
| Tampa | .5475 | .5024 | .4860 | .4786 | .4914 | .5292 | .5254 | .5400 | .5242 | .4880 | .5553 | .5551 | .5926 |
| Tulsa | .5684 | .5501 | .5369 | .5282 | .5498 | .5454 | .5334 | .5288 | .5472 | .5107 | .5414 | .5968 | .6327 |
| Vallejo | .4040 | .3940 | .3826 | .3452 | .3713 | .3606 | .2836 | .3570 | .3959 | .2872 | .4532 | .5269 | .5617 |

*Calculated using Equation 11.9 in text and assuming  = -.5, using the estimates of  from Table 8.3 and land's share from Table 11.1.

Table 11.4.   Price Elasticity of Derived Demand
for Residential Land for Various Cities:
1966–1978*

Assuming $\eta = -1.5$

| City | 1966 | 1967 | 1968 | 1969 | 1970 | 1971 | 1972 | 1973 | 1974 | 1975 | 1976 | 1977 | 1978 |
|---|---|---|---|---|---|---|---|---|---|---|---|---|---|
| Albuquerque | .6320 | .5226 | .5135 | .5259 | .5483 | .5779 | .7537 | .5741 | .6631 | .6128 | .6627 | .7148 | .7327 |
| Charlotte | .8473 | .8161 | .8467 | .8193 | .7997 | .8091 | .7982 | .7976 | .8514 | .8298 | .8815 | .9137 | .9030 |
| Columbus, OH | .8163 | .7782 | .7160 | .7221 | .6970 | .7078 | .7221 | .6974 | .7532 | .7222 | .7823 | .7989 | .8224 |
| Dallas | .6696 | .6402 | .6131 | .6130 | .6337 | .6498 | .6245 | .6247 | .6384 | .5899 | .6433 | .7095 | .7265 |
| Dayton | .8538 | .8210 | .7787 | .7828 | .8072 | .7411 | .7813. | .7889 | .7848 | .7842 | .8543 | .8431 | .8482 |
| Denver | .7706 | .6381 | .6061 | .6205 | .6869 | .7225 | .7276 | .6850 | .5465 | .6862 | .7437 | .7741 | .7757 |
| El Paso | .6155 | .5962 | .6068 | .5422 | .5514 | .5670 | .5788 | .5280 | .5335 | .5720 | .6213 | .6662 | .6948 |
| Fresno | .6137 | .4888 | .5395 | .2855 | .5135 | .5658 | .6055 | .5502 | .6455 | .6006 | .6483 | .7499 | .7895 |
| Greensboro, NC | .8471 | .7884 | .7669 | .7649 | .7764 | .7730 | .8106 | .8045 | .6720 | .7931 | .8287 | .9022 | .9223 |
| Houston | .6442 | .5441 | .5267 | .5106 | .4931 | .4995 | .5528 | .5697 | .5349 | .5269 | .6046 | .6907 | .7288 |
| Jacksonville | .7404 | .6072 | .6284 | .6128 | .6365 | .6605 | .7006 | .6509 | .7781 | .7315 | .7296 | .8318 | .8351 |
| Las Vegas | .6276 | .5456 | .5105 | .4699 | .4992 | .6386 | .5422 | .5661 | .6034 | .6133 | .6669 | .6862 | .7336 |
| Los Angeles | .6859 | .5662 | .5398 | .6545 | .6265 | .6478 | .6385 | .6659 | .6267 | .6265 | .7060 | .7946 | .6873 |
| Louisville | .8262 | .7663 | .7770 | .7543 | .7466 | .7724 | .8071 | .7716 | .7917 | .7770 | .7872 | .8623 | .8626 |
| Memphis | .7769 | .7224 | .7709 | .7429 | .6931 | .6948 | .6777 | .7059 | .7812 | .7288 | .7610 | .8006 | .8216 |
| Miami | .7733 | .7240 | .6718 | .7216 | .6717 | .5900 | .6684 | .7416 | .7824 | .7413 | .6500 | .7458 | .7760 |
| Nashville | .9112 | .8748 | .8502 | .8413 | .8396 | .8504 | .8547 | .8398 | .8445 | .8903 | .8908 | .9237 | .9502 |
| Oklahoma City | .7449 | .6852 | .6598 | .6798 | .6740 | .6845 | .6848 | .6723 | .6562 | .6280 | .6681 | .7130 | .7367 |
| Orlando | .6523 | .6945 | .6653 | .6965 | .6867 | .6831 | .7206 | .6623 | .7377 | .7627 | .8129 | .8170 | .8137 |
| Phoenix | .6046 | .7103 | .5197 | .6064 | .5783 | .5629 | .4417 | .5831 | .6115 | .7144 | .7055 | .7429 | .7045 |
| Sacramento | .7227 | .6068 | .6123 | .6663 | .5911 | .6450 | .6213 | .5955 | .6254 | .5948 | .6667 | .7344 | .7339 |
| San Diego | .7630 | .6314 | .7302 | .7141 | .6721 | .6437 | .6212 | .6719 | .7241 | .7133 | .7035 | .7746 | .8232 |
| San Francisco | .6814 | .6055 | .5683 | .6435 | .5561 | .4133 | .4910 | .4474 | .4452 | .5890 | .6231 | .8216 | .8586 |
| San Jose | .6031 | .5011 | .5261 | .5898 | .4824 | .5042 | .5132 | .5607 | .6333 | .6600 | .6851 | .7904 | .8842 |
| Seattle | .7369 | .7413 | .7469 | .7572 | .7474 | .7542 | .7777 | .7213 | .7729 | .7259 | .7649 | .7989 | .8379 |
| Shreveport | .8391 | .7218 | .8228 | .8183 | .6506 | .6954 | .6253 | .6356 | .6599 | .7383 | .7828 | .7690 | .8266 |
| Spokane | .8128 | .6509 | .6551 | .7996 | .7326 | .7807 | .7644 | .7475 | .7714 | .8061 | .8325 | .9845 | .9167 |
| Stockton | .6381 | .5495 | .6292 | .6004 | .5343 | .5830 | .6174 | .5612 | .5601 | .5837 | .6444 | .6830 | .7137 |
| Tampa | .7305 | .6712 | .6609 | .6871 | .6396 | .6821 | .6822 | .6933 | .6740 | .6553 | .7434 | .7309 | .7681 |
| Tulsa | .7382 | .7194 | .7151 | .7169 | .7246 | .7116 | .6886 | .6930 | .6983 | .6564 | .6868 | .7569 | .7869 |
| Vallejo | .6435 | .6369 | .6271 | .6408 | .6042 | .5999 | .5077 | .5932 | .5989 | .6031 | .6479 | .7102 | .8040 |

Note:   *Calculated using Equation 11.9 in text and assuming  = -1.5, using the estimates of    from Table 8.3
and land's share from Table 11.1.

Table 11.5. Price Elasticity of Derived Demand
for Residential Land for Various Cities:
1966-1978[*][a]

Assuming $\eta = -2.0$

| City | 1966 | 1967 | 1968 | 1969 | 1970 | 1971 | 1972 | 1973 | 1974 | 1975 | 1976 | 1977 | 1978 |
|------|------|------|------|------|------|------|------|------|------|------|------|------|------|
| Albuquerque | .7092 | .6006 | .5879 | .6012 | .6225 | .6528 | .8259 | .6459 | .7330 | .6806 | .7378 | .7918 | .8111 |
| Charlotte | .9407 | .9036 | .9294 | .9004 | .8720 | .8869 | .8792 | .8780 | .9320 | .9129 | .9675 | .9895 | .9808 |
| Columbus, OH | .9165 | .8821 | .8192 | .8236 | .7886 | .8004 | .9144 | .7926 | .8475 | .8107 | .8752 | .8957 | .9151 |
| Dallas | .7438 | .7151 | .6907 | .6931 | .7200 | .7460 | .7204 | .7211 | .7360 | .6699 | .7297 | .7956 | .8145 |
| Dayton | .9601 | .9379 | .8952 | .8967 | .9205 | .8425 | .8780 | .8873 | .8853 | .8784 | .9521 | .9386 | .9388 |
| Denver | .8581 | .7223 | .6876 | .7027 | .7662 | .8071 | .8076 | .7629 | .6203 | .7543 | .8120 | .8450 | .8438 |
| El Paso | .6934 | .6719 | .6789 | .6096 | .6218 | .6401 | .6512 | .5989 | .6069 | .6402 | .6924 | .7362 | .7640 |
| Fresno | .7049 | .5834 | .6340 | .6458 | .6086 | .6642 | .7032 | .6490 | .7360 | .6946 | .7572 | .8600 | .9000 |
| Greensboro, NC | .9271 | .8628 | .8479 | .8445 | .8519 | .8512 | .8943 | .8793 | .8318 | .8782 | .9077 | .9871 | 1.0085 |
| Houston | .7236 | .6222 | .6041 | .5886 | .5705 | .5755 | .6232 | .6420 | .6035 | .5995 | .6848 | .7804 | .8304 |
| Jacksonville | .8181 | .6765 | .6983 | .6777 | .7003 | .7258 | .7703 | .7170 | .8947 | .8130 | .8136 | .9276 | .9142 |
| Las Vegas | .7183 | .6373 | .6040 | .6674 | .5972 | .7528 | .6563 | .6728 | .7037 | .7042 | .7680 | .7874 | .8367 |
| Los Angeles | .8215 | .7131 | .6958 | .8264 | .7858 | .8167 | .8025 | .8193 | .7608 | .7664 | .8470 | .9422 | .7823 |
| Louisville | .9274 | .8637 | .8722 | .8497 | .8339 | .8691 | .9040 | .8647 | .8843 | .8657 | .8789 | .9513 | .9497 |
| Memphis | .8580 | .8042 | .8525 | .8417 | .7682 | .7734 | .7565 | .7905 | .8634 | .8047 | .3458 | .8873 | .0938 |
| Miami | .8798 | .8263 | .7732 | .8440 | .7616 | .6711 | .7621 | .8751 | .9060 | .8662 | .7736 | .8719 | .9037 |
| Nashville | 1.0011 | .9640 | .9377 | .9377 | .9208 | .9382 | .9414 | .9247 | .9318 | .9769 | .9813 | 1.0167 | 1.0402 |
| Oklahoma City | .8222 | .7613 | .7330 | .7658 | .7437 | .7562 | .7561 | .7437 | .7245 | .6904 | .7323 | .7777 | .8046 |
| Orlando | .7148 | .7817 | .7490 | .7968 | .7673 | .7615 | .7982 | .7356 | .8379 | .8715 | .9193 | .9121 | .9056 |
| Phoenix | .7006 | .8055 | .6134 | .7259 | .6732 | .6566 | .5279 | .6678 | .6988 | .8104 | .7988 | .8351 | .7926 |
| Sacramento | .8406 | .7234 | .7245 | .8028 | .6963 | .7452 | .7216 | .6938 | .7158 | .6786 | .7543 | .8263 | .8240 |
| San Diego | .8930 | .7620 | .8635 | .8625 | .7913 | .7624 | .7379 | .8021 | .8596 | .8420 | .8435 | .9208 | .9806 |
| San Francisco | .8090 | .7263 | .6956 | .8005 | .6830 | .5380 | .6245 | .5805 | .5819 | .7226 | .7493 | .9543 | 1.0079 |
| San Jose | .7291 | .6264 | .6600 | .7376 | .6052 | .6328 | .6447 | .6984 | .7720 | .8059 | .8248 | .9443 | 1.0767 |
| Seattle | .8278 | .8436 | .8450 | .8635 | .8483 | .8569 | .8767 | .8153 | .8632 | .8099 | .8506 | .8881 | .9334 |
| Shreveport | .9178 | .7997 | .9025 | .9098 | .7216 | .7728 | .7019 | .7079 | .7391 | .8152 | .8666 | .8626 | .9164 |
| Spokane | .8713 | .7026 | .7076 | .8743 | .7841 | .8357 | .8185 | .8014 | .8262 | .8611 | .8096 | .9640 | .9963 |
| Stockton | .7384 | .6537 | .7296 | .7070 | .6278 | .6888 | .7147 | .6581 | .6488 | .6679 | .7313 | .7668 | .8047 |
| Tampa | .8220 | .7556 | .7483 | .7913 | .7137 | .7585 | .7606 | .7699 | .7489 | .7389 | .8374 | .8186 | .8558 |
| Tulsa | .8231 | .8040 | .8042 | .8112 | .8120 | .7947 | .7663 | .7751 | .7738 | .7292 | .7595 | .8369 | .8640 |
| Vallejo | .7632 | .7583 | .7493 | .7886 | .7207 | .7198 | .6197 | .7113 | .7004 | .7110 | .7452 | .8018 | .9224 |

Note: [*]Calculated using Equation 11.9 in text and assuming   = -2.0, using the estimates of   from
Table 8.3, and land's share from Table 11.1.

$$\Omega_{it} = .5863 + .0077(\text{Time}) + .0084(\text{Size1}) +$$
$$\phantom{\Omega_{it} = }(.0120) \quad (.0011) \quad\quad\quad (.0099)$$

$$\phantom{\Omega_{it} = }.0592(\text{Size2}) - .1044(\text{West})$$
$$\phantom{\Omega_{it} = }(.0100) \quad\quad\quad (.0089)$$

where:

$\Omega_{it}$ = the price elasticity of demand for land (in absolute value) for the $i^{th}$ time period,

Time = the time variable with 1966 equal to 1,

Size1 = dummy variable for cities of population less than one-half million,

Size2 = dummy variable for cities of population between one-half and one million, and

West = dummy variable for cities in the west.

The standard errors are in parentheses below the coefficients. The excluded size category was cities with population greater than one million. The total sample size was 403 (thirty-one cities for thirteen time periods). The adjusted $R^2$ for the price elasticity equation was .43. These pooled results follow the same general pattern as the individual city and time period results. All coefficients are significant at traditional levels with the exception of the dummy variable for small cities in the price elasticity equation.

Table 11.6 gives the cross-sectional estimates for variation in for each year between 1966 and 1978. These results indicate that the price elasticity is significantly lower in western cities. For the size variable, the price elasticity is significantly higher in the larger cities. The individual city results indicated that the price elasticity increase significantly over time for 25 of the 31 cities.

## Table 11.6. Cross-Sectional Estimates of Variation in Price Elasticity of Land: 1966-1978[a]

| Variable | 1966 | 1967 | 1968 | 1969 | 1970 | 1971 | 1972 | 1973 | 1974 | 1975 | 1976 | 1977 | 1978 |
|---|---|---|---|---|---|---|---|---|---|---|---|---|---|
| Constant | .6910* (.0282) | .6220* (.0302) | .6178* (.0326) | .6229* (.0319) | .6017* (.0332) | .5840* (.0366) | .6142* (.0408) | .6205* (.0316) | .6286* (.0318) | .6320* (.0276) | .6582* (.0277) | .7016* (.0243) | .7184* (.0243) |
| Size 1 | -.0149 (.0303) | -.0164 (.0325) | .0189 (.0351) | -.0005 (.0343) | -.0122 (.0357) | .0333 (.0394) | .0183 (.0439) | -.0157 (.0340) | .0210 (.0342) | .0231 (.0297) | .0311 (.0298) | .0039 (.0261) | .0162 (.0240) |
| Size 2 | .0404* (.0304) | .0692* (.0325) | .0618* (.0351) | .0485* (.0344) | .0675* (.0357) | .0842* (.0394) | .0571* (.0439) | .0553* (.0340) | .0703* (.0343) | .0636* (.0297) | .0612* (.0298) | .0558* (.0262) | .0589* (.0278) |
| West | -.1095* (.0269) | -.1181* (.0288) | -.1335* (.0311) | -.1148* (.0305) | -.1050* (.0316) | -.0905* (.0349) | -.1116* (.0389) | -.1126* (.0301) | -.1190* (.0304) | -.1082* (.0263) | -.0962* (.0264) | -.0644* (.0232) | -.0605* (.0241) |
| $\bar{R}^2$ | .469 | .536 | .485 | .421 | .432 | .338 | .279 | .457 | .469 | .491 | .429 | .373 | .378 |

Notes: [a]Standard errors in parentheses.

* = significant at 10% level.

187

### 11.3.3. Price Elasticity of Land with Variable $\eta$

In a recent article, Gerking and Boyes (1980) provided some preliminary estimates of the price elasticity of demand for housing in various cities. In the previous section, we assumed that $\eta$ was constant across cities. The evidence by Gerking and Boyles suggests that there may be significant difference in $\eta$ across various cities. Their estimates of $\eta$ include nine of the thirty-one cities that we have examined. Using their estimates of $\eta$, shown in Table 11.7, we can derive the estimates of $\Omega$ by dropping the assumption that $\eta$ is constant.

Table 11.7 contains the estimates of the price elasticity of demand for land using the Gerking and Boyes (1980) estimates of $\eta$. Their price elasticity of housing estimates ($\eta$) are generally below .5. Their estimates would tend to make the price elasticity of demand for land closer to the estimation in Table 11.4 where $\eta$ was assumed to be equation to $-.5$ and constant across the various cities.

If one uses the estimates of $\eta$ from Gerking and Boyes (1980), the demand for land is even more inelastic as compared to over estimates in Table 11.2. One of the most fruitful areas of future research would be to examine the interurban variations in the price elasticity of demand to housing and thus land.

### 11.4 Summary

This chapter has examined interurban variations over time in the price elasticity of derived demand for urban residential land. The theory of derived demand for an input factor, as developed in Marshall's well known four rules, indicates that the price elasticity depends on the price elasticity of the output, the elasticity of substitution between input factors, the elasticity of supply of other input factors and the relative importance of the input factor. Little empirical research has investigated the responsiveness of the demand for land with respect to its price.

Table 11.7. Price Elasticity of Demand for Land
Using Variable Estimates of $\eta$: 1970

| City | Price Elasticity of Demand for Housing, [a] | Land Price Elasticity, [b] |
|------|------|------|
| Dayton | −.40 | −.5578 |
| Denver | −.39 | −.5276 |
| Houston | −.55 | −.3461 |
| Los Angeles | −.40 | −.2761 |
| Nashville | −.44 | −.6673 |
| Orlando | −.47 | −.5205 |
| San Diego | −.29 | −.3834 |
| San Francisco | −.26 | −.2412 |
| Seattle | −.30 | −.5051 |

Notes:

[a] From Gerking and Boyes (1980).

[b] Calculated using Equation 11.9, using the land share by city for 1970 from Table 11.1, the estimates of $\sigma$ from Table 8.3, and the Gerking and Boyes (1980) estimates of $\eta$.

Using the interurban estimates of the elasticity of substitution from Chapter 8, the relative share of land, and assuming that the elasticity of demand for housing services and the elasticity of supply of capital inputs are constant across housing areas, estimates of the demand price elasticity for land were made for 31 FHA housing market areas over the period 1966 to 1978. These estimates indicate an inelastic demand for residential sites in all housing areas for all time periods. In general, the demand for land was less inelastic in the latter time periods.

While the estimates should be interpreted as preliminary, they are the first to investigate this neglected area of urban analysis. More refined estimates can be developed when research examines the interurban variations in the price elasticity of demand for housing services and the elasticity of supply for other inputs in housing production.

## NOTES

1. See Rubenfeld (1972) for a discussion of the literature.

2. For examples of the former, see Kau and Sirmans (1978) and Downing (1970). For examples of the latter, see Muth (1971) and Witte (1975, 1977).

3. See Mills (1977), chapter 3.

4. Muth (1964, 1969) has recently developed a model of land for land assuming a constant elasticity of substitution production function in housing production. Witte (1977) has provided some empirical estimates of interurban demand for land.

5. Witte (1977) recently estimates the price elasticity for aggregate U.S. data at $-.8$. Another area which has been neglected is possible intraurban variations in the price elasticity of land.

6. For a good discussion of the theory of derived demand, see Stigler (1966). Some recent literature is Bronfenbrenner (1961), Muth (1961), Ferguson (1966), Mundlak (1968), Andrieu (1974) and Sato and Koizumi (1970). Early literature includes Hicks (1963, 1961), Marshall (1920) and Pigou (1932).

7. See Sato and Koizumi (1970) for the derivation of this equation. The Hicks (1963) formulation is

$$\Omega = \frac{E_K \alpha_L [\eta-\sigma] + \sigma[\eta+E_K]}{[\eta+ E_K] - \alpha_L [\eta-\sigma]}$$

8. Andrieu has recently generalized Equation (11.8) in the case of non-constant returns to scale in production. Andrieu's generalization can be written

$$\Omega = \frac{E_K \alpha_L [\eta-\sigma G] + \sigma[\eta+E_K G]}{[\eta+E_K G] - \alpha_L [\eta-\sigma G]}$$

where $G = \eta(1-v) + v$. v is the degree of homogeneity of the production function. Obviously, if v is equal to one, this equation reduces to the Hicks formulation in footnote 7. Sato and Koizumi (1970) have introduced different degrees of substitutability and complimentarity among factors of production to the theory of derived demand.

9. Kau and Lee (1976c) required an estimate of $\alpha_L$ which was not available in their sample.

10. See Chapter 4 for a discussion of the VES production function and Chapter 8 for empirical estimates.

11. The data are the average values for FHA new houses. While the data have some limitations [see Muth (1971) for a discussion], they are the most comprehensive data available. The data were taken from FHA Homes (various years) published by the Department of Housing and Urban Development. The structure input (K) is the average improved living area for new houses, L is the average lot size, r is the estimated land price per square foot, and n

is the estimated construction cost per square foot of living area. See appendix C for the data.

12. The excluded category was cities with population greater than one million.

Chapter 12


SPATIAL VARIATIONS IN LAND VALUES


12.1.   Introduction


The rate of return on land is a frequent discussion among real estate professionals and a topic of research among academicians. There has been a significant movement toward tangible assets such as land in recent years. Land appreciation is treated as a fact of life without historical evidence to support it. Many standard references support the idea that an excess risk-premium is available for housing land as an investment (see Hodges (1971), Ricks (1968), Case (1960), Davis (1973), and Achtenhagen (1974)). Others [see Hallengren (1974) and Friedman (1971)] observe that real estate is no more risky than corporate bonds. This would suggest no excess risk-premium over bonds for land investment.

Suprisingly, there are no long-term historical studies on the return to holding land. Following the approach developed by Krasker (1979) this chapter develops a model for measuring the return to land and examines those returns using a random coefficient estimation procedure [see Swamy (1970)] for specific periods from 1836-1970. This statistical model provides a mean rate of return for land and a predictor for each time period. The results suggest that the expected long-term return to holding land is no higher than the rate of return to holding high grade bonds. This chapter also examines the variations in the return to land over space.

## 12.2. Model of Excess Returns

The data base is the Chicago land values over the period 1836 to 1970 used in Chapter 10. The same cross-sectional parcel was used for corresponding time period comparisons within the two separate samples: Hoyt (1933) estimates of land values for 1836, 1857, 1873, 1892, 1910, and 1928 and Olcott (1970) land values are for 1910, 1920, 1930, 1940, 1950, 1960, and 1970. Both the Hoyt and Olcott data have been used by others for research [see Mills (1971b), McDonald and Bowman (1979), Yeates (1969), and Kau and Sirmans (1979)]. The samples used are actual sale prices for land. The rates of returns and statistical tests were conducted for each data set separately since they are not directly comparable.[1] Rates of return for land are compared with the return to holding premium bonds. This was done because no continuous approximation to a risk-free rate is available for the time period used.[2]

Assume that land is purchased at price $PL_t$ and sold for $PL_{t+1}$ after a specific period, with net revenue from renting the land equal to $\xi$. The net revenue of holding land represents the rental income minus the holding cost and taxes.[3] The expected risk-premium for holding land would be:

$$E(\psi_t) = E \left( \frac{PL_{t+1} - PL_t - \xi}{PL_t} \right) - \omega_t \qquad (12.1)$$

where $\omega$ = the bond rate,

$E(\psi)$ = the expected risk-premium,

$\xi$ = the net revenue, and

$t$ = time

There are two reasons why may differ from zero. The real return on land might be correlated with the real return on other assets and the land market may not be competitive. Equation (12.1) can be rearranged to obtain the estimable form:

$$\left(\frac{PL_{t+1} - PL_t}{PL_t}\right) - \omega_t = \psi_t + \xi\frac{1}{PL_t} \tag{12.2}$$

The statistical model used to obtain estimates of and   is written as:[4]

$$RL_{it} = \sum_{k=1}^{K} \Phi_{kt} \cdot X_{kit} + e_{it} \tag{12.3}$$

where:   $RL_{it}$ = the rate-of-return for the ith parcel of land in the tth time period,

$\Phi_{kt}$ = the coefficient for $\psi_t(\Phi_{1t})$ and $\xi_t(\Phi_{2t})$ for each time period, and

$X_{kit}$ = the variables $X_{1it}$ (the constant term) and $X_{2it}$ the direct cost variable for each parcel of land for each time period.

When the response coefficients are fixed parameters, Equation (12.2) can be viewed as a seemingly unrelated regression model [see Zellner (1962)], or when $\Phi_{kt}$'s are random, it is equivalent to a random coefficient model [see Swamy (1970)].

The initial test will be to determine whether the co-efficients are fixed or random. The null hypotheses is:

$$H_o: \quad \Phi_1 = \Phi_2 = \ldots = \Phi_n = \bar{\Phi}. \tag{12.4}$$

If this null is accepted, the rates of return for land each time period are not random and they are all identical to the mean [see Swamy (1970)]. Generally one would expect random variations in returns between time periods because of exogenous shocks to the economic and social system.

Assuming the null is rejected, $\Phi_t$ can be regarded as a probability distribution with mean $\bar{\Phi}$. For the tth time period, the model is:

$$RL_t = X_t(\bar{\Phi} + \mu_t) + e_t \qquad t = 1 \ldots n \qquad (12.5)$$

where $RL_t$ and $X_t$ contain observations on the dependent and independent variables, respectively, with $e_t$ the disturbance vector and $\mu$ the random component. Thus

$$\Phi_t = \bar{\Phi} + \mu_t \quad \text{with} \qquad (12.6)$$

$E(\mu_t) = 0$, $E(\mu_t \mu'_t) = \nabla$, and $E(\mu_t \mu'_j) = 0$ for $t \neq j$. This implies that the disturbances across time are heteroscedastic but uncorrelated.

In this model we use a generalized least squares (GLS) estimator for $\bar{\Phi}$. This gives the mean rate of return $\bar{\Phi}$ and the best linear unbiased predictor $\hat{\Phi}_t$ for each time period. The prediction of the individual components ($\Phi_t$) is of interest because it provides information for each time period and also because it provides a basis for predicting values of the dependent variable for a given time period. The predictor $\hat{\Phi}_t$ can be viewed as an estimate of the mean, $\bar{\Phi}$, plus a predictor for $\mu_t$, the random component. A Bayesian argument leads to the same predictor [see Smith (1973) and Leamer (1978, p.274)]. Judge et al. (1980) provides a detailed description of the Swamy approach.

## 12.3. The Empirical Estimates of Returns Over Time

The OLS results are presented in Table 12.1. The $\Phi_t$'s seem to vary with each time period. Before adopting the random coefficient approach to estimate (12.3), we conduct a preliminary test of:

$$H_o: \quad \Phi_1 = \Phi_2 \ldots = \Phi_N = \bar{\Phi}$$

for the two sample periods. The $x^2$ value for the Olcott data is 5310.38 and for the Hoyt data 1193.37, both of which are significant. We conclude that the $\beta_t$'s (rates of return to holding land) are not fixed coefficients.

The resulting GLS estimates with t-values in parentheses are:

Table 12.1. The OLS and Predicted Rates of Return on Land for Selected Time Periods 1836-1970

| Holding Period | 1836-1857 | 1857-1873 | 1873-1892 | 1892-1910 | 1910-1928 | 1910-1920 | 1920-1930 | 1930-1940 | 1940-1950 | 1950-1960 | 1960-1970 |
|---|---|---|---|---|---|---|---|---|---|---|---|
| Premium Rate of Return (Constant Term) | 0.056 | 0.0899 | 0.000164 | -0.0476 | 0.0473 | -0.00816 | 0.0405 | -0.1410 | -0.0311 | 0.0074 | 0.0157 |
| | 0.056 (11.40)* | 0.0907 (14.16)* | 0.000046 (0.01) | -0.0480 (-10.99)* | 0.04559 (8.26)* | -0.00808 (-2.07)* | 0.0408 (7.76)* | -0.1413 (-48.58)* | -0.0311 (-12.50)* | 0.0059 (1.29)* | 0.0157 (7.35)* |
| Direct Cost | 0.0599 | 0.7451 | 8.726 | 17.481 | 34.029 | 0.2516 | 0.4820 | 1.236 | 0.629 | 1.431 | -0.0059 |
| | 0.0594 (2.52)* | 0.7146 (2.22)* | 8.709 (6.05)* | 17.749 (3.62)* | 37.338 (6.57)* | 0.2503 (7.69)* | 0.4793 (6.18)* | 1.244 (8.79)* | 0.628 (11.45) | 1.492 (10.34)* | -0.0085 (-0.24) |

Note: * t-values significant at the .05 level

197

Hoyt Data                          Olcott Data

$(\bar{\beta}_1) \psi = 0.0293$              $(\bar{\beta}_1) \psi = -0.0194$
$\quad\quad (1.21)$                   $\quad\quad (-0.74)$

$(\bar{\beta}_2) \xi = 12.208$              $(\bar{\beta}_2) \xi = 0.670$
$\quad\quad (1.77)$                   $\quad\quad (2.83)$

the mean $\bar{\Phi}$, the premium to holding land, is not significantly different from zero. This would indicate that the
return to land does not exceed the bond rate. The net revenue variable is significant and positive. Indicating as
expected that rental income exceeds holding costs and
taxes.

The $\hat{\Phi}_t$ estimates for each time period are presented in
Table 12.1. As with the OLS estimates there are significant variations between time periods. For the 1910-1970
periods holding land led to significantly less than a bond
return in 3 out of the 6 years with an additional year insignificant. For the 1836-1928 periods the rate of return
was significantly greater than the bond rate for 3 out of 5
periods.

Overall, the results indicate no risk premium for land
relative to bonds. The Olcott data contains a period that
involved the depression. During this period that was a
significant negative rate on land (-14%). Excluding this
period does not change the insignificance for the mean rate
of return for the 1910-1970 period.

The insignificant risk-premium and the significant net
revenue of holding land would indicate that land is not a
risk premium asset relative to bonds. The results suggest
that future research should investigate the accepted view
that markets in land are inefficient. The evidence presented in this paper indicates that the efficient market
hypothesis might well be applied to real estate investments.

12.4. Spatial Variations in Rates of Return

To examine the variations in the rate of return over space, the following equation was estimated.

$$RL_{ij} = \Phi_0 + \Phi_1(u_i) + \varepsilon \qquad (12.7)$$

where:

$RL_{ij}$ = the rate of return on the ith parcel of land for the ith combination of years,

$u_i$ = the distance from the center of the city.

As in the previous section, the rates of return were calculated using the Hoyt and Olcott estimates of the land value.

Table 12.2 presented OLS estimates of Equation (12.7) for various pairs of years from the Hoyt data. Table 12.3 contains the estimates for the Olcott data. The distance variable was significant. The sign, however, is positive in some pairs of years and negative in others. The rate of return were significantly negative for the Hoyt 1936-1857 time period and insignificant for the 1892-1910 time period. For the Olcott data, rates of return were significantly positive with distance for five of the six time periods. The rate of return was significantly negative with respect to distance for the 1960-1970 time span.

Table 12.4 and 12.5 present the estimates of rate of return as a function of distance using Equation (12.3). These estimates were the inverse of the land value in the initial time period in order to examine the impact of the holding costs. These estimates follow the same general pattern as those in Table 12.2 and 12.3. The distance coefficient is smaller in these estimates. Holding costs, as indicated by the coefficient, in general, increase over time.

Table 12.2. OLS Estimates of Rates of Return on Land in Chicago*
as a Function of Distance for Various Holding Periods: 1836-1928

| Independent Variable | 1836-1857 | 1857-1873 | Years 1873-1892 | 1892-1910 | 1910-1928 |
|---|---|---|---|---|---|
| Constant | .1315 (20.26) | .1093 (11.88) | .0134 (1.74) | .0068** (.79) | .0748 (6.50) |
| Distance | -.00196 (2.56) | .00681 (6.32) | .00489 (5.50) | -.0013** (-1.19) | .00490 (3.42) |
| $\bar{R}^2$ | .03 | .16 | .15 | .01 | .08 |

Note: * t-values are in parentheses

** = insignificant at .05 level.

200

Table 12.3. OLS Estimates of Rates of Return on Land in Chicago*
as a Function of Distance for Various Holding Periods: 1910-1970

| Independent Variable | 1910-1920 | 1920-1930 | 1930-1940 | 1940-1950 | 1950-1960 | 1960-1970 |
|---|---|---|---|---|---|---|
| Constant | .0132 (1.77) | .0351 (3.69) | .0991 (-18.11) | -.0064 (-1.32) | .03654 (5.60) | .0981 (21.16) |
| Distance | .0062 (6.10) | .0108 (8.36) | .0020 (2.66) | .0033 (5.10) | .0064 (7.22) | -.0055 (-8.81) |
| $\bar{R}^2$ | .12 | .20 | .02 | .09 | .16 | .22 |

Note: * t-values are in parentheses

Table 12.4. OLS Estimates of Rates of Return on Land in Chicago: 1836-1928

| Independent Variable | 1836-1857 | 1857-1873 | 1873-1892 | 1892-1910 | 1910-1928 |
|---|---|---|---|---|---|
| Constant | .1260 (21.97) | .1050 (7.75) | .0130 (1.41) | .0068 (3.16) | .0748 (4.11) |
| Distance | -.0144 (-13.52) | .00309 (2.35) | .00109* (1.01) | -.00364 (-3.28) | .00037** (.237) |
| 1/LV1 | .3071 (13.66) | .7820 (4.55) | 8.9420 (5.52) | 24.9191 (4.75) | 35.7393 (5.28) |
| $\bar{R}^2$ | .49 | .24 | .28 | .16 | .25 |

Notes: * t-values are in parentheses

** = insignificant at .05 level.

Table 12.5.  OLS Estimates of Rates of Return on Land in Chicago: 1910-1970

| Independent Variable | 1910-1920 | 1920-1930 | 1930-1940 | 1940-1950 | 1950-1960 | 1960-1970 |
|---|---|---|---|---|---|---|
| Constant | .0178 (2.48) | .0365 (3.90) | -.1070 (-31.40) | -.0153 (-3.63) | .0048** (.760) | .0778 (12.89) |
| Distance | .0031 (2.71) | .0088 (6.29) | .0004** (.525) | .0017 (2.97) | .0055 (7.23) | -.0049 (-8.00) |
| 1/LV | .1972 (5.21) | .2620 (3.25) | 1.2241 (8.31) | .5834 (10.35) | 1.3872 (10.35) | 1.3043 (4.99) |

Note:  * t-values are in parentheses

    ** = insignificnt at .05 level.

203

### 12.5. Returns Over Long Holding Periods

To examine the impact of longer holding periods on the rate of return over space, the Hoyt data was used to compute the rate of return over the following holding periods: 1836–1873, 1836–1892, 1836–1910, 1836–1928, 1857–1910, 1892–1910, 1857–1928, 1873–1910, 1873–1928, and 1892–1928.

The OLS estimates of the rates of return on these longer holding periods are in Table 12.6. For these longer holding periods, the rate of return were positively related to distance in each pair of years.

### 12.6. Summary

The purpose of this chapter has been to examine variations in the changes in land values for the Chicago area. Using data from Hoyt and Olcott, we estimated equations using rates of appreciation as the dependent variable.

The results indicate that rates of land return appear comparable to that of high grade bonds over the long-run. Spatial variations were observed when distance was used as an explanatory variable.

### NOTES

1. The Hoyt (1933) data is value per acre whereas the Olcott (1970) data are measured in value per front foot. The values are estimated using actual sale prices for a sample of land parcels. The two data sets also have different parcels, hence the two sets are not comparable.

2. Homer (1963) has provided a detailed analysis of historical interest rates. The bond rate used in the study for the Hoyt data 1936–1928 was the average return over the various periods for the New England Municipal Bond yields. The data were from Homer (1963) pp. 286–288. For the Olcott data set, the Homer estimates of prime corporate

Table 12.6. Rates of Return on Land in Chicago
for Long Holding Periods:
1836-1928*

| Independent Variable | 1836-1873 | 1836-1892 | 1836-1910 | 1836-1928 | 1857-1892 | 1857-1910 | 1857-1928 | 1873-1910 | 1823-1928 | 1892-1928 |
|---|---|---|---|---|---|---|---|---|---|---|
| Constant | .1224 (29.64) | .0848 (25.50) | .0688 (22.27) | .0690 (26.40) | .0608 (12.81) | .0449 (13.65) | .0525 (17.70) | .0144 (3.48) | .0354 (10.07) | .0408 (6.06) |
| Distance | .0016 (3.22) | .0026 (6.80) | .00108 (2.81) | .0020 (6.47) | .0049 (8.95) | .0023 (5.62) | .0029 (8.36) | .0015 (2.81) | .0021 (5.24) | .0015 (1.88) |
| $\bar{R}^2$ | .04 | .21 | .05 | .23 | .32 | .20 | .34 | .05 | .16 | .02 |

Note: * t-values are in parentheses

205

bond yields were used. These were from Homer (1963) pp. 340, 350, and 359.

3. It would appear that taxes vary with the value of land thus making Equation (12.1) an inappropriate specification. This is not the case. The tax rate is the same regardless of the value. This means that the rate of return to holding land does not vary with value because of taxes, therefore Equation (12.1) is still the correct specification.

4. The rate of return was calculated using the following equation

$$PL_t = \frac{PL_n}{(1+RL_i)^n}$$

where: $PL_t$ is the land value in the initial period, $PL_n$ is the land value at the end of n periods, and n is the number of periods. $RL_i$ is thus the rate of return on each parcel (i). The sample size was equal to 119 for the Hoyt data and 282 for the Olcott data.

PART V


URBAN POPULATION DENSITY
_____

Introduction

The last major section of the book concentrates on population densities.  The functional form of the density gradient
is analyzed in Chapter 13 by a Box and Cox procedure to determine the best alternative.  The results suggest that
functional forms other than exponential should be considered.  Chapter 14 uses various statistical techniques such
as a random coefficient model to investigate the stability
and uncertainty of urban spatial structure.  The model indicates significant structural change and stochastic behavior
of the density gradient.  In general the OLS density gradient estimates have over-stated the impact of distance on
population density and understated the importance of other
urban factors.  Chapter 15 uses a varying coefficient model
to expand the usefulness of the exponential density gradient.  Thus, allowing urban density functions to be used as
a tool for policy analysis.  This is accomplished by incorporating other urban variables into the function.

Chapter 13


FUNCTIONAL FORM AND URBAN POPULATION DENSITY


13.1.  Introduction


The spatial pattern of population densities is important in urban economic analysis.  Changing population densities influence the intensity of demand for municipal services and the design of transport systems.  Clark (1951) initially employed the negative exponential function to investigate the relationship between density and distance.[1]  Muth (1969) using Cobb-Douglas supply and demand functions for housing derived the necessary and sufficient conditions for the existence of an exponential function between density and distance.  One of the necessary conditions for the existence of an exponential function is that the price elasticity of demand for housing services be minus one.  This condition is relatively restrictive and the price elasticity of demand for housing has been subject to discussion.[2]  However, the question of whether the exponential function is the true functional form, and correspondingly, whether the price elasticity of demand for housing is greater or less than minus one, has never been determined conclusively on statistical ground.

The main purpose of this chapter is to examine the "true" functional relationship between the population density and distance for fifty United States SMSA's.  A Box and Cox (1964) transformation technique is used to introduce a functional form parameter to generalize the relationship between the population density and distance.  It will be shown that the functional form parameter can be used to test whether the negative exponential function accurately describes the density-distance relationship. In addition, the functional form parameter can be used to test whether the price elasticity of demand for housing services is minus one.

This chapter is divided into five sections. In Section 13.2 the economic theory and assumptions used to derive the negative exponential function will be reviewed. In Section 13.3 the general relationship between the population density and distance discussed in Section 13.2 will be used to derive a generalized functional form. It will be shown that the Box and Cox (1964) transformation technique can be employed to use the generalized functional form to test whether the negative exponential function is a true relationship. The procedures used to estimate and to test the functional form parameter will also be specified. Section 13.4 presents the statistical model and in Section 13.5 the data, which consist of a random sample of 45 census tract densities and distance from the central business district for each of fifty United States cities in 1970,[3] will be used to test the negative exponential. In Section 13.6 the price elasticity of demand is derived. The generalized functional relationships will be discussed in Section 13.7 and the implications of the findings of this chapter will be discussed in detail. Finally, Section 13.8 will summarize the results of this chapter.

## 13.2. Derivation of the Negative Exponential Function

In accordance with Muth (1969) and following Mills' exposition (see Chapter 2) the output of housing services at distance u, Xs(u), is defined as

$$Xs(u) = AL(u)^{\alpha}K(u)^{\alpha-1} \tag{13.1}$$

where K(u) and L(u) represent inputs of capital and land in the production of housing services u miles from the center. A and $\alpha$ are scale and distribution parameters, respectively, for a Cobb-Douglas production function.

In deriving a negative exponential function to describe the relationship between the land rent r(u) and the distance u, Mills and Muth have also defined a demand function for housing services at u, Xd(u), as

$$xd(u) = Bw^{\theta_1} p(u)^{\theta_2} \tag{13.2}$$

where

B = a scale parameter and depends upon the units in which housing services are measured;

w = income for workers;

p(u) = price of housing services at distance u;

$\theta_1$ = income elasticity; and

$\theta_2$ = price elasticity.

By using the first order conditions of Equation (13.1), the aggregate demand derived from Equation (13.2) and other equilibrium conditions, Mills (1981, pp. 226–228) has derived the following relationship between population density D(u) and distance as[4]

$$D(u) = E[\bar{r}^{-\beta} + \beta TE(\bar{u}-u)]^{\frac{1-\beta}{\beta}} \quad \text{if } \beta \neq 0 \tag{13.3}$$

and

$$D(u) = E(\bar{r}e^{TEu})e^{-TEu} \quad \text{if } \beta = 0 \tag{13.4}$$

where

D(u) = density at distance u;

$$\beta = \alpha(1 + \theta_2); \tag{13.5}$$

$$E = Bw^{\theta_1}[A\alpha^{\alpha}(1-\alpha)^{1-\alpha}]^{-(1+\theta_2)} n^{(1-\alpha)(1+\theta_2)}; \tag{13.6}$$

n = rental rate for housing capital;

T = the commuting cost per mile;

$\bar{u}$ = the distance from the center to the edge of the urban area;

$\bar{r}$ = rent on nonurban uses of land; and

$r(\bar{u}) = \bar{r}$.

From Equation (13.4) we know that the population density declines exponentially with distance if and only if $\beta$ is equal to zero. This result also implies that the population density declines exponentially with distance if and only if the price elasticity $\theta_2$ is minus one. This is one of the null hypotheses to be tested in Section 13.6.

## 13.3. The Generalized Functional Form

After some rearrangements, Equation (13.3) can be rewritten as

$$\frac{D(u)^{\frac{\beta}{1-\beta}}-1}{\frac{\beta}{1-\beta}} = \frac{(ER^{\frac{\beta}{1-\beta}})^{\frac{\beta}{1-\beta}}-1}{\frac{\beta}{1-\beta}} + (1-\beta)TE^{\frac{1}{1-\beta}}(\bar{u}-u). \tag{13.7}$$

It can be shown that Equation (13.7) will become Equation (13.4) when $\beta$ approaches zero. Let $\beta/1-\beta$ be equal to $\lambda$, then Equation (13.7) will reduce to

$$\frac{D^{\lambda}(u)-1}{\lambda} = [\frac{(C^{\lambda}-1)}{\lambda} + \gamma\bar{u}] - \gamma u \tag{13.8}$$

where $C = ER^{\frac{L}{1-\beta}}$ , $\gamma = (1-\beta)TE^{\frac{1}{1-\beta}}$. Since there exists only two observable variables, $D(u)$ and $u$, in Equation (13.7), it can be rewritten based on the technique of Box and Cox's (1964) transformation procedure.

## 13.4.  The Statistical Model

Based on Box and Cox (1964) and Zarembka (1968), two generalized functional forms for describing the relationship between the population density (D) and distance (u) are defined as

$$(D^\lambda - 1)/\lambda = D_0 - \gamma u + \epsilon \tag{13.9}$$

and

$$(D^{\lambda^\prime} - 1)/\lambda^\prime = D_0 - \gamma_1^\prime(u^{\lambda^\prime} - 1)/\lambda^\prime + \epsilon^\prime, \tag{13.10}$$

where $\gamma_0$, $\gamma_1$, $\gamma_0^\prime$, and $\gamma_1^\prime$ are regression parameters, $\lambda$ and $\lambda^\prime$
are functional form parameters and the disturbance terms
($\epsilon_i$ and $\epsilon_i^\prime$) are normally distributed with zero means and
variances of $\sigma^2$ and $\sigma^{\prime 2}$, respectively.

For (13.9), if $\lambda = 1$, linear density is regressed on
distance.  If $\lambda$ approaches zero, the dependent variable is
the natural logarithm of density.  Similarly, (13.10) will
reduce to the linear form when $\lambda^\prime$ is equal to one and to a
double logarithmic form when $\lambda^\prime$ approaches zero.  Following
Taylor's theorem, (13.9) can be approximated as

$$\log D = D_0 - \gamma u + \gamma^\prime u^2, \tag{13.11}$$

where $\gamma^\prime = 1/2\lambda\gamma$ and $\lambda < 1$.

This demonstrates that the negative quadratic exponential form used by Latham and Yeates (1970) is a special case
of (13.9).  Using maximum likelihood techniques developed by
Box and Cox (1964), both $\lambda$ and $\lambda^\prime$ and the regression coefficients are estimated from the data [see Chapter 5, 6 and
10].

Under the assumption of normality, the probability density function for $\epsilon_i$ in (13.9) is written as

$$f(\xi) = (2\pi\sigma^2)^{-\frac{1}{2}} \exp(-\tfrac{1}{2}(\epsilon^2/\sigma^2)). \tag{13.12}$$

If the $\epsilon$'s are identically and independently distributed, the log likelihood function for (13.12) can be written as

$$\log L = -\frac{n}{2} \log 2\pi\sigma^2 + (\lambda - 1) \sum_{i-1}^{n} \log D_i$$

$$-\frac{1}{2\sigma^2} \sum_{i=1}^{n} \left[ \frac{D_i^\lambda - 1}{\lambda} - \gamma_0 + \gamma_1 u_i \right]^2 \qquad (13.13)$$

The logarithmic likelihood is maximized with respect to $\sigma^2$, $\gamma_0$ and $\gamma_2$, given $\lambda$. The maximum likelihood estimates of $\sigma^2$ for the given $\lambda$, $\hat{\sigma}^2 (\lambda)$, is then the estimated variance of the disturbances of regressing $(D_i^\lambda - 1)/\lambda$ on u. Replacing $\sigma^2$ by $\hat{\sigma}^2 (\lambda)$, the maximum log likelihood $[L_{max}(\lambda)]$ for (13.9) is

$$L_{max}(\lambda) = -\frac{n}{2} \log 2\pi \, \hat{\sigma}(\lambda) - \frac{n}{2} + (\lambda - 1) \sum_{i=1}^{n} \log D_i. \qquad (13.14)$$

Box and Cox [1964, p. 216] indicate that an approximate 95 percent confidence region for $\lambda$ is obtained from

$$L_{max}(\hat{\lambda}) - L_{max}(\lambda) < \tfrac{1}{2}\chi^2(.05) = 1.92. \qquad (13.15)$$

Equations (13.14) and (13.15) with $\lambda´$ can also be derived for (13.10) by a similar procedure. Equation (13.15) is used to test whether the functional form parameters, $\lambda$ and $\lambda´$, are significantly different from zero and/or one.[5]

To test the importance of the quadratic term of distance in explaining the population density, the log likelihood for (13.16) and (13.17) are estimated:

$$D_i = \beta_0 - \beta_1 u_i + \beta_2 u_i^2 + e_i , \qquad (13.16)$$

$$\log D_i = \beta_0´ - \beta_1´ u_i + \beta_2´ u_i^2 + e_i´ , \qquad (13.17)$$

where $e_i$ and $e_i´$ = the disturbance terms, $\beta_0$, $\beta_1$, $\beta_2$, $\beta_0´$, $\beta_1´$ and $\beta_2´$ are regression parameters.

13.5.  Empirical Estimates


The data for this chapter consist of a random sample of 45 census tract densities measured u miles from the Central Business District for each of 50 U.S. cities in 1970.

The appropriate power transformation for (13.9) and (13.10) is determined by iterating $\lambda$ and $\lambda'$ between -.50 and 1.50 at intervals of 0.1.  The maximum likelihood estimates (Table 13.1) of these iterations for each 50 cities indicate that the functional form parameters ($\lambda$ and $\lambda'$) for 45 cities in this study are significantly different from one, and approximately 50 percent of them are significantly different from zero at the .05 level.  A summary of Table 13.1 is:

| Estimated $\lambda$ values | Number of cities | Estimated $\lambda'$ values | Number of cities |
|---|---|---|---|
| $\hat{\lambda} \neq 0$ | 23 | $\hat{\lambda}' \neq 0$ | 29 |
| $\hat{\lambda} \neq 1$ | 45 | $\hat{\lambda}' \neq 1$ | 45 |

In most cases it is preferred to use simple transformations to facilitate interpretation of the empirical results. Five alternative specifications are examined - linear ((13.9) with $\lambda = 1$), semi-log ((13.9) with $\lambda \to 0$), double-log ((13.9) with $\lambda' \to 0$), quadratic ((13.16) and semi-log quadratic (13.17).  The log likelihood for each specification is calculated using (13.15).  These formulations encompass the Clark and Muth exponential models ((13.9) with $\lambda \to 0$) and the Latham and Yeates model (13.17) with the addition of other alternative specifications for comparison.

Using the critical value of 1.92 from (13.15), the results indicate that the logarithmic specifications dominate the linear specifications.  But is is difficult to differentiate the semi-log from the double-log functional forms, since their log likelihood values are similar.  Also, there exist some cities in which the optimal functional form is either linear or linear quadratic.

Table 13.1.  The Maximum Likelihood Estimates
of the Optimum $\lambda$

| City | $\hat{\lambda}$ | 95% Confidence Region for $\hat{\lambda}$ |
|------|------|------|
| 1. Akron | -.20 | -.39~0.18 |
| 2. Baltimore | .00 | -.13~0.13 |
| 3. Birmingham | .40 | .18~0.76* |
| 4. Boston | .10 | -.19~0.50 |
| 5. Buffalo | .30 | .02~0.59* |
| 6. Chicago | -.10 | -.55~0.31 |
| 7. Cincinnati | .20 | -.09~0.49 |
| 8. Cleveland** | --- | --- --- |
| 9. Columbus | .50 | .08~0.92* |
| 10. Dallas | .60 | .31~0.91* |
| 11. Dayton | -.30 | -.55~0.02 |
| 12. Denver | .20 | -.50~0.35 |
| 13. Detroit | .50 | .20~0.72* |
| 14. Flint | .10 | -.13~0.39 |
| 15. Fort Worth | .60 | .27~1.05* |
| 16. Houston | .50 | .27~0.89* |
| 17. Jacksonville | .20 | .04~0.43* |
| 18. Kansas City | .40 | .05~0.82* |
| 19. Los Angeles | -.20 | -.55~0.31 |
| 20. Louisville | .10 | -.19~0.30 |
| 21. Memphis | .40 | .03~0.67* |
| 22. Miami | .20 | -.02~0.46 |
| 23. Milwaukee | -.10 | -.45~0.19 |
| 24. Nashville | .20 | -.04~0.42 |
| 25. New Haven | .10 | -.09~0.37 |
| 26. New Orleans | .10 | -.29~0.48 |
| 27. Oklahoma City | .80 | .29~1.15* |
| 28. Omaha | -.20 | -.55~0.12 |
| 29. Philadelphia | .20 | -.09~0.49 |
| 30. Phoenix | .90 | .55~1.49* |
| 31. Pittsburgh | .40 | -.19~0.92 |
| 32. Portland, Or. | .50 | .09~0.91* |
| 33. Providence | .30 | .02~0.58* |
| 34. Richmond | .10 | -.06~0.31 |
| 35. Rochester | .20 | .04~0.41* |
| 36. Sacramento | .50 | .23~0.90* |

Table 13.1 (continued)

| | | |
|---|---|---|
| 37. Salt Lake City | .50 | .27~0.81* |
| 38. San Antonio | .40 | -.02~0.85 |
| 39. San Diego | .50 | -.07~1.13 |
| 40. San Jose | 1.20 | .65~1.80* |
| 41. Seattle | -.10 | -.22~0.19 |
| 42. St. Louis | .20 | -.02~0.45 |
| 43. Spokane | .50 | .27~0.81* |
| 44. Syracuse | .20 | .04~0.33* |
| 45. Tacoma | .40 | .02~0.78* |
| 46. Toledo | .10 | -.12~0.20 |
| 47. Tuscon | .60 | .31~1.05* |
| 48. Utica | .10 | -.39~0.29 |
| 49. Washington, D.C. | .00 | -.29~0.35 |
| 50. Wichita | .80 | .38~1.25* |

Notes:

*Indicates significantly different from zero at 0.05 level.

**Cleveland's minimum $\lambda$ value was outside the -.50 to 1.50 range.

(Text Continues)

The results would suggest that the functional form varies among cities. For both the semi-log and the double-log functional forms, there is no statistical justification for preferring a priori one specification over another. The variation among all functional forms for all cities is of enough significance to warrant empirical investigation for each particular case.

## 13.6. The Price Elasticity of Demand for Housing

After the optimum point estimate, $\lambda$ and the confidence region for the $\hat{\lambda}$'s are determined [see Table 13.1]. The point estimate and the confidence region for $\hat{\beta}$ will be calculated using the relationship between $\hat{\beta}$ and $\hat{\lambda}$, i.e.,

$$\hat{\beta} = \frac{\hat{\lambda}}{1+\hat{\lambda}} \tag{13.18}$$

It should be noted that $\hat{\beta}$ will be significantly different from zero if and only if $\lambda$ is significantly different from zero. From the relationship between $\beta$ and $\theta_2$ which is defined in Equation (13.5), the assumption of unity price elasticity can also be tested statistically. Using Equation (13.18), the point estimate and the 95% confidence region for are calculated and listed in Table 13.2.

From Table 13.2 it is shown that approximately 50% of the $\beta$'s are significantly different from zero. Since $\beta = \alpha(1 + \theta_2)$ it can be concluded that the price elasticity of demand for housing services is significantly different from minus one when the is significantly different from zero. Given downward sloping demand curves for housing then $\alpha > \beta$ when $\beta > 0$. In all significant cases $\hat{\beta}$ is greater than zero implying an inelastic demand for housing services. In no cases did the results indicate significant elastic demands for housing.

## 13.7. A Generalized Density Gradient

As an example the Lmax ($\lambda$)s for two cities are plotted in Figure 13.1. The maximum likelihood estimate of $\lambda$ can then

Table 13.2.  The Maximum Likelihood Estimates
of the Optimum β Values

| City | $\hat{\beta}$ | 95% Confidence Region for $\hat{\beta}$ |
|---|---|---|
| 1. Akron | -.25 | -.15~.15 |
| 2. Baltimore | .00 | -.14~.12 |
| 3. Birmingham | .29 | .15~.43* |
| 4. Boston | .09 | -.23~.33 |
| 5. Buffalo | .23 | .02~.37* |
| 6. Chicago | -.11 | -1.22~.24 |
| 7. Cincinnati | .17 | -.10~.33 |
| 8. Cleveland | --- | --- --- |
| 9. Columbus | .33 | .07~.48* |
| 10. Dallas | .38 | .24~.48* |
| 11. Dayton | -.43 | -1.22~.02 |
| 12. Denver | .17 | -1.00~.26 |
| 13. Detroit | .33 | .17~.42* |
| 14. Flint | .09 | -.15~.28 |
| 15. Fort Worth | .38 | .21~.51* |
| 16. Houston | .33 | .21~.47* |
| 17. Jacksonville | .17 | .04~.30* |
| 18. Kansas City | .29 | .04~.45* |
| 19. Los Angeles | -.25 | -1.22~.24 |
| 20. Louisville | .09 | -.23~.23 |
| 21. Memphis | .29 | .03~.40* |
| 22. Miami | .17 | -.08~.32 |
| 23. Milwaukee | -.11 | -.31~.16 |
| 24. Nashville | .17 | -.04~.30 |
| 25. New Haven | .09 | -.10~.27 |
| 26. New Orleans | .10 | -.41~.32 |
| 27. Oklahoma City | .44 | .22~.47* |
| 28. Omaha | -.25 | -1.22~.11 |
| 29. Philadelphia | .17 | -.10~.33 |
| 30. Phoenix | .47 | .35~.60* |
| 31. Pittsburgh | .29 | -.23~.48 |
| 32. Portland | .33 | .92~.48* |
| 33. Providence | .23 | .02~.37* |
| 34. Richmond | .09 | -.06~.24 |
| 35. Rochester | .17 | .04~.29* |
| 36. Sacramento | .33 | .18~.47* |

(continued)

Table 13.2 (continued)

| | | |
|---|---|---|
| 37. Salt Lake City | .33 | .21~.45* |
| 38. San Antonio | .29 | -.02~.46 |
| 39. San Diego | .33 | -.08~.53 |
| 40. San Jose | .45 | .39~.64* |
| 41. Seattle | -.11 | -.28~.16 |
| 42. St. Louis | .17 | -.02~.31 |
| 43. Spokane | .33 | .21~.45* |
| 44. Syracuse | .17 | .04~.25* |
| 45. Tacoma | .29 | .02~.49* |
| 46. Toledo | .09 | -.14~.17 |
| 47. Tuscon | .38 | .23~.51* |
| 48. Utica | -.11 | -.64~.22 |
| 49. Washington, D.C. | .00 | -.41~.26 |
| 50. Wichita | .44 | .28~.56* |

Notes:

*Indicates significantly different from zero at .05 level.

**Cleveland's minimum $\lambda$ value was outside the -.05 to 1.50 range.

(Text Continues)

be read off the plot. Note that in the two cases below, is significantly different from zero.

Figure 13.1. Log Maximum Values for Alternative $\lambda$'s for the Cities of Dallas and Birmingham

Log Likelihood

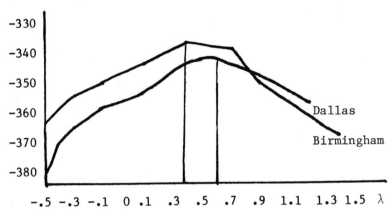

To derive a generalized density gradient, Equation (13.9) is rewritten as

$$D(u) = [\lambda D_0 - 1 - \lambda \gamma u]^{\frac{1}{\gamma}} . \qquad (13.19)$$

Taking the derivative of Equation (13.19) with respect to u and rearranging terms we have

$$-\gamma = (\frac{\partial D(u)}{\partial u}) \cdot (\frac{D^{\lambda}}{D}) . \qquad (13.20)$$

This is the generalized density gradient. The elasticity of density with respect to distance is

$$E_d = \frac{\partial D}{\partial u} \cdot \frac{u}{D} = \frac{-\gamma u}{D\lambda} \qquad (13.21)$$

if $\lambda = 0$, $E_d = -\gamma u$ which is the elasticity for the exponential function. If $\hat{\lambda}$ is significantly different from zero, then $\lambda$ should be interpreted as the absolute population density change per unit of distance. In other words, the generalized density gradient and its elasticity are a function not only of distance u but also of D(u).

The effect of this additional term D(u) is to reduce the elasticity of the generalized density gradient relative to the exponential gradient. If we accept that current density is partially a function of the character of past development, Equation (13.21) allows us to measure the impact of this past development on current density gradients.[6]

In accordance with Taylor's series formula, Equation (13.9) can be expanded as[7]

$$\text{Log } D(u) = D_0 - \gamma'u - \delta[\text{Log } D(u)]^2 \qquad (13.22)$$

where

$$\delta = 1/2\lambda, \quad \lambda > 1 \text{ and } \gamma' = \text{unbias density gradient.}$$

This implies that the estimated density gradient obtained from Equation (13.9) will be biased unless $\lambda$ is not significantly different from zero. Following the specification analysis technique, the relationship between $\gamma$ and $\gamma'$ can be defined as

$$\gamma = \gamma' + \omega\delta \qquad (13.23)$$

where $\omega$ is the auxiliary regression coefficient between u and $[\text{log}D(u)]^2$. Since u and log D(u) are always larger than zero and the Cov(u, D(u)) is negative, then $\gamma$ will be downward biased estimate of $\gamma'$. Generalized density gradient estimates of Equation (13.20) should be employed to obtain unbiased density gradients.

## 13.8. Summary and Conclusions

In this chapter evidence is presented on the correct specification of the functional form of the relationship between density and distance. The data show that the exponential function is, in 50% of the cases, not the appropriate specification. Evidence also suggests that where the exponential function is inappropriate and the $\lambda$ value positive, the price elasticity of demand for housing is greater than minus one. This suggests that future studies should use the generalized functional form to avoid specification bias of the estimated density gradient. The variation of the functional form among cities would indicate that future research should investigate the relationship between the characteristics of a city and the density gradient.

## NOTES

1. Numerous authors have provided studies of the relationship between density and distance. This paper will not attempt to review all of them, See Alonso, W. (1964); Beckman, M. (1969), (1974); Harrison, D., Jr. and Kain, J. F. (1974); Kain, J. F. (1962); Mills, E. S. (1967), (1970); Montesano, A. (1972); Muth, R. (1969); Solow, R. (1972); Wendt, P. and Goldner, W. (1966); and Wingo, L. (1961).

2. For discussions on the price elasticity for housing, see de Leeuw, F., "The Demand for Housing: A Review of Cross-Section Evidence," (1971); Muth R., "The Demand for Nonfarm Housing," (1962); Reid, M., Housing and Income, (1962).

3. Population data for the tracts are from the 1970 census tract statistics (1970). Areas in square miles were measured with a polar planimeter using tract maps. Distance in miles was measured with a ruler on the tract maps from the center of the CBD to the center of the tract. Density is in terms of population per square mile.

4. This equation is obtained by substituting Mills' Equation (A-14a, p. 227 (1981)) into Equation (A.17, p. 228 (1981)).

5. The Lmax ($\lambda$) values are calculated using estimates for $\gamma_0$ and $\gamma_1$ derived from regression using $\hat{\lambda}$. This may overstate the misspecification for alternative $\lambda$'s, since

the maximum likelihood technique implies other values for $\gamma_0$ and $\gamma_1$ in general. However, this technique derived by Box and Cox (1964) used by Zarembka (1968), White (1972), Heckman and Polachek (1974) and others, seems to be the best available procedure for determining the optimal functional form parameter.

6.   See Harrison and Kain (1974) for a discussion on the cumulative impact of time in the density gradient.

7.   By the Taylor expansion, the left hand side of Equation (13.9) can be written as

$$\frac{D^{\lambda}(u)-1}{\lambda} = \log D(u) + 1/2\lambda[\log D(u)]^2 + 1/6\lambda^2[\log D(u)]^3 + \ldots$$

Substituting this result into Equation (13.11) and omitting the items with second or higher powers of $\lambda$ we can obtain Equation (13.22).

Chapter 14


THE STABILITY AND UNCERTAINTY OF URBAN SPATIAL STRUCTURE


14.1.  Introduction


One of the implications of Chapter 13 on the density patterns for urban areas is the rejection of the negative-
exponential function.  The exponential function was first
noted by Colin Clark (1951) and elaborated on by Richard
Muth (1969) and Edwin Mills (1981).  In Chapter 2 we theoretically showed that the functional relationship between
population density and distance in an urban area is not negative exponential unless the production function is Cobb-
Douglas and the price elasticity of demand for housing services is a negative one.

Mills and Muth's estimated density gradients seem significantly different.[1]  Why are these estimates different?  The theory and Muth's (1969) regression procedure,
to investigate the effects of income, transportation and
other structural and population characteristics on population density, suggest that distance is not the sole determinant of density.  Muth (1969) found that there exists
variables other than distance which should be included in
an analysis of population density.  However, both Mills and
Muth did not examine the degree of uncertainty in the density gradient associated with omitting the various explanatory variables.

Most recently, Arnott (1980), Brueckner (1980, 1981)
and Wheaton (1982) have theoretically and empirically developed growth and vintage models of urban areas.  Their theoretical and empirical results indicate that a growing city

227

generally has a sawtooth-shaped spatial contour of building ages, a feature which in turn yields strikingly discontinuous contours for structural and population density. Brueckner's and Wheaton's findings have further indicated that it is necessary to empirically investigate the stability of urban spatial structure.

The main purpose of this chapter is to investigate the stability of urban structure by using three alternative econometric techniques. This study will shed more light on the stability of the density gradient and provide new econometric techniques for researchers in urban economics. This will also supply guidelines to future researchers in using density gradients in urban planning and location theory.

The second section uses Goldfeld and Quandt's (1965) F-statistic to detect the possibility of heteroskedastic behavior of the residuals. In the third section, Farley, Hinich and McGuire (1975, FHM) shifting regression technique is used to detect the possibility of structural changes in the density gradient within an urban area. In the fourth section two random coefficient methods are used, one by Theil (1971), the other by Singh, Nagar, Choudhry and Raj (1976 [SNCR]). Both are used to detect the stochastic behavior and the possibile structural changes in the density gradient within an urban area. This procedure would capture any changes due to population shifts or transportation routes. The fifth section discusses possible implications of the empirical results. Finally the results are summarized.

## 14.2. The Existence of Heterogeneous Residuals

Based upon the negative exponential function, the empirical relationship can be defined as

$$\log D_i(u) = \gamma_0 - \gamma u_i + \varepsilon_i \tag{14.1}$$

where $D_i(u)$ = population density per square mile for each $i^{th}$ tract,

$u_i$ = the distance from the CBD to each tract, and

$\varepsilon_i$ = a random error term.

To estimate $\gamma$, the density gradient, sample data were collected for each $D_i(u)$ and $u_i$ in an urban area. One of the necessary conditions to obtain an efficient density gradient estimate is that the residual errors ( $\varepsilon_i$ ) be homogeneous. A Goldfeld and Quandt's F statistic is used to test for heteroskedasticity for 50 U.S. urban areas.[2] The Goldfeld and Quandt method can briefly be described as

1. Order the observations (log $D_i(u)$, u) by increasing values of u

2. omit two control observations and run separate OLS regressions to the first $[((n/2)-1)]$ and the last $[((n/2)-1)]$ observations of $(\log D_i(u)$ ,u)

3. use the sum of squares from each regression to compute the F-statistic as $F_j = S_{2_j} / S_{1_j}$.

The F-statistics for the 50 urban areas are listed in Table 14.1. It was found that 31 out of 50 areas had heterogeneous residuals. Therefore, the OLS estimated density gradient for these 31 urban areas are not efficient.

## 14.2.1. Implications of Heteroskedasticity

The implications of heteroskedasticity fall into three possible areas: (i) possible inefficient estimators, (ii) a misleading tendency to fail to reject the null in hypothesis testing, and (iii) coefficient of determination ($R^2$) is understated. First, since the estimators do not have the smallest variance in a class of unbiased estimators, they are inefficient. Thus, the estimators may miss the mark for any urban area more than they would if heteroskedasticity were not present. Johnston (1972, pp. 216-127) indicates that, for a specific example the OLS estimators in the presence of heteroskedasticity were only 56-83 percent as efficient as the GLS estimators. This tendency may imply that the density gradient for some urban areas tend to be unstable over distance. Secondly, the estimated covariance matrix for estimating regression parameters is

Table 14.1. Goldfeld and Quandt F-Statistic[1]
for Heteroscadasticity.
$$F = S_2/S_1.$$

| City | | | | | | | | | |
|------|--------|-----|--------|-----|--------|-----|--------|-----|--------|
| 1. | 6.366* | 13. | 2.124* | 25. | 2.855* | 38. | 1.838* | | |
| 2. | 1.744* | 14. | 1.856* | 26. | 2.207* | 39. | 1.347 | | |
| 3. | 6.429* | 15. | 4.661* | 27. | 0.505 | 40. | 1.424 | | |
| 4. | 2.108* | 16. | 2.053* | 28. | 2.949* | 41. | 3.288* | | |
| 5. | 1.305 | 17. | 2.356* | 29. | 0.615 | 42. | 0.778 | | |
| 6. | 0.480 | 18. | 2.259* | 30. | 1.518 | 43. | 0.618 | | |
| 7. | 2.041* | 19. | 0.710 | 31. | 5.566* | 44. | 1.245 | | |
| 8. | 2.104* | 20. | 0.767 | 32. | 1.141 | 45. | 6.168* | | |
| 9. | 0.699 | 21. | 6.785* | 33. | 1.467 | 46. | 7.399* | | |
| 10. | 1.391 | 22. | 0.916 | 34. | 2.893* | 47. | 2.475* | | |
| 11. | 3.119* | 23. | 1.215 | 35. | 3.979* | 48. | 1.436 | | |
| 12. | 2.918* | 24. | 2.430* | 36. | 3.569* | 49. | 3.919* | | |
| | | | | 37. | 3.394* | 50. | 3.056* | | |

Note:

1. * Significant at the 10% level.

(Text Continues)

biased in the presence of heteroskedasticity. If large variances tend to be associated with large values of distance, u, then the bias will be negative and the estimated variance will be smaller, leading to narrower confidence intervals [see Kmenta (1971, p. 256)]. Consequently, hypothesis tests about the estimators will be made with a higher type I error than the assumed value. Finally, Kmenta (1971, pp. 259-264) has shown that the presence of heteroskedasticity will reduce the $R^2$ of OLS regression. The effect of reducing $R^2$ is to understate the role of distance in explaining population distribution.

## 14.3. Structural Shifts of Population in an Urban Area

To test for possible shifts of the density gradient within an urban area the Farley, Hinich and McGuire (FHM) method is used. The FHM model is defined as

$$\log D_i(u) = a_0 - a_1 u_i + a_2 Z(u) + \varepsilon_i \qquad (14.2)$$

where $\quad Z(u_i) = iu_i$ and $i = \frac{1}{n}, \frac{2}{n}, \ldots 1,$ $\qquad (14.3)$

$\qquad$ n = sample size.

If the estimated $a_2$ is significantly different from zero, it implies that there exists some shifts of the density gradient. This indicates that the density gradient is not smooth and that other variables are important in explaining changes in the density gradient. The regression coefficients ($a_2$) for the 50 urban areas are listed in Table 14.1. It was found that 20 urban areas had density gradients with structural shifts. Of these, 20 urban areas had a positive estimated $a_2$ and 9 urban areas had a negative estimated $a_2$. Graphically, these two structural shifts can be found in Figures 1.A and 1.B. These graphs demonstrate the typical irregular details in urban landscape.

Possible explanation of the structural shift of the density gradient are: (1) multi-centers of an urban area and (ii) different vintage characteristics of an urban area as demonstrated by Brueckner (1980, 1981) and dynamic urban

Figure 1.A

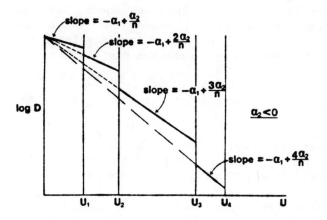

$\alpha_2 < 0$

Figure 1.B

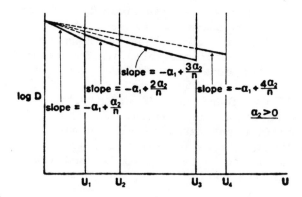

$\alpha_2 > 0$

growth by Harrison and Kain (1974). FMH's method does give us an objective technique to detect the possible shift of urban density gradients. However, FMH method does not explicitly specify the distance variable in the functional relationship and take possible randomness of estimated $\gamma$ into account. To reduce the above-mentioned weakness, a generalized random coefficient model will be used in the next section to simultaneously consider the randomness and the stationarity of an estimated density gradient.

## 14.4. The Theil Method for Uncertainty

In accordance with Muth (1969), the fixed coefficient models of estimating the density gradient can be defined as

$$\log D_i = \log D_o - \bar{\gamma} u_i + \varepsilon_i \qquad (14.4)$$

and

$$\log D_i = \log D_o - b u_i + c X_i + d Y_i + e Z_i + \varepsilon_i' \qquad (14.5)$$

where

$D_i$ = population density,

$u_i$ = distance from the central business district (CBD),

$\bar{\gamma}$ = fixed coefficient density gradient,

$D_o$ = the density of the central area of the city,

$\varepsilon_i$ and $\varepsilon_i'$ = the disturbance terms with mean zero and variance $\sigma_o^2$ and $\sigma_o^2$

b, c, d, and e = regression coefficients and $X_i$,

$Y_i$, and $Z_i$ represent various explanatory variables.

Equations (14.4) and (14.5) imply that the regression coefficient of u in responsiveness to $\log D_i$ is fixed instead of stochastic. However, it is clear that distance u is only one of the important factors determining the density gradient of a city. It is obvious that Equation (14.4) is a misspecified equation unless c, d, and e are not significantly different from zero. In principal, $X_i$, $Y_i$ and $Z_i$ should be explicitly included in an empirical study. However because of collection costs, measurement error and multi-collinearity, specification 14.4 is still used. If X, Y, and Z are omitted from the equation, it then seems much more reasonable to regard $\bar{\gamma}$ as only a mean value of a random response of population density to distance.[3] A random coefficient model is proposed to substitute for the fixed coefficient model as described by Equation (14.4) to estimate the mean value and variance of the stochastic density gradient.

In accordance with Theil's (1971) random coefficient model, Equation (14.4) is rewritten as[4]

$$\log D_i = \log D_o - \bar{\bar{\gamma}}_i u_i + \varepsilon_i \qquad (14.6)$$

where $\bar{\gamma}_i$ is a random coefficient estimate of the density gradient and is normally distributed with mean $\bar{\gamma}$ and variance $\sigma_i^2$. In addition, it is assumed that $\varepsilon_i$ is independent of $(\bar{\gamma}_i - \bar{\gamma})$.

Equation (14.6) is a linear regression model with random slope $\bar{\gamma}_i$. It can be rewritten into a fixed coefficient model as

$$\log D_i = \log D_o - \gamma u_i + \varepsilon_i^* \qquad (14.7)$$

where $\gamma$ = fixed coefficient density gradient with

$$\varepsilon_i^* = \varepsilon_i + (\bar{\bar{\gamma}} r_i - \bar{\gamma})u_i \sim N(0, \ \sigma_o^2 + u_i^2 \sigma_i^2)$$

This is a fixed coefficient regression model with a heteroskedastic error term, therefore the generalized least squares method (G.L.S.) instead of the ordinary least squares method (O.L.S.) should be employed to estimate $\gamma$ to improve its efficiency. Note that the point estimate of $\bar{\gamma}$ from Equation (14.4) will not be significantly different from the estimated $\gamma$ in Equation (14.7), but the estimated $\gamma$ from Equation (14.7) permits a derivation of the population interval-estimate (variance) for the density gradient.

Theil has presented a technique that can be used to estimate both $\sigma_0^2$ , the residual variance of the dependent variable density, and $\sigma_\omega^2$ , the population variance of the density gradient, simultaneously [see Chapter 5]. The next section provides empirical estimates of the fixed and random coefficient of the density gradients and of $\sigma_0^2$ and $\sigma_1^2$ .

## 14.5.   Empirical Results for the Theil Method

The data are the same as used in Chapter 13. The data are employed to estimate the density gradients by both fixed and random coefficient models. The results of the fixed coefficient model (O.L.S.) are listed in Table 14.3. The average $\bar{R}^2$ and density gradient of the fifty cities are .37 and .18 respectively. In employing the random coefficient model to estimate the density gradient Theil's multiple regression method is used to estimate $\sigma_0^2$ and $\sigma_1^2$. The results indicate that in Theil's regression method 13 out of 50 $\sigma_1^2$ 's are negative.[5] Since all the negative $\sigma_1^2$ 's are insignificantly different from zero the density gradient of these cities can be treated as certainty, i.e. the density gradient has a fixed mean with zero population variance. Therefore, the density gradient for these 13 cities can be estimated by the traditional O.L.S. method. For the remaining 37 cities a G.L.S. method is used to deal with the heteroskedastic nature of their residual terms.[6]

The G.L.S. equation is

$$\frac{\log D_i}{H_i} = \gamma(\frac{u_i}{H_i} + \bar{\eta}_i/T_i) \qquad (14.8)$$

where $\lambda_i = \log D_o/\bar{\gamma}$ and $H_i = (\sigma_0^2 + \sigma_1^2 k_i)^{1/2}$

Both $\log D_o$ and $\bar{\gamma}$ are estimated by the fixed coefficient model as reported in Table 14.3. The justification of employment the O.L.S. estimators of $\log D_o$ and $\bar{\gamma}$ as prior information is that even though they are not efficient they are unbiased.[7]

Table 14.2.   FHM Test for Structural Shifts
in the Density Gradient.

| | | | | | | | |
|---|---|---|---|---|---|---|---|
| 1. | -0.0707<br>(0.186) | 14. | 0.0797<br>(0.247) | 27. | -0.1134<br>(0.744) | 40. | -0.1568<br>(0.968) |
| 2. | 0.2650<br>(0.654)* | 15. | 0.160<br>(0.927) | 28. | 0.0978<br>(0.335) | 41. | -0.2862<br>(1.440)* |
| 3. | 0.2660<br>1.539)* | 16. | -0.1641<br>(1.307)* | 29. | -0.1063<br>(0.605) | 42. | 0.1694<br>(0.635) |
| 4. | -0.2346<br>(1.640)* | 17. | -0.1554<br>(1.076) | 30. | 0.7167<br>(2.512)* | 43. | 0.4818<br>(2.920) |
| 5. | 0.0245<br>(0.099) | 18. | -0.0924<br>(0.878) | 31. | -0.2572<br>(2.343)* | 44. | -0.1990<br>(1.540)* |
| 6. | -0.1554<br>(1.513)* | 19. | -0.0045<br>(0.029) | 32. | -0.2774<br>(0.986) | 45. | 0.0357<br>(0.124) |
| 7. | 0.2076<br>(1.1412)* | 20. | 0.1525<br>(0.830) | 33. | -0.0734<br>(0.497) | 46. | 0.1206<br>(0.405) |
| 8. | 0.2369<br>(0.844) | 21. | -0.0814<br>(0.505) | 34. | 0.2365<br>(1.545)* | 47. | 0.6946<br>(2.696)* |
| 9. | 0.2501<br>(1.167) | 22. | -0.0302<br>(0.295) | 35. | 0.3246<br>(1.015) | 48. | -0.00487<br>(0.0170) |
| 10. | 0.1364<br>(1.518)* | 23. | 0.2793<br>(1.585)* | 36. | 0.0485<br>(0.325) | 49. | 0.1859<br>(0.783) |
| 11. | -0.1641<br>(1.307)* | 24. | 0.2247<br>(0.919) | 37. | -0.0459<br>(0.322) | 50. | 0.5306<br>(1.606)* |
| 12. | -0.1263<br>(1.291)* | 25. | 0.4514<br>(1.906)* | 38. | 0.1239<br>(0.950) | | |
| 13. | 0.3473<br>(1.354)* | 26. | 0.2113<br>(1.078) | 39. | 0.2898<br>(2.500)* | | |

Note:   *Significant at the 10% level.

Table 14.3.  OLS and GLS Density-Distance
Regressions, 50 U.S. Cities, 1970.

| City[1] | OLS $\log D_0$ | GLS $\log D_0$ | OLS - | GLS | OLS $\bar{R}^2$ | GLS $\bar{R}^2$ | Interval Estimate ( ± ) | Index of Uncertainty |
|---|---|---|---|---|---|---|---|---|
| 1 | 9.30 | 9.31 | -.23 (-4.86)* | -.23 (-45.97)* | .35 | .98 | -.44⁻.22 | 1.22 |
| 2 | 9.78 | 10.12 | -.19 (-13.12)* | -.20 (-29.30)* | .80 | .95 | -.26⁻.14 | .28 |
| 3 | 9.01 | 9.01 | -.19 (-6.76)* | -.19 (-6.76)* | .51 | .51 | point est. | 0.0 |
| 4 | 10.27 | 10.64 | -.12 (-2.91)* | -.13 (-24.80)* | .51 | .93 | -.27⁻.01 | 1.09 |
| 5 | 10.16 | 10.08 | -.24 (-8.27)* | -.24 (-27.68)* | .61 | .95 | -.31⁻.17 | .31 |
| 6 | 9.74 | 9.74 | -.04 (-1.64)* | -.04 (-1.64)* | .06 | .06 | point est. | 0.0 |
| 7 | 9.64 | 9.81 | -.16 (-4.96)* | -.16 (-29.43)* | .36 | .95 | -.26⁻.06 | .61 |
| 8 | 9.99 | 9.65 | -.14 (-4.08)* | -.14 (-32.71)* | .28 | .96 | -.29⁻.01 | 1.08 |
| 9 | 9.12 | 9.18 | -.13 (-3.07)* | -.13 (-17.19)* | .16 | .87 | -.22⁻.04 | .73 |
| 10 | 9.21 | 9.13 | -.13 (-4.56)* | -.13 (-16.24)* | .31 | .86 | -.20⁻.06 | .52 |
| 11 | 9.23 | 9.66 | -.18 (-4.64)* | -.18 (-57.20)* | .32 | .99 | -.39⁻.03 | 1.17 |
| 12 | 9.62 | 9.80 | -.21 (-5.53)* | -.21 (-46.63)* | .40 | .98 | -.39⁻.03 | .84 |
| 13 | 9.70 | 9.56 | -.07 (-4.02)* | -.07 (-57.75)* | .26 | .99 | -.18⁻.06 | 1.75 |
| 14 | 9.47 | 9.45 | -.38 (-7.03)* | -.38 (-29.49)* | .52 | .95 | -.58⁻.18 | .52 |
| 15 | 8.39 | 8.47 | -.06 (-2.42)* | -.06 (-41.11)* | .10 | .97 | -.19⁻.07 | 2.02 |
| 16 | 9.12 | 12.17 | -.15 (-5.94)* | -.19 (-14.81)* | .45 | .83 | -.24⁻.14 | .29 |
| 17 | 8.74 | 10.20 | -.24 (-6.79)* | -.28 (-61.03)* | .51 | .99 | -.49⁻.07 | .76 |
| 18 | 8.90 | 8.91 | -.10 (-3.54)* | -.10 (-14.15)* | .21 | .82 | -.16⁻.04 | .57 |
| 19 | 9.27 | 9.27 | -.02 (-.96) | -.02 (-.96) | .02 | .02 | point est. | 0.0 |
| 20 | 8.65 | 8.65 | -.14 (-7.16)* | -.14 (-7.16)* | .54 | .54 | point est. | 0.0 |
| 21 | 9.47 | 9.45 | -.17 (-6.56)* | -.17 (-64.14)* | .49 | .99 | -.30⁻.04 | .77 |
| 22 | 9.66 | 9.71 | -.14 (-6.26)* | -.14 (-17.09)* | .47 | .87 | -.18⁻.14 | .26 |
| 23 | 9.99 | 10.09 | -.20 (-6.31)* | -.21 (-29.02)* | .47 | .95 | -.29⁻.13 | .39 |
| 24 | 9.07 | 9.25 | -.27 (-8.61)* | -.27 (-27.86)* | .62 | .94 | -.35⁻.19 | .31 |
| 25 | 9.78 | 9.78 | -.51 (-10.97)* | -.51 (-10.97)* | .73 | .73 | point est. | 0.0 |

(continued)

## Table 14.3 (Cont.)

| | | | | | | | | |
|---|---|---|---|---|---|---|---|---|
| 26 | 9.84 | 9.84 | -.19 (-4.62)* | -.19 (-4.62)* | .32 | .32 | point est. | 0.0 |
| 27 | 8.90 | 8.66 | -.17 (-4.00)* | -.16 (-11.66)* | .26 | .76 | -.23~.09 | .42 |
| 28 | 8.86 | 8.86 | -.10 (-2.46)* | -.10 (-2.41)* | .10 | .10 | point est. | 0.0 |
| 29 | 10.63 | 10.62 | -.20 (-6.22)* | -.20 (-6.22)* | .47 | .47 | point est. | 0.0 |
| 30 | 8.94 | 8.62 | -.10 (-3.94)* | -.10 (-61.79)* | .25 | .99 | -.23~.03 | 1.31 |
| 31 | 9.67 | 9.67 | -.11 (-2.50)* | -.11 (-2.50)* | .13 | .13 | point est. | 0.0 |
| 32 | 9.15 | 9.17 | -.14 (-4.49)* | -.14 (-34.10)* | .32 | .96 | -.26~.02 | .90 |
| 33 | 9.09 | 9.08 | -.13 (-4.46)* | -.13 (-13.45)* | .31 | .81 | -.19~.07 | .44 |
| 34 | 8.67 | 8.74 | -.22 (-6.80)* | -.22 (-26.96)* | .52 | .96 | -.35~.09 | .60 |
| 35 | 9.90 | 9.90 | -.35 (-10.95)* | -.35 (-10.95)* | .74 | .73 | point est. | 0.0 |
| 36 | 8.95 | 8.30 | -.12 (-5.13)* | -.12 (-17.50)* | .38 | .88 | -.18~.06 | .50 |
| 37 | 9.01 | 9.10 | -.13 (-5.27)* | -.13 (-45.19)* | .39 | .98 | -.24~.02 | .86 |
| 38 | 9.20 | 9.23 | -.18 (-6.36)* | -.18 (-16.07)* | .48 | .86 | -.22~.14 | .21 |
| 39 | 9.06 | 9.14 | -.05 (-2.48)* | -.05 (-36.03)* | .11 | .97 | -.12~.02 | 1.34 |
| 40 | 8.68 | 8.73 | -.01 (-.27)* | -.01 (-15.33)* | .00 | .84 | -.07~.06 | 8.79 |
| 41 | 9.13 | 9.31 | -.13 (-5.73)* | -.14 (-12.00)* | .42 | .76 | -.18~.10 | .29 |
| 42 | 9.99 | 9.91 | -.17 (-7.75)* | -.17 (-27.01)* | .58 | .94 | -.23~.11 | .38 |
| 43 | 8.69 | 8.69 | -.25 (-5.02)* | -.25 (-5.02)* | .35 | .35 | point est. | 0.0 |
| 44 | 9.91 | 9.99 | -.49 (-15.63)* | -.49 (-27.01)* | .85 | .94 | -.56~.42 | .14 |
| 45 | 9.07 | 8.91 | -.18 (-4.30)* | -.18 (-6.20)* | .30 | .46 | -.21~.13 | .23 |
| 46 | 9.94 | 9.82 | -.36 (-8.27)* | -.35 (-22.26)* | .61 | .92 | -.48~.22 | .42 |
| 47 | 8.51 | 8.51 | -.13 (-3.41)* | -.13 (-3.41)* | .20 | .20 | point est. | 0.0 |
| 48 | 9.41 | 9.38 | -.37 (-5.70)* | -.37 (-6.52)* | .43 | .49 | -.40~.34 | .09 |
| 49 | 9.97 | 9.97 | -.14 (-4.08)* | -.14 (-4.08)* | .28 | .28 | point est. | 0.0 |
| 50 | 9.18 | 9.71 | -.29 (-6.17)* | -.27 (-75.94)* | .47 | .99 | -.54~.00 | .98 |

Note: [1]*Name of city, see Table 14.5, $\underline{t}$ statistics in parentheses, * indicates significance at the 10% level.

The main purpose of a random coefficient model is to improve the efficiency of the O.L.S. estimators and to maintain the original unbiased property of the O.L.S. estimators [see Theil (1971, p. 602)].

If $\sigma_1$ (the population standard deviation) is not insignificant for a city it immplies that the residual variance of the model used to estimate the density gradient is heterogeneous. In this circumstance, the G.L.S. instead of the O.L.S. should be used in the estimation process because the density gradient obtained from O.L.S. will be inefficient. In addition, the coefficient of determination from G.L.S. is generally larger than that from O.L.S. as indicated in Table 14.3. Essentially, G.L.S. is a weighted regression and the weight used in this study is

$$( \sigma_0^2 + \sigma_1^2 u_i^2 )^{-1/2}.$$

This weighting scheme implies that a less important role is assigned to the population density and distance further away from the central business district. However, an equal weight is assigned to each observation if the population standard dewviation of the density gradient, $\sigma_1$, is insignificant. In this case the distance variable itself is sufficient to explain the population density pattern of a city. If the $\sigma_1$ of a city is significant, then $\sigma_1$ itself can be used as additional information in explaining the population density pattern of a city. Thus the three point estimates ($\gamma$, $\sigma_0$ and $\sigma_1$) give a better understanding of the population density pattern without relying upon other economic variables of a city.

In sum, the random coefficient model can be used as a compromise model in explaining the variation of density gradient by combining the essence of the simple regression fixed coefficient model and the multiple regression fixed coefficient model. The resulting $\gamma$ obtained from Equation (14.8) is listed in Table 14.1. It is obvious that the student t for the density gradient obtained from the G.L.S. method is higher than those obtained by the O.L.S. method.

The existence of possible trade-offs between efficiency and data collection in terms of additional variables necessitates the use of an arbitrary decision function as to when to collect additional data. An index-of-uncertainty defined as $\sigma_1/\gamma$ is suggested as a possible indicator of the marginal benefit of additional data and is listed in Table 14.3. As the index approaches or equals zero this implies that $\gamma$ is an efficient population estimate and requires no additional data. An arbitrarily assumed positive value such as .5 which implies a population standard deviation equation to $1/2\sigma_1$ could be used to indicate the necessity of additional explanatory variables to reduce the population variance. Previous studies implicitly assume the density gradient estimate to have a zero population standard deviation. Comparing the density gradients among cities and between studies requires the assumption of zero or equal index-of-uncertainty which this study shows does not usually exist.

### 14.6. A Generalized Random Coefficient Model for Examining the Density Gradient

The possible stochasticity of the density gradient was investigated by Kau and Lee (1977) using Theil (1971, pp. 622-627) random coefficient model. However, Theil's method cannot take the structural shifts of the density gradient into consideration. Therefore the interpretation of Kau and Lee's results do not take into account the possible structural changes within urban areas.

SNCR's (1976) generalized random coefficient method is used in this paper to simultaneously correct for possible stochastic behavior and structural shifts in the density gradient. The spatial structure model is represented as [8]

$$\log D_i = \alpha_i + \gamma_i U_i + \varepsilon_i, \tag{14.9}$$

where

$$\alpha_i = \bar{\alpha} + \eta_{oi}, \tag{14.10a}$$

$$\gamma_i = \bar{\gamma} + \beta T_i + \eta_{1i}, \tag{14.10b}$$

$$T_i = i \text{ and } i = 1,2,\ldots,n.$$

$\eta_{1i}$ and $\eta_{oi}$ represent the stochastic density gradient and intercept, respectively. This specification is similar to SNCR's time ordering in examining the possible structural shifts of the consumption function (as before, the observations are arranged in increasing order of distance).

The estimation procedure for estimating the parameters of Equations (14.9) and (14.10) is now discussed. Substituting Equation (14.10a) and (14.10b) into Equation (14.9), the following is obtained:

$$\log D_i = \bar{\alpha} + \bar{\gamma}U_i + \beta T_i U_i + [\eta_{1i}U_i + \varepsilon_i + \eta_{oi}] \quad (14.11)$$
$$= \bar{\alpha} + \bar{\gamma}U_i + \beta T_i U_i + \omega_i \cdot .$$

The assumptions are

$$E[\eta_{ki}] = 0 \qquad\qquad k = 0,1, i = 1,2,\ldots,n,$$

$$E[\varepsilon_i] = 0,$$

$$E[\eta_{ki}\eta_{k'i'}] = \sigma_{kk} \qquad \text{when} \quad k = k', i = i',$$

$$= 0 \qquad\qquad k \neq k', i = i',$$

$$E[\varepsilon_i \varepsilon_{i'}] = \sigma_\varepsilon^2 \qquad \text{when} \quad i = i',$$

$$= 0 \qquad\qquad i \neq i',$$

$$E[\eta_{ki}\varepsilon_{i'}] = 0 \qquad \text{for all} \quad k,i,i',$$

Therefore,   $E[\omega_i] = 0$

$$E[\omega_i^2] = \sigma_{oo} + \sigma_{11}U_i^2 + \sigma_\varepsilon^2, \qquad\qquad (14.12)$$

$$E[\omega_i, \omega_j] = 0, \qquad i \neq j. \qquad\qquad (14.12a)$$

If we let $\Omega$ be the variance-covariance matrix of $\omega$, then the diagonal elements of $\Omega$ are $E[\omega_i^2]$, off diagonal elements are zero. Equations (14.12) and (14.12a) can be rewritten together as

$$E(\omega\omega') = \begin{bmatrix} \Omega_1 & & 0 \\ & \Omega_2 & \\ 0 & & \Omega_n \end{bmatrix} = \Omega, \quad (14.13)$$

where

$$\Omega_i = \sigma_{oo} + \sigma_{11} U_o^2 + \sigma_\varepsilon^2 . \quad (14.14)$$

Since an intercept term is allowed in Equation (14.9), the estimation of $\sigma_{oo}$ and $\sigma_\varepsilon^2$ can be combined together. This is because variance of $\varepsilon_i$ is not separate from the variance of $\eta_{oi}$. $\sigma_{oo}$ is hereafter referred to as a combination of $\sigma_{oo}$ and $\sigma_\varepsilon^2$.

If we let $\dot{U}$ denote a n x 2 matrix whose elements are 1 and $U_i^2$, and $\sigma$ represent a 2 x 1 column vector with elements $\sigma_{kk}$, then a column vector of order n with elements being the diagonal elements in Equation (8) can be written as

$$\bar{\Omega} = \dot{U}\sigma \quad (14.15a)$$

or

$$\begin{bmatrix} \Omega_1 \\ \Omega_2 \\ \cdot \\ \cdot \\ \cdot \\ \Omega_n \end{bmatrix} = \begin{bmatrix} 1 & U_1^2 \\ 1 & U_2^2 \\ \cdot & \cdot \\ \cdot & \cdot \\ \cdot & \cdot \\ 1 & U_n^2 \end{bmatrix} \begin{bmatrix} \sigma_{oo} \\ \sigma_{11} \end{bmatrix}$$

Therefore, Equation (14.15a) is comparable to Equation (14.14a).

If we let D represent a n x 1 vector of observations

in the dependent variable log $D_i$, Z represents a n x 3 matrix of regressors $(1, U_i, R_i U_i)$, and $\theta$ represents a 3 x 1 vector of parameters $(\bar{\alpha}, \bar{\gamma}, \text{and } \beta)$, Equation (6) can be written in a matrix as

$$D = Z\theta + \omega \tag{14.16}$$

Since the variance of $\omega_i$ is not constant, an ordinary least squares estimate of $\theta$ is unbiased but generally inefficient. A best linear unbiased estimate of $\theta$, according to SNCR, is thus

$$\theta = (Z'\Omega^{-1}Z)^{-1}Z'\Omega^{-1}D. \tag{14.17}$$

To estimate $\theta' = [\bar{\alpha}, \bar{\gamma}, \beta]$, first apply OLS to Equation (9) to compute

$$\hat{\omega} = D - Z\tilde{\theta} = M\omega, \tag{14.18}$$

where $\tilde{\theta}$ is the OLS estimate of $\theta$, and M is a symmetric, idempotent matrix of order n such that

$$M = I - Z(Z'Z)^{-1}Z'. \tag{14.19}$$

From Equation (14.18) the variance-covariance matrix of $\hat{}$ is thus

$$E(\hat{\omega}\hat{\omega}') = E[M\omega\omega'M]$$

$$= ME(\omega\omega')M$$

$$= M\Omega M. \tag{14.20}$$

From Equations (14.15b) and (14.20), the diagonal elements of $E(\hat{\omega}\hat{\omega}')$ can thus be written as

$$E(\hat{\omega}) = MU , \tag{14.21}$$

where $\hat{\omega}$ and M are vectors and matrices of the squared elements of $\omega$ and M, respectively. Alternatively, Equation (14.21) can be written as

$$E(\hat{\omega}_i^2) = \sum_{j=1}^{n} M_{ji}^2 (U_j^2 \sigma_{11} + \sigma_{oo}) \tag{14.22}$$

for $i = 1, 2, \ldots, n$. Therefore, Equations (14) and (15) can be written as

$$\hat{\ddot{\omega}} = \dot{M}\dot{U}\sigma + e = G\sigma + e \qquad (14.23)$$

where e is a vector of random error and is also assumed to be $IID(0, \sigma_e^2)$.

Therefore, OLS can be applied to Equation (16) and can be estimated as

$$\hat{\sigma} = (G'G)^{-1}G'\hat{\omega}, \qquad (14.24)$$

with $\sigma = [\sigma_{oo}, \sigma_{11}]'$ estimated (note again, here $\sigma_{oo}$ is not separated from $\sigma_\varepsilon^2$, $\Omega$ can be constructed following Equations (14.15a) and (14.15), and GLS estimate of $\theta$ can be obtaind through Equation (14.17).

The GLS empirical results are listed in Table 14.4. Included in the Table are the OLS density gradient $\gamma$, GLS$\bar{\gamma}$, and GLS $\sigma_{11}$. Also reported are the estimates for the GLS$\beta$, which indicate significant structural shifts for 17 cities, and demonstrate that 28 cities have significant positive random density gradients. From Table 14.4 it is demonstrated that there exist some structural shifts of the density gradient. This is determined by the t statistic associated with $\beta$ listed in Table 14.3. From the estimated $\sigma_{11}$, the standard deviation of the random fluctuations associated with structural shifts in the density gradient are determined. These results suggest that the random coefficient approach is important for analyzing the density gradient, as pointed out by Kau and Lee (1977).

The generalized random coefficient model as indicated in Equations (14.9) and (14.10) allows us to decompose the OLS density gradient into three components, (i) pure density gradient, (ii) structural shift component, and (iii) random component. Conceptually, only the first component indicates the relationship between population density and distance (or transportation cost). The second and the third components represent the impacts of other urban characteristics on the population density of a particular city tract. Results of Table 14.4 indicate that 48 out of 50

Table 14.4.    Generalized Random Coefficient
Model Results[1].

| City[1] | OLS $\gamma$ | GLS Const. | GLS $\gamma$ | GLS a1 | GLS $\sigma_{11}$ |
|---|---|---|---|---|---|
| 1 | -0.23 (4.86)* | 8.926 (20.58)* | 0.094 (0.26) | -0.0063 (0.79) | 0.0343 (1.52)* |
| 2 | -0.19 (13.12)* | 10.418 (20.56)* | -0.390 (2.41)* | 0.00434 (1.21) | 0.00059 (0.94) |
| 3 | -0.19 (6.76)* | 9.832 (22.37)* | -0.504 (3.12)* | 0.00685 (1.92)* | 0.004767 (2.44)* |
| 4 | -0.12 (2.91)* | 9.638 (29.30)* | 0.0268 (0.17) | -0.0056 (1.75)* | 0.00144 (0.52) |
| 5 | -0.24 (8.27)* | 9.539 (12.88)* | -0.289 (1.03) | 0.00278 (0.53) | 0.00622 (1.68)* |
| 6 | -0.04 (1.64)* | 8.939 (14.05)* | 0.158 (1.07) | -0.00361 (1.36)* | -0.00116 (1.02) |
| 7 | -0.16 (4.96)* | 10.139 (34.51)* | -0.413 (2.81)* | 0.0054 (1.65)* | 0.00382 (1.30) |
| 8 | 0.14 (4.08)* | 10.342 (19.43)* | -0.473 (1.51)* | 0.00536 (0.85) | -0.00264 (0.12) |
| 9 | -0.13 (3.07)* | 10.943 (20.66)* | -0.449 (1.74)* | 0.00582 (1.13) | -0.00264 (0.55) |
| 10 | -0.13 (4.56)* | 10.164 (37.37)* | -0.309 (3.42)* | 0.00351 (1.77)* | 0.00181 (1.39)* |
| 11 | -0.18 (4.64)* | 10.023 (32.06)* | -0.390 (2.59)* | 0.00375 (1.09) | 0.00942 (2.19)* |

(continued)

Table 14.4 (Continued)

| City[1] | OLS $\gamma$ | GLS Const. | GLS $\gamma$ | GLS a1 | GLS $\sigma_{11}$ |
|---|---|---|---|---|---|
| 12 | -0.21 (5.53)* | 8.729 (52.60)* | 0.239 (3.88)* | -0.00719 (4.37)* | 0.00564 (5.29)* |
| 13 | -0.07 (4.02)* | 9.739 (28.40)* | -0.366 (1.09) | -0.00041 (0.58) | 0.0139 (4.96)* |
| 14 | -0.38 (7.03)* | 9.450 (17.95)* | -0.367 (1.09) | -0.000402 (0.58) | 0.00971 (1.69)* |
| 15 | -0.06 (2.42)* | 8.254 (30.64)* | 0.0248 (0.19) | -0.00209 (0.678) | 0.00642 (3.48)* |
| 16 | -0.15 (5.94)* | 8.771 (22.42)* | -0.0557 (0.49) | -0.00147 (0.58) | 0.00487 (1.84)* |
| 17 | -0.24 (6.79)* | 8.798 (34.26)* | -0.151 (1.23) | -0.00409 (1.42)* | 0.00717 (1.94)* |
| 18 | -0.10 (3.54)* | 9.247 (29.62)* | -0.151 (1.55)* | 0.000544 (0.231) | 0.00549 (2.43)* |
| 19 | -0.02 (0.96) | 8.928 (24.43)* | -0.116 (0.71) | 0.00020 (0.057) | 0.00217 (0.723) |
| 20 | -0.14 (7.16)* | 9.082 (15.35)* | -0.317 (1.44)* | 0.00355 (0.81) | -0.000710 (0.49) |
| 21 | -0.17 (6.56)* | 9.534 (27.37)* | -0.214 (1.30)* | 0.00099 (0.27) | 0.00508 (1.84)* |
| 22 | -0.14 (6.26)* | 9.206 (20.10)* | 0.00604 (0.045) | -0.000703 (0.27) | -0.00123 (1.21) |
| 23 | -0.20 (6.31)* | 11.277 (18.37)* | -0.647 (3.07)* | 0.00805 (2.08)* | 0.00228 (1.58)* |
| 24 | -0.27 (8.61)* | 10.16 (28.12)* | -0.771 (4.05)* | 0.00535 (1.02) | 0.0069 (1.15) |

Table 14.4 (Continued)

| | OLS $\gamma$ | GLS Const. | GLS $\gamma$ | GLS a1 | GLS $\sigma_{11}$ |
|---|---|---|---|---|---|
| 25 | -0.51 (10.97)* | 9.859 (22.20)* | -0.718 (2.79)* | 0.00945 (1.69)* | 0.0037 (1.68)* |
| 26 | -0.19 (4.62)* | 9.252 (27.05)* | -0.423 (2.43)* | 0.00652 (1.72)* | 0.0102 (2.03)* |
| 27 | -0.17 (4.00)* | 9.503 (19.37)* | 0.0496 (0.22) | -0.00264 (0.62) | -0.006001 (1.909)* |
| 28 | -0.10 (2.46)* | 9.0754 (17.83)* | -0.248 (0.82) | 0.00264 (0.41) | 0.00535 (0.54) |
| 29 | -0.20 (6.22)* | 10.28 (15.99)* | -0.0768 (0.37) | -0.00247 (0.57) | -0.00241 (0.89) |
| 30 | -0.10 (3.94)* | 11.138 (18.86)* | -1.010 (2.90)* | 0.1667 (2.59)* | -0.000394 (0.073) |
| 31 | -0.11 (2.50)* | 8.680 (101.76)* | -0.0322 (0.616) | -0.00126 (0.82) | 0.00786 (4.62)* |
| 32 | -0.14 (4.49)* | 8.649 (14.38)* | 0.08179 (0.278) | -0.00479 (0.76) | 0.00184 (0.847) |
| 33 | -0.13 (4.46)* | 9.012 (24.58)* | -0.0504 (0.314) | -0.00187 (0.56) | 0.000225 (0.098) |
| 34 | -0.22 (6.80)* | 9.262 (23.63)* | -0.433 (3.07)* | 0.00484 (1.48)* | 0.00712 (3.20)* |
| 35 | -0.35 (10.95)* | 10.295 (20.82)* | -0.608 (1.85)* | 0.00610 (0.81) | 0.00959 (4.19)* |
| 36 | -0.12 (5.13)* | 9.018 (30.74)* | -0.173 (1.31)* | 0.00151 (0.48) | 0.00327 (1.91)* |
| 37 | -0.13 (5.27)* | 9.095 (34.35)* | -0.102 (0.75) | -0.00233 (0.78) | 0.00578 (1.50)* |

(continued)

Table 14.4 (Continued)

|    | OLS $\gamma$ | GLS Const. | GLS $\gamma$ | GLS al | GLS $\sigma_{11}$ |
|----|------|-------|-------|-------|-------|
| 38 | -0.18 | 9.393 | -0.176 | 0.00234 | 0.00288 |
|    | (6.36)* | (32.22)* | (1.46)* | (0.92) | (3.08)* |
| 39 | -0.05 | 10.133 | -0.457 | 0.0067 | 0.000077 |
|    | (2.48)* | (25.66)* | (3.67)* | (2.59)* | (0.06) |
| 40 | -0.01 | 8.744 | -0.00465 | -0.00101 | 0.0075 |
|    | (0.27) | (26.66)* | (0.031) | (0.31) | (1.58)* |
| 41 | -0.13 | 8.745 | -0.141 | -0.000043 | 0.0178 |
|    | (5.73)* | (142.2)* | (2.20)* | (0.02) | (3.67)* |
| 42 | -0.17 | 9.227 | -0.335 | 0.00452 | 0.00156 |
|    | (7.75)* | (19.85)* | (1.26)* | (0.77) | (0.438) |
| 43 | -0.25 | 11.56 | -0.696 | 0.01121 | -0.00190 |
|    | (5.02)* | (18.55)* | (3.39)* | (2.76)* | (0.89) |
| 45 | -0.18 | 8.739 | -0.227 | -0.000903 | 0.01189 |
|    | (4.30)* | (16.23)* | (0.802) | (0.141) | (2.01)* |
| 46 | -0.36 | 9.9945 | -0.520 | 0.000510 | 0.00851 |
|    | (8.27)* | (30.59)* | (1.68)* | (0.069) | (2.22)* |
| 47 | -0.13 | 10.099 | -0.949 | 0.01615 | -0.00118 |
|    | (3.41)* | (24.76)* | (3.30)* | (2.71)* | (0.27) |
| 48 | -0.37 | 9.829 | -0.320 | 0.00018 | 0.00221 |
|    | (5.70)* | (21.28)* | (1.12) | (0.029) | (0.311) |
| 49 | -0.14 | 8.865 | -0.346 | 0.00378 | 0.00698 |
|    | (4.08)* | (17.88)* | (1.38)* | (0.72) | (0.885) |
| 50 | -0.29 | 10.294 | -1.0622 | 0.0138 | 0.0128 |
|    | (6.17)* | (23.61)* | (3.11)* | (1.89)* | (1.36)* |

Table 14.4 (Continued)

---

Note:

[1]t-values (absolute values) are in parentheses, * indicates significant at the 10% level. For name of the
city see Table 14.5.

Table 14.5. List of Sample Cities.

---

| 1. Akron | 18. Kansas City | 35. Rochester |
| 2. Baltimore | 19. Los Angeles | 36. Sacramento |
| 3. Birmingham | 20. Louisville | 37. Salt Lake City |
| 4. Boston | 21. Memphis | 38. San Antonio |
| 5. Buffalo | 22. Miami | 39. San Diego |
| 6. Chicago | 23. Milwaukee | 40. San Jose |
| 7. Cincinnati | 24. Nashville | 41. Seattle |
| 8. Cleveland | 25. New Haven | 42. St. Louis |
| 9. Columbus | 26. New Orleans | 43. Spokane |
| 10. Dallas | 27. Oklahoma City | 44. Syracuse |
| 11. Dayton | 28. Omaha | 45. Tacoma |
| 12. Denver | 29. Philadelphia | 46. Toledo |
| 13. Detroit | 30. Phoenix | 47. Tuscon |
| 14. Flint | 31. Pittsburgh | 48. Utica |
| 15. Fort Worth | 32. Portland | 49. Washington, DC |
| 16. Houston | 33. Providence | 50. Wichita |
| 17. Jacksonville | 34. Richmond | |

---

(Text Continues)

OLS density gradient estimates are negative and significantly different from zero. However, there are only 20 GLS $\gamma$ estimates that are negative and significantly different from zero. These results imply that the OLS estimates have misled researchers and planners on the importance of distance in determining population distribution in an urban area.[9]

The relationship between the results obtained for the two models is now explored. By comparing Equation (14.10) with Equation (14.3), it is found that $\beta = \alpha_2/nb$. Results of Tables 1 and 2 show that the structural shifts detected by Equation (14.2) are qualitatively identical to those obtained by Equation (4.9). However, the model of Equation (14.9) has given us some additional information, i.e., the degree of randomness associated with estimated density gradient. The existence of random coefficients associated with density gradient estimates implies that the errors of an OLS density gradient regression might be heteroskedastic.

## 14.7. Implications for Urban Spatial Research

Previous studies [Latham and Yeates (1970), McDonald and Bowman (1976) and Mills (1972b)] of spatial structure have not accounted for heteroskedasticity or structural shifts in the estimation procedure. This may lead to seriously biased and inefficient estimates leading to misguided policy conclusions. Especially, the impact of distance on the population density has been over-estimated by the traditional OLS density gradient estimates. The density gradient model has been used often by regional planners and urban economists. The results of this study suggest that other variables such as race, various amenities, school districts, mass transit and their interactions must be taken into account. Chapter 15 will demonstrate by using a varying coefficient model the relevance of including other variables in explaining population shifts. Harrison and Kain's (1974) study of the influence of past development suggests that the principal differences in urban structures are due to differences in the timing of development. Many studies [Ali and Greenbaum (1977) and Kemper and Schmenner

(1974)] have used density gradient specifications to obtain estimates of population or employment patterns. If the applications of the density model neglect the possible problems pointed out in this study, then their empirical results will be subject to bias. The results of this paper are useful to give the researcher using this kind of model some further insight into the problems.

## 14.8. Summary and Conclusions

In this chapter Goldfeld and Quandt's F-statistic has been used to detect the existence of heterogeneous residuals in estimating the relationship between population density and distance. FHM's shifting regressions technique has been used to detect the possible change in the structure of the density gradient. Theil's and SNCR's generalized random coefficient technique has been used to simultaneously detect the possible structural change and stochastic behavior of the density gradient. In all cases significant structural shifts and biases were found. In general the OLS density gradient estimates have over-estimated the impact of distance (transportation cost) on the population density of an urban area and understated the importance of other urban factors.

### NOTES

1. The reasons given by Mills for the differences were, briefly: the years are different, different data base, differing methodology and measurement error. Given the above, differences may still exist because of variations in the population value of the density gradient.

2. There are several other methods which can be used to test the existence of heteroskedasticity. Goldfeld and Quandt's method and Bartlett's method are two more popular methods. In addition, Harvey and Phillips (1974) has found that Goldfeld and Quandt method is similar to other methods.

3.   Hildreth and Houck (1968) have employed two examples to justify the necessity of random coefficient models, i.e.,

  (a) Response of a plant to nitrogen fertilizer, and

  (b) Response of a household to the level of income.

For case (a), the random coefficient assumption can be used to take care of the variation of the regression coefficients associated with the omitted factors, e.g., temperature and rainfall;

For case (b), the random coefficient assumption can be used to take care of the variation of the coefficient associated with the omitted demographic factors.

4.   Under this circumstance, the negative exponential functional relationship is defined as

$$D_i = D_o e - \gamma_{ui} - (\bar{\gamma}_i - \gamma)u_i + \varepsilon_i \qquad (14.1A)$$

where $e^{(-(\bar{\gamma}_i - \gamma)u + \varepsilon_i)}$ is log-normally distributed with mean

$e^{\sigma_0^2 + u_i^2 \sigma_i^2}$ and variance $(e^{\sigma_0^2 + u_i^2})(e^{\sigma_0^2 + u_i^2 \sigma_i^2} - 1)$.

However, $\log [e - (\bar{\gamma}_i - \gamma)u_i + \varepsilon_i]$ is normally distributed

with mean zero and variance $\sigma_0^2 + u_i^2\sigma^2$ .   This is an

important property which allows us to apply regression technique to the logarithmic transformation of (14.1A).

5.   Theoretically, Hildreth and Houck (1968) dynamic programming method can be employed to avoid the negative variance estimates, their estimates are not unbiased.

6.   In principles, both weighted least square and maximum likelihood methods can be used to estimate $\gamma$.   The function used in this paper belongs to the exponential

family, and therefore both methods will give us equivalent results.

7. This approach has been discussed by Kmenta (1971, pp. 305-386).

8. Alternatively, $\gamma_i(u) = \bar{\gamma} = ay_i + \bar{\eta}(i)$ can be estimated. The results are similar, however SNCR have shown that the estimators obtained from this specification is not consistent.

9. Lee and Chen (1982) have successfully applied this generalized coefficient model to determine the stock rates-of-return generating process.

Chapter 15


POLICY DECISIONS AND URBAN SPATIAL STRUCTURE:

AN ANALYSIS WITH A VARYING COEFFICIENT MODEL


## 15.1. Introduction


The density-distance relationship, or more generally the density gradient, has been used in recent years to explain urban spatial structure. The standard functional form assumed for te density gradient is the negative exponential, i.e.,

$$D(u) = D_o e^{-\gamma u} \qquad (15.1)$$

where $D(u)$ is density $u$ distance from the urban center, $D_o$ is the density at the urban center and $\gamma$, the density gradient, is the percentage by which $D(u)$ falls as distance increases. Previous models of urban economies have focused on explaining the intensity of land use and employment by distance from the urban center with modification incorporated to include transportation cost, income, past development and selected other socio-economic factors.

This chapter proposes an alternative method for analyzing the variable nature of the process of urban growth and change. The varying coefficient model (VCM) depicts urban growth as a dynamic process, allowing for changes in factors reflecting differences in time and urban characteristics. Using the negative exponential density function as a theoretical base, the VCM provides a means for systematically incorporating hypothesized effects of current and past levels of population, income, commuting costs, and other factors identified with present urban spatial structures. Since a number of the structural factors exhibit

255

high secondary relationships with time, the VCM also represents a basis for sharpening existing forecasting tools. Also, the VCM can be used with little additional computational or data collecting effort so it is attractive for exploratory statistical analyses of urban structure and other applied economic problems.

The present chapter applies the VCM to estimate an urban density function conditioned on factors which vary within and among cities. Section 15.2 discusses the problems with past urban spatial structure models. Data and the theoretical and empirical results on density gradients are reviewed. The theoretical basis for the hypothesized effects of the conditioning variables to be investigated are discussed in Section 15.3. Section 15.4 presents the data. The VCM as applied for changing density functions is developed in Section 15.5. The method for estimating parameters of the VCM using vailable cross section data is discussed in Section 15.6. Section 15.7 contains the results of an application of the VCM to the generalized urban density function problem. Simulated forecasts for selected cities and analyses of structural changes are reported in Section 15.8. The final section provides a brief summary and some conclusions.

## 15.2. Problems with Urban Spatial Structure Models

Clark (1951) initially employed the negative exponential function to describe the relationship between density and distance. Subsequently, Muth (1969), using Cobb-Douglas supply and demand functions for housing, derived necessary and sufficient conditions for the existence of an exponential function relating density and distance. Since Muth's work a number of theoretical results providing additional justification for the exponential density function have been obtained.[2]

More sophisticated empirical studies have also followed Muth's application of his own model to the analysis of urban density. We have derived a stochastic density gradient employing a random coefficient regression model [see Chapter 14 and Kau and Lee (1977)]. An index of uncertainty for the density gradient was constructed to determine whether distance is a sufficient variable for measuring the variation of the population density patterns in cities. The deterministic density gradient developed by Clark (1951) and Muth (1969) is, of course, a special case of this formulation. Interestingly for this chapter, the index of uncertainty for the density gradient [Derived in Chapter 14] indicated that for a number of the cities distance is not sufficient for explaining observed variations in population density patterns. We have also applied the Box and Cox (1964) technique to examine the hypothesized functional form for the density gradient [see Chapter 13]. Data for 50 cities indicated that the exponential function is not an appropriate specification in one-half of the cases. The variation in the functional form among cities and the results for the uncertainty index both suggest further investigation of the relationship between the characteristics of a city and the density gradient.

Adding to the uncertainty regarding the simple density gradient, Muth (1975), using a constant-elasticity of substitution (CES) production function and alternative values of the elasticity of substitution between land and structures, demonstrated the inappropriateness of an exponential function derived from the Cobb-Douglas production function in predicting the actual distribution of population densities. More generally, density equations derived from CES production functions, while theoretically more sound, are difficult to estimate because of limited data [see Chapter 3 and Fallis (1975), Koenker (1972), and Muth (1975)].

Relatedly, Muth (1969) found significant variations from linearity but was unable to draw meaningful conclusions about the role of an included quadratic distance term in a polynomial model explaining urban structure. McDonald and Bowman (1976) studied alternative functional forms and found that the explanatory power of the negative exponential function was improved in some cases by adding a quadratic term. Latham and Yeates (1970) developed the use of a negative quadratic exponential and Mills (1970) has compared linear and log forms of a distance-density relationship. Kemper and Schemenner (1974) have concluded that the exponential function form is not completely satisfactory in describing the variation of manufacturing densities with distance. Finally, Fales and Moses (1973) relate density to a variety of variables other than distance. Their results suggest that these other locational characteristics reduce the explanatory power of the distance variable, but represent a means of specializing the results to particular urban structure problems.

In summary, the theory and empirical results indicate that the exponential density function is misspecified because of different functional forms or omitted variables. An equally plausible interpretation suggests the possibility that additional specializing arguments may be required to measure intracity and intercity differences in the density function. For example, variations in density may result from nonhomogeneous physical characteristics of the land, transportation costs which are not independent of direction, producers with nonidentical production functions, zoning laws, the rigidity of past development, and concentration of noncentral employment. Muth's (1969) model cannot accomodate intraurban variations in the density function. Muth (1961) developed a procedure to explain interurban variations; his technique is compared with the VCM in note 7.

### 15.3. The Theory of Urban Population Density

The theoretical foundation for the density gradient by Muth (1969) and Mills (1981) and further developed in Chapters 3 and 4 can be used to determine qualitative effects of alternative specifications on the intercept and slope of the resulting exponential function. Briefly, housing is produced by using land which surrounds the Central Business District (CBD). Workers residing in these households are assumed to commute to and from jobs in the CBD.[3] The optimum household location for a cost minimizing worker employed in a CBD occurs when

$$p'(u)xd(u) + T = 0 \qquad (15.2)$$

where p and Xs are the price and quantity of housing services, respectively; and T represents transport cost.

Thus, p'(u) is the reduction in expenditure necessary to purchase a given quantity of housing (Xs) that results from moving a unit distance (u) away from the CBD. The T represents the increase in transport costs incurred by making such a move [see Chapters 2, 3, and 4 for a detailed discussion of the theory.]

It is further assumed that the demand for housing services is given by the expression

$$Xd(u) = Bw^{\theta_1} p(u)^{\theta_2} \qquad (15.3)$$

where w is household money income, and B, $\theta_1$ and $\theta_2$ are parameters. Clearly, $\theta_1$ is the income elasticity of housing demand and $\theta_2$ is the price elasticity. Using Equation (15.3) and relating formulations of the demand for housing, Mills (1981) was able to derive qualitative effects for a number of variables on optimum location. Since the model is well known, this discussion only reviews the qualitative results as specialized for the variables selected for empirical analysis in this chapter.

## 15.4. Data for Policy Analysis

Data employed consist of a random sample of 43 census tract densities measured u distance from the CBD for each of 39 United States cities in 1970.[4] Two corresponding sets of additional data were also used. The first of these consists of observations for each of the 43 tracts in the various cities, referred to as tract-specific variables.

### 15.4.1. Tract-Specific Variables

The tract-specific variables are the percent of commuters using public transportation ($X_1$) and income ($X_2$). Percent of public transportation commuters is used to reflect the impact, introduction and continued use of subways or bus systems on urban structures. Relative costs of private versus public transportation are, of course, difficult to determine. Instead of making non-testable statements about relative costs, this study uses observed behavior to establish the importance of the transportation variable.

Muth's model shows that an increase in either the fixed or the marginal costs of transport decreases the equilibrium distance from the CBD for any household.

The relation of the optimal household location and income is important because it determines housing consumption patterns in different parts of the city. For example, consider a general increase in the level of income for the residents of a city. The increase in income would increase housing consumption [(Xs) in Equation (15.3)] and, assuming this outweighed effects of increased transport cost and housing prices, the equilibrium distance from the CBD would increase for all households. On the basis of this reasoning, the density gradient is expected to vary inversely with the income level.

### 15.4.2. City-Wide Data

The second set of concomitant data is city-wide and designed to explain differences among cities due to variations in past development. Harrison and Kain (1974) have demonstrated the importance of past development on current land use. In fact, they have suggested that the principle differences in urban structures among United States cities are due to differences in the timing of their development. For example, in the Los Angeles metropolitan area dwelling units constructed between 1950 and 1960 accounted for almost 40 percent o.f the total in 1960, whereas in Boston it was only 16 percent, [Harrison and Kain (1974, p. 65)]. Two variables used to capture these effects in the present study are relative age ($X_3$) of the city and population ($X_4$). Age, based on the last signfiicant growth spurt, pinpoints the timing of the significant structural changes which occurred in the city.[5] Population levels are used to represent overall scale effects due to past development. Generally, and again based on the Muth results, recent growth spurts and population increases would tend to reduce the density gradient because of technological changes affecting transportation, e.g., freeways and the automobile.

## 15.5.  The VCM for Urban Areas

The review of previous work and discussion of the theory and data shows that the density function hypothesis for explaining urban structure has broad empirical support.  At the same time it raises a number of questions.  These questions concern the appropriateness of the exponential functional form and relatedly, the possibility that additional specializing arguments may be required to  obtain consistency among estimates and improved predictive performance. The present model provides a basis for examining both of these questions using a conventionally specified density function.

### 15.5.1.  The Appropriateness of the Exponential Functional Form

Consider the density function represented by the solid line in Figure 15.1.  For convenience, the natural log of the density function has been used, i.e.,

$$\ln D(u) = \ln D_o - \gamma u. \tag{15.4}$$

Data typical of those used to estimate the parameters of such functions are also plotted in Figure 15.1.  These data points have been selected to suggest some ambiguity in the appropriateness of the log linear functional form; a systematic pattern of errors indicates the possibility of misspecification.  Different functional forms and omitted variables are alternative explanation for this result.

An equally plausible, but slightly altered, interpretation is that the sampled units (cities and/or tracks) each had a different density function.  The plotted sample data would then represent points from a collection of density functions.  Some density functions conforming to this interpretation are illustrated by the broken lines in Figures 15.2.  The interpretation is consistent with both the partial success in empirically supporting the exponential functional form hypotheses and the inclusion of additional explanatory variables.  The latter would, of course, be based on the more complex population density theory discussed in Section 15.3.

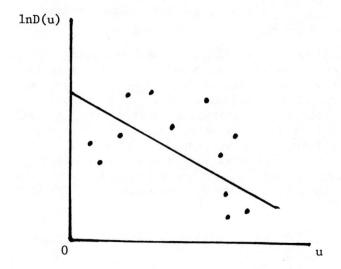

Figure 15.1.   Illustrative Fitted Density Gradient

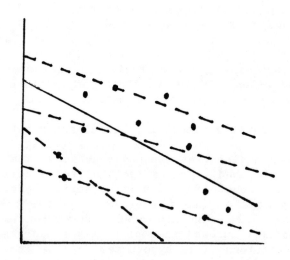

Figure 15.2.   Alternative Functional Forms
for Various Data Points

The approach employed in specifying a model consistent with the theory and data presented in Sections 15.3 and 15.4 is to use the exponential density function but to introduce systematic parameter changes. That is, the parameters of the density function are hypothesized to vary as a result of the interplay of city and tract-specific variables. As indicated in Section 15.3, the a priori basis for relating parameters of the exponential density function to city and tract-specific variables is somewhat limited. Generally, the theory only yields conclusions for signs of anticipated parameter changes.

## 15.5.2. A Polynominal Specification

Owing to the limited prior information, a VCM with a polynomial as the structure for possible parameter changes is posited.[6] Since the specification locally approximates more complex relationships it is appealing for exploratory work. To implement the polynomial specification let

$$\ln D_o = \ln D_o(X_1, X_2, X_3, X_4)$$

$$= \sum_{n_1=0}^{g_{o1}} \sum_{n_2=0}^{g_{o2}} \sum_{n_3=0}^{g_{o3}} \sum_{n_4=0}^{g_{o4}} \beta^o_{n_1,n_2,n_3,n_4} X_1^{n_1} X_2^{n_2} X_3^{n_3} X_4^{n_4} . \quad (15.5)$$

And similarly for the slope coefficient, $\gamma$, in model (15.4), let

$$\gamma = \gamma(X_1, X_2, X_3, X_4)$$

$$= \sum_{n_1=0}^{g_{11}} \sum_{n_2=0}^{g_{12}} \sum_{n_3=0}^{g_{13}} \sum_{n_4=0}^{g_{14}} \beta^1_{n_1,n_2,n_3,n_4} X_1^{n_1} X_2^{n_2} X_3^{n_3} X_4^{n_4} . \quad (15.6)$$

The parameters $\ln D_o$ and $\gamma$ are thus polynomials of orders $g_o$ and $g_1$, respectively, in the four city and tract-specific variables, $X_1$, $X_2$, $X_3$, $X_4$. Application of this revised specification to the data represented in Figures 15.1 and 15.2 is straightforward. The parameters

$$\beta^o_{n_1,n_2,n_3,n_4} \quad \text{and} \quad \beta^1_{n_1,n_2,n_3,n_4}$$

along with values for city and tract-specific variables corresponding to the data points, determine exponential density function of the type represented by the dotted lines in Figure 15.2. The special case $n_1 = n_2 = n_3 = n_4 = 0$ is illustrated by the solid line in Figures 15.1 and 15.2, i.e., the constant coefficient, log linear density function.

### 15.5.3.  Advantages of the VCM

The advantages of the VCM provided by Equations (15.5) and (15.6), combined with the log linear density function hypothesis, should be apparent. The VCM generates city and tract-specific results but within the context of a functional form which has theoretical and empirical support. Moreover, the flexibility of the VCM would appear to make the exponential density function more useful for policy analysis and prediction. Since the selected city and tract-specific characteristics may be subject to control by policy action and/or themselves comparatively easily projected on the basis of time, the model can be used for both forecasting and policy analysis, even though estimated from cross sectional data. While not without statistical limitations, the latter feature should prove especially useful given the data bases available for studying density patterns in urban economies.

### 15.6.  Estimation Methods for the VCM

The estimation procedure follows from the error assumptions, and additional information restricting the numbers of parameters for the model is expressed in Equations (15.4) and (15.5), and (15.6). To begin, the polynomials relating $\ln D_0$ and $\gamma$ to the conditioning variables $X_1$, $X_2$, $X_3$, $X_4$ are assumed to be of second order. Even with this assumption, application of the standard formula for permutations shows there are 1320 parameters for each of the hypothesized conditioning structures on the two coefficients, $\ln D_0$ and $\gamma$. The data, though extensive by comparison to some other studies, obviously cannot support this ambitious specification. Accordingly, the number of parameters required to determine the variable coefficients of the log linear density model was further limited.

## 15.6.1. Specification Restrictions

The approach one uses to obtain these restrictions is based on intended model uses and preliminary tests in the sample data. Although there are some obvious statistical problems with the latter method [Wallace and Ashar (1972)], the situation offers no alternative. First, four versions of the density function model are estimated, each with the coefficients a function of only one conditioning variable. For example, in the case of the tract-specific variable, percentage of commuters using public transportation $(X_1)$, is assumed to be

$$g_{o_2} = g_{o_3} = g_{o_4} = 0 \text{ and } g_{1_1} = g_{1_2} = g_{1_3} = 0,$$

implying structures for the VCM determined on the basis of six parameter estimates. Letting i denote the city and j the tract for this specialized case, the model given in Equations (15.4), (15.5), and (15.6) can be expressed as

$$\ln D(u)_{ij} = \ln D_{o_{ij}} - \gamma_{ij} u + \varepsilon_{ij} \tag{15.7}$$

for the 43 x 39 observations in the sample. An additive error term $\varepsilon_{ij}$ with a subsequently specified structure has been included as well. Applying the specialized assumptions to Equations (15.5) and (15.6) yields

$$\ln D_o(X_1, X_2, X_3, X_4) = \ln D_o(X_1) = \ln D_{o_{ij}} = \sum_{n_1 = o}^{g_{o_1}} \beta^o_{n_1} X^{n_1}_{ij} \tag{15.8}$$

and

$$\gamma(X_1, X_2, X_3, X_4) = \gamma(X_1) = \ln \gamma_{ij} = \sum_{n_1 = o}^{g_{1_1}} \beta^1_{n_1} X^{n_1}_{ij} \tag{15.9}$$

where the subscripts for $\beta^o$ and $\beta^1$ corresponding to the excluded conditioning variables have been omitted for convenience.

The model specified in Equations (15.7), (15.8), and (15.9) includes coefficient restrictions across tracts and cities. It is clear, therefore, that pooling of the tract and city data is necessary to estimate the required parameters.[7] In addition, plausible assumptions for the distribution for the structural disturbance, $\varepsilon_{ij}$, point to advantages of pooling [Balstra and Nerlove (1966), Wallace and Hassan (1969), and Zellner (1962)]. Although the estimation problem is not of the classic time series cross section type, it seems reasonable to specify an error structure allowing for different variances between the cities and across city effects. In particular, the error term is assumed to be normally distributed with mean zero with the covariance structure having additive components for identically numbered cities and tracts. Thus, the across city relationship for the errors assumes between tract independence except for those identically numbered. The latter is motivated by the selection procedure for tracts. Where possible, tracts were chosen to correspond between cities, with relative distance being the major characteristic used in the ordering.

## 12.6.2. A Generalized Least Squares Model

With the assumed error stucture and the across tract and city coefficient restrictions, the application of generalized least squares results in estimators which are asymptotically more efficient than those obtained by applying ordinary least squares [Oberhofer and Kamenta (1973)]. For discussing the generalized least squares estimation procedure and tests of homogeneity, a matrix representation is useful. For this representation, let $y_i$ denote the vector of 43 tract observations on the $i$th city. Similarly define $Z_i$ and $\varepsilon_i$, $Z_i$ being the matrix of observations on newly defined variables obtained by combining Equations (15.9) and (15.8) with Equation (15.7) and $\varepsilon_i$ an error vector corresponding to $y_i$. For the set of observations across cities the vectors $y_i$ are stacked, i.e., $y = (y_1, y_2, \ldots, y_{39})'$. Again the same notational convention carries over to the $Z_i$'s and $\varepsilon_i$'s. Specifically,

$$\hat{Z} = (\hat{Z}_1, \hat{Z}_2, \ldots, \hat{Z}_{39})' \text{ and } \varepsilon = (\varepsilon_1, \varepsilon_2, \ldots, \varepsilon_{39})'.$$

Finally, defining

$$\beta = (\beta_0^0, \beta_1^0, \beta_2^0, \beta_0^1, \beta_1^1, \beta_2^1)' ,$$

the set of 39 x 43 observations on tracts and cities with coefficients varying on the basis of public to private transport, the model can be written as

$$y = \hat{Z}\beta + \varepsilon \qquad (15.10)$$

Estimators of the parameter vector, $\beta$, and its sampling variance are straight-forwardly obtained, e.g.,

$$\bar{b} = [\bar{Z}'(\hat{\Sigma}^{-1} \otimes I)^{-1}\bar{Z}'(\hat{\Sigma}^{-1} \otimes I)y \qquad (15.11)$$

and

$$VAR(\bar{b}) = [\bar{Z}'(\hat{\Sigma}^{-1} \otimes I)\bar{Z}]^{-1} \qquad (15.12)$$

where the $\Sigma$ is the 39 x 43 covariance matrix, the estimate $\hat{\Sigma}$ is formed using OLS residuals, $\otimes$ is the Kronecker product, and I is a 43 x 43 identity matrix.

The four models provided by considering the variables conditioning the coefficients one at a time present the basis for the preliminary tests on which the final VCM was formulated. Comparing Equation (15.4) and the model given by Equations (15.7), (15.8), and (15.9), it is apparent that abstracting, from the errors assumptions, they differ by only a set of 4 exclusionary restrictions on the structure. These restrictions can be written,

$$\bar{R}\beta = 0 \qquad (15.13)$$

where $\bar{R}$ is a 4 x 6 matrix with rows containing only one non-zero element. The restrictions are

$$\beta_1^0 = \beta_2^0 = \beta_1^1 = \beta_2^2 = 0.$$

Two tests of this restriction are made. Both involve a structural norm. The first uses a simple F statistic and evaluates the restrictions on the basis of the improvement in variances of the coefficient estimators [Fisher (1970)]. The second weighs bias and variance – a reasonable norm given the exploratory nature of the hypothesized varying coefficient structure. This second test involves a weak mean square error norm [Wallace (1972). As shown, a sufficient condition and the lowest bound that will always hold for the restricted estimator to be superior to the unrestricted estimator is when

$$\gamma = \frac{1}{2d_L} \text{tr. } [S^{-1}\bar{R}(\bar{R}S^{-1}\bar{R}')^{-1}\bar{R}S^{-1}]$$  (15.14)

where $S = [Z'(\hat{\Sigma}^{-1} \otimes I)Z]$ and $d_L$ is the largest given value of the expression under the trace operator (tr.). This inequality can be tested straightforwardly since under the null hypothesis, the f statistic

$$\bar{\mu} = \frac{RSS(\bar{b}_R) - RSS(\bar{b})}{6 - 2} \div \frac{RSS(\bar{b})}{43 \times 39 - 6}$$  (15.15)

is distributed as non-central F with (6-2) and (43x39-6) degrees of freedom and a non-centrality parameter [Wallace (1972)]. is just the test statistic for the first norm [Fisher (1970)] with $RSS(\bar{b}_R)$ and $RSS(\bar{b})$ defined as the residual sums of squares under the restricted and unrestricted hypotheses, respectively.

### 15.6.3. The Final VCM Model

Based on the results from the four simplified VCM's and prior information to be subsequently discussed, a model incorporating effects of all of the coefficient conditioning variables was specified. In terms of Equation (15.5) and (15.6) the structure for the density function coefficient variation for this final model was

$$\ln D_o = \beta^o_{oooo} + \beta^o_{1ooo}X_1 + \beta^o_{o1oo}X_2 + \beta^o_{oo1o}X_3 + \beta^o_{ooo1}X_4,$$  (15.16)

and

$$\gamma = \beta^1_{oooo} + \beta^1_{1ooo}X_1 + \beta^1_{2ooo}X_1^2 + \beta^1_{o1oo}X_2 + \beta^1_{o2oo}X_2^2$$

$$+ \beta^1_{oo1o}X_3 + \beta^1_{oo2o}X_3^2 + \beta^1_{ooo1}X_4 + \beta^1_{ooo2}X_4^2 .$$  (15.17)

As should be apparent, final specification concentrates on

variation in the density gradient, $\gamma$. By argument analogous to that made for Equation (15.7), this variable coefficient structure can be substituted to reparameterize the exponential density function model and generalized least squares method applied to obtain estimates with desirable asymptotic properties. Based on the procedures just described, the central and noncentral F statistics can be used to test the null-constant coefficient density function model hypothesis for appropriateness given the sample data.

## 15.7. Empirical Results

Results from an application of the constant coefficient density function model on a city-by-city basis are contained in Table 15.1. These estimates provide a source of comparison to the alternative VCM's subsequently presented. The results in Table 15.1 demonstrate the aforementioned concern for the appropriateness of the constant coefficient exponential density hypothesis. Both estimated parameters ($\ln D_0$ and $\gamma$) are, for most of the 39 cities, statistically significant. There are, however, important differences in their magnitudes, especially for the density gradient $\gamma$. Also, the estimated density function for the pooled data did not explain a high proportion of the observed variation in the dependent variables. In all cases the explained variation for the city-by-city density function estimates is higher than for the model using pooled data. Although pointing up the limitations of empirical generalizations based on the constant coefficient density function hypothesis, the results are typical of others obtained using data from U.S. cities [see Mills (1970) and Muth (1969)].

Formal statistical tests of the similarity of the density function coefficients presented in Table 15.1 are equally discouraging regarding the generality of the constant coefficient model. Applications of the F statistic and the test based on the first weak mean square error norm underscore these observed differences. The null hypothesis that the constant coefficient density function, given in Equation (15.4), is appropriate for all cities, is rejected at the 1% level using both norms. Obviously, more elaborate hypotheses are required for explaining population density within and across cities.

Table 15.1.  Ordinary Least Squares Estimates of
Coefficients for the Exponential Density Function for
39 Cities and for the Pooled City Data

| City | Density Function Coefficient Estimates | | |
|------|------|------|------|
| | $lnD_o$ | $\gamma$ | $R^2$ |
| Akron | 9.273 | −0.202 (−2.86) | .167 |
| Baltimore | 9.767 | −0.186 (−12.37) | .783 |
| Birmingham | 9.017 | −0.190 (−6.38) | .498 |
| Chicago | 9.745 | −0.039 (−1.60) | .059 |
| Cincinnati | 9.669 | −0.162 (−4.78) | .358 |
| Dayton | 9.245 | −0.179 (−4.62) | .342 |
| Denver | 9.624 | −0.206 (−5.37) | .413 |
| Detroit | 9.714 | −0.075 (−3.86) | .281 |
| Flint | 9.482 | −0.386 (−6.82) | .532 |
| Fort Worth | 8.399 | −0.059 (−2.38) | .121 |
| Houston | 9.209 | −0.153 (−5.17) | .395 |

Table 15.1.  (Continued)

| City | Density Function Coefficient Estimates | | $R^2$ |
| | $\ln D_o$ | $\gamma$ | |
|------|------|------|------|
| Jacksonville | 9.205 | −0.343 (−10.34) | .723 |
| Louisville | 8.619 | −0.139 (−6.12) | .478 |
| Memphis | 9.463 | −0.173 (−5.79) | .450 |
| Milwaukee | 10.013 | −0.207 (−6.53) | .509 |
| Nashville | 9.078 | −0.269 (−8.42) | .634 |
| New Haven | 9.791 | −0.510 (−10.75) | .738 |
| Omaha | 8.845 | −0.114 (−2.41) | .124 |
| Philadelphia | 10.612 | −0.195 (−6.05) | .471 |
| Phoenix | 9.089 | −0.134 (−4.54) | .335 |
| Pittsburgh | 9.689 | −0.121 (−2.14) | .100 |
| Portland | 9.193 | −0.139 (−4.75) | .355 |
| Providence | 9.090 | −0.135 (−4.54) | .335 |

(continued)

Table 15.1 (Continued)

| City | Density Function Coefficient Estimates | | $R^2$ |
| | $\ln D_o$ | $\gamma$ | |
|---|---|---|---|
| Richmond | 8.716 | −0.221 (−6.71) | .523 |
| Rochester | 9.845 | −0.327 (−10.32) | .722 |
| Salt Lake City | 8.883 | −0.128 (−4.17) | .298 |
| San Antonio | 9.300 | −0.212 (−6.44) | .503 |
| San Diego | 9.141 | −0.065 (−2.79) | .159 |
| San Jose | 8.990 | −0.085 (−2.12) | .099 |
| Seattle | 9.220 | −0.140 (−6.02) | .469 |
| St. Louis | 10.029 | −0.170 (−7.48) | .577 |
| Spokane | 8.762 | −0.256 (−5.24) | .404 |
| Syracuse | 9.938 | −0.487 (−15.62) | .856 |
| Tacoma | 9.078 | −0.177 (−4.20) | .284 |
| Toledo | 9.835 | −0.317 (−7.12) | .553 |

Table 15.1 (Continued)

| City | Density Function Coefficient Estimates | | $R^2$ |
|------|-------|-------|-------|
| | $\ln D_o$ | $\gamma$ | |
| Tuscon | 8.459 | −0.146 (−2.88) | .169 |
| Utica | 9.421 | −0.374 (−5.78) | .449 |
| Washington, DC | 9.980 | −0.138 (−3.96) | .277 |
| Wichita | 9.000 | −0.227 (−4.63) | .343 |
| Pooled Data | 8.41 | −.010 | .010 |

(Text Continues)

### 15.7.1.  The VCM with Quadratic Specifications

Estimates for the pooled data with the parameters varying according to the scheme given in Equations (15.8) and (15.9) are presented in Table 15.2.  Recall that the conditioning variables are public to private transportation $(X_1)$, income $(X_2)$, age $(X_3)$, and population $(X_4)$.  The specification is that the coefficients for the density gradient are quadratic functions of these conditioning variables.  Examining of the significance levels of the parameters on the linear and quadratic terms for the specifications shown in Table 15.2 indicates that each of the conditioning variables is important in shifting the density from city to city and between tracts.  This general observation is confirmed by comparing the $R^2$'s in Table 15.2 with that of the 15.1.  High $R^2$'s for the VCM's based on each of the four separate conditioning arguments are confirmed as statistically significant by an application of the central and non-central F tests.  Both indicate a rejection of the restricted hypothesis at the 1% level.

### 15.7.2.  The Impact of Social Economic Variables

On a more specific basis, results obtained using public/private transportation to condition the density function coefficients show that its major effect is on the distance coefficient, $\gamma$.  For the constant term, the estimated parameter on the linear term is not statistically significant and the parameter estimate for the quadratic is only marginally so.  Estimates on the constant, linear, and quadratic terms for the distance coefficient are $-.0867$, $.456$ and $-.0517$, respectively, and all are statistically significant.  The estimates show that the public/private transport variable first increases and then, with increase usage, decreases density.

More precise interpretations of this and the other results presented in Table 15.2 require inspection of the sample data.  For this purpose, means and standard deviations of the conditioning variables as well as some other variables required in the subsequent discussion are presented in Table 15.3.  Using this information, it is apparent that the value for the distance coefficient estimate

Table 15.2. Exponential Density Function Estimated with
Coefficients Jointly Conditioned on Selected Income,
Public to Private Transportation, Age and Population Variables

| Conditioning Variable | Constant Coefficient $(lnD_o)^{a,b}$ | | | Distance Coefficient $(\ )^a$ | | | Coefficient of Determination $(R^2)$ |
| --- | --- | --- | --- | --- | --- | --- | --- |
| | Constant | Linear$(X_k)$ | Quadratic$(X_k^2)$ | Constant | Linear$(X_k)$ | Quadratic$(X_k^2)$ | |
| Public/private Transportation $(X_1)$ | 8.545 (86.08)[c] | -.179 (.87) | .222 (1.91) | -.0867 (13.92) | .456 (12.76) | -.0517 (2.14) | .32 |
| Income $(X_2)$ | 8.895 (87.68) | 5.91E-5 (2.72) | -4.714E-9 (4.36) | 6.59E-3 (2.81) | -2.17E-5 (12.54) | 8.75E-10 (7.33) | .26 |
| Age $(X_3)$ | 8.689 (85.88) | .015 (4.81) | -9.96E-5 (5.86) | -.120 (1.42) | -1.19E-3 (2.50) | 1.23E-5 (5.03) | .21 |
| Population $(X_4)$ | 9.367 (119.59) | -1.33E-6 (8.55) | 5.10E-13 (8.51) | -2.90 (22.18) | 4.20E-7 (20.92) | -1.14E-13 (16.05) | .28 |

Notes:

[a] Constant, linear and quadratic parameters for the indicated conditioning variables on $lnD_o$ and $\ $ -- the traditional density function coefficients.

[b] The index k takes on values 1, 2, 3, and 4, indicating public/private transportation, income, age, and population, respectively.

[c] Values in parentheses are estimated students t statistics.

Table 15.3. Mean Values and Standard Deviation
for Variables Used in the Analysis of the Pooled City Data

| Variable | Mean | Standard Deviation |
|----------|---------|--------------------|
| Dist | 5.625 | 10.144 |
| Pub/PR | .2144 | .1899 |
| Age | 55.897 | 42.228 |
| Pop | 567492. | 587355. |
| Inc | 9735.6 | 4026.31 |

(Text Continues)

at the sample mean for the public/private transportation variable is

$$\dot{Y} = -.0867 + .456(.2144) - .0517(.2144)^2$$

$$= .01344.$$

What this result shows is that for cities and/or tracts with a low value for the public/private transportation variable, the density gradient is lower than in cities for which it has a high value. Thus, other things equal, cities with below average levels for public to private transport and contemplating policy measures designed to increase it should expect a decrease in the absolute value of the density.

The mean for income in the sampled cities and tracts is $9,735. From Table 15.2 observe that when the density function coefficient are conditioned on income, all are significant. Evaluated at the sample mean the constant term is 9.470 and the distance coefficient is −0.2046. For the constant term, the results show that higher income cities tend to have higher densities at the center. The positive sign on the quadratic term for the distance coefficient indicates that at higher income levels cities and tracts away from the center tend to become less dense.

Age and population are city-specific conditioning variables. Results for the density functions conditioned on age are of interest in that the significant parameter estimates on the quadratic terms show that older cities are less dense at the center and have flatter density gradients. For population, signs on the quadratic terms indicate that larger cities are less dense at the center but have steeper density gradients. These results are somewhat at variance with commonly held views, possibly due to the highly simplified conditioning of the coefficients. This observation is supported by the results for the more complex function.

### 15.7.3. The VCM with a Linear Constant Term

Parameter estimates for the density function specified with coefficients conditioned as hypothesized in Equations

(15.16) and (15.17) are presented in Table 15.4. The table is constructed similar to Table 15.2 except that estimates in the constant columns are repeated for reference. The table shows all parameters statistically significant and the $R^2$ for the pooled data improved to .49. In general, the parameter estimates are interpreted as were those presented in Table 15.2.

For the constant coefficient ($\ln D_0$) the estimated parameters on the linear terms show that densities in the CBD increase with increased public and private transportation, income, and age and decrease with population. The significant parameter estimates on the linear and quadratic terms on the distance coefficient show that $\gamma$ increases at higher public/private transport use and income levels and decreases with city age and population. The former two effects would indicate a flatter density gradient in cities with higher average income and greater public transportation usage.

### 15.7.4. VCM Density Gradients

Perhaps the best way to assess the implications of this final version of the VCM is to evaluate the function for each of the cities included in the within-city sample means. The results are shown in Table 15.5. Means for income, public/private transportation for each of the cities along with mean, maximum, minimum and variance for distance, $\mu$, are given in Appendix Table 15.1A. With such information, specialized analyses for particular cities can be made using the estimates from Table 15.4. More generally, in comparing Tables 15.5 and 15.1, it is apparent that the VCM produces estimates for the density function which are reasonable. The advatnage of the VCM is thus the improved fit, the increases realiability of parameter estimates and, most importantly, the increased possibility for functional analysis of population density based on the common advanced socio-economic conditioning arguments.

### 15.8. Policy Applications of the VCM

The results presented in Section 15.7 have been argued as

Table 15.4. Exponential Density Function Estimated with Coefficients Jointly Conditioned on Selected Income, Public to Private Transportation, Age and Population Variables

| Conditioning Variable | Constant Coefficient $(\ln D_o)$[a,b] | | | Distance Coefficient ( )[a] | | | Coefficient of Determination$(R^2)$ |
|---|---|---|---|---|---|---|---|
| | Constant | Linear$(X_k)$ | Quadratic$(X_k^2)$ | Constant | Linear$(X_k)$ | Quadratic$(X_k^2)$ | |
| Public/private transportation $(X_1)$ | 8.8746[c] (91.88) | 2.3102E-1 (1.71) | -- | -2.0146E-1 (11.53) | 2.4260E-1 (6.42) | -3.7874E-3 (11.21) | 0.49 |
| Income $(X_2)$ | 8.8746 (91.81) | 1.2194E-5 (1.42) | -- | -2.0146E-1 (-11.53) | -9.6841E-6 (-7.78) | 1.2931E-10 (3.30) | 0.49 |
| Age $(X_2)$ | 8.8746 (91.88) | 5.8489E-4 (0.80) | -- | -2.0146E-1 (-11.53) | -6.3914E-6 (3.56) | -6.3914E-6 (4.67) | 0.49 |
| Population $(X_4)$ | 8.8746 (91.88) | -3.2657E-8 (-0.41) | -- | -2.0146E-1 (-11.53) | 2.5331E-7 (15.20) | -6.6665E-14 (-14.54) | 0.49 |

Notes:

[a] Constant, linear and quadratic parameters for the indicated conditioning variables on $\ln D_o$ and — the traditional density function coefficients.

[b] The index k takes on values 1, 2, 3, and 4, indicating public/private transportation, income, age, and population, respectively.

[c] Values in parentheses are estimated students t statistics.

**Table 15.5.**  Estimates of the Density Function
Coefficients Based on the VCM

| City | Density Function Coefficient Estimates $lnD_o$ | | City | Density Function Coefficient Estimates $lnD_o$ | |
|------|---------|---------|------|---------|---------|
| Akron | 9.0223 | -0.1754 | Providence | 9.0587 | -0.19157 |
| Baltimore | 9.1219 | -0.0865 | Richmond | 9.0846 | -0.12926 |
| Birmingham | 9.0055 | -0.14101 | Rochester | 9.0772 | -0.15185 |
| Chicago | 9.1495 | 0.0785 | Salt Lake City | 9.0096 | -0.2151 |
| Cincinnati | 9.0504 | -0.08339 | San Antonio | 9.0016 | -0.10121 |
| Dayton | 9.0676 | -0.16836 | San Diego | 8.9008 | -0.11302 |
| Denver | 9.0399 | -0.11955 | San Jose | 9.0112 | -0.19152 |
| Detroit | 9.0373 | -0.0187 | Seattle | 9.0423 | -0.12774 |
| Flint | 9.4459 | -0.29751 | St. Louis | 9.0911 | 0.08084 |
| Fort Worth | 9.0097 | -0.1650 | Spokane | 8.9996 | -0.2067 |
| Houston | 8.9848 | -0.04485 | Syracuse | 9.0781 | -0.16427 |
| Jacksonville | 9.0128 | -0.10718 | Tacoma | 9.0094 | -0.20905 |
| Louisville | 9.081 | -0.125008 | Toledo | 9.0388 | -0.15614 |
| Memphis | 9.0308 | -0.04447 | Tuscon | 8.9777 | -0.2071 |
| Milwaukee | 9.0907 | -0.05699 | Utica | 9.0841 | -0.2345 |
| Nashville | 9.024 | -0.1098 | Washington, DC | 9.1478 | -0.000955 |
| New Haven | 9.1092 | -0.19926 | Wichita | 9.000 | -0.20338 |
| Omaha | 9.0436 | -0.13125 | | | |
| Philadelphia | 9.1784 | 0.07524 | | | |
| Phoenix | 8.9984 | -0.15133 | | | |
| Pittsburgh | 9.1589 | 0.03081 | | | |
| Portland | 9.0365 | -0.13139 | | | |

important for policy and prediction purposes. In this section, two examples are provided to demonstrate how the empirical results can be used in policy and forecasting contexts. One example involves a representative city, obtained by setting the density function coefficient conditioning variables at mean sample values. The sample example used in specializing the empirical results is Washington, D.C.

15.8.1. The Impact of Economic Variables on Density

The analysis of impacts of changes in public transportation, income, age and population is made on a partial basis. That is, the value for one of the conditioning variables is changed while others are held at current levels for the two example cities. Initially, three levels are considered for each of the variables assumed to condition the density function coefficients; the current level and 50 and 100 percent increases in it. Results obtained using these assumptions are presented in Table 15.6. These results show for example, that in the typical city setting public/private transport at the current level increases the constant coefficient, $\ln D_o$, by .0494 and the gradient, $\gamma$, by .0517. By contrast, increasing the public/private transport variable by 100 percent raises the value of the constant by .0989 and the gradient by .10304. Similar interpretations of the results apply for the second example city, Washington, D.C., and for the other conditioning variables.

What the results in Table 15.6 show is that the major impact of the conditioning variables is on the density gradient. This is not surprising since the specification of the structure for the varying coefficients featured possible changes in the gradient. What is encouraging is that the results are reasonable for the changes considered even though some are for values of the conditioning variables far from the sample means. This indicates that the surface being approximated by the polynomial is sufficiently stable so that projections or forecasts based on assumed valued of the conditioning variables can be viewed with some confidence.

Table 15.6. Impact of the Explanatory Variables on Central Densities ($\log D_o$) and the Density Gradient ($\gamma$) for the Typical City and Washington, D.C.; Current Values, 50 Percent and 100 Percent Increases in Levels of the Conditioning Variables

| | Conditioning Variables | | | |
| --- | --- | --- | --- | --- |
| | Public Transportation $(X_1)$ | Income $(X_2)$ | Age $(X_3)$ | Population $(X_4)$ |
| Typical City | | | | |
| **Current** | | | | |
| $D_o$ | .0494 | .1187 | .3269 | .0185 |
| $r^o$ | .0517 | -.0823 | .0326 | .1223 |
| **50% Increase** | | | | |
| $D_o$ | .0742 | .1781 | .4907 | .0278 |
| $r^o$ | .0775 | -.1138 | .0343 | .1673 |
| **100% Increase** | | | | |
| $D_o$ | .0989 | .2374 | .6539 | .0371 |
| $r^o$ | .10314 | -.1395 | .0253 | .2016 |
| Washington, D.C. | | | | |
| **Current** | | | | |
| $D_o$ | .1003 | .1965 | .4094 | -.0247 |
| $r^o$ | .1046 | -.1030 | .0345 | .1535 |
| **50% Increase** | | | | |
| $D_o$ | .1504 | .2347 | .6141 | -.0371 |
| $r^o$ | .1563 | -.1385 | .0283 | .2016 |
| **100% Increase** | | | | |
| $D_o$ | .2005 | .3130 | .8189 | -.0494 |
| $r^o$ | .2077 | -.1634 | .0063 | .2306 |

## 15.8.2. A Graphic Technique for Policy Analysis

To further illustrate the results for the VCM, impacts of changes in the explanatory variables on the gradient, $\gamma$, are plotted in Figure 15.3 - 15.6 along with representative structural shifts in the density function. The interpretation for the shifted density functions is that they are cross section and thus refer to equilibrium levels. Thus, shifts resulting from changes in the conditioning variables represent density relationships to which the cities would gravitate as a result of policy changes or other possible exogenous effects. Finally, the similarity in the shifting density gradients presented in Figures 15.3B - 15.6B and Figure 15.2 shows that the VCM can be consistent with cities and tracts with differing characteristics. In doing so the VCM explains much of what, on a simpler hypothesis, would be attributed to spurious variation.

## 15.8.3. The Impact of Transportation on Density

Mills (1971b), Mohring (1961), Muth (1969), Pendleton (1963), and others have found empirical evidence that improvements in transportation tend to reduce the density gradient. The evidence provided by the VCM indicates that as the percentage of public transit users increases the density gradient ($\gamma$) decreases; in fact as shown in Figure 15.3A , became positive when the number of public transit riders exceeds 30 percent. This occurs in four cities: Chicago, Philadelphia, Pittsburgh and Washington, D.C. Referring to Table 15.5 the estimates of the gradient, $\gamma$, based on city specific values for the conditioning variables show that in all cases it was positive except for Washington, D.C., which was essentially zero. Thus, the city specific results based on the VCM, (and the ordinary least squares estimates shown in Table 15.1) corroborate the findings of the more general analysis of the impact of transportation on the density gradient.

Additional information for policy analysis is contained in Figure 15.3C which assumes that a relatively substantial number of riders consistently use public transit for some predetermined distance from the CBD with eventually a decrease in riders at further distances. Since the marginal cost of public transport is mostly time related, this result would apply if identical income groups

Figure 15.3A.  The Impact of Public Transportation
on the Density Gradient (r)

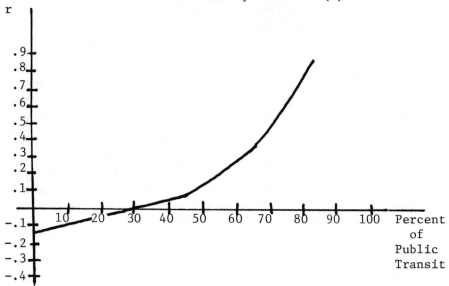

Figure 15.3B.  The Impact of Public Transportation
on the Density Function.  Examples for
50%, 10% and 0% Public Transit Passengers

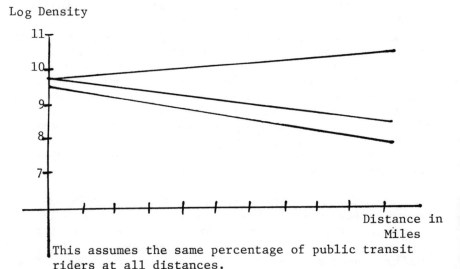

This assumes the same percentage of public transit
riders at all distances.

Figure 15.3C.  Impact of Public Transit (Special Case).

Log Density

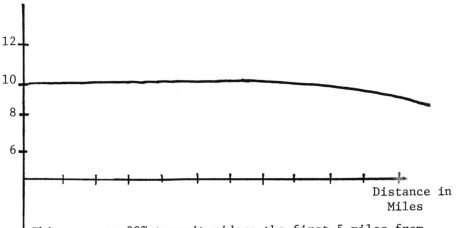

Distance in
Miles

This assumes 30% transit riders the first 5 miles from
the city center with a decreasing percentage after 5
miles.

have a tendency to locate approximately equal distances from the CBD. In general then, subsidies to increase public transit riders would result in decentralization. Since the percentage of public transit is a tract-specific variable, the VCM approach can measure changes in density patterns with a particular area of a city due to a shift in the number of riders. For example, the impact of the new mass-transit system in Washington, D.C. could be approximated for each specific tract. This allows for the development of spatial or more generally three-dimensional density functions.

### 15.8.4. The Impact of Income on Density

The other tract-specific variable is income. Again, the analysis is conducted for the representative city and Washington, D.C. The theoretical results as expressed by Equation (15.2) suggest that higher income households locate at greater distances from the CBD. The empirical results as presented in Table 15.5 and Figures 15.4A, B and C, suggest a somewhat different behavior. For incomes between $0 and $37,500, the density gradient ($\gamma$) decreases; for greater incomes $\gamma$ increases and in all cases it is negative. In all the cities average income fell within the 0 to 38 thousand range. Thus, it would seem that the increased income effect, i.e., increasing housing consumption, on location might be offset by the increased transport costs resulting from the greater value of time. These results combined with the previous analysis on public transportation are consistent with the proposition that changes in transport cost relative to income have dominated the decentralization process.

### 15.8.5. The Effect of City-Age on Density

Age has a definite tendency to reduce the density gradient ($\gamma$). This was expected because of the rigidity of older cities in adjusting to the technological development of the automobile, (see Figures 15.5A, B and C). Figure 15.5C demonstrates that if the assumption of decreasing age with distance is accepted then the effects of age lead to an exponential density function of classical shape. This was approximately the result obtained when assuming increasing income with distance (see Figure 15.4C).

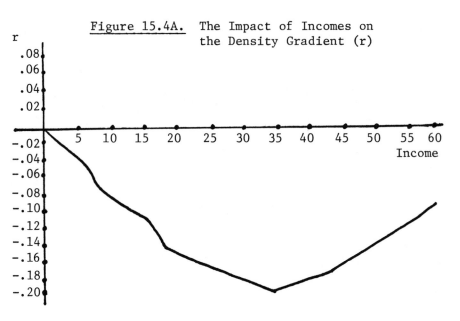

Figure 15.4A.   The Impact of Incomes on
the Density Gradient (r)

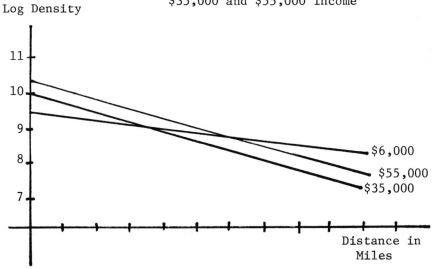

Figure 15.4B.   The Impact of Income on the Density
Function.   Examples for $6,000,
$35,000 and $55,000 Income

Figure 15.4C. The Impact of Income on the Density
Function Assuming Income Increases
with Distance

Log Density

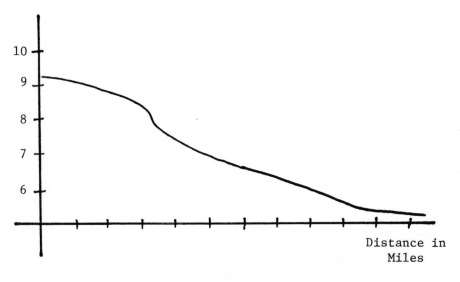

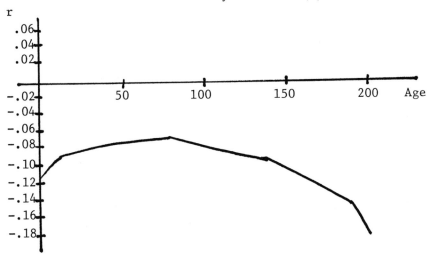

Figure 15.5A.  The Impact of Age on the
Density Gradient (r)

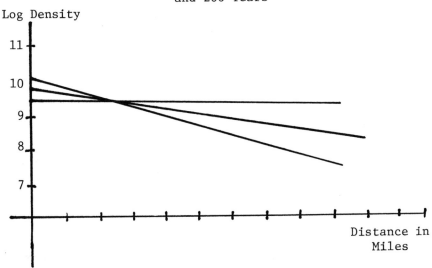

Figure 15.5B.  The Impact of Age on the Density
Function.  Examples for 90, 150
and 200 Years

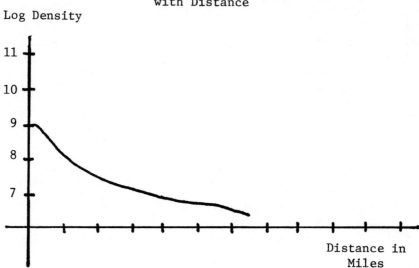

Figure 15.5C. The Impact of Age on the Density Function Assuming Age Decreases with Distance

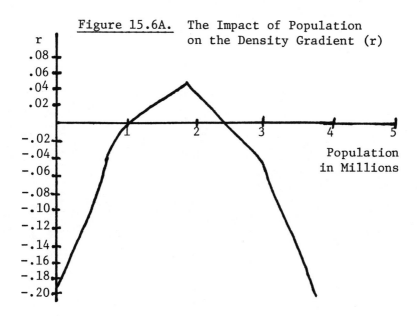

Figure 15.6A. The Impact of Population on the Density Gradient (r)

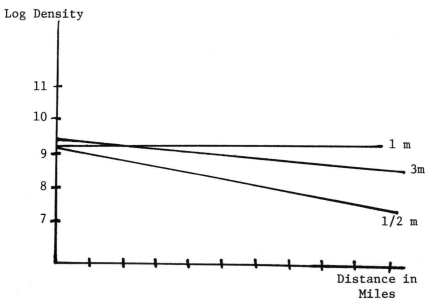

Figure 15.6B. The Impact of Population on the Density Function. Examples for 1/2, 1 and 3 Million Population

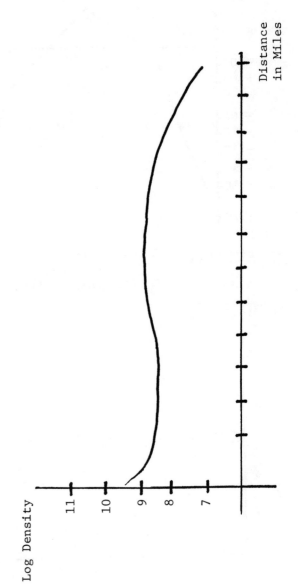

Figure 15.6C. The Impact of Population on the Density
Function Assuming Population Decreases with Distance

15.8.6.  The Effect of Population Density

For the population, as with the age variable, variation results from comparisons across cities.  Within the
relevant range for the sample used in this study, population has the effect of increasing r.  Associated results
plotted for smaller cities must result in economics of
scale for services (perhaps public transportation) leading
to decentralization.  At much larger levels of population
(over 1,900,000), diseconomies of scale seem to set in
making a city inflexible and possibly not responsive to
technological changes of the type brought on by the automobile.

15.9.  Summary and Conclusions

The VCM has been proposed as a method for introducing
city and tract-specific variables into the exponential density functions used to study urban structure.  A major advantage of the VCM is that it permits the introduction of
such variables while retaining an interpretation which can
be reconciled with the body of theory justifying the use of
the exponential functional form.  This facilitates comparisons of results obtained by applying the VCM with the massive empirical literature on urban density functions.  Most
estimated density functions are but special cases of the
general VCM with a polynomial structure relating the density function coefficients to the socio-economic conditioning variables.

Application of the VCM specification to data from 43
randomly selected census tracts in each of 39 U.S. cities
for the year 1970 provided a number of interesting results.
First, the results point to the resolution of a problem
raised by recent applied density function studies.  It is
shown that apparent questions about the appropriateness of
the exponential functional form and specification errors
associated with the omission of city and tract-specific
variables can be handled within the context of applied density function studies using the VCM framework.  In the present study the explanatory power of the density function

and the significance levels of the structural parameters were greatly enhanced by the application of the VCM in studying the 1970 data.

Second, the results showed that the conditioning variables reflecting transport mode, age of city, household income and population could be used to provide reasonable explanations of apparent structural differences between cities and tracts. Of these results, perhaps the most interesting relates income and transport mode to density trade-offs. Analysis of the polynomial structure relating these tract-specific variables to the density gradient gave results which have a natural interpretation based on the opportunity cost of travel time as incomes increase. Other results while, perhaps less novel, are consistent with the hypotheses which emerge from the more elaborate theories supporting the exponential density function.

The most important results which come out of the application and VCM specification concern the use of the urban density function as a tool for policy analysis and projection. Until the present, the empirical work on urban density functions has been largely descriptive; including tests of the density function form and exploratory analyses of possible additional variables for explaining density patterns. The present study, by introducing a method for including possible policy control variables and additional uncontrollable variables directly related to time, offers an expanded area of application for the density function hypothesis. As shown in the specialized analysis of the typical city and Washington, D.C., effects of policies designed to influence transport mode and income can be directly examined in the context of an estimated density function. Provided that density is a target for urban planning, estimated VCM's of the type presented in this study can assume an important role in the structure of planning models. Regarding projection, the relationship between age and population and time provides an illustration of how the model can be used in forecasting. Since these uncontrollable variables can be accurately projected on the basis of simple expressions in time, the cross sectionally estimated density function can be used for forecasting changes in urban structure. Although such forecasts can yield little information about the adjustment to

new equilibrium levels, they should provide urban economists with a tool of some value. Furthermore, the void in
the information on rates of adjustment from the cross section data, indicates an area of high potential for further
research.

NOTES

1. The research for this section was done in collaboration with S. R. Johnson.

2. Neidercorn, using a more general model, established the negative exponential as appropriate for population and employment (1969). More recent theoretical work
has been rooted in Wilson's (1976) entropy spatial systems.
Following a different approach, Beckmann and Wallace (1969)
and Golob and Beckmann (1971) have modeled individual trip
preferences using interrelationships between opportunity
interactions and trips. In these studies net utility for
the individual is derived from potential utility of interaction for each spatial opportunity minus the reduction in
utility due to traveling time. Smith (1975), following a
similar line of argument, presents a theory of travel preferences leading to distance-dependent utility functions.
Trip-makers are assumed to discount anticipated opportunity
interaction for the distance. Smith (1974) also demonstrates the possibility of exponential spatial discounting
behavior within an axiomatic framework. Finally, Isard
(1975) in an associated development, provides a rationale
for travel behavior consistent with both gravity model trip
patterns and exponential spatial discounting.

3. The VCM does not require that all employment be
concentrated in the CBD. The CBD is used as the convenient
reference point established in previous theoretical and empirical studies.

4. The tract-specific data, the ratio of public to
private commuters' income, and population used to compute
density for each tract are from the 1970 census tract statistic (1970). City-wide data, population and age were taken from the statistical abstract. Areas in square miles

were measured with a polar planimeter using tract maps.
Distance in miles was measured with a rule in the tract
maps from the center of the CBD to the center of the tract.
Density is in terms of population per square miles.

5. Urban age was determined by examining the historical profile of each city's decennial population growth
rate. Each city was assigned a date which correponded to
the decade in which the city experienced its last growth
spurt exceeding the growth rate of the national urban population. This technique was taken from a study by Alfred
Watkins (1976). For common cities the age data were taken
from Watkins' study. Age data for the additional cities
were computed using the Watkins technique. The authors
wish to thank Watkins for his help.in supplying some data
and the computational procedure.

6. It should be noted that Brown, Durbin and Evans
(1975) have proposed a similar scheme for dealing with the
problem of regression relationships which may change over
time. In this case the potential change is across tracts
and cities. The method of parameterizing the change is,
however, the same. In a somewhat different context with
random coefficients, models for parameter change have been
specified with the conditioning variable time [Rosenberg
(1973), Rosenberg and McKibben (1973)]. The problem with
random coefficients is that they are estimated with a more
complex error structure. Also, the fact that time as an
artificial variable is unbounded, restricts the structures
which can be used to condition the random coefficients and
still maintain consistent parameter estimates.

7. An alternative approach used by Muth (1961) to estimate the density gradient with coefficients conditioned
on these variables would be to form city and tract specific
subsamples. A two stage procedure could then be applied.
First, least squares estimates of the density gradient
would be calculated from the sub-samples. Second, polynomials in the conditioning variables would be estimated with
the first stage coefficient estimates as dependent variables. This method has several drawbacks as compared to the
one currently employed. First, the additional efficiency
gained from the covariance structure for the pooled data
used to estimate the VCM would be lost. Second, the gains

in efficiency from simultaneous imposition of the restrictions could not, in general, be obtained. Finally, a part
of the variance being explained in the second stage of the
process would be due to sample size unless more complex
random coefficient procedures were applied in the first
stage. If the coefficients are treated as random variables
in the second stage of the estimation process they must be
correspondingly specified in the first stage. Thus, the
present method for estimating the VCM by reparameterizing
and pooling the data is, in general, more efficient and, in
fact, more simple.

(Appendix follows)

Appendix

Table 15.A1. Mean Values of Distance, Income and
Public Transportation with Minimum and
Maximum Values and Variance for Distance

|       | Akron  | Baltimore | Birmingham | Chicago | Cincinnati |
|-------|--------|-----------|------------|---------|------------|
| MDIST | 2.939  | 9.756     | 7.159      | 8.214   | 4.974      |
| MINC  | 9,642  | 11,371    | 7,524      | 9,880   | 8.584      |
| MPT   | 9.042  | 0.191     | 0.109      | 0.940   | 0.244      |
| MIND  | 0.874  | 1.002     | 1.048      | 2.138   | 0.699      |
| MAXD  | 6.50   | 29.00     | 16.5       | 14.966  | 9.873      |
| VD    | 2.19   | 64.99     | 16.84      | 10.70   | 6.99       |

|       | Dayton  | Denver  | Detroit | Flint   | Fort Worth |
|-------|---------|---------|---------|---------|------------|
| MDIST | 4.225   | 5.301   | 9.256   | 3.54    | 6.523      |
| MINC  | 10,482  | 10,404  | 11,148  | 10,215  | 10,100     |
| MPT   | 0.113   | 0.086   | 0.202   | 0.029   | 0.056      |
| MIND  | 1.223   | 0.786   | 1.781   | 0.874   | 1.000      |
| MAXD  | 10.992  | 10.485  | 29.000  | 8.38    | 15.75      |
| VD    | 5.53    | 7.11    | 28.40   | 3.21    | 17.02      |

|       | Houston | Jacksonville | Louisville | Memphis | Milwaukee |
|-------|---------|--------------|------------|---------|-----------|
| MDIST | 8.27    | 5.544        | 6.145      | 5.489   | 5.738     |
| MINC  | 10,191  | 8,844        | 8,556      | 7,644   | 11,424    |
| MPT   | 0.088   | 0.130        | 0.1868     | 0.259   | 0.230     |
| MIND  | 1.625   | 0.625        | 1.50       | 1.311   | 1.50      |
| MAXD  | 21.25   | 12.75        | 16.875     | 11.009  | 16.875    |
| VD    | 17.25   | 8.79         | 11.89      | 8.28    | 5.13      |

|       | Nashville | New Haven | Omaha  | Philadelphia | Phoenix |
|-------|-----------|-----------|--------|--------------|---------|
| MDIST | 4.656     | 3.487     | 4.128  | 7.188        | 6.360   |
| MINC  | 8,751     | 11,548    | 9,452  | 10,349       | 10,836  |
| MPT   | 0.172     | 0.145     | 0.154  | 0.611        | 0.020   |
| MIND  | 1.223     | 0.601     | 0.601  | 0.961        | 0.750   |
| MAXD  | 11.000    | 8.750     | 10.623 | 17.823       | 12.750  |
| VD    | 7.97      | 3.74      | 5.68   | 16.16        | 9.16    |

|       | Pittsburg | Portland | Providence | Richmond | Rochester |
|-------|-----------|----------|------------|----------|-----------|
| MDIST | 3.414     | 5.259    | 5.555      | 7.371    | 4.792     |
| MINC  | 8,125     | 9,281    | 9,927      | 10,239   | 11,602    |
| MPT   | 0.646     | 0.112    | 0.069      | 0.276    | 0.179     |
| MIND  | 1.01      | 0.699    | 0.699      | 1.50     | 1.136     |
| MAXD  | 7.827     | 12.844   | 13.875     | 19.50    | 12.500    |
| VD    | 2.27      | 8.10     | 13.28      | 15.92    | 11.27     |

Table 15.A1 (Continued)

|        | Salt Lake City | San Antonio | San Diego | San Jose | Seattle |
|--------|---------------|-------------|-----------|----------|---------|
| MDIST  | 5.051         | 4.747       | 5.677     | 5.016    | 7.651   |
| MINC   | 9,884         | 9,340       | 9,143     | 11,901   | 11,454  |
| MPT    | 0.037         | 0.098       | 0.049     | 0.026    | 0.145   |
| MIND   | 0.699         | 1.000       | 1.398     | 0.961    | 0.437   |
| MAXD   | 13.50         | 9.000       | 11.009    | 10.485   | 22.50   |
| VD     | 12.54         | 5.18        | 7.65      | 5.67     | 22.11   |

|        | St. Louis | Spokane | Syracuse | Tacoma | Toledo |
|--------|-----------|---------|----------|--------|--------|
| MDIST  | 8.194     | 5.196   | 3.783    | 3.479  | 4.238  |
| MINC   | 10,969    | 8,809   | 10,268   | 9,217  | 10,907 |
| MPT    | 0.191     | 0.049   | 0.163    | 0.068  | 0.012  |
| MIND   | 0.874     | 0.869   | 0.612    | 0.334  | 0.454  |
| MAXD   | 17.50     | 12.25   | 13.00    | 8.485  | 12.00  |
| VD     | 18.80     | 9.41    | 9.07     | 4.29   | 7.19   |

|        | Tuscon | Utica | Washington, DC | Wichita |
|--------|--------|-------|----------------|---------|
| MDIST  | 4.589  | 3.057 | 6.641          | 3.287   |
| MINC   | 8,708  | 9,355 | 12,832         | 10,092  |
| MPT    | 0.024  | 0.069 | 0.434          | 0.0234  |
| MIND   | 0.786  | 0.534 | 1.804          | 0.349   |
| MAXD   | 10.66  | 8.125 | 15.25          | 6.728   |
| VD     | 5.93   | 2.81  | 11.31          | 1.94    |

PART VI


SUMMARY
_____

Chapter 16

# SUMMARY AND IMPLICATIONS FOR FUTURE RESEARCH

## 16.1. Summary

Mills and Muth developed models that provided detailed information concerning the requirements for the existence of a negative exponential population density gradient. Their results indicate that with a Cobb-Douglas production function the main conditions are that the price elasticity of demand must be equal to minus one and the elasticity of substitution between capital and land must be unitary.

The properties of the production function used in any urban study are of importance. The CES and VES production functions allow more flexibility and provide more information about urban structure. The elasticity of substitution (the present change in the capital-land ratio divided by the percentage change in their price) for the CES production function is the same at all points on the isoquant mapping, and is thus independent of output and the K/L ratio. The VES production function does not require that the elasticity of substitution be the same. Thus the elasticity can vary with output and with changes in the K/L ratio. It can increase steadily from zero to infinity. In terms of the isoquants, this is demonstrated by their becoming more flattened with increased output. This study demonstrates that the production function for housing (isoquant) becomes flatter with a decrease in the K/L ratio for the same output.

These properties of the VES production function are important since the studies of Mills and Muth have demonstrated the existence of a downward sloping rent gradient; therefore the K/L ratio will decrease with increasing distance from the urban center. This means that firms producing urban structures will become more capital-intensive near the urban center. Second the VES is useful because urban structures may have significantly different production functions relative to output. Third because of technological limitation the ability to substitute capital for land decreases with increasing capital intensity. All of these attributes of cities and housing construction indicate that using all but the most flexible form will lead to specification bias. The results of this study demonstrate that using a Cobb-Douglas or a CES leads to significant specification bias. That is, all of the above factors, changing K/L ratios, changing output and changing technology are significant in the production process. This means that a production function must be used to take account of these characteristics and at this time the VES serves a useful purpose in this regards.

Both the theoretical and empirical results throughout the entire book continually support the main theme of this study, i.e., the development of more sophisticated production functions leads to a better understanding of urban structure. One only has to review the empirical results to understand and accept such a conclusion.

First, Part II provided clear evidence; by using the Box and Cox functional form procedure, that the VES production function is the more correct specification. Using the VES function, the elasticity ranged from 0.95 to 0.66. The above estimates were for single-family housing. The same procedure was followed to determine the elasticity for multi-family housing. In this case the elasticity of substitution varied from 0.09 to 0.929. Next regional and time series values of the elasticity of substitution were estimated. The results were conclusive, the elasticity varied significantly over time and space. Finally Part II providews clear evidence that technological charge in housing has occurred. This again means that more sophisticated production functions are necessary.

Second, Part III examines the functional form of land value gradients. The result indicates that the price elasticity for housing has shifted from elastic to unitary elasticity of demand. Further evidence in Chapter 11 has shown that this shift may have gone into the inelastic range. Again, the negative exponential form proved to be incorrect in most cases. If the land-value gradient is not exponential and the price elasticity not unitary we again reach the conclusion that the VES is the appropriate production functions. This is aside from the fact that the estimates themselves have value for future studies of urban planning.

Finally, Part V concentrates on population densities. Again, functional form tests were performed. The data show that the exponential population density gradient is in 50% of the cases; not the appropriate specification. The evidence again demonstrates an inelastic price elasticity for housing services. The last sections of Part 5 accept that the Cobb-Douglas and CES functions are inappropriate and answers the question of what types of empirical techniques can essentially incorporate the sophistication of the VES format. One approach was to use a random coefficient model to adjust for uncertainty caused by missing variables. The approach is useful when there is no hope of using any data except distance from the city center to explain urban spatial structure. If, on the other hand, additional data such as transportation cost, and income are available, a varying coefficient model can be used to incorporate this additional information into a standard model. Both of these empirical models provide a way to add empirical sophistication to the analysis without having to rely on direct estimates of the VES production function.

Thus the VES provides both theoretical and empirical insights into the formation of urban structure. This was demonstrated throughout the book by the empirical estimates of the elasticity of substitution, the price elasticity and technological change. The VCM accepts the theoretical evidence provided by the VES and provides a different way of including this information empirically into the model.

## 16.2. Implications for Future Research

In recent years a great deal of theoretical and econometric work has focused attention on the form of production functions. Technological progress, exploitation of economics of scale and the elasticity of substitution are of special interest. Our book concentrated on three different production functions, the Cobb-Douglas, the CES and the VES. Future studies must concentrate their efforts in developing new techniques for the study of housing.

It is well known that optimizing behavior on the part of economic agents in housing implies certain restrictions on observed behavior. However, empirical studies in urban structure have not always checked whether these theoretical restrictions are consistent with the functional forms which are used in applied studies of housing and urban structure. Thus the problem arises of finding functional forms which are (1) consistent with the theory; (2) sufficiently flexible so that technological change may be estimated; and (3) simple enough so that existing econometric techniques may be used.

Two familiar functional forms of production that have been widely used in housing under the restriction of constant elasticity of substitution are the Cobb-Douglas and the CES production function. Our study has shown that the VES adds significant flexibility to the empirical model. Recently several additional flexible functional forms for production functions have been proposed which move away from the restricted assumptions of the Cobb-Douglas or CES. These are the Generalized Leontief [Diewart; (1971)], the Translog [Christensen, Jorgenson and Lau (1973)], and Generalized Square Root Quadratic [Denney; (1974)] functional forms. These functional forms are flexible in the sense that they do not constrain elasticity of substitution to some a priori base point.

Unfortunately it is impossible to choose among the available forms on theoretical grounds. A common practice in econometrics and in our study is to choose between the linear functional term and the linear-in-logarithms functional form. This was done throughout our study by comparing the log-linear CES with the linear VES functional form. This was accomplished in our study by using the Box and Cox transformation function. This transformation of variables is very useful which the functional form is not suggested by theory.

The next major step in the study of production functions and urban structural form will use a generalized Box-Cox functional form. The first application of this approach was by Khaled (1977) and Berndt and Khaled (1980). The major characteristic of this generalized Box and Cox functional form is that it provides a clear break between the major functional forms currently in use. Essentially it is assumed that there exists a dual cost function reflecting the production technology. An alternative notion of total factor productivity can be obtained from the point of view of the dual cost function.

Thus future research in housing and urban spatial structure will benefit by incorporating duality theory into the study of urban shape. This will provide a superior method of estimation the elasticity of substitution, returns to scale and technological change.

Appendix A

HOYT'S CHICAGO LAND VALUE DATA

| CODE* | DISTANCE* | LAND VALUE/ACRE FOR YEAR* | | | | | |
|-------|-----------|------|------|------|------|------|------|
|       |           | 1836 | 1857 | 1873 | 1892 | 1910 | 1928 |
| 1  | 12.58 | 3  | 20  | 300  | 1000  | 850   | 13000  |
| 2  | 11.72 | 3  | 20  | 500  | 1000  | 650   | 5700   |
| 3  | 11.15 | 3  | 25  | 1000 | 1000  | 1920  | 10308  |
| 4  | 10.29 | 3  | 30  | 500  | 500   | 1250  | 16000  |
| 5  | 9.43  | 3  | 30  | 500  | 400   | 1000  | 10550  |
| 6  | 8.86  | 5  | 40  | 500  | 400   | 600   | 11500  |
| 7  | 8.29  | 5  | 50  | 500  | 400   | 435   | 25000  |
| 8  | 8.00  | 10 | 100 | 500  | 500   | 1000  | 35000  |
| 9  | 8.86  | 5  | 50  | 500  | 400   | 428   | 30000  |
| 10 | 8.29  | 10 | 90  | 1000 | 1000  | 4710  | 63000  |
| 11 | 8.00  | 15 | 150 | 1500 | 2000  | 17000 | 200000 |
| 12 | 7.43  | 15 | 125 | 1000 | 2000  | 4300  | 43300  |
| 13 | 7.15  | 20 | 200 | 1500 | 5000  | 13000 | 119000 |
| 14 | 11.43 | 3  | 20  | N/A  | 500   | N/A   | N/A    |
| 15 | 10.58 | 3  | 25  | N/A  | 500   | N/A   | N/A    |
| 16 | 9.72  | 3  | 50  | 500  | 1000  | N/A   | N/A    |
| 17 | 8.86  | 3  | 60  | 500  | 500   | N/A   | N/A    |
| 18 | 8.00  | 5  | 75  | 875  | 500   | N/A   | N/A    |
| 19 | 7.43  | 10 | 100 | 875  | 500   | N/A   | N/A    |
| 20 | 6.86  | 20 | 125 | 1000 | 1000  | N/A   | N/A    |
| 21 | 6.58  | 20 | 150 | 1500 | 2500  | N/A   | N/A    |
| 22 | 6.00  | 25 | 250 | 2000 | 7500  | N/A   | N/A    |
| 23 | 9.15  | 3  | 50  | 300  | 400   | 1000  | 16670  |
| 24 | 8.29  | 5  | 60  | 2000 | 800   | 2820  | 36235  |
| 25 | 7.43  | 10 | 100 | 2000 | 1000  | 3150  | 26400  |
| 26 | 6.86  | 15 | 125 | 1000 | 1500  | 4000  | 52500  |
| 27 | 6.29  | 20 | 150 | 1000 | 3750  | 4780  | 46250  |
| 28 | 6.00  | 20 | 200 | 1500 | 7500  | 10950 | 65000  |
| 29 | 5.15  | 35 | 400 | 3000 | 12500 | 13500 | 128000 |
| 30 | 10.86 | 3  | 25  | 100  | N/A   | N/A   | 6000   |

| | | | | LAND | VALUE/ACRE | FOR | YEAR |
|---|---|---|---|---|---|---|---|
| Code* | Distance* | 1836 | 1857 | 1873 | 1892 | 1910 | 1928 |
| 31 | 10.29 | 3 | 25 | 100 | 400 | 500 | 8000 |
| 32 | 9.43 | 3 | 50 | 100 | 400 | 750 | 12200 |
| 33 | 8.58 | 5 | 75 | 300 | 400 | 750 | 20200 |
| 34 | 7.72 | 5 | 75 | 1000 | 425 | 1000 | 34000 |
| 35 | 6.86 | 10 | 100 | 3000 | 1000 | 3580 | 31770 |
| 36 | 6.00 | 20 | 150 | 3000 | 1600 | 5600 | 34300 |
| 37 | 5.43 | 25 | 250 | 2000 | 1900 | 4000 | 18000 |
| 38 | 4.86 | 30 | 400 | 2000 | 4000 | 9430 | 42000 |
| 39 | 4.58 | 50 | 800 | 4500 | 7500 | 15400 | 71700 |
| 40 | 4.29 | 50 | N/A | 7000 | 20000 | 36000 | 200000 |
| 41 | 9.15 | 3 | 50 | 150 | 500 | N/A | N/A |
| 42 | 8.29 | 5 | 73 | 300 | 800 | N/A | N/A |
| 43 | 7.43 | 5 | 100 | 1000 | 1000 | N/A | N/A |
| 44 | 6.29 | 10 | 125 | 1000 | 2000 | N/A | N/A |
| 45 | 5.43 | 20 | 125 | 3000 | 3000 | N/A | N/A |
| 46 | 4.58 | 30 | 300 | 3000 | 3500 | N/A | N/A |
| 47 | 4.29 | 40 | 300 | 4000 | 5000 | N/A | N/A |
| 48 | 3.43 | 50 | 400 | 7500 | 10000 | N/A | N/A |
| 49 | 2.86 | 75 | 800 | 25000 | 25000 | N/A | N/A |
| 50 | 8.86 | 3 | 75 | 200 | 1000 | 1800 | 17720 |
| 51 | 8.00 | 5 | 100 | 300 | 1500 | 2222 | 16600 |
| 52 | 6.86 | 5 | 125 | 1000 | 2000 | 1500 | 27500 |
| 53 | 6.00 | 10 | 150 | 1200 | 2500 | 2530 | 27500 |
| 54 | 5.15 | 20 | 175 | 2000 | 4000 | 5730 | 38500 |
| 55 | 4.29 | 35 | 300 | 2500 | 8000 | 9250 | 43000 |
| 56 | 3.43 | 50 | 500 | 5000 | 10000 | 10450 | 22300 |
| 57 | 2.86 | 75 | 1400 | 10000 | 11000 | 4650 | 26600 |
| 58 | 2.29 | 150 | 5000 | 25000 | 30000 | 24600 | 115000 |
| 59 | 7.43 | 5 | 100 | N/A | 2500 | 4500 | 50000 |
| 60 | 6.86 | 5 | 200 | 1000 | 3000 | 4000 | 32800 |

| CODE* | DISTANCE* | LAND VALUE/ACRE FOR YEAR | | | | | |
|---|---|---|---|---|---|---|---|
| | | 1836 | 1857 | 1873 | 1892 | 1910 | 1928 |
| 61 | 5.72 | 15 | 200 | 1500 | 5000 | 5300 | 26200 |
| 62 | 4.86 | 25 | 300 | 2000 | 8400 | 4120 | 27400 |
| 63 | 4.72 | 75 | 500 | 3000 | 11750 | 10600 | 33000 |
| 64 | 2.86 | 100 | 2000 | 7500 | 13000 | 14700 | 40500 |
| 65 | 2.00 | 300 | 3000 | 10000 | 17250 | 27000 | 40000 |
| 66 | 1.43 | 500 | 12000 | 48000 | 85000 | 52600 | 153650 |
| 67 | 1.15 | 600 | N/A | 36000 | 100000 | 80000 | 382500 |
| 68 | 7.15 | 5 | 200 | 1000 | N/A | N/A | N/A |
| 69 | 6.58 | 10 | 300 | 1500 | N/A | N/A | N/A |
| 70 | 5.72 | 25 | 300 | 3000 | N/A | N/A | N/A |
| 71 | 4.58 | 30 | 300 | 5000 | N/A | N/A | N/A |
| 72 | 3.43 | 125 | 1200 | 9000 | N/A | N/A | N/A |
| 73 | 2.58 | 200 | 3000 | 25000 | N/A | N/A | N/A |
| 74 | 1.72 | 750 | 12000 | 30000 | N/A | N/A | N/A |
| 75 | 0.86 | 1500 | 16000 | 72000 | N/A | N/A | N/A |
| 76 | 0.58 | 2000 | 25000 | 240000 | N/A | N/A | N/A |
| 77 | 7.15 | 5 | 200 | 1000 | 4500 | 4500 | 4500 |
| 78 | 6.58 | 10 | 300 | 1000 | 7000 | 6400 | 59000 |
| 79 | 5.72 | 25 | 300 | 2000 | 10500 | 8000 | 42800 |
| 80 | 4.58 | 50 | 300 | 3000 | 18500 | 13000 | 66700 |
| 81 | 3.72 | 125 | 500 | 5000 | 19000 | 11100 | 32000 |
| 82 | 2.58 | 200 | 2500 | 12000 | 30000 | 17600 | 48000 |
| 83 | 1.72 | 500 | 8000 | 20000 | 40000 | 32600 | 80000 |
| 84 | 0.86 | 1000 | 20000 | 25000 | 120000 | 130000 | 200000 |
| 85 | 0.58 | 3000 | 50000 | 7000 | N/A | N/A | N/A |
| 86 | 5.43 | 15 | 200 | 1500 | 3500 | 4000 | 27500 |
| 87 | 4.86 | 25 | 300 | 2500 | 9000 | 8750 | 45300 |
| 88 | 3.72 | 100 | 500 | 3500 | 10800 | 12500 | 28500 |
| 89 | 2.86 | 150 | 1500 | 6000 | 13000 | 13800 | 24000 |
| 90 | 2.29 | 500 | 5000 | 15000 | 20000 | 24200 | 37400 |
| 91 | 1.72 | 500 | 10000 | 28000 | 25000 | N/A | N/A |
| 92 | 1.15 | 600 | 20000 | 62500 | 150000 | 110000 | 125000 |
| 93 | 6.00 | 10 | 150 | 1200 | N/A | N/A | N/A |
| 94 | 5.43 | 15 | 250 | 2500 | N/A | N/A | N/A |
| 95 | 4.29 | 40 | 500 | 3500 | N/A | N/A | N/A |

| | | | LAND | VALUE/ACRE | FOR | YEAR | |
|---|---|---|---|---|---|---|---|
| CODE* | DISTANCE* | 1836 | 1857 | 1873 | 1892 | 1910 | 1928 |
| 96 | 3.72 | 60 | 1000 | 1000 | N/A | N/A | N/A |
| 97 | 3.15 | 100 | 3000 | 10000 | N/A | N/A | N/A |
| 98 | 2.58 | 250 | 4000 | 15000 | N/A | N/A | N/A |
| 99 | 2.29 | 300 | 7500 | 40000 | N/A | N/A | N/A |
| 100 | 6.58 | 10 | 100 | 800 | 1500 | 2700 | 10700 |
| 101 | 5.72 | 15 | 250 | 1000 | 2000 | 3000 | 12000 |
| 102 | 5.15 | 40 | 450 | 3000 | 2500 | 3665 | 28500 |
| 103 | 4.29 | 40 | 500 | 2000 | 5000 | 5000 | 10600 |
| 104 | 4.00 | 40 | 500 | 4000 | 8000 | 11000 | 24000 |
| 105 | 3.72 | 40 | 1000 | 8000 | 12500 | 11600 | 17300 |
| 106 | 3.43 | 150 | 1500 | 30000 | 60000 | 30000 | 42000 |
| 107 | 7.43 | 10 | 50 | 600 | 2000 | 540 | 5782 |
| 108 | 6.58 | 15 | 100 | 1000 | 2500 | 1100 | 13090 |
| 109 | 6.00 | 30 | 150 | 2000 | 3000 | 2160 | 19000 |
| 110 | 5.15 | 30 | 200 | 2000 | 4000 | 3125 | 41000 |
| 111 | 4.86 | 30 | 300 | 4000 | 7000 | 7700 | 42000 |
| 112 | 4.58 | 30 | 500 | 6000 | 12500 | 7700 | 10700 |
| 113 | 4.58 | 35 | 500 | 20000 | 36500 | 24500 | 31250 |
| 114 | 4.58 | 60 | 600 | 20000 | 60000 | 40000 | 100000 |
| 115 | 10.29 | N/A | 20 | N/A | N/A | N/A | N/A |
| 116 | 9.43 | N/A | 25 | N/A | N/A | N/A | N/A |
| 117 | 8.58 | N/A | 30 | 500 | N/A | N/A | N/A |
| 118 | 7.72 | 5 | 40 | 600 | 2000 | N/A | N/A |
| 119 | 7.15 | 15 | 75 | 1000 | 2500 | N/A | N/A |
| 120 | 6.58 | 20 | 100 | 1000 | 3000 | N/A | N/A |
| 121 | 6.00 | 20 | 100 | 2000 | 3000 | N/A | N/A |
| 122 | 5.72 | 20 | 300 | 3000 | N/A | N/A | N/A |
| 123 | 5.43 | 25 | 300 | 3000 | N/A | N/A | N/A |
| 124 | 5.43 | 25 | 500 | 15000 | N/A | N/A | N/A |
| 125 | 5.43 | 40 | 600 | 15000 | N/A | N/A | N/A |
| 126 | 10.58 | 3 | 20 | 200 | 500 | 300 | 4360 |
| 127 | 10.00 | 3 | 25 | 200 | 500 | 300 | 6500 |
| 128 | 9.15 | 3 | 30 | 300 | 1000 | 300 | 4400 |
| 129 | 8.29 | 3 | 40 | 400 | 2000 | 763 | 9387 |
| 130 | 7.72 | 5 | 75 | 600 | 2500 | 1380 | 16668 |

| CODE* | DISTANCE* | LAND VALUE/ACRE FOR YEAR | | | | | |
|---|---|---|---|---|---|---|---|
| | | 1836 | 1857 | 1873 | 1892 | 1910 | 1928 |
| 131 | 7.15 | 75 | 100 | 800 | 3000 | 880 | 29000 |
| 132 | 6.58 | 75 | 100 | 2000 | 4500 | 3100 | 17300 |
| 133 | 6.29 | 10 | 125 | 3000 | 6000 | 9200 | 29900 |
| 134 | 6.00 | 125 | 200 | 3000 | 12500 | 11440 | 29200 |
| 135 | 6.29 | 15 | 300 | 10000 | 33334 | 22667 | 40000 |
| 136 | 6.58 | 25 | 300 | 5000 | 40000 | 20000 | 116000 |
| 137 | 6.86 | 30 | 400 | N/A | N/A | 28800 | 320000 |
| 138 | 9.15 | 3 | 30 | 300 | 2000 | 500 | 6000 |
| 139 | 8.58 | 3 | 40 | 300 | 2500 | 900 | 12370 |
| 140 | 8.00 | 3 | 50 | 600 | 3000 | 1300 | 25500 |
| 141 | 7.72 | 5 | 75 | 1000 | 4000 | 2600 | 16700 |
| 142 | 7.43 | 75 | 100 | 1500 | 5000 | 6700 | 30000 |
| 143 | 7.15 | 10 | 150 | 3000 | 25000 | 13800 | 51400 |
| 144 | 7.15 | 125 | 200 | 3000 | 15000 | 6000 | 25300 |
| 145 | 7.15 | 25 | 200 | 4000 | 20000 | 10000 | 72300 |
| 146 | 7.72 | 25 | 300 | 3000 | 15000 | 7000 | 106000 |
| 147 | 9.72 | 3 | 30 | 300 | 1500 | N/A | N/A |
| 148 | 9.43 | 3 | 40 | 500 | 2000 | N/A | N/A |
| 149 | 8.86 | 3 | 50 | 500 | 3000 | N/A | N/A |
| 150 | 8.58 | 3 | 60 | 1000 | 3500 | N/A | N/A |
| 151 | 8.29 | 5 | 75 | 1500 | 4000 | N/A | N/A |
| 152 | 8.00 | 75 | 100 | 2500 | 5000 | N/A | N/A |
| 153 | 8.00 | 125 | 100 | 2000 | N/A | N/A | N/A |
| 154 | 8.29 | 25 | 100 | 2000 | N/A | N/A | N/A |
| 155 | 8.58 | 25 | 100 | 1500 | N/A | N/A | N/A |
| 156 | 8.58 | 25 | 200 | 20000 | N/A | N/A | N/A |
| 157 | 10.58 | 3 | 30 | 300 | 1000 | 300 | 3000 |
| 158 | 10.29 | 3 | 40 | 500 | 1500 | 750 | 7000 |
| 159 | 9.72 | 3 | 50 | 500 | 2500 | 650 | 8430 |
| 160 | 9.43 | 3 | 60 | 1000 | 3000 | 850 | 22000 |
| 161 | 9.15 | 5 | 75 | 1500 | 3500 | 2500 | 38700 |
| 162 | 9.15 | 5 | 100 | 2000 | 3500 | 3500 | 23200 |
| 163 | 8.86 | 75 | 125 | 1500 | 5000 | 1100 | 28700 |
| 164 | 9.15 | 125 | 100 | 1500 | 7500 | 2222 | 33333 |
| 165 | 9.72 | 125 | 75 | 1500 | 3200 | 1436 | 32000 |

| | | LAND VALUE/ACRE FOR YEAR | | | | | |
|---|---|---|---|---|---|---|---|
| CODE* | DISTANCE* | 1836 | 1857 | 1873 | 1892 | 1910 | 1928 |
| 166 | 10.00 | 125 | 75 | 1500 | 5000 | 4700 | 44000 |
| 167 | 10.29 | 15 | 100 | 2000 | 12500 | N/A | N/A |
| 168 | 10.58 | 3 | 35 | 1000 | 2500 | N/A | 28250 |
| 169 | 10.29 | 3 | 35 | 1500 | 1800 | N/A | 32000 |
| 170 | 10.00 | 5 | 35 | 1500 | 3000 | N/A | 7000 |
| 171 | 10.29 | 5 | 35 | 1000 | 2000 | 1925 | 11000 |
| 172 | 10.29 | 5 | 35 | 1000 | 2000 | 1320 | 9650 |
| 173 | 10.58 | 5 | 50 | 1000 | 2000 | 1280 | 9440 |
| 174 | 10.58 | 10 | 50 | 1000 | 6000 | 6222 | 22667 |
| 175 | 10.86 | 25 | 100 | 3000 | N/A | N/A | N/A |
| 176 | 11.43 | 3 | 35 | 1200 | 2500 | N/A | N/A |
| 177 | 11.15 | 3 | 35 | 1200 | 1800 | N/A | N/A |
| 178 | 11.15 | 3 | 35 | 600 | 1500 | N/A | N/A |
| 179 | 11.15 | 3 | 35 | 600 | N/A | N/A | N/A |
| 180 | 11.43 | 3 | 10 | 600 | N/A | N/A | N/A |
| 181 | 11.43 | 3 | 10 | 600 | N/A | N/A | N/A |
| 182 | 11.72 | 10 | 5 | 1000 | N/A | N/A | N/A |
| 183 | 12.00 | 25 | 50 | 2000 | N/A | N/A | N/A |
| 184 | 12.86 | 2 | 20 | 500 | 1000 | N/A | N/A |
| 185 | 12.58 | 2 | 25 | 800 | 1000 | N/A | 6900 |
| 186 | 12.29 | 2 | 30 | 1200 | 1500 | N/A | 27000 |
| 187 | 12.29 | 3 | 30 | 1200 | 1800 | N/A | 11860 |
| 188 | 12.29 | 3 | 30 | 600 | 2200 | N/A | 14260 |
| 189 | 12.00 | 3 | 30 | 500 | 5000 | 6000 | 30000 |
| 190 | 12.29 | 3 | 25 | N/A | N/A | 2000 | 4000 |
| 191 | 12.29 | 3 | 25 | 700 | 1500 | 1000 | 2850 |
| 192 | 12.58 | 3 | 25 | 700 | 1500 | 2500 | 6000 |
| 193 | 12.86 | 3 | 25 | 600 | 1500 | 4040 | 11250 |
| 194 | 13.43 | N/A | 20 | 500 | N/A | N/A | 3000 |
| 195 | 12.86 | N/A | 25 | 800 | N/A | N/A | N/A |
| 196 | 13.43 | 2 | 20 | 800 | 1200 | N/A | 16350 |
| 197 | 13.15 | 2 | 20 | 500 | 2500 | N/A | 6330 |
| 198 | 12.86 | 2 | 20 | 500 | 3500 | N/A | 18500 |
| 199 | 13.15 | 2 | 75 | 500 | 5000 | N/A | 25800 |
| 200 | 13.43 | 2 | 25 | 150 | 1500 | 750 | 2000 |

| CODE* | DISTANCE* | LAND VALUE/ACRE FOR YEAR | | | | | |
|-------|-----------|------|------|------|------|------|------|
| | | 1836 | 1857 | 1873 | 1892 | 1910 | 1928 |
| 201 | 13.43 | 2 | 25 | 150 | 1500 | 1690 | 4000 |
| 202 | 13.72 | 2 | 25 | 100 | 1500 | 720 | 3745 |
| 203 | 13.72 | N/A | 4 | 300 | 2250 | N/A | N/A |
| 204 | 14.00 | 2 | 20 | 300 | 2500 | N/A | N/A |
| 205 | 13.72 | 2 | 25 | 500 | N/A | N/A | N/A |
| 206 | 14.00 | 2 | N/A | N/A | N/A | N/A | N/A |
| 207 | 14.29 | 2 | 25 | 150 | 1500 | N/A | N/A |
| 208 | 14.29 | 2 | 25 | 150 | 1500 | N/A | N/A |
| 209 | 14.58 | 2 | 25 | 100 | 1500 | N/A | N/A |
| 210 | 14.58 | N/A | N/A | N/A | N/A | N/A | 6000 |
| 211 | 14.86 | 2 | 25 | 300 | 1500 | N/A | 4850 |
| 212 | 14.86 | 2 | 25 | 150 | 1500 | 863 | 1500 |
| 213 | 15.15 | 2 | 25 | 100 | 1500 | 700 | 1500 |
| 214 | 15.15 | 2 | 25 | 100 | 1500 | 1000 | 5000 |
| 215 | 15.43 | 2 | 25 | 100 | 1500 | 600 | 1500 |

Source: Homer Hoyt, One Hundred Years of Land Values in Chicago. University of Chicago Press, 1933.

Notes:

* Code number represents a square mile (or one and one-half sq. mile) as outlined in Figure A1.

Airline distance from corner of State and Madison Streets to approximate center of one square mile areas in Figure A1.

N/A indicates that data was not available.

Appendix B

## OLCOTT'S CHICAGO LAND VALUE DATA

| STREET ADDRESS* | DISTANCE* | LAND VALUE/FRONT FOOT FOR YEAR* | | | | | | |
|---|---|---|---|---|---|---|---|---|
| | | 1910 | 1920 | 1930 | 1940 | 1950 | 1960 | 1970 |
| ISHAM OKETO | 12.394 | N/A | 10 | 40 | 25 | 40 | 140 | 400 |
| ESTES OLCOTT | 12.223 | N/A | 6 | 73 | 40 | 50 | 150 | 275 |
| ESTES MOBILE | 11.368 | N/A | N/A | 35 | 17 | 33 | 160 | 280 |
| WILDWOOD HIAWATHA | 10.941 | N/A | N/A | 22 | 35 | 65 | 195 | 300 |
| CALDWELL Waukesha | 10.855 | N/A | N/A | 40 | 35 | 50 | 175 | 300 |
| FARGO SACRAMENTO | 9.744 | N/A | N/A | 60 | 28 | 55 | 195 | 300 |
| ARTHUR RICHMOND | 8.975 | N/A | 21 | 125 | 45 | 70 | 195 | 450 |
| FARGO WINCHESTER | 9.402 | 15 | 40 | 250 | 75 | 90 | 200 | 400 |
| LUNT RAVENSWOOD | 8.975 | 20 | 30 | 275 | 75 | 95 | 200 | 300 |
| ARTHUR CLAREMONT | 8.548 | 10 | 20 | 185 | 75 | 85 | 190 | 400 |
| SHERWIN GREENVIEW | 9.402 | 60 | 100 | 550 | 130 | 90 | 300 | 500 |
| LUNT SHERIDAN | 8.975 | 100 | 200 | 800 | 140 | 150 | 300 | 700 |
| ALBION GLENWOOD | 8.462 | 35 | 75 | 350 | 115 | 100 | 225 | 400 |
| ROSEMONT GRNVIEW | 7.864 | 40 | 60 | 250 | 70 | 70 | 130 | 275 |
| ARDMORE KENMORE | 7.265 | 70 | 220 | 725 | 135 | 120 | 350 | 1000 |
| BERWYN GLENWOOD | 7.009 | 45 | 90 | 325 | 80 | 80 | 135 | 300 |
| CARMEN MOBILE | 9.830 | N/A | 12 | 35 | 15 | 40 | 160 | 250 |
| PARK MENARD | 9.317 | N/A | N/A | 55 | 35 | 43 | 165 | 350 |
| BELEPLNE MONITR | 9.231 | N/A | N/A | 90 | 35 | 50 | 175 | 260 |
| CARMEN LARAMIE | 9.146 | 8 | 13 | 75 | 30 | 38 | 150 | 300 |
| MILWAUKEE WILSON | 8.889 | 30 | 60 | 375 | 75 | 100 | 225 | 350 |
| CULLOM LINDER | 8.377 | 8 | 22 | 125 | 45 | 55 | 165 | 250 |
| ROSEMONT BELL | 8.120 | 10 | 15 | 175 | 70 | 70 | 190 | 400 |
| OLIVE ASHLAND | 7.607 | 30 | 50 | 250 | 70 | 65 | 125 | 300 |
| FARRAGUT WINCHSTR | 7.265 | 25 | 35 | 125 | 45 | 45 | 110 | 250 |
| ROSEMONT CALIF | 8.548 | 3 | 16 | 200 | 50 | 55 | 200 | 450 |
| ARDMORE LINCOLN | 7.693 | 20 | 35 | 225 | 60 | 60 | 350 | 500 |
| BALMORAL ROCKWELL | 7.778 | 20 | 25 | 150 | 60 | 70 | 225 | 400 |
| ROSEMONT CENTRALP | 8.975 | N/A | N/A | 70 | 20 | 45 | 225 | 300 |
| HOLLYWOOD KIMBALL | 8.206 | N/A | 11 | 160 | 40 | 70 | 200 | 400 |
| FOSTER BERNARD | 8.291 | N/A | 30 | 200 | 60 | 85 | 200 | 350 |
| DEVON KILDARE | 9.659 | N/A | N/A | 35 | 15 | 35 | 185 | 275 |
| GRANVILLE KARLOV | 8.975 | N/A | N/A | 35 | 17 | 65 | 195 | 300 |
| HOLLYWOOD KENNETH | 8.889 | N/A | N/A | 40 | 25 | 60 | 165 | 300 |
| DEVON LEROY | 10.086 | N/A | N/A | 38 | 20 | 45 | 180 | 275 |
| LAWSON LEMONT | 9.317 | N/A | 8 | 18 | 12 | 40 | 155 | 290 |
| BALMORAL LUNA | 9.402 | N/A | 18 | 50 | 35 | 43 | 160 | 350 |
| MILWAUKEE HAFT | 10.684 | N/A | 20 | 175 | 55 | 50 | 225 | 400 |
| ARDMORE MOODY | 10.171 | N/A | 8 | 55 | 30 | 40 | 175 | 350 |
| BERWYN MOODY | 10.086 | N/A | 9 | 25 | 13 | 34 | 150 | 275 |

(Continued)

| STREET ADDRESS* | DISTANCE* | LAND VALUE/FRONT FOOT FOR YEAR* | | | | | | |
| | | 1910 | 1920 | 1930 | 1940 | 1950 | 1960 | 1970 |
|---|---|---|---|---|---|---|---|---|
| HIGHLAND NEWCASTL | 11.539 | N/A | N/A | 55 | 25 | 42 | 150 | 260 |
| THORNDALE NATOMA | 11.112 | N/A | N/A | 70 | 35 | 65 | 175 | 300 |
| BERWYN NORDICA | 10.770 | N/A | N/A | 16 | 12 | 28 | 140 | 260 |
| DEVON ORIOLE | 11.966 | N/A | 5 | 60 | 25 | 35 | 130 | 230 |
| ARDMORE OKETO | 11.624 | N/A | N/A | 35 | 10 | 27 | 130 | 250 |
| BERWYN ORIOLE | 11.539 | N/A | N/A | 15 | 15 | 40 | 130 | 250 |
| CARMEN KOSTNER | 8.377 | 5 | 14 | 90* | 35 | 45 | 145 | 200 |
| WILSON KNOX | 7.864 | 12 | 14 | 100 | 30 | 40 | 145 | 250 |
| BERTEAU KENNETH | 7.778 | 12 | 28 | 75 | 25 | 35 | 140 | 250 |
| CARMEN HAMLIN | 7.693 | 8 | 20 | 135 | 50 | 60 | 135 | 200 |
| WILSON CENTRALPK | 7.265 | 14 | 35 | 175 | 45 | 50 | 125 | 275 |
| BERTEAU BERNARD | 7.095 | 14 | 20 | 125 | 35 | 45 | 110 | 225 |
| ARGYLE CALIF | 7.265 | 10 | 30 | 175 | 50 | 60 | 135 | 250 |
| WILSON MOZART | 7.180 | 32 | 50 | 200 | 70 | 70 | 140 | 175 |
| BERTEAU RICHMOND | 6.496 | 10 | 20 | 125 | 45 | 55 | 125 | 225 |
| AINSLIE SEELEY | 6.838 | 18 | 40 | 175 | 45 | 50 | 125 | 250 |
| WILSON RAVENSWD | 6.411 | 100 | 125 | 375 | 80 | 125 | 225 | 300 |
| BERTEAU BELL | 5.983 | 25 | 40 | 100 | 50 | 55 | 125 | 200 |
| CARMEN GLENWOOD | 6.496 | 45 | 70 | 325 | 80 | 70 | 75 | 225 |
| ESTWD CLARENDON | 6.069 | 80 | 100 | 750 | 100 | 90 | 100 | 800 |
| GRACE OKETO | 10.599 | N/A | N/A | 20 | 13 | 35 | 150 | 300 |
| ROSCOE OLLOTT | 10.257 | N/A | N/A | 18 | 13 | 35 | 150 | 300 |
| BARRY ODELL | 10.000 | N/A | N/A | 25 | 14 | 37 | 155 | 300 |
| BYRON NEVA | 9.659 | N/A | 6 | 40 | 22 | 45 | 160 | 300 |
| ROSCOE OAKPARK | 9.317 | N/A | 6 | 50 | 30 | 50 | 170 | 300 |
| GEORGE NWCASTLE | 9.231 | N/A | 7 | 42 | 25 | 50 | 170 | 280 |
| ROSCOE CHURCHLND | 8.548 | N/A | N/A | 50 | 25 | 50 | 165 | 300 |
| GEORGE MERRIMAC | 9.317 | N/A | 8 | 50 | 30 | 55 | 165 | 300 |
| DAKIN LOCKWD | 8.120 | 8 | 25 | 100 | 35 | 50 | 155 | 300 |
| NEWPOR TAMON | 7.693 | 7 | 45 | 85 | 30 | 50 | 160 | 300 |
| WELLINGTON LAVERN | 7.607 | 8 | 20 | 90 | 40 | 55 | 160 | 300 |
| GRACE KILDARE | 7.009 | 22 | 40 | 105 | 60 | 55 | 140 | 275 |
| HENDERSON KEELER | 6.582 | 8 | 22 | 85 | 35 | 40 | 115 | 225 |
| WELLINGTON KOLMAR | 6.838 | 6 | 14 | 100 | 35 | 45 | 120 | 210 |
| GRACE MONTICELLO | 6.667 | 25 | 25 | 125 | 40 | 45 | 110 | 225 |
| ROSCOE AVERS | 6.411 | 20 | 25 | 115 | 45 | 50 | 125 | 225 |
| GEORGE HAMLIN | 5.812 | 16 | 25 | 100 | 30 | 35 | 110 | 175 |
| BYRON WHIPPLE | 5.983 | 14 | 20 | 80 | 32 | 40 | 100 | 225 |
| ROSCOE ALBANY | 5.812 | 16 | 25 | 60 | 30 | 33 | 80 | 160 |
| GEORGE ROCKWELL | 5.043 | 14 | 20 | 75 | 30 | 35 | 80 | 150 |

(Continued)

| STREET ADDRESS* | DISTANCE* | 1910 | 1920 | 1930 | 1940 | 1950 | 1960 | 1970 |
|---|---|---|---|---|---|---|---|---|
| | | | LAND VALUE/FRONT FOOT FOR YEAR* | | | | | |
| BYRON LEAVITT | 5.471 | 25 | 40 | 140 | 60 | 65 | 125 | 100 |
| SCHOOL WOLCOTT | 4.787 | 30 | 45 | 75 | 40 | 40 | 100 | 120 |
| WELLINGTON HOYNE | 4.787 | 25 | 35 | 60 | 35 | 32 | 85 | 150 |
| GRACE WAYNE | 5.129 | 40 | 50 | 225 | 70 | 55 | 110 | 175 |
| ROSCOE GREENVIEW | 4.701 | 40 | 40 | 175 | 50 | 50 | 110 | 175 |
| DALE SEMINARY | 4.103 | 60 | 100 | 175 | 50 | 55 | 110 | 175 |
| GRACE GROVE | 4.701 | 100 | 215 | 750 | 150 | 200 | 250 | 1000 |
| ALDINE SHERIDAN | 4.189 | 225 | 275 | 1750 | 450 | 400 | 800 | 2000 |
| OAKDALE BROADWAY | 3.847 | 80 | 125 | 750 | 225 | 250 | 250 | 500 |
| SCHUBERT SAYRE | 8.975 | N/A | 20 | 60 | 35 | 50 | 175 | 350 |
| PALMER NORDICA | 8.889 | N/A | 20 | 60 | 40 | 55 | 170 | 275 |
| WABANSIA NAGLE | 8.462 | N/A | 10 | 95 | 52 | 70 | 215 | 350 |
| SCHUBERT MENARD | 7.778 | N/A | 10 | 50 | 27 | 45 | 145 | 350 |
| PALMER MEADE | 7.949 | N/A | 10 | 40 | 20 | 45 | 95 | 300 |
| WABANSIA AUSTIN | 7.778 | N/A | 10 | 85 | 40 | 50 | 140 | 300 |
| PARKER LONG | 7.436 | 3 | 14 | 60 | 35 | 50 | 140 | 275 |
| PALMER LAWLER | 6.753 | 16 | 19 | 70 | 28 | 37 | 110 | 250 |
| WABANSIA LARAMIE | 7.095 | 10 | 14 | 80 | 40 | 50 | 115 | 275 |
| DEMING KOSTNER | 6.411 | 6 | N/A | 110 | 45 | 50 | 120 | 200 |
| PALMER KEELER | 5.983 | 16 | 25 | 65 | 30 | 38 | 100 | 200 |
| WABANSIA KILDARE | 5.983 | 14 | 20 | 65 | 35 | 43 | 100 | 200 |
| SCHUBERT LAWNDALE | 5.812 | 18 | 25 | 85 | 35 | 45 | 90 | 150 |
| PALMER DRAKE | 5.471 | 16 | 30 | 130 | 35 | 40 | 85 | 150 |
| WABANSIA DRAKE | 5.129 | 20 | 28 | 85 | 30 | 37 | 70 | 135 |
| LOGAN FAIRFIELD | 4.701 | 70 | 100 | 125 | 40 | 35 | 150 | 200 |
| MILWAUKEE ARMITAG | 4.274 | 200 | 1000 | 800 | 150 | 250 | 350 | 300 |
| WABANSIA WHIPPLE | 4.616 | 25 | 35 | 100 | 35 | 35 | 60 | 135 |
| WRIGHTWD MARSHFLD | 3.932 | 30 | 35 | 40 | 25 | 35 | 80 | 100 |
| PALMER LEAVITT | 3.932 | 40 | 45 | 60 | 30 | 30 | 65 | 100 |
| WABANSIA WOLCOTT | 3.590 | 40 | 45 | 50 | 27 | 25 | 50 | 100 |
| SCHUBERT MAGNOLIZ | 3.761 | 40 | 40 | 80 | 30 | 30 | 75 | 125 |
| WEBSTER RACINE | 3.248 | 70 | 90 | 70 | 40 | 40 | 70 | 200 |
| WILLOW DAYTON | 2.736 | 40 | 70 | 70 | 35 | 28 | 70 | 140 |
| DEMING CLARK | 3.334 | 125 | 200 | 800 | 150 | 250 | 275 | 700 |
| WEBSTER CLEVELAND | 2.992 | 70 | 60 | 400 | 80 | 90 | 110 | 500 |
| WILLOW VINE | 2.479 | 50 | 70 | 90 | 35 | 65 | 65 | 200 |
| HIRSCH MONITOR | 7.436 | 6 | 30 | 55 | 55 | 70 | 135 | 200 |
| AUGUSTA MENARD | 7.265 | 16 | 30 | 150 | 45 | 55 | 115 | 250 |
| RACE MENARD | 7.265 | 40 | 50 | 200 | 55 | 75 | 125 | 200 |
| LEMOYNE LARAMIE | 6.667 | 7 | 18 | 125 | 50 | 60 | 125 | 250 |

(Continued)

| STREET ADDRESS* | DISTANCE* | LAND VALUE/FRONT FOOT FOR YEAR* | | | | | | |
|---|---|---|---|---|---|---|---|---|
| | | 1910 | 1920 | 1930 | 1940 | 1950 | 1960 | 1970 |
| AUGUSTA LAVERGNE | 6.411 | 12 | 22 | 125 | 40 | 50 | 115 | 200 |
| RACE LAMON | 6.325 | 28 | 32 | 60 | 20 | 25 | 80 | 155 |
| HIRSCH KILDARE | 5.727 | 18 | 25 | 80 | 30 | 30 | 85 | 150 |
| WALTON KOSTNER | 5.642 | 10 | 16 | 55 | 20 | 20 | 65 | 140 |
| OHIO KENTON | 5.727 | 22 | 30 | 40 | 18 | 18 | 70 | 150 |
| LEMOYNE HAMLIN | 5.129 | 20 | 30 | 75 | 30 | 35 | 70 | 150 |
| AUGUSTA CENTRALPK | 4.787 | 16 | 25 | 95 | 35 | 38 | 75 | 135 |
| OHIO HOMAN | 4.530 | 20 | 25 | 85 | 35 | 38 | 80 | 140 |
| LEMOYNE TALMAN | 4.018 | 40 | 45 | 125 | 30 | 32 | 40 | 150 |
| AUGUSTA MOZART | 3.932 | 35 | 45 | 85 | 30 | 40 | 50 | 140 |
| OHIO TROY | 3.932 | 25 | 20 | 50 | 25 | 30 | 55 | 100 |
| JULIAN PAULINA | 3.077 | 40 | 40 | 45 | 25 | 25 | 50 | 125 |
| CORTEZ LEAVITT | 3.419 | 28 | 55 | 90 | 30 | 35 | 75 | 135 |
| OHIO WOLCOTT | 2.821 | 40 | 40 | 40 | 25 | 25 | 50 | 110 |
| BLACKHWK GRNVIEW | 2.565 | 75 | 72 | 70 | 25 | 25 | 55 | 100 |
| AUGUSTA MILWAUKEE | 2.137 | 175 | 250 | 350 | 70 | 80 | 125 | 250 |
| OHIO OGDEN | 1.966 | 55 | 75 | 100 | 25 | 60 | 95 | 115 |
| EVERGRN CLYBORN | 1.881 | 80 | N/A | 100 | 65 | 75 | 150 | 200 |
| HOBBIE MOHAWK | 1.539 | 60 | 70 | 60 | 25 | 30 | 85 | 150 |
| ILLINOIS FRANKLIN | 1.624 | 350 | 500 | 750 | 175 | 175 | 325 | 700 |
| ERIE MCCLURG | 1.453 | 150 | 700 | 1250 | 250 | 325 | 850 | 3000 |
| GRAND PESHTIGO | 1.283 | 250 | 400 | 1000 | 250 | 425 | 750 | 2500 |
| ILLINOIS OUTTER | 1.197 | 450 | 600 | 700 | 700 | 450 | 850 | 3500 |
| LAKE LONG | 6.667 | 40 | 40 | 225 | 70 | 70 | 125 | 250 |
| ADAMS LAVERENE | 6.154 | 10 | 30 | 250 | 80 | 80 | 135 | 175 |
| LEXINGTN LOCKWD | 6.667 | 10 | 18 | 60 | 30 | 35 | 85 | 150 |
| CARROLL KEELER | 5.300 | 25 | 30 | 45 | 25 | 25 | 60 | 80 |
| ADAMS KILDARE | 5.214 | 34 | 40 | 200 | 60 | 60 | 65 | 125 |
| GRENSHAW KEELER | 5.385 | 18 | 25 | 90 | 30 | 35 | 50 | 95 |
| CARROLL HOMAN | 4.189 | 30 | 50 | 70 | 30 | 40 | 40 | 100 |
| ADAMS SPRINGFIELD | 5.403 | 45 | 70 | 225 | 65 | 70 | 75 | 125 |
| POLK LAWNDALE | 4.445 | 45 | 45 | 115 | 40 | 50 | 55 | 100 |
| FULTON SACRAMENTO | 3.590 | 40 | 50 | 60 | 30 | 30 | 40 | 95 |
| ADAMS FAIRFIELD | 3.248 | 50 | 40 | 90 | 35 | 35 | 40 | 100 |
| TAYLOR MOZART | 3.419 | 30 | 30 | 60 | 25 | 30 | 35 | 100 |
| MAYPOLE LEAVITT | 2.565 | 60 | 65 | 70 | 25 | 25 | 30 | 100 |
| ADAMS WOOD | 2.223 | 65 | 55 | 200 | 30 | 35 | 40 | 115 |
| GRENSHAW WESTERN | 2.906 | 50 | 40 | 125 | 75 | 75 | 100 | 200 |
| JACKSON RACINE | 1.283 | 150 | 300 | 400 | 45 | 70 | 125 | 250 |
| RANDOLPH JEFFERSN | 0.599 | 800 | 750 | 1000 | 225 | 350 | 625 | 1000 |

(Continued)

| STREET ADDRESS* | DISTANCE* | LAND VALUE/FRONT FOOT FOR YEAR* | | | | | | |
|---|---|---|---|---|---|---|---|---|
| | | 1910 | 1920 | 1930 | 1940 | 1950 | 1960 | 1970 |
| STATE MADISON | 0.000 | 8000 | 7000 | 4000 | 6800 | 8000 | 8000 | 5000 |
| 13TH KEOVALE | 5.300 | 16 | 25 | 160 | 40 | 35 | 40 | 95 |
| CULLERTON KILDARE | 5.556 | 8 | 34 | 60 | 30 | 30 | 35 | 75 |
| 25TH KEELER | 5.642 | 22 | 40 | 70 | 40 | 35 | 60 | 100 |
| 13TH MILLARD | 4.530 | 35 | 60 | 200 | 40 | 30 | 35 | 85 |
| OGDEN CHRISTIANA | 4.530 | 80 | 155 | 235 | 60 | 85 | 150 | 175 |
| 24TH HAMLIN | 5.043 | 20 | 35 | 65 | 40 | 45 | 80 | 100 |
| 12TH ROCKWELL | 3.419 | 40 | 40 | 100 | 50 | 25 | 35 | 100 |
| 19TH MARSHALL | 3.932 | 35 | 60 | 125 | 45 | 65 | 75 | 110 |
| 25TH WHIPPLE | 4.274 | 20 | 35 | 50 | 30 | 32 | 55 | 100 |
| HASTINGS WOOD | 2.565 | 40 | 40 | 45 | 20 | 20 | 35 | 85 |
| 19TH LEAVITT | 3.077 | 45 | 40 | 45 | 30 | 25 | 50 | 100 |
| CERMARK PAULINA | 2.992 | 50 | 50 | 50 | 25 | 30 | 60 | 150 |
| MAXWELL MILLER | 1.710 | 50 | 100 | 175 | 45 | 25 | 50 | 100 |
| ELEANOR THROOP | 2.565 | 40 | 50 | 30 | 35 | 20 | 35 | 90 |
| 12TH HALSTED | 1.368 | 450 | 2500 | 3500 | 550 | 500 | 550 | 450 |
| 18TH DEARBORN | 1.624 | 300 | 200 | 175 | 65 | 80 | 125 | 100 |
| 24TH PRINCETON | 2.137 | 45 | 50 | 55 | 25 | 18 | 30 | 125 |
| 13TH WABASH | 1.283 | 600 | 600 | 350 | 200 | 225 | 250 | 450 |
| CULLERTON MICH | 2.052 | 400 | 400 | 400 | 125 | 180 | 225 | 500 |
| 24TH PRAIRIE | 2.308 | 200 | 200 | 300 | 90 | 140 | 160 | 300 |
| 27TH KEELER | 5.983 | 18 | 25 | 60 | 35 | 38 | 75 | 100 |
| 30TH KENNETH | 6.325 | 8 | 14 | 40 | 20 | 25 | 60 | 90 |
| 27TH SPRINGFIELD | 5.300 | 15 | 30 | 65 | 40 | 40 | 85 | 100 |
| 32ND RIDGEWAY | 5.471 | 8 | 10 | 35 | 20 | 25 | 55 | 80 |
| 38TH HOMAN | 5.642 | 10 | 14 | 40 | 15 | 18 | 40 | 100 |
| 26TH TROY | 4.445 | 35 | 50 | 125 | 25 | 60 | 85 | 200 |
| 38TH ALBANY | 5.214 | 20 | 20 | 50 | 20 | 22 | 45 | 150 |
| 33RD HOYNE | 3.847 | 10 | 16 | 40 | 22 | 20 | 50 | 125 |
| 34TH HONORE | 3.847 | 20 | 35 | 40 | 25 | 27 | 55 | 125 |
| 37TH WOLCOTT | 4.445 | 25 | 40 | 55 | 30 | 32 | 60 | 150 |
| ELEANOR LOOMIS | 2.992 | 15 | 30 | 30 | 20 | 15 | 35 | 90 |
| 34TH LITUANCIA | 3.505 | 25 | 35 | 45 | 18 | 18 | 45 | 135 |
| 36TH SANGAMON | 3.761 | 25 | 30 | 40 | 15 | 25 | 40 | 125 |
| 28TH UNION | 3.334 | 30 | 20 | 45 | 22 | 14 | 45 | 125 |
| 32ND WELLS | 3.505 | 40 | 52 | 55 | 25 | 18 | 40 | 100 |
| 38TH DEARBORN | 3.847 | 40 | 30 | 45 | 17 | 20 | 50 | 100 |
| 29TH SOUTHPARK | 3.077 | 80 | 60 | 350 | 45 | 35 | 85 | 150 |
| 35TH RHODES | 3.590 | 125 | 100 | 100 | 35 | 60 | 150 | 150 |
| 38TH PRAIRIE | 3.932 | 60 | 35 | 50 | 20 | 25 | 50 | 125 |

(Continued)

| STREET ADDRESS* | DISTANCE* | LAND VALUE/FRONT FOOT FOR YEAR* | | | | | | |
|---|---|---|---|---|---|---|---|---|
| | | 1910 | 1920 | 1930 | 1940 | 1950 | 1960 | 1970 |
| 37TH LAKE PARK | 3.590 | 80 | 60 | 250 | 65 | 35 | 70 | 150 |
| 43RD KEATING | 7.265 | 3 | 3 | 12 | 5 | 13 | 75 | 100 |
| 45TH KEOVALE | 7.180 | 3 | 6 | 18 | 9 | 17 | 80 | 175 |
| 49TH KILDARE | 7.522 | 4 | 9 | 36 | 27 | 40 | 110 | 200 |
| 45TH HARDING | 6.582 | 5 | 10 | 32 | 17 | 30 | 85 | 175 |
| 50TH RIDGEWAY | 6.924 | 5 | 6 | 12 | 6 | 25 | 75 | 110 |
| 44TH TALMAN | 5.727 | 6 | 16 | 50 | 27 | 32 | 80 | 160 |
| 50TH TALMAN | 6.411 | 5 | 12 | 40 | 20 | 23 | 65 | 140 |
| 47TH DAMEN | 5.642 | 40 | 60 | 80 | 30 | 30 | 90 | 200 |
| 50TH OAKLEY | 5.983 | 12 | 14 | 35 | 18 | 18 | 55 | 125 |
| 45TH ASHLAND | 5.129 | 50 | 300 | 250 | 50 | 65 | 110 | 175 |
| 48TH ADA | 5.385 | 30 | 25 | 30 | 15 | 17 | 45 | 110 |
| 50TH MORGAN | 5.556 | 16 | 20 | 32 | 22 | 18 | 50 | 85 |
| 45TH WALLACE | 4.872 | 25 | 25 | 35 | 20 | 14 | 40 | 85 |
| 48TH PRINCETON | 5.471 | 25 | 25 | 30 | 17 | 15 | 40 | 70 |
| 40TH INDIANA | 4.445 | 100 | 150 | 150 | 45 | 40 | 55 | 110 |
| 50TH MICHIGAN | 5.556 | 60 | 125 | 150 | 55 | 55 | 65 | 125 |
| 40TH ELLIS | 4.701 | 125 | 90 | 175 | 55 | 55 | 70 | 150 |
| 46TH GREENWOOD | 5.129 | 150 | 150 | 400 | 90 | 80 | 90 | 160 |
| 50TH DORCHESTER | 5.642 | 100 | 100 | 350 | 90 | 85 | 150 | 250 |
| 51ST NEWLAND | 10.513 | N/A | 2 | 10 | 6 | 20 | 100 | 175 |
| 56TH NEWCASTLE | 10.428 | N/A | 4 | 14 | 9 | 22 | 110 | 200 |
| 61ST NORMANDY | 10.941 | N/A | 8 | 10 | 6 | 12 | 90 | 200 |
| 52ND MOBILE | 9.659 | N/A | 8 | 15 | 9 | 20 | 105 | 180 |
| 57TH MASON | 9.402 | N/A | 8 | 13 | 7 | 16 | 95 | 190 |
| 61ST AUSTIN | 10.342 | N/A | 12 | 35 | 15 | 25 | 100 | 200 |
| 51ST LUNA | 8.975 | N/A | 10 | 40 | 10 | 20 | 105 | 160 |
| ARCHER LOCKWOOD | 9.317 | N/A | 14 | 100 | 25 | 45 | 150 | 300 |
| 55TH LARAMIE | 9.659 | N/A | 10 | 60 | 20 | 25 | 70 | 200 |
| ARCHER KEATING | 8.291 | 7 | 60 | 150 | 35 | 80 | 175 | 300 |
| 61ST KOLIN | 8.975 | 4 | 10 | 28 | 23 | 36 | 140 | 250 |
| 52ND AVERS | 7.607 | 4 | 6 | 17 | 9 | 22 | 115 | 160 |
| 57TH LAWNDALE | 8.035 | 4 | 13 | 22 | 18 | 30 | 135 | 165 |
| 61ST HOMAN | 8.206 | 10 | 21 | 65 | 30 | 37 | 135 | 220 |
| 52ND RICHMOND | 7.095 | 4 | 12 | 50 | 32 | 37 | 120 | 185 |
| 57TH MOZART | 7.265 | 3 | 16 | 60 | 35 | 40 | 140 | 170 |
| 61ST TALMAN | 7.864 | 3 | 25 | 95 | 40 | 45 | 140 | 220 |
| 52ND WOLCOTT | 6.753 | 10 | 27 | 45 | 28 | 25 | 65 | 110 |
| 57TH WINCHESTER | 6.838 | 16 | 22 | 55 | 30 | 28 | 55 | 100 |
| 62ND HONORE | 7.351 | 14 | 18 | 60 | 32 | 30 | 60 | 100 |

(Continued)

| STREET ADDRESS* | DISTANCE* | LAND VALUE/FRONT FOOT FOR YEAR* | | | | | | |
|---|---|---|---|---|---|---|---|---|
| | | 1910 | 1920 | 1930 | 1940 | 1950 | 1960 | 1970 |
| 52ND LAFLIN | 6.240 | 25 | 30 | 50 | 30 | 27 | 55 | 100 |
| 57TH CARPENTER | 6.753 | 35 | 35 | 55 | 30 | 28 | 50 | 85 |
| 62ND MORGAN | 7.180 | 30 | 35 | 60 | 30 | 30 | 40 | 80 |
| 52ND UNION | 6.154 | 25 | 25 | 50 | 22 | 24 | 35 | 85 |
| 56TH NORMAL | 6.582 | 30 | 28 | 35 | 30 | 30 | 40 | 75 |
| 61ST STEWART | 7.009 | 65 | 55 | 100 | 45 | 35 | 40 | 80 |
| 53RD MICHIGAN | 6.582 | 40 | 60 | 175 | 80 | 75 | 110 | 130 |
| 58TH INDIANA | 6.496 | 75 | 75 | 90 | 40 | 40 | 70 | 100 |
| 61ST LAWRENCE | 7.009 | 50 | 80 | 125 | 55 | 75 | 100 | 110 |
| 52ND ELLIS | 6.325 | 60 | 100 | 225 | 80 | 70 | 85 | 300 |
| 56TH BLACKSTONE | 6.753 | 70 | 115 | 350 | 160 | 135 | 160 | 400 |
| 62ND WOODLAWN | 7.180 | 70 | 115 | 325 | 90 | 85 | 100 | 150 |
| HYDEPARK CORNELL | 6.496 | 175 | 400 | 1000 | 300 | 250 | 350 | 800 |
| 54TH EASTVIEW | 6.924 | 100 | 165 | 225 | 225 | 275 | 350 | 1200 |
| 56TH SOUTH | 7.522 | 100 | 250 | 400 | 400 | 350 | 700 | 1500 |
| 63RD KOSTNER | 9.402 | 4 | 20 | 30 | 24 | 60 | 175 | 350 |
| 66TH KNOX | 9.744 | 5 | 8 | 25 | 19 | 28 | 110 | 200 |
| 68TH KEDVALE | 10.171 | 3 | 12 | 30 | 17 | 35 | 130 | 200 |
| 63RD SPRINGFIELD | 9.060 | 6 | 18 | 40 | 80 | 42 | 135 | 210 |
| 67TH LAWNDALE | 9.231 | 4 | 10 | 23 | 14 | 25 | 135 | 200 |
| 73RD ST. LOUIS | 9.830 | 5 | 3 | 22 | 15 | 28 | 130 | 170 |
| 64TH WHIPPLE | 8.548 | 7 | 20 | 90 | 40 | 50 | 155 | 220 |
| 68TH MABLEWOOD | 8.718 | 5 | 13 | 75 | 35 | 43 | 145 | 220 |
| 73RD FAIRFIELD | 9.402 | 3 | 10 | 40 | 15 | 32 | 140 | 170 |
| 64TH HOYNE | 8.206 | 9 | 16 | 30 | 25 | 27 | 60 | 110 |
| 68TH WOOD | 8.718 | 10 | 20 | 40 | 28 | 28 | 60 | 110 |
| 73RD WOLCOTT | 9.146 | 5 | 15 | 27 | 20 | 17 | 50 | 90 |
| 64TH LAFLIN | 7.864 | 25 | 30 | 65 | 40 | 35 | 40 | 80 |
| 69TH MORGAN | 8.291 | 40 | 45 | 65 | 32 | 30 | 45 | 110 |
| 74TH MORGAN | 8.889 | 10 | 30 | 60 | 30 | 25 | 35 | 75 |
| 64TH EGGLESTON | 7.607 | 50 | 50 | 175 | 80 | 55 | 60 | 90 |
| 68TH UNION | 8.035 | 50 | 50 | 200 | 60 | 45 | 70 | 100 |
| 74TH PERRY | 8.718 | 20 | 25 | 65 | 35 | 32 | 40 | 100 |
| 64TH RHODES | 7.778 | 30 | 30 | 40 | 22 | 35 | 50 | 100 |
| 69TH MICHIGAN | 8.206 | 25 | 35 | 100 | 40 | 35 | 50 | 90 |
| 74TH RHODES | 8.889 | 10 | 30 | 90 | 45 | 38 | 55 | 90 |
| 64TH DREXEL | 8.035 | 40 | 60 | 200 | 60 | 55 | 55 | 100 |
| 68TH DANTE | 8.462 | 25 | 50 | 225 | 75 | 70 | 75 | 100 |
| 76TH ESSEX | 10.000 | 18 | 125 | 230 | 75 | 100 | 145 | 160 |
| 74TH DANTE | 8.975 | 25 | 30 | 125 | 45 | 50 | 60 | 95 |

(Continued)

| STREET ADDRESS* | DISTANCE* | LAND VALUE/FRONT FOOT FOR YEAR* | | | | | | |
|---|---|---|---|---|---|---|---|---|
| | | 1910 | 1920 | 1930 | 1940 | 1950 | 1960 | 1970 |
| 68TH CREGIER | 8.120 | 20 | 70 | 250 | 120 | 150 | 135 | 150 |
| 70TH MERRILL | 8.889 | 20 | 70 | 400 | 125 | 125 | 150 | 200 |
| 74TH CLYDE | 9.146 | 15 | 40 | 150 | 90 | 90 | 115 | 125 |
| 71ST SOUTHSHORE | 9.659 | 50 | 200 | 1000 | 225 | 225 | 250 | 350 |
| 73RD EXCHANGE | 9.744 | 15 | 125 | 250 | 200 | 200 | 200 | 200 |
| 74TH COLES | 9.659 | 30 | 80 | 450 | 100 | 140 | 120 | 250 |
| 77TH KILPATRICK | 10.941 | N/A | N/A | 18 | 5 | 11 | 115 | 200 |
| 83ST KENNETH | 11.112 | N/A | N/A | 10 | 4 | 8 | 115 | 200 |
| 86TH KOLIN | 11.966 | N/A | N/A | 10 | 5 | 10 | 115 | 200 |
| HAYFORD HAMLIN | 10.428 | 3 | 4 | 12 | 4 | 8 | 90 | 185 |
| 80TH ST. LOUIS | 10.855 | 4 | 4 | 35 | 16 | 25 | 135 | 175 |
| 85TH LAWNDALE | 11.368 | 4 | 4 | 16 | 6 | 15 | 135 | 180 |
| 77TH WHIPPLE | 9.915 | 3 | 3 | 21 | 7 | 12 | 85 | 175 |
| 81ST FAIRFIELD | 10.428 | 3 | 4 | 25 | 10 | 30 | 150 | 200 |
| 85TH CALIFORNIA | 10.855 | 2 | 4 | 25 | 10 | 25 | 150 | 220 |
| 76TH WOLCOTT | 9.744 | 4 | 12 | 60 | 30 | 45 | 125 | 155 |
| 81ST DAMEN | 10.000 | 3 | 9 | 45 | 25 | 45 | 140 | 165 |
| 86TH PAULINA | 10.684 | 4 | 10 | 75 | 35 | 52 | 150 | 200 |
| 76TH CARPENTER | 9.573 | 8 | 25 | 75 | 35 | 45 | 125 | 130 |
| 81ST ADA | 10.086 | 10 | 20 | 110 | 45 | 55 | 140 | 160 |
| 86TH MORGAN | 10.599 | 10 | 20 | 70 | 35 | 40 | 120 | 150 |
| 76TH UNION | 9.402 | 20 | 40 | 80 | 30 | 35 | 80 | 110 |
| 80TH PRINCETON | 9.915 | 6 | 12 | 50 | 30 | 28 | 65 | 70 |
| 86TH PARNELL | 10.513 | 6 | 10 | 25 | 12 | 17 | 60 | 75 |
| 76TH INDIANA | 9.402 | 6 | 15 | 90 | 45 | 42 | 75 | 80 |
| 80TH RHODES | 9.915 | 5 | 22 | 180 | 55 | 60 | 85 | 125 |
| 85TH VERNON | 10.428 | 5 | 11 | 75 | 40 | 50 | 85 | 90 |
| 76TH DREXEL | 9.573 | 12 | 30 | 100 | 35 | 40 | 75 | 110 |
| 81ST KENWOOD | 10.171 | 5 | 18 | 85 | 50 | 55 | 110 | 110 |
| 85TH ENGLESIDE | 10.513 | 6 | 10 | 150 | 50 | 60 | 100 | 150 |
| 80TH PAXTON | 10.257 | 6 | 14 | 105 | 50 | 75 | 135 | 100 |
| 80TH ESCANABA | 10.599 | 16 | 22 | 135 | 35 | 40 | 105 | 110 |
| 86TH BURNHAM | 11.112 | 14 | 23 | 60 | 35 | 45 | 95 | 110 |
| 83RD BUFFALO | 10.770 | 15 | 40 | 35 | 20 | 20 | 40 | 90 |
| 85TH BURLEY | 11.398 | 15 | 23 | 75 | 40 | 50 | 75 | 125 |
| HUNT PLEASANT | 11.368 | N/A | 14 | 100 | 95 | 85 | 155 | 250 |
| 93RD HOYNE | 11.624 | N/A | 20 | 100 | 80 | 100 | 170 | 240 |
| 98TH DAMEN | 12.223 | N/A | N/A | 105 | 70 | 85 | 160 | 185 |
| 88TH ELIZABETH | 11.112 | N/A | 16 | 75 | 38 | 45 | 125 | 175 |
| 92ND BISHOP | 11.710 | N/A | 12 | 100 | 45 | 65 | 145 | 210 |

(Continued)

| STREET ADDRESS* | DISTANCE* | LAND VALUE/FRONT FOOT FOR YEAR* | | | | | | |
|---|---|---|---|---|---|---|---|---|
| | | 1910 | 1920 | 1930 | 1940 | 1950 | 1960 | 1970 |
| 98TH MORGAN | 12.223 | N/A | 10 | 40 | 20 | 32 | 100 | 100 |
| 88TH LOWE | 11.026 | 9 | 14 | 48 | 25 | 35 | 75 | 100 |
| 94TH LASALLE | 11.539 | 4 | 7 | 13 | 8 | 20 | 65 | 95 |
| 98TH LOWE | 12.052 | 5 | 8 | 30 | 10 | 30 | 75 | 100 |
| 93RD VERNON | 11.539 | 10 | 16 | 42 | 15 | 17 | 70 | 90 |
| 98TH FOREST | 12.137 | 6 | 26 | 45 | 20 | 37 | 75 | 95 |
| 88TH DAUPHIN | 11.197 | 18 | 16 | 70 | 25 | 35 | 85 | 135 |
| 92ND HARPER | 11.539 | 10 | 16 | 60 | 27 | 32 | 120 | 130 |
| 98TH ELLIS | 12.137 | 9 | 23 | 37 | 22 | 24 | 90 | 100 |
| 88TH RIDGELAND | 11.368 | 4 | 12 | 45 | 22 | 34 | 135 | 160 |
| 93RD CRANDON | 11.881 | 10 | 16 | 80 | 30 | 30 | 95 | 125 |
| 97TH MERRILL | 12.479 | 5 | 10 | 18 | 5 | 35 | 95 | 150 |
| 88TH MUSKEGON | 11.624 | 16 | 25 | 65 | 30 | 32 | 85 | 125 |
| 93RD COLFAX | 11.966 | 8 | 14 | 45 | 25 | 30 | 80 | 110 |
| 98TH ESCANABA | 12.650 | 10 | 12 | 40 | 18 | 17 | 65 | 100 |
| 88TH BUFFALO | 11.966 | 20 | 30 | 50 | 22 | 17 | 50 | 75 |
| 92ND BURLEY | 12.479 | 45 | 100 | 35 | 18 | 12 | 45 | 125 |
| 98TH AVENUEL | 12.992 | 25 | 30 | 35 | 20 | 22 | 50 | 85 |
| 105TH ALBANY | 13.590 | N/A | N/A | 15 | 6 | 18 | 115 | 160 |
| 110TH CAMPBELL | 14.018 | N/A | N/A | 20 | 25 | 47 | 145 | 160 |
| 99TH BELL | 12.906 | N/A | N/A | 80 | 55 | 65 | 155 | 200 |
| 110TH BELL | 13.847 | N/A | N/A | 70 | 50 | 60 | 130 | 190 |
| 100TH CHARLES | 12.821 | N/A | 16 | 70 | 30 | 45 | 95 | 115 |
| 104TH PEORIA | 13.248 | N/A | 8 | 30 | 20 | 36 | 100 | 110 |
| 110TH RACINE | 13.676 | N/A | 6 | 14 | 10 | 17 | 55 | 110 |
| 100TH LOWE | 12.650 | 5 | 8 | 45 | 22 | 33 | 60 | 100 |
| 104TH WENTWORTH | 13.163 | 10 | 14 | 50 | 25 | 22 | 75 | 100 |
| 109TH WALLACE | 12.052 | 6 | 12 | 60 | 22 | 44 | 135 | 130 |
| 101ST PRAIRIE | 12.650 | 15 | 30 | 60 | 19 | 42 | 110 | 120 |
| 105TH MAPLE | 13.163 | 15 | 32 | 50 | 25 | 45 | 125 | 125 |
| 109TH MICHIGAN | 13.761 | 80 | 125 | 1000 | 100 | 200 | 300 | 250 |
| 104TH MARYLAND | 12.821 | N/A | N/A | 37 | 10 | 15 | 35 | 80 |
| 100TH PAXTON | 13.077 | N/A | N/A | 12 | 4 | 20 | 80 | 100 |
| 103RD CRANDON | 13.334 | N/A | N/A | 15 | 4 | 20 | 70 | 100 |
| 99TH CALHOUN | 13.248 | N/A | N/A | 22 | 6 | 22 | 80 | 96 |
| 105TH YATES | 13.505 | N/A | 10 | 20 | 15 | 19 | 55 | 100 |
| 109TH HOXIE | 14.018 | N/A | 14 | 20 | 8 | 17 | 50 | 80 |
| 101ST AVENUEM | 13.590 | N/A | 20 | 35 | 20 | 25 | 75 | 125 |
| 105TH AVENUEF | 14.189 | N/A | 14 | 45 | 30 | 25 | 85 | 100 |
| 110TH GREENBAY | 14.530 | N/A | 10 | 25 | 8 | 18 | 70 | 85 |

(Continued)

| STREET ADDRESS* | DISTANCE* | LAND VALUE/FRONT FOOT FOR YEAR* | | | | | | |
|---|---|---|---|---|---|---|---|---|
| | | 1910 | 1920 | 1930 | 1940 | 1950 | 1960 | 1970 |
| 112TH OAKLEY | 14.445 | N/A | 35 | 75 | 55 | 55 | 115 | 175 |
| 117TH VINCENNES | 14.616 | N/A | 12 | 60 | 15 | 18 | 50 | 80 |
| 111TH THROOP | 14.359 | N/A | 8 | 16 | 10 | 30 | 55 | 95 |
| 117TH SANGAMON | 14.787 | N/A | N/A | 35 | 15 | 20 | 45 | 100 |
| 122ND LOOMIS | 15.385 | N/A | 6 | 12 | 5 | 20 | 70 | 110 |
| 112TH PARNELL | 14.359 | N/A | 14 | 80 | 35 | 40 | 125 | 125 |
| 117TH YALE | 14.616 | N/A | 18 | 55 | 25 | 30 | 100 | 120 |
| 122ND NORMAL | 15.300 | N/A | 16 | 60 | 25 | 30 | 95 | 125 |
| 112TH INDIANA | 14.274 | N/A | 60 | 150 | 50 | 50 | 100 | 150 |
| 117TH PRAIRIE | 15.043 | N/A | N/A | 45 | 12 | 17 | 45 | 110 |
| 121ST MICHIGAN | 15.471 | N/A | 16 | 175 | 25 | 50 | 75 | 110 |
| 119TH BENSLEY | 14.958 | N/A | 4 | 10 | 4 | 4 | 4 | 4 |
| 112TH GREENBAY | 15.043 | N/A | 8 | 24 | 7 | 17 | 45 | 85 |
| 113TH AVENUEH | 15.471 | N/A | N/A | 35 | 25 | 32 | 90 | 135 |
| 117TH AVENUED | 15.983 | N/A | 5 | 8 | 5 | 10 | 40 | 75 |
| 124TH EMERALD | 15.812 | N/A | 10 | 28 | 25 | 35 | 80 | 135 |
| BRAYTON STATE | 16.069 | N/A | N/A | 35 | 17 | 25 | 80 | 125 |
| 128TH WALLACE | 16.496 | N/A | N/A | 24 | 25 | 35 | 105 | 135 |
| 124TH STATE | 15.983 | N/A | 12 | 60 | 15 | 25 | 50 | 110 |
| 131ST RHODES | 16.154 | N/A | N/A | 40 | 20 | 18 | 55 | 80 |
| 131ST CORLISS | 16.069 | N/A | N/A | 12 | 3 | 30 | 65 | 85 |
| 135TH DREXEL | 16.667 | N/A | N/A | 10 | 3 | 25 | 40 | 70 |
| 135TH MERRILL | 17.009 | N/A | 3 | 9 | 2 | 2 | 2 | 2 |
| 123RD YATES | 16.411 | N/A | 4 | 8 | 3 | 3 | 10 | 50 |
| 128TH MANISTER | 16.838 | N/A | 4 | 22 | 5 | 8 | 40 | 100 |
| 134TH BRANDON | 17.265 | N/A | 20 | 125 | 35 | 40 | 60 | 100 |
| 130TH BUFFALO | 16.496 | N/A | 8 | 16 | 5 | 7 | 20 | 80 |
| 134TH AVENUEL | 16.924 | N/A | 5 | 20 | 8 | 17 | 40 | 85 |
| 135TH BURLEY | 17.522 | N/A | 20 | 30 | 18 | 22 | 45 | 100 |

Source:  Olcott's Land Values Blue Book of Chicago, George C.
Olcott and Co., Chicago, Ill.

Notes:

*Land value is in dollars per front foot.

Distance is measured in airline miles from the corner of
State and Madison Streets.

Street address is at the intersection of two streets.

N/A indicates that data was not available at those particular
street intersections.

Appendix C

FHA DATA FOR VARIOUS CITIES

| 1966 | | | AVERAGES FOR NEW HOUSES | | |
| CITY | SALE PRICE* | LOT SIZE* | LIVING AREA* | CONSTR. COST* | LAND VALUE* |
|---|---|---|---|---|---|
| ALBUQUERQUE, NM | $19008 | 8612 | 1499 | $11.27 | $2934 |
| CHARLOTTE, NC | 17151 | 13188 | 1313 | 11.34 | 3204 |
| COLUMBUS, OH | 16753 | 8973 | 1036 | 12.60 | 3357 |
| DALLAS, TX | 16415 | 8558 | 1346 | 10.74 | 2436 |
| DAYTON, OH | 16537 | 10974 | 1160 | 11.40 | 3517 |
| DENVER, CO | 18425 | 8790 | 1119 | 13.43 | 3226 |
| EL PASO, TX | 15534 | 8075 | 1460 | 9.21 | 2420 |
| FRESNO, CA | 18608 | 7722 | 1490 | 10.79 | 3394 |
| GREENSBORO, NC | 16289 | 14051 | 1251 | 11.25 | 2607 |
| HOUSTON, TX | 16325 | 8275 | 1411 | 10.15 | 2593 |
| JACKSONVILLE, FL | 17111 | 10497 | 1384 | 10.87 | 2659 |
| LAS VEGAS, NV | 21382 | 6998 | 1307 | 13.77 | 3880 |
| LOS ANGELES, CA | 21976 | 7094 | 1448 | 10.81 | 5963 |
| LOUISVILLE, KY | 14077 | 8864 | 1007 | 11.58 | 2851 |
| MEMPHIS, TN | 16731 | 11097 | 1336 | 10.52 | 2714 |
| MIAMI, FL | 16508 | 9521 | 1331 | 10.30 | 3518 |
| NASHVILLE, TN | 15579 | 16658 | 1204 | 11.05 | 2801 |
| OKLAHOMA CITY, OK | 15280 | 8900 | 1154 | 11.33 | 2363 |
| ORLANDO, FL | 24002 | 9186 | 1427 | 10.65 | 3002 |
| PHOENIX AZ | 17115 | 7555 | 1516 | 9.47 | 3286 |
| SACRAMENTO, CA | 18237 | 7852 | 1345 | 10.92 | 4302 |
| SAN DIEGO, CA | 20355 | 8319 | 1364 | 10.79 | 5294 |
| SAN FRANCISCO, CA | 23025 | 7528 | 1491 | 11.84 | 5877 |
| SAN JOSE, CA | 22575 | 6550 | 1511 | 11.32 | 5689 |
| SEATTLE, WA | 19369 | 8975 | 1283 | 13.17 | 3522 |
| SHREVEPORT, LA | 19986 | 16200 | 1516 | 11.64 | 3145 |
| SPOKANE, WA | 18347 | 14154 | 1277 | 13.32 | 2148 |
| STOCKTON, CA | 17210 | 6610 | 1263 | 11.24 | 3452 |
| TAMPA, FL | 14718 | 8087 | 1184 | 10.51 | 2694 |
| TULSA, OK | 16245 | 8834 | 1220 | 11.34 | 2758 |
| VALLEJO, CA | 18112 | 6296 | 1304 | 11.84 | 4337 |

* See footnotes at end of Appendix.

| 1967 | | | | AVERAGES FOR NEW HOUSES | |
| --- | --- | --- | --- | --- | --- |
| CITY | SALE PRICE* | LOT SIZE* | LIVING AREA* | CONST. COST* | LAND VALUE* |
| ALBUQUERQUE, NM | $20759 | 8581 | 1575 | $11.88 | $3237 |
| CHARLOTTE, NC | 19123 | 14730 | 1355 | 11.81 | 3347 |
| COLUMBUS, OH | 17545 | 9294 | 1071 | 12.66 | 3645 |
| DALLAS, TX | 17342 | 9249 | 1318 | 11.47 | 2597 |
| DAYTON, OH | 16992 | 11061 | 1195 | 11.74 | 3973 |
| DENVER, CO | 19862 | 8744 | 1311 | 12.70 | 3344 |
| EL PASO, TX | 16258 | 8764 | 1386 | 10.32 | 2462 |
| FRESNO, CA | 19536 | 7240 | 1515 | 11.31 | 3698 |
| GREENSBORO, NC | 18009 | 13811 | 2198 | 11.92 | 2682 |
| HOUSTON, TX | 18268 | 8274 | 1461 | 10.63 | 2856 |
| JACKSONVILLE, FL | 16734 | 8764 | 1317 | 11.43 | 3419 |
| LAS VEGAS, NV | 25079 | 7473 | 1419 | 14.58 | 4599 |
| LOS ANGELES, CA | 24564 | 6521 | 1498 | 11.25 | 7219 |
| LOUISVILLE, KY | 15324 | 9198 | 1059 | 11.98 | 2985 |
| MEMPHIS, TN | 17492 | 10980 | 1310 | 11.04 | 2794 |
| MIAMI, FL | 16813 | 9767 | 1296 | 10.84 | 3440 |
| NASHVILLE, TN | 16637 | 16711 | 1228 | 11.20 | 2968 |
| OKLAHOMA CITY, OK | 15606 | 8905 | 1150 | 11.90 | 2377 |
| ORLANDO, FL | 17997 | 10202 | 1360 | 11.68 | 3138 |
| PHOENIX, AZ | 18167 | 7072 | 1465 | 10.24 | 3461 |
| SACRAMENTO, CA | 19959 | 7463 | 1385 | 11.32 | 4657 |
| SAN DIEGO, CA | 23331 | 7795 | 1471 | 11.36 | 6096 |
| SAN FRANCISCO, CA | 25059 | 7593 | 1513 | 12.40 | 6557 |
| SAN JOSE, CA | 23950 | 6296 | 1465 | 12.02 | 6005 |
| SEATTLE, WA | 19747 | 9818 | 1149 | 14.59 | 3648 |
| SHREVEPORT, LA | 20783 | 12372 | 1461 | 12.29 | 3241 |
| SPOKANE, WA | 18982 | 10627 | 1326 | 13.41 | 1962 |
| STOCKTON, CA | 17862 | 6567 | 1285 | 11.29 | 3725 |
| TAMPA, FL | 15655 | 8764 | 1214 | 10.88 | 2643 |
| TULSA, OK | 16270 | 9401 | 1159 | 12.05 | 2754 |
| VALLEJO, CA | 18449 | 7050 | 1265 | 12.19 | 4482 |

*See footnotes at end of Appendix

| 1968 | | | | AVERAGES FOR NEW HOUSES | |
|---|---|---|---|---|---|
| CITY | SALE PRICE* | LOT SIZE* | LIVING AREA* | CONST. COST* | LAND VALUE* |
| ALBUQUERQUE, NM | $20902 | 8405 | 1520 | $12.19 | $3110 |
| CHARLOTTE, NC | 20039 | 16681 | 1306 | 12.25 | 3340 |
| COLUMBUS, OH | 18134 | 7935 | 1061 | 13.61 | 3743 |
| DALLAS, TX | 17925 | 8657 | 1309 | 11.93 | 2782 |
| DAYTON, OH | 18024 | 10065 | 1222 | 12.54 | 4201 |
| DENVER, CO | 20351 | 8499 | 1325 | 12.92 | 3318 |
| EL PASO, TX | 16869 | 9461 | 1409 | 10.35 | 2415 |
| FRESNO, CA | 19554 | 7884 | 1480 | 11.67 | 3698 |
| GREENSBORO, NC | 19096 | 12702 | 1306 | 12.44 | 3095 |
| HOUSTON, TX | 19579 | 8204 | 1468 | 11.26 | 2987 |
| JACKSONVILLE, FL | 16054 | 9052 | 1275 | 11.44 | 2246 |
| LAS VEGAS, NV | 25350 | 7429 | 1464 | 14.46 | 4743 |
| LOS ANGELES, CA | 26529 | 6026 | 1484 | 11.56 | 8276 |
| LOUISVILLE, KY | 15212 | 9562 | 1030 | 12.44 | 2898 |
| MEMPHIS, TN | 18345 | 12787 | 1300 | 11.59 | 2993 |
| MIAMI, FL | 17732 | 8874 | 1316 | 11.70 | 3596 |
| NASHVILLE, TN | 18108 | 15635 | 1242 | 11.79 | 3169 |
| OKLAHOMA CITY, OK | 16560 | 9071 | 1210 | 12.54 | 2425 |
| ORLANDO, FL | 19064 | 10139 | 1397 | 12.35 | 3192 |
| PHOENIX, AZ | 18834 | 7621 | 1481 | 10.45 | 3529 |
| SACRAMENTO, CA | 21061 | 8125 | 1437 | 11.88 | 4727 |
| SAN DIEGO, CA | 24072 | 9254 | 1399 | 11.97 | 6420 |
| SAN FRANCISCO, CA | 25082 | 7385 | 1518 | 12.64 | 6385 |
| SAN JOSE, CA | 24888 | 6566 | 1495 | 12.22 | 6665 |
| SEATTLE, WA | 20756 | 9504 | 1142 | 15.13 | 4072 |
| SHREVEPORT, LA | 20191 | 15930 | 1342 | 12.92 | 3220 |
| SPOKANE, WA | 18852 | 10484 | 1283 | 14.09 | 1982 |
| STOCKTON, CA | 19509 | 8070 | 1305 | 12.16 | 3919 |
| TAMPA, FL | 15640 | 8347 | 1188 | 11.90 | 2736 |
| TULSA, OK | 19004 | 13025 | 1633 | 9.99 | 3387 |
| VALLEJO, CA | 20763 | 7267 | 1305 | 12.34 | 5077 |

* See footnotes at end of Appendix

| 1969 | | | | AVERAGES FOR NEW HOUSES | |
|------|------|------|------|------|------|
| CITY | SALE PRICE* | LOT SIZE* | LIVING AREA* | CONST. COST* | LAND VALUE* |
| ALBUQUERQUE, NM | $21443 | 8564 | 1523 | $12.81 | $3231 |
| CHARLOTTE, NC | 21415 | 15882 | 1366 | 13.35 | 3475 |
| COLUMBUS, OH | 19332 | 8107 | 1062 | 15.03 | 3926 |
| DALLAS, TX | 19862 | 8610 | 1419 | 13.89 | 3183 |
| DAYTON, OH | 19654 | 10494 | 1234 | 13.65 | 4479 |
| DENVER, CO | 21399 | 8200 | 1248 | 14.03 | 3518 |
| EL PASO, TX | 17654 | 8175 | 1367 | 11.15 | 2379 |
| FRESNO, CA | 20483 | 8028 | 1485 | 12.12 | 3898 |
| GREENSBORO, NC | 19773 | 12442 | 1285 | 13.48 | 3150 |
| HOUSTON, TX | 21794 | 8255 | 1527 | 11.96 | 3403 |
| JACKSONVILLE, FL | 19646 | 9273 | 1330 | 13.08 | 2553 |
| LAS VEGAS, NV | 22460 | 5991 | 1232 | 15.43 | 3933 |
| LOS ANGELES | 26028 | 6217 | 1348 | 12.57 | 8952 |
| LOUISVILLE, KY | 16550 | 9038 | 1052 | 13.22 | 3159 |
| MEMPHIS, TN | 16951 | 11325 | 1381 | 12.95 | 3350 |
| MIAMI, FL | 16885 | 9339 | 1364 | 13.15 | 4133 |
| NASHVILLE, TN | 17004 | 14581 | 1268 | 12.90 | 3280 |
| OKLAHOMA CITY, OK | 14191 | 8816 | 1194 | 13.39 | 2442 |
| ORLANDO, FL | 17108 | 10700 | 1489 | 13.38 | 3434 |
| PHOENIX, AZ | 15956 | 8040 | 1461 | 11.36 | 3721 |
| SACRAMENTO, CA | 17517 | 7942 | 1410 | 13.11 | 4783 |
| SAN DIEGO, CA | 19087 | 7690 | 1309 | 12.76 | 5667 |
| SAN FRANCISCO, CA | 21429 | 7397 | 1521 | 13.35 | 6731 |
| SAN JOSE, CA | 23260 | 6605 | 1443 | 12.91 | 6879 |
| SEATTLE, WA | 19816 | 9304 | 1134 | 16.36 | 4215 |
| SHREVEPORT, LA | 15430 | 13761 | 1268 | 13.10 | 2823 |
| SPOKANE, WA | 15105 | 14762 | 1315 | 16.18 | 2256 |
| STOCKTON, CA | 16959 | 7126 | 1258 | 13.24 | 3616 |
| TAMPA, FL | 13207 | 7983 | 1159 | 13.36 | 2754 |
| TULSA, OK | 14841 | 8859 | 1137 | 13.29 | 2801 |
| VALLEJO, CA | 18161 | 6963 | 1381 | 13.09 | 5368 |

*See footnotes at end of Appendix.

| 1970 | AVERAGES FOR NEW HOUSES | | | | |
|------|------------------|------------|--------------|----------------|-------------|
| CITY | SALE PRICE* | LOT SIZE* | LIVING AREA* | CONSTR. COST* | LAND VALUE* |
| ALBUQUERQUE, NM | $23153 | 8590 | 1578 | $13.29 | $3436 |
| CHARLOTTE, NC | 24614 | 15170 | 1434 | 14.37 | 3561 |
| COLUMBUS, OH | 20435 | 7869 | 1131 | 15.03 | 3746 |
| DALLAS, TX | 21890 | 8454 | 1381 | 13.17 | 3779 |
| DAYTON, OH | 20895 | 10246 | 1206 | 15.11 | 4737 |
| DENVER, CO | 24443 | 8676 | 1204 | 15.50 | 3880 |
| EL PASO, TX | 20130 | 8158 | 1466 | 11.71 | 2835 |
| FRESNO, CA | 22349 | 7661 | 1639 | 12.35 | 4251 |
| GREENSBORO, NC | 20220 | 11956 | 1258 | 14.13 | 3055 |
| HOUSTON, TX | 23838 | 7622 | 1570 | 12.57 | 3691 |
| JACKSONVILLE, FL | 22578 | 9701 | 1420 | 14.32 | 2884 |
| LAS VEGAS, NV | 25287 | 5916 | 1314 | 16.62 | 4958 |
| LOS ANGELES, CA | 27929 | 5954 | 1387 | 13.78 | 8898 |
| LOUISVILLE, KY | 19850 | 8945 | 1098 | 14.36 | 3466 |
| MEMPHIS, TN | 24320 | 10827 | 1449 | 13.81 | 3656 |
| MIAMI, FL | 24302 | 8944 | 1360 | 15.50 | 4373 |
| NASHVILLE, TN | 21533 | 14819 | 1281 | 13.72 | 3500 |
| OKLAHOMA CITY, OK | 20040 | 9262 | 1269 | 14.08 | 2793 |
| ORLANDO, FL | 20984 | 10065 | 1406 | 14.31 | 3385 |
| PHOENIX, AZ | 21683 | 7556 | 1439 | 12.64 | 4115 |
| SACRAMENTO, CA | 22577 | 7360 | 1430 | 13.61 | 4751 |
| SAN DIEGO, CA | 25032 | 7674 | 1340 | 14.00 | 5970 |
| SAN FRANCISCO, CA | 26464 | 6162 | 1403 | 14.65 | 6720 |
| SAN JOSE, CA | 24526 | 5526 | 1399 | 13.97 | 6025 |
| SEATTLE, WA | 23042 | 8664 | 1144 | 16.96 | 4652 |
| SHREVEPORT, LA | 21402 | 8704 | 1271 | 14.08 | 3040 |
| SPOKANE, WA | 24368 | 11900 | 1265 | 18.00 | 2513 |
| STOCKTON, CA | 20946 | 6344 | 1300 | 13.51 | 3919 |
| TAMPA, FL | 19007 | 7707 | 1173 | 14.02 | 2817 |
| TULSA, OK | 19379 | 9307 | 1221 | 13.59 | 3387 |
| VALLEJO, CA | 23751 | 6602 | 1371 | 13.93 | 5533 |

* See footnotes at end of Appendix.

| 1971 | | | AVERAGES | FOR NEW | HOUSES |
|------|------|------|------|------|------|
| CITY | SALE PRICE | LOT SIZE* | LIVING AREA* | CONSTR. COST* | LAND VALUE* |
| ALBUQUERQUE, NM | $22667 | 8551 | 1498 | $13.34 | $3416 |
| CHARLOTTE, NC | 23381 | 14221 | 1352 | 14.63 | 3638 |
| COLUMBUS, OH | 22823 | 8380 | 1181 | 16.67 | 4226 |
| DALLAS, TX | 23098 | 8729 | 1437 | 13.07 | 4444 |
| DAYTON, OH | 21569 | 8483 | 1147 | 15.76 | 4377 |
| DENVER, CO | 23668 | 8691 | 1126 | 17.89 | 3999 |
| EL PASO, TX | 21067 | 8269 | 1463 | 12.19 | 3083 |
| FRESNO, CA | 21262 | 7312 | 1447 | 12.99 | 4186 |
| GREENSBORO, NC | 21654 | 12000 | 1295 | 14.45 | 3387 |
| HOUSTON, TX | 24179 | 7741 | 1574 | 13.11 | 3677 |
| JACKSONVILLE, FL | 22378 | 9699 | 1345 | 14.88 | 2923 |
| LAS VEGAS, NV | 26405 | 7037 | 1298 | 16.48 | 6031 |
| LOS ANGELES, CA | 27941 | 5681 | 1337 | 14.27 | 9442 |
| LOUISVILLE, KY | 20415 | 9257 | 1111 | 14.02 | 3948 |
| MEMPHIS, TN | 24375 | 10440 | 1427 | 14.27 | 3833 |
| MIAMI, FL | 26907 | 7566 | 1327 | 17.51 | 4365 |
| NASHVILLE, TN | 21108 | 14265 | 1227 | 13.86 | 3708 |
| OKLAHOMA CITY, OK | 20980 | 9590 | 1297 | 14.28 | 3010 |
| ORLANDO, FL | 21133 | 9705 | 1359 | 14.44 | 3316 |
| PHOENIX, AZ | 23208 | 7167 | 1400 | 13.77 | 4350 |
| SACRAMENTO, CA | 24053 | 8370 | 1424 | 14.03 | 4822 |
| SAN DIEGO, CA | 25455 | 7040 | 1311 | 14.62 | 6045 |
| SAN FRANCISCO, CA | 25142 | 4803 | 1359 | 14.66 | 6272 |
| SAN JOSE, CA | 24045 | 5268 | 1323 | 14.38 | 6187 |
| SEATTLE, WA | 23762 | 9052 | 1185 | 16.68 | 4883 |
| SHREVEPORT, LA | 21356 | 8879 | 1202 | 14.70 | 3307 |
| SPOKANE, WA | 23576 | 12883 | 1183 | 18.76 | 2594 |
| STOCKTON, CA | 20077 | 6171 | 1222 | 14.16 | 4250 |
| TAMPA, FL | 19878 | 8200 | 1141 | 14.49 | 3040 |
| TULSA, OK | 19674 | 8991 | 1200 | 13.80 | 3270 |
| VALLEJO, CA | 23747 | 6650 | 1358 | 13.85 | 5687 |

*See footnotes at end of Appendix.

| 1972 | | | AVERAGES FOR NEW HOUSES | | |
| --- | --- | --- | --- | --- | --- |
| CITY | SALE PRICE* | LOT SIZE* | LIVING AREA* | CONSTR. COST* | LAND VALUE* |
| ALBUQUERQUE, NM | $23922 | 8576 | 1526 | $13.56 | $3454 |
| CHARLOTTE, NC | 26104 | 13133 | 1408 | 15.42 | 4230 |
| COLUMBUS, OH | 23238 | 7811 | 1128 | 17.55 | 4293 |
| DALLAS, TX | 23303 | 7896 | 1458 | 13.18 | 4472 |
| DAYTON, OH | 22066 | 9001 | 1113 | 16.93 | 4270 |
| DENVER, CO | 24764 | 8126 | 1083 | 18.14 | 3961 |
| EL PASO, TX | 22192 | 7845 | 1435 | 13.03 | 3213 |
| FRESNO, CA | 21159 | 7024 | 1365 | 13.94 | 4136 |
| GREENSBORO, NC | 23907 | 12881 | 1340 | 14.80 | 4002 |
| HOUSTON, TX | 24068 | 7635 | 1460 | 14.10 | 3388 |
| JACKSONVILLE, FL | 25096 | 10218 | 1393 | 15.86 | 3498 |
| LAS VEGAS, NV | 28156 | 5752 | 1353 | 16.85 | 6427 |
| LOS ANGELES, CA | 29411 | 5441 | 1348 | 14.48 | 9649 |
| LOUISVILLE, KY | 20562 | 9107 | 1042 | 15.01 | 3987 |
| MEMPHIS, TN | 24682 | 9092 | 1372 | 14.68 | 3892 |
| MIAMI, FL | 26118 | 7493 | 1244 | 17.22 | 4896 |
| NASHVILLE, TN | 21758 | 13425 | 1194 | 14.13 | 3773 |
| OKLAHOMA CITY, OK | 21407 | 8664 | 1237 | 15.21 | 3055 |
| ORLANDO, FL | 21536 | 9361 | 1256 | 15.02 | 3342 |
| PHOENIX, AZ | 22727 | 5509 | 1358 | 15.01 | 3921 |
| SACRAMENTO, CA | 23585 | 6989 | 1329 | 15.06 | 4730 |
| SAN DIEGO, CA | 25618 | 6125 | 1258 | 15.21 | 5982 |
| SAN FRANCISCO, CA | 26649 | 4837 | 1347 | 15.08 | 7117 |
| SAN JOSE, CA | 25925 | 4905 | 1307 | 15.25 | 6819 |
| SEATTLE, WA | 24423 | 9489 | 1202 | 16.74 | 4836 |
| SHREVEPORT, LA | 22944 | 7539 | 1276 | 15.35 | 3515 |
| SPOKANE, WA | 24426 | 11219 | 1150 | 19.03 | 2642 |
| STOCKTON, CA | 21950 | 6640 | 1255 | 14.92 | 4273 |
| TAMPA, FL | 19694 | 7692 | 1145 | 14.79 | 3088 |
| TULSA, OK | 20076 | 8360 | 1217 | 14.42 | 3117 |
| VALLEJO, CA | 24267 | 5409 | 1338 | 14.97 | 5437 |

*See footnotes at end of Appendix.

| 1973 | | | AVERAGES FOR NEW HOUSES | | |
| CITY | SALE PRICE* | LOT SIZE* | LIVING AREA* | CONSTR. COST* | LAND VALUE* |
|---|---|---|---|---|---|
| ALBUQUERQUE, NM | $25094 | 8591 | 1556 | $14.22 | $3603 |
| CHARLOTTE, NC | 26029 | 12343 | 1302 | 16.49 | 4187 |
| COLUMBUS, OH | 24334 | 7239 | 1109 | 18.67 | 4634 |
| DALLAS, TX | 23010 | 8059 | 1470 | 13.27 | 4437 |
| DAYTON, OH | 23511 | 9440 | 1135 | 17.95 | 4628 |
| DENVER, CO | 24357 | 6957 | 1006 | 20.12 | 3796 |
| EL PASO, TX | 21948 | 6625 | 1305 | 14.35 | 3112 |
| FRESNO, CA | 21472 | 6181 | 1314 | 15.25 | 4244 |
| GREENSBORO, NC | 23493 | 12634 | 1252 | 16.36 | 3514 |
| HOUSTON, TX | 23702 | 7338 | 1342 | 15.43 | 3428 |
| JACKSONVILLE, FL | 24714 | 8693 | 1299 | 17.12 | 3267 |
| LAS VEGAS, NV | 29064 | 6260 | 1338 | 17.75 | 6202 |
| LOS ANGELES, CA | 27842 | 5954 | 1302 | 14.95 | 8542 |
| LOUISVILLE, KY | 21937 | 8885 | 1092 | 15.44 | 4085 |
| MEMPHIS, TN | 22729 | 8243 | 1167 | 15.47 | 3849 |
| MIAMI, FL | 24404 | 7896 | 1089 | 18.55 | 5381 |
| NASHVILLE, TN | 21525 | 12454 | 1140 | 15.24 | 3657 |
| OKLAHOMA CITY, OK | 21520 | 8306 | 1204 | 15.75 | 3072 |
| ORLANDO, FL | 24896 | 8619 | 1296 | 15.45 | 3649 |
| PHOENIX, AZ | 24468 | 7228 | 1362 | 15.65 | 4142 |
| SACRAMENTO, CA | 24217 | 6510 | 1270 | 16.23 | 4764 |
| SAN DIEGO, CA | 27126 | 6434 | 1241 | 15.84 | 7063 |
| SAN FRANCISCO, CA | 27242 | 4714 | 1373 | 15.94 | 7252 |
| SAN JOSE, CA | 26662 | 5088 | 1260 | 16.17 | 7343 |
| SEATTLE, WA | 26329 | 9167 | 1307 | 17.42 | 4953 |
| SHREVEPORT, LA | 24542 | 7968 | 1268 | 16.61 | 3549 |
| SPOKANE, WA | 23986 | 10251 | 1094 | 20.21 | 2587 |
| STOCKTON, CA | 24049 | 6324 | 1313 | 15.80 | 4664 |
| TAMPA, FL | 21119 | 7811 | 1102 | 15.69 | 3237 |
| TULSA, OK | 21374 | 8445 | 1223 | 15.35 | 3509 |
| VALLEJO, CA | 24821 | 5913 | 1263 | 15.91 | 5863 |

* See footnotes at end of Appendix.

| 1974 | | | AVERAGES FOR NEW HOUSES | | |
|---|---|---|---|---|---|
| CITY | SALE PRICE* | LOT SIZE* | LIVING AREA* | CONSTR. COST* | LAND VALUE* |
| ALBUQUERQUE, NM | $27214 | 9005 | 1425 | $16.42 | $3829 |
| CHARLOTTE, NC | 30385 | 14604 | 1325 | 18.83 | 4897 |
| COLUMBUS, OH | 26455 | 7518 | 1050 | 21.55 | 4989 |
| DALLAS, TX | 24631 | 8128 | 1534 | 14.00 | 4808 |
| DAYTON, OH | 27946 | 9821 | 1292 | 20.37 | 5648 |
| DENVER, CO | 27125 | 4995 | 1029 | 21.49 | 4003 |
| EL PASO, TX | 25971 | 6388 | 1351 | 16.27 | 3822 |
| FRESNO, CA | 24616 | 7427 | 1344 | 16.50 | 4458 |
| GREENSBORO, NC | 28601 | 10115 | 1310 | 17.99 | 4570 |
| HOUSTON, TX | 28091 | 6988 | 1438 | 17.74 | 3854 |
| JACKSONVILLE, FL | 28627 | 8002 | 1177 | 19.91 | 6676 |
| LAS VEGAS, NV | 31511 | 6426 | 1332 | 19.66 | 6320 |
| LOS ANGELES, CA | 31385 | 6364 | 1471 | 15.95 | 8419 |
| LOUISVILLE, KY | 23625 | 8151 | 1004 | 19.14 | 4378 |
| MEMPHIS, TN | 25446 | 9765 | 1176 | 17.71 | 4185 |
| MIAMI, FL | 27464 | 7447 | 1123 | 19.20 | 6792 |
| NASHVILLE, TN | 27284 | 11971 | 1179 | 20.91 | 4767 |
| OKLAHOMA CITY, OK | 23808 | 7673 | 1219 | 18.38 | 3254 |
| ORLANDO, FL | 29492 | 8653 | 1306 | 20.07 | 5914 |
| PHOENIX, AZ | 25845 | 6810 | 1309 | 18.19 | 4514 |
| SACRAMENTO, CA | 28144 | 6779 | 1279 | 18.94 | 5089 |
| SAN DIEGO, CA | 31004 | 6532 | 1230 | 17.73 | 8404 |
| SAN FRANCISCO, CA | 30197 | 4063 | 1289 | 17.98 | 8260 |
| SAN JOSE, CA | 31153 | 5726 | 1335 | 18.11 | 8645 |
| SEATTLE, WA | 29501 | 8185 | 1055 | 21.70 | 5327 |
| SHREVEPORT, LA | 29296 | 7892 | 1311 | 18.83 | 4642 |
| SPOKANE, WA | 26765 | 10124 | 1073 | 22.63 | 2933 |
| STOCKTON, CA | 25963 | 5847 | 1254 | 18.00 | 4607 |
| TAMPA, FL | 29353 | 7801 | 1223 | 19.27 | 4398 |
| TULSA, OK | 24653 | 8280 | 1225 | 18.11 | 3724 |
| VALLEJO, CA | 31108 | 6489 | 1362 | 18.42 | 6315 |

* See footnotes at end of Appendix.

| 1975 | | | | AVERAGES FOR NEW HOUSES | |
| CITY | SALE PRICE* | LOT SIZE* | LIVING AREA* | CONSTR. COST* | LAND VALUE* |
| --- | --- | --- | --- | --- | --- |
| ALBUQUERQUE, NM | $32415 | 8395 | 1472 | $18.80 | $4400 |
| CHARLOTTE, NC | 32858 | 13658 | 1374 | 19.91 | 5464 |
| COLUMBUS, OH | 31598 | 7307 | 1084 | 23.61 | 5596 |
| DALLAS, TX | 30510 | 8066 | 1561 | 17.07 | 4884 |
| DAYTON, OH | 28361 | 9072 | 1152 | 21.84 | 5346 |
| DENVER, CO | 34231 | 7410 | 1092 | 25.50 | 4665 |
| EL PASO, TX | 29187 | 7169 | 1367 | 18.44 | 3984 |
| FRESNO, CA | 28282 | 6905 | 1395 | 17.42 | 5320 |
| GREENSBORO, NC | 32596 | 11880 | 1386 | 19.63 | 5551 |
| HOUSTON, TX | 31221 | 6947 | 1474 | 18.78 | 4521 |
| JACKSONVILLE, FL | 33110 | 9399 | 1311 | 21.84 | 5400 |
| LAS VEGAS, NV | 35979 | 7190 | 1397 | 20.91 | 6540 |
| LOS ANGELES, CA | 33484 | 5842 | 1384 | 17.43 | 9371 |
| LOUISVILLE, KY | 31144 | 8776 | 1107 | 22.89 | 5527 |
| MEMPHIS, TN | 31852 | 9602 | 1308 | 20.55 | 4835 |
| MIAMI, FL | 31303 | 7123 | 1208 | 20.84 | 7822 |
| NASHVILLE, TN | 31781 | 15375 | 1214 | 22.07 | 5506 |
| OKLAHOMA CITY, OK | 28181 | 7952 | 1313 | 20.39 | 3521 |
| ORLANDO, FL | 29780 | 8760 | 1288 | 21.35 | 6480 |
| PHOENIX, AZ | 30596 | 8760 | 1378 | 20.06 | 5877 |
| SACRAMENTO, CA | 33084 | 6907 | 1339 | 22.08 | 5479 |
| SAN DIEGO, CA | 39037 | 7088 | 1321 | 20.28 | 10050 |
| SAN FRANCISCO, CA | 40823 | 5819 | 1437 | 21.20 | 10906 |
| SAN JOSE, CA | 37439 | 5915 | 1347 | 20.65 | 10926 |
| SEATTLE, WA | 33588 | 8303 | 1185 | 23.02 | 5641 |
| SHREVEPORT, LA | 35165 | 10714 | 1423 | 21.47 | 5407 |
| SPOKANE, WA | 29969 | 11198 | 1045 | 25.45 | 3295 |
| STOCKTON, CA | 28502 | 6157 | 1232 | 21.63 | 4799 |
| TAMPA, FL | 29924 | 7001 | 1198 | 21.79 | 5005 |
| TULSA, OK | 27971 | 7832 | 1269 | 20.85 | 4076 |
| VALLEJO, CA | 36176 | 6259 | 1341 | 21.21 | 7812 |

* See footnotes at end of Appendix.

| 1976 | | | AVERAGES FOR NEW HOUSES | | |
|------|------|------|------|------|------|
| CITY | SALE PRICE* | LOT SIZE* | LIVING AREA* | CONSTR. COST* | LAND VALUE* |
| ALBUQUERQUE, NM | $33879 | 8332 | 1445 | $20.19 | $5090 |
| CHARLOTTE, NC | 34154 | 15393 | 1349 | 21.78 | 5865 |
| COLUMBUS, OH | 34451 | 8172 | 1108 | 26.04 | 6402 |
| DALLAS, TX | 30342 | 7877 | 1506 | 17.82 | 5247 |
| DAYTON, OH | 30434 | 10089 | 1090 | 24.71 | 5956 |
| DENVER, CO | 36259 | 7808 | 1050 | 27.12 | 4954 |
| EL PASO, TX | 29526 | 7034 | 1317 | 19.31 | 4202 |
| FRESNO, CA | 30848 | 6719 | 1409 | 18.32 | 6722 |
| GREENSBORO, NC | 33416 | 13145 | 1395 | 19.88 | 5279 |
| HOUSTON, TX | 34823 | 7406 | 1497 | 20.29 | 5590 |
| JACKSONVILLE, FL | 32763 | 8432 | 1280 | 22.53 | 5518 |
| LAS VEGAS, NV | 37876 | 6816 | 1320 | 23.28 | 7658 |
| LOS ANGELES, CA | 39666 | 6427 | 1386 | 19.55 | 11185 |
| LOUISVILLE, KY | 30633 | 8391 | 1116 | 23.14 | 5620 |
| MEMPHIS, TN | 36024 | 9887 | 1371 | 22.15 | 6111 |
| MIAMI, FL | 30642 | 5219 | 1172 | 21.10 | 7603 |
| NASHVILLE, TN | 32067 | 13612 | 1187 | 22.46 | 5808 |
| OKLAHOMA CITY, OK | 30089 | 8155 | 1319 | 21.21 | 3863 |
| ORLANDO, FL | 29293 | 9117 | 1217 | 22.29 | 6238 |
| PHOENIX, AZ | 32053 | 8143 | 1386 | 21.31 | 5982 |
| SACRAMENTO, CA | 34633 | 6906 | 1260 | 24.01 | 6070 |
| SAN DIEGO, CA | 41790 | 6149 | 1326 | 21.84 | 11690 |
| SAN FRANCISCO, CA | 41848 | 5752 | 1381 | 23.75 | 10565 |
| SAN JOSE, CA | 41310 | 5903 | 1331 | 23.87 | 11546 |
| SEATTLE, WA | 35184 | 8506 | 1172 | 24.37 | 6029 |
| SHREVEPORT, LA | 38007 | 11193 | 1439 | 22.12 | 6374 |
| SPOKANE, WA | 29553 | 10570 | 961 | 26.67 | 3433 |
| STOCKTON, CA | 30582 | 6304 | 1201 | 22.88 | 5317 |
| TAMPA, FL | 28591 | 7701 | 1185 | 21.65 | 5379 |
| TULSA, OK | 30616 | 7903 | 1272 | 22.39 | 4450 |
| VALLEJO, CA | 38311 | 6879 | 1371 | 24.09 | 7459 |

*See footnotes at end of Appendix.

| 1977 | | | | AVERAGES FOR NEW HOUSES | |
| --- | --- | --- | --- | --- | --- |
| CITY | SALE PRICE* | LOT SIZE* | LIVING AREA* | CONSTR. COST* | LAND VALUE* |
| ALBUQUERQUE, NM | $36149 | $7848 | 1392 | 22.14 | $5571 |
| CHARLOTTE, NC | 35659 | 15537 | 1233 | 23.23 | 5409 |
| COLUMBUS, OH | 36516 | 7760 | 1186 | 27.60 | 7086 |
| DALLAS, TX | 31723 | 7920 | 1483 | 18.71 | 5461 |
| DAYTON, OH | 35936 | 9933 | 1284 | 25.22 | 6868 |
| DENVER, CO | 41121 | 7614 | 1089 | 25.86 | 5833 |
| EL PASO, TX | 31844 | 6749 | 1309 | 20.66 | 4459 |
| FRESNO, CA | 34693 | 7495 | 1431 | 20.10 | 7641 |
| GREENSBORO, NC | 34831 | 15596 | 1422 | 21.60 | 5918 |
| HOUSTON, TX | 37207 | 7200 | 1449 | 21.47 | 6674 |
| JACKSONVILLE, FL | 33686 | 9380 | 1263 | 23.90 | 6459 |
| LAS VEGAS, NV | 42484 | 6343 | 1361 | 24.64 | 8599 |
| LOS ANGELES, CA | 42598 | 6542 | 1355 | 21.20 | 12573 |
| LOUISVILLE, KY | 33372 | 9680 | 1106 | 24.84 | 5943 |
| MEMPHIS, TN | 34949 | 9018 | 1289 | 23.56 | 6061 |
| MIAMI, FL | 33680 | 5720 | 1199 | 22.26 | 8486 |
| NASHVILLE, TN | 32628 | 13641 | 1172 | 23.55 | 6072 |
| OKLAHOMA CITY, OK | 33213 | 7900 | 1319 | 22.64 | 4300 |
| ORLANDO, FL | 32657 | 9497 | 1347 | 21.78 | 6215 |
| PHOENIX, AZ | 35828 | 8028 | 1422 | 22.28 | 6607 |
| SACRAMENTO, CA | 37525 | 6825 | 1237 | 27.86 | 6896 |
| SAN DIEGO, CA | 46571 | 6048 | 1311 | 23.17 | 13617 |
| SAN FRANCISCO, CA | 47471 | 7578 | 1328 | 26.23 | 12597 |
| SAN JOSE, CA | 44602 | 5641 | 1225 | 26.05 | 13729 |
| SEATTLE, WA | 38689 | 7607 | 1111 | 27.05 | 6902 |
| SHREVEPORT, LA | 39215 | 8349 | 1378 | 23.82 | 7341 |
| SPOKANE, WA | 33044 | 11894 | 1002 | 28.93 | 4592 |
| STOCKTON, CA | 35930 | 6343 | 1264 | 26.49 | 6020 |
| TAMPA, FL | 31678 | 6795 | 1217 | 22.20 | 5570 |
| TULSA, OK | 32916 | 7937 | 1265 | 23.08 | 5270 |
| VALLEJO, CA | 40756 | 6827 | 1320 | 26.36 | 7471 |

*See footnotes at end of Appendix.

| 1978 | | | AVERAGES FOR NEW HOUSES | | |
| --- | --- | --- | --- | --- | --- |
| CITY | SALE PRICE* | LOT SIZE* | LIVING AREA* | CONSTR. COST* | LAND VALUE* |
| ALBUQUERQUE, NM | $43956 | 7883 | 1447 | $24.79 | $6891 |
| CHARLOTTE, NC | 40138 | 14781 | 1372 | 25.58 | 6250 |
| COLUMBUS, OH | 40530 | 8153 | 1218 | 30.61 | 7518 |
| DALLAS, TX | 37839 | 7871 | 1548 | 21.36 | 6663 |
| DAYTON, OH | 40392 | 9648 | 1280 | 28.10 | 7321 |
| DENVER, CO | 47704 | 7270 | 1104 | 28.50 | 6500 |
| EL PASO, TX | 35449 | 6662 | 1297 | 23.31 | 4905 |
| FRESNO, CA | 38734 | 7443 | 1380 | 22.70 | 8563 |
| GREENSBORO, NC | 37606 | 14292 | 1279 | 26.41 | 6485 |
| HOUSTON, TX | 42749 | 7187 | 1507 | 23.26 | 8686 |
| JACKSONVILLE, FL | 37872 | 10221 | 1329 | 24.78 | 5982 |
| LAS VEGAS, NV | 48851 | 6549 | 1368 | 28.07 | 10080 |
| LOS ANGELES, CA | 44774 | 6146 | 1391 | 25.05 | 8513 |
| LOUISVILLE, KY | 37704 | 9416 | 1151 | 27.04 | 6568 |
| MEMPHIS, TN | 39945 | 9536 | 1337 | 25.44 | 6567 |
| MIAMI, FL | 34894 | 5536 | 1172 | 23.73 | 8911 |
| NASHVILLE, TN | 34758 | 14437 | 1117 | 26.33 | 6303 |
| OKLAHOMA CITY, OK | 37219 | 7668 | 1321 | 24.47 | 5055 |
| ORLANDO, FL | 36519 | 8865 | 1360 | 22.96 | 6711 |
| PHOENIX, AZ | 41001 | 7020 | 1470 | 23.98 | 7225 |
| SACRAMENTO, CA | 44428 | 6655 | 1300 | 30.04 | 8007 |
| SAN DIEGO, CA | 59164 | 5924 | 1297 | 24.99 | 18631 |
| SAN FRANCISCO, CA | 55936 | 6624 | 1232 | 31.24 | 16702 |
| SAN JOSE, CA | 54870 | 5276 | 1185 | 30.23 | 21125 |
| SEATTLE, WA | 43250 | 7460 | 1064 | 29.93 | 8267 |
| SHREVEPORT, LA | 47472 | 10364 | 1497 | 28.13 | 8526 |
| SPOKANE, WA | 39076 | 11831 | 1025 | 32.91 | 6220 |
| STOCKTON, CA | 41622 | 6212 | 1286 | 29.51 | 7573 |
| TAMPA, FL | 34835 | 7161 | 1244 | 23.35 | 6114 |
| TULSA, OK | 36557 | 8322 | 1279 | 24.99 | 5636 |
| VALLEJO, CA | 48949 | 6928 | 1279 | 30.73 | 11598 |

*See footnotes at end of Appendix.

## NOTES FOR APPENDIX C

SALE PRICE:  The price stated in the sales agreement, ex-excluding closing costs and non-real estate costs.

LIVING AREA:  The total square foot area of a house appro-priately improved for the intended use and in compliance with the minimum standards for new homes and with general acceptability criteria for existing homes.  It includes practically all improved areas in the house.

CONSTRUCTION COSTS:  Is replacement cost of property less estimated market price of equivalent site (land) divided by improved living area in square feet.

LAND VALUE:  The FHA estimated price for an equivalent site.

LOT SIZE is in square feet.


SOURCE:  U.S. Department of Housing and Urban Development, FHA Homes 1966-1978, Washington, D.C.

Appendix D

DISTANCE, POPULATION AND AREA FOR SELECTED
CENSUS TRACTS BY CITY:   1970.*

| CITY: AKRON, OH | | | | CITY: BALTIMORE, MD | | | |
|---|---|---|---|---|---|---|---|
| TRACT | DIST. | POP. | AREA | TRACT | DIST. | POP. | AREA |
| 5011 | 0.874 | 2794 | 0.821 | 104 | 1.002 | 2125 | 0.114 |
| 5012 | 0.874 | 2223 | 0.297 | 601 | 1.403 | 3483 | 0.091 |
| 5014 | 0.961 | 3038 | 0.391 | 908 | 2.138 | 7777 | 0.354 |
| 5017 | 0.874 | 2754 | 0.195 | 1505 | 4.276 | 2192 | 0.434 |
| 5018 | 1.485 | 3009 | 0.382 | 1606 | 3.675 | 6699 | 0.172 |
| 5021 | 2.796 | 8855 | 2.462 | 2303 | 2.004 | 1703 | 0.695 |
| 5022 | 2.010 | 7899 | 1.798 | 50402 | 4.009 | 5412 | 0.302 |
| 5024 | 1.311 | 3238 | 0.313 | 60202 | 3.608 | 6752 | 0.491 |
| 5027 | 3.757 | 8119 | 2.134 | 4206 | 4.810 | 5393 | 0.654 |
| 5033 | 3.233 | 7653 | 1.251 | 4208 | 4.944 | 4066 | 0.787 |
| 5034 | 2.272 | 3622 | 0.406 | 30101 | 4.543 | 3872 | 0.571 |
| 5036 | 3.495 | 5947 | 1.915 | 4302 | 4.410 | 3204 | 0.709 |
| 5041 | 1.311 | 2171 | 0.422 | 2607 | 2.205 | 3504 | 0.366 |
| 5042 | 1.398 | 3233 | 0.461 | 1509 | 5.345 | 7192 | 0.649 |
| 5044 | 2.272 | 2766 | 0.313 | 1510 | 5.813 | 8018 | 0.583 |
| 5045 | 2.184 | 2632 | 0.320 | 70702 | 5.813 | 2465 | 0.329 |
| 5047 | 2.709 | 5822 | 0.782 | 2711 | 5.679 | 4435 | 0.617 |
| 5048 | 3.320 | 6944 | 0.938 | 71501 | 6.882 | 5545 | 1.623 |
| 5052 | 2.184 | 3258 | 0.547 | 70501 | 6.748 | 5603 | 1.060 |
| 5053 | 1.747 | 3598 | 0.391 | 80101 | 7.750 | 4494 | 0.662 |
| 5057 | 3.844 | 42080 | 0.508 | 80401 | 6.080 | 4384 | 0.686 |
| 5061 | 3.408 | 5585 | 2.345 | 4006 | 6.948 | 3409 | 0.416 |
| 6301 | 2.446 | 13356 | 1.719 | 2403 | 7.750 | 2658 | 0.811 |
| 5064 | 1.922 | 4484 | 0.391 | 4202 | 5.879 | 3563 | 0.984 |
| 5065 | 1.747 | 4917 | 0.469 | 4012 | 7.416 | 3422 | 0.823 |
| 5067 | 1.835 | 4035 | 0.336 | 21102 | 5.211 | 3268 | 0.421 |
| 5068 | 0.961 | 3371 | 0.274 | 4402 | 7.483 | 1895 | 0.878 |
| 5072 | 3.320 | 12401 | 4.455 | 4503 | 7.951 | 3545 | 1.088 |
| 5073 | 1.747 | 4919 | 0.703 | 50501 | 8.084 | 6024 | 1.097 |
| 5075 | 2.709 | 7638 | 2.501 | 90501 | 7.082 | 1352 | 1.142 |
| 5076 | 2.621 | 5963 | 0.625 | 4910 | 6.948 | 2700 | 0.544 |
| 5202 | 3.000 | 9477 | 1.600 | 4915 | 7.617 | 5680 | 0.457 |
| 5204 | 3.000 | 7645 | 0.960 | 3012 | 18.000 | 3418 | 10.560 |
| 5206 | 3.500 | 5427 | 0.688 | 3031 | 26.250 | 3433 | 21.888 |
| 5307 | 4.000 | 3637 | 1.520 | 4048 | 19.000 | 860 | 7.936 |
| 5037 | 4.893 | 12701 | 2.423 | 4072 | 23.000 | 825 | 10.240 |
| 5058 | 4.369 | 7195 | 1.993 | 11301 | 11.250 | 6505 | 7.520 |
| 5071 | 4.543 | 9706 | 3.126 | 5073 | 28.000 | 2960 | 6.080 |
| 5101 | 6.000 | 5861 | 1.120 | 5081 | 27.500 | 2176 | 8.160 |
| 5103 | 5.500 | 10229 | 2.560 | 5130 | 29.000 | 3106 | 15.860 |
| 5105 | 6.500 | 5870 | 0.832 | 6021 | 13.250 | 2006 | 5.888 |
| 5318 | 5.500 | 10449 | 8.800 | 6061 | 15.500 | 2596 | 5.120 |
| 32201 | 5.000 | 2714 | 3.200 | 7013 | 27.500 | 2738 | 37.760 |

341

| CITY: | BIRMINGHAM, AL | | | CITY: | BOSTON, MA | | |
|---|---|---|---|---|---|---|---|
| TRACT | DIST. | POP. | AREA | TRACT | DIST. | POP. | AREA |
| 11202 | 14.250 | 6660 | 9.088 | 2052 | 10.125 | 5759 | 0.600 |
| 119 | 8.500 | 10084 | 15.680 | 2057 | 8.750 | 5062 | 0.620 |
| 120 | 7.250 | 8056 | 26.880 | 2062 | 9.625 | 4910 | 0.204 |
| 12301 | 10.250 | 7765 | 15.040 | 3536 | 3.312 | 5146 | 0.276 |
| 12701 | 10.000 | 2491 | 9.280 | 3541 | 3.750 | 3426 | 0.240 |
| 110 | 15.000 | 6697 | 8.832 | 3421 | 4.312 | 9552 | 0.648 |
| 129 | 5.500 | 18812 | 21.120 | 3423 | 4.000 | 7081 | 0.270 |
| 14101 | 16.500 | 3471 | 15.360 | 3397 | 4.375 | 5106 | 0.488 |
| 14201 | 16.000 | 5028 | 39.040 | 3734 | 7.375 | 3532 | 0.400 |
| 144 | 7.750 | 16109 | 41.600 | 3738 | 7.125 | 5244 | 0.880 |
| 2 | 5.679 | 3960 | 0.860 | 3681 | 10.500 | 8371 | 0.292 |
| 21 | 6.728 | 4382 | 1.079 | 3567 | 6.500 | 8702 | 1.080 |
| 36 | 5.592 | 5049 | 0.782 | 3572 | 6.000 | 3757 | 0.560 |
| 53 | 7.776 | 8235 | 3.595 | 3701 | 7.250 | 15978 | 1.380 |
| 57 | 5.592 | 11451 | 2.579 | 4004 | 3.875 | 5522 | 0.280 |
| 5901 | 10.310 | 7275 | 4.221 | 4012 | 5.750 | 5440 | 2.600 |
| 101 | 11.271 | 7009 | 1.235 | 2 | 5.000 | 9245 | 0.440 |
| 103 | 11.446 | 9242 | 2.501 | 511 | 3.875 | 6724 | 1.200 |
| 100 | 12.232 | 7095 | 3.048 | 924 | 4.187 | 7489 | 0.220 |
| 106 | 7.077 | 14369 | 3.361 | 1005 | 4.687 | 7369 | 0.272 |
| 109 | 5.242 | 6835 | 2.814 | 1010 | 6.000 | 11189 | 1.080 |
| 131 | 7.776 | 4397 | 2.579 | 1105 | 6.437 | 8840 | 0.520 |
| 133 | 8.737 | 4810 | 1.485 | 1202 | 4.375 | 4423 | 0.256 |
| 136 | 10.223 | 3796 | 2.032 | 1303 | 7.000 | 6210 | 0.540 |
| 138 | 11.796 | 5202 | 3.830 | 1404 | 6.375 | 7360 | 0.760 |
| 125 | 7.864 | 6554 | 10.473 | 1701 | 4.250 | 6846 | 0.532 |
| 5 | 3.145 | 7330 | 2.188 | 1707 | 4.500 | 6672 | 0.712 |
| 8 | 2.883 | 6288 | 1.641 | 3531 | 1.812 | 5601 | 0.520 |
| 11 | 4.893 | 5819 | 2.931 | 3502 | 3.187 | 7742 | 0.260 |
| 12 | 3.670 | 8352 | 3.283 | 0 | 0.0 | 0 | 0.0 |
| 15 | 1.048 | 7967 | 0.938 | 7 | 3.812 | 9730 | 0.240 |
| 18 | 4.281 | 4042 | 1.055 | 104 | 1.875 | 9620 | 0.260 |
| 2302 | 3.844 | 8328 | 2.970 | 201 | 0.687 | 5443 | 0.152 |
| 29 | 1.485 | 6228 | 0.469 | 301 | 0.812 | 3204 | 0.040 |
| 31 | 4.019 | 4678 | 0.930 | 403 | 1.625 | 3623 | 0.080 |
| 33 | 5.068 | 6128 | 1.329 | 407 | 2.187 | 2208 | 0.420 |
| 39 | 3.320 | 2955 | 0.899 | 502 | 1.937 | 4453 | 0.088 |
| 40 | 2.971 | 7486 | 1.329 | 509 | 2.375 | 4366 | 0.380 |
| 47 | 2.184 | 9946 | 1.954 | 605 | 1.562 | 4661 | 0.420 |
| 4901 | 1.485 | 2571 | 0.313 | 610 | 1.687 | 3709 | 0.068 |
| 51 | 2.446 | 9132 | 1.032 | 821 | 3.437 | 5523 | 0.156 |
| 56 | 4.893 | 6636 | 1.915 | 911 | 2.687 | 6281 | 0.160 |
| 7 | 2.709 | 7831 | 1.407 | 918 | 3.375 | 4279 | 0.160 |

| CITY: BUFFALO, NY | | | | CITY: CHICAGO, IL | | | |
|---|---|---|---|---|---|---|---|
| TRACT | DIST. | POP. | AREA | TRACT | DIST. | POP. | AREA |
| 2 | 3.495 | 7043 | 0.492 | 103 | 13.763 | 6751 | 0.366 |
| 12 | 1.398 | 5464 | 0.719 | 305 | 11.091 | 8117 | 0.457 |
| 15 | 1.398 | 8350 | 0.461 | 1103 | 14.966 | 5838 | 0.914 |
| 2502 | 0.874 | 6863 | 0.563 | 1407 | 10.690 | 7724 | 0.503 |
| 2703 | 2.272 | 7820 | 0.383 | 1608 | 9.487 | 5111 | 0.480 |
| 31 | 1.398 | 11135 | 0.703 | 2106 | 8.485 | 6864 | 0.480 |
| 3301 | 2.709 | 6378 | 0.313 | 4005 | 8.619 | 5250 | 0.297 |
| 35 | 2.709 | 10257 | 0.664 | 4112 | 9.020 | 2429 | 0.366 |
| 5202 | 3.145 | 4157 | 0.234 | 2241 | 10.690 | 2241 | 0.229 |
| 61 | 2.534 | 7428 | 0.547 | 11492 | 13.362 | 11492 | 0.846 |
| 6301 | 2.883 | 6713 | 0.313 | 7974 | 13.630 | 7974 | 1.006 |
| 6501 | 2.359 | 4267 | 0.156 | 5273 | 10.690 | 5273 | 0.754 |
| 6701 | 1.660 | 4846 | 0.250 | 3192 | 10.422 | 3192 | 0.640 |
| 69 | 1.747 | 13029 | 0.469 | 5501 | 10.824 | 5501 | 0.480 |
| 7101 | 1.223 | 7910 | 1.172 | 3106 | 9.888 | 3106 | 0.283 |
| 7 | 5.068 | 5403 | 0.399 | 3291 | 12.494 | 3291 | 0.480 |
| 10 | 4.543 | 9261 | 0.930 | 6004 | 13.964 | 6004 | 0.823 |
| 19 | 3.757 | 4806 | 0.547 | 321 | 8.084 | 10292 | 0.297 |
| 22 | 3.844 | 2951 | 0.328 | 505 | 8.285 | 6513 | 0.527 |
| 39 | 4.107 | 6142 | 0.719 | 604 | 7.683 | 4038 | 0.279 |
| 42 | 4.718 | 5654 | 0.469 | 620 | 6.481 | 3680 | 0.192 |
| 45 | 4.980 | 7303 | 0.782 | 701 | 5.078 | 6967 | 0.731 |
| 47 | 5.242 | 7246 | 0.606 | 715 | 3.608 | 4019 | 0.777 |
| 50 | 4.718 | 3326 | 0.547 | 810 | 2.138 | 3989 | 0.229 |
| 55 | 4.019 | 5506 | 0.703 | 2212 | 7.750 | 3976 | 0.448 |
| 58 | 5.242 | 10731 | 1.172 | 2227 | 7.149 | 2441 | 0.183 |
| 122 | 5.125 | 5011 | 2.160 | 2313 | 8.218 | 6195 | 0.754 |
| 1251 | 5.375 | 7161 | 1.120 | 2411 | 5.412 | 6995 | 0.283 |
| 76 | 7.750 | 4865 | 0.880 | 2426 | 5.412 | 10334 | 0.411 |
| 78 | 8.000 | 7754 | 1.760 | 2607 | 7.483 | 6043 | 0.283 |
| 7902 | 7.250 | 10111 | 1.376 | 2702 | 5.545 | 3494 | 0.366 |
| 8001 | 5.875 | 8559 | 0.976 | 2716 | 6.080 | 2494 | 0.178 |
| 8101 | 6.750 | 7414 | 1.280 | 2805 | 4.142 | 4953 | 0.366 |
| 8202 | 5.750 | 5320 | 0.496 | 2828 | 4.343 | 2422 | 0.146 |
| 87 | 5.000 | 6766 | 0.400 | 2839 | 2.939 | 8703 | 0.480 |
| 9002 | 10.500 | 7693 | 6.000 | 2915 | 5.078 | 4776 | 0.366 |
| 9104 | 8.500 | 5717 | 1.152 | 2925 | 8.084 | 7162 | 0.754 |
| 96 | 9.000 | 3829 | 4.800 | 3016 | 7.349 | 3549 | 0.283 |
| 10002 | 7.500 | 11963 | 2.160 | 3113 | 5.345 | 4254 | 1.006 |
| 10802 | 7.125 | 12344 | 3.872 | 3402 | 2.940 | 4375 | 0.594 |
| 113 | 5.000 | 5484 | 2.320 | 3511 | 5.145 | 7182 | 0.274 |
| 12002 | 7.500 | 7906 | 3.168 | 3801 | 5.946 | 6170 | 0.320 |
| 13101 | 9.500 | 4918 | 2.720 | 3817 | 7.216 | 7619 | 0.146 |

| CITY: CINCINNATTI, OH | | | | CITY: CLEVELAND, OH | | | |
|---|---|---|---|---|---|---|---|
| TRACT | DIST. | POP. | AREA | TRACT | DIST. | POP. | AREA |
| 301 | 1.048 | 3048 | 0.078 | 1011 | 4.343 | 7707 | 0.777 |
| 9 | 0.699 | 3562 | 0.203 | 1016 | 4.410 | 3119 | 0.187 |
| 13 | 0.961 | 2043 | 0.156 | 1027 | 3.608 | 5821 | 0.517 |
| 16 | 1.136 | 3055 | 0.149 | 1033 | 1.537 | 2631 | 0.366 |
| 19 | 1.485 | 2855 | 0.547 | 1038 | 2.071 | 4282 | 0.343 |
| 22 | 1.573 | 4384 | 0.305 | 1043 | 1.403 | 2822 | 0.091 |
| 25 | 1.660 | 3351 | 0.164 | 1047 | 2.004 | 3316 | 0.649 |
| 29 | 2.534 | 5423 | 0.449 | 1053 | 3.675 | 4243 | 0.283 |
| 33 | 2.097 | 3054 | 0.188 | 1058 | 4.677 | 5763 | 1.097 |
| 36 | 2.796 | 2834 | 0.391 | 1084 | 1.537 | 2502 | 0.229 |
| 39 | 3.058 | 3764 | 0.258 | 1089 | 1.603 | 3675 | 0.091 |
| 42 | 2.883 | 2752 | 0.281 | 1093 | 1.069 | 2425 | 0.183 |
| 50 | 4.718 | 6822 | 0.782 | 1105 | 2.539 | 1899 | 0.133 |
| 66 | 3.670 | 3493 | 0.352 | 1109 | 1.871 | 2761 | 0.233 |
| 69 | 3.582 | 6621 | 0.782 | 1114 | 3.875 | 5511 | 0.722 |
| 72 | 3.233 | 3496 | 0.399 | 1119 | 3.541 | 4466 | 0.320 |
| 78 | 4.806 | 3762 | 0.297 | 1124 | 2.405 | 6139 | 0.283 |
| 8601 | 3.408 | 5842 | 0.547 | 1131 | 2.806 | 3421 | 0.183 |
| 88 | 4.107 | 4584 | 1.016 | 1136 | 3.541 | 3131 | 0.366 |
| 91 | 2.184 | 3187 | 0.625 | 1141 | 3.007 | 3070 | 0.119 |
| 96 | 3.145 | 6366 | 0.954 | 1146 | 2.940 | 3052 | 0.640 |
| 100 | 4.893 | 11288 | 2.188 | 1152 | 3.741 | 2197 | 0.137 |
| 256 | 4.369 | 5155 | 0.485 | 1158 | 4.810 | 6541 | 0.690 |
| 21402 | 4.980 | 5531 | 1.978 | 1185 | 4.677 | 3982 | 0.183 |
| 4601 | 6.815 | 4824 | 1.798 | 1189 | 3.474 | 7514 | 0.389 |
| 47 | 5.155 | 5048 | 2.970 | 1193 | 4.209 | 6083 | 0.539 |
| 53 | 6.116 | 7885 | 1.368 | 1204 | 4.543 | 5213 | 0.370 |
| 56 | 7.864 | 8666 | 1.016 | 1021 | 5.545 | 7517 | 0.617 |
| 58 | 8.038 | 6789 | 1.094 | 1065 | 5.946 | 3254 | 0.571 |
| 61 | 7.077 | 3291 | 0.860 | 1163 | 5.345 | 4775 | 0.274 |
| 63 | 6.029 | 7323 | 0.625 | 1168 | 5.479 | 8771 | 0.361 |
| 75 | 5.330 | 2683 | 0.782 | 1175 | 7.349 | 4702 | 0.503 |
| 8201 | 7.689 | 4908 | 0.703 | 1179 | 7.884 | 5950 | 0.814 |
| 84 | 6.640 | 5223 | 2.032 | 1197 | 5.278 | 7320 | 0.503 |
| 10202 | 5.679 | 3030 | 0.547 | 1209 | 5.412 | 3848 | 0.361 |
| 252 | 6.029 | 6066 | 0.625 | 1214 | 6.414 | 6920 | 0.640 |
| 20703 | 9.262 | 16620 | 5.315 | 1221 | 8.084 | 4859 | 0.686 |
| 211 | 9.436 | 7922 | 8.832 | 1232 | 6.681 | 4302 | 0.640 |
| 21801 | 8.650 | 8267 | 1.172 | 1237 | 10.824 | 6828 | 3.611 |
| 21802 | 8.475 | 4096 | 0.743 | 1245 | 8.619 | 5289 | 1.600 |
| 229 | 8.650 | 1476 | 0.313 | 1501 | 6.280 | 6097 | 0.411 |
| 234 | 7.077 | 5170 | 0.625 | 1507 | 5.211 | 5835 | 0.366 |
| 23701 | 9.873 | 3840 | 0.485 | 1601 | 7.817 | 2680 | 0.503 |

| CITY: COLUMBUS, OH | | | | CITY: DALLAS, TX | | | |
|---|---|---|---|---|---|---|---|
| TRACT | DIST. | POP. | AREA | TRACT | DIST. | POP. | AREA |
| 0 | 6.764 | 4631 | 0.768 | 320 | 17.250 | 11819 | 4.480 |
| 0 | 7.576 | 1119 | 1.420 | 9602 | 9.250 | 8696 | 1.920 |
| 0 | 10.011 | 6885 | 2.879 | 13602 | 13.125 | 7639 | 4.928 |
| 0 | 8.117 | 9589 | 1.324 | 13701 | 12.250 | 4561 | 0.560 |
| 0 | 8.496 | 2600 | 1.765 | 139 | 11.750 | 8439 | 1.568 |
| 0 | 12.446 | 4510 | 1.535 | 18103 | 14.250 | 5418 | 19.840 |
| 0 | 8.929 | 3704 | 4.107 | 182 | 13.750 | 12170 | 3.840 |
| 0 | 6.763 | 4506 | 0.652 | 189 | 12.750 | 3810 | 1.568 |
| 0 | 7.034 | 5632 | 0.864 | 19005 | 11.875 | 14626 | 2.560 |
| 0 | 6.764 | 5195 | 0.729 | 162 | 12.500 | 6543 | 1.280 |
| 0 | 5.952 | 4055 | 0.768 | 143 | 11.375 | 22950 | 5.280 |
| 0 | 5.574 | 3700 | 0.518 | 174 | 12.500 | 3923 | 1.152 |
| 0 | 4.491 | 4168 | 0.557 | 180 | 9.750 | 8446 | 1.520 |
| 0 | 3.247 | 6113 | 0.461 | 19207 | 14.000 | 9555 | 2.544 |
| 0 | 4.058 | 5087 | 0.518 | 13703 | 14.500 | 6797 | 18.560 |
| 0 | 3.788 | 12479 | 2.744 | 152 | 10.125 | 8995 | 2.720 |
| 0 | 2.706 | 6557 | 1.362 | 16503 | 11.125 | 6605 | 3.216 |
| 0 | 3.247 | 2977 | 0.883 | 168 | 13.750 | 6107 | 18.960 |
| 0 | 4.600 | 2954 | 0.461 | 171 | 12.250 | 4412 | 17.440 |
| 0 | 4.870 | 2815 | 0.384 | 177 | 11.500 | 10056 | 4.400 |
| 0 | 4.329 | 2935 | 0.710 | 191 | 12.500 | 6106 | 1.744 |
| 0 | 3.788 | 6243 | 0.576 | 18101 | 15.500 | 5624 | 13.280 |
| 0 | 4.329 | 3506 | 0.384 | 5 | 2.000 | 4582 | 0.560 |
| 0 | 1.894 | 5059 | 0.480 | 1101 | 3.000 | 4132 | 0.480 |
| 0 | 2.570 | 3795 | 0.461 | 16 | 1.500 | 6007 | 0.560 |
| 0 | 1.894 | 3715 | 0.288 | 23 | 2.250 | 2553 | 0.352 |
| 0 | 2.165 | 3704 | 0.365 | 29 | 1.625 | 3778 | 0.320 |
| 0 | 5.952 | 8499 | 2.648 | 37 | 2.500 | 5855 | 0.624 |
| 0 | 5.682 | 2911 | 0.960 | 42 | 2.250 | 4638 | 0.960 |
| 0 | 4.329 | 3907 | 0.998 | 49 | 3.000 | 7597 | 0.960 |
| 0 | 5.140 | 3993 | 1.094 | 5901 | 5.750 | 8621 | 1.136 |
| 0 | 2.976 | 2490 | 1.267 | 64 | 5.500 | 5979 | 0.800 |
| 0 | 5.952 | 2310 | 1.727 | 7102 | 4.750 | 7662 | 1.040 |
| 0 | 6.331 | 1332 | 0.326 | 7601 | 7.500 | 2302 | 1.088 |
| 0 | 5.411 | 5800 | 0.672 | 7901 | 5.500 | 7769 | 2.160 |
| 0 | 2.705 | 2796 | 0.652 | 86 | 4.375 | 4121 | 3.360 |
| 0 | 2.976 | 3802 | 0.768 | 9102 | 7.250 | 8818 | 0.944 |
| 0 | 2.976 | 4672 | 1.055 | 102 | 3.875 | 6511 | 0.920 |
| 0 | 3.247 | 1884 | 1.036 | 110 | 7.125 | 10217 | 2.480 |
| 0 | 5.412 | 7400 | 2.360 | 115 | 4.625 | 6782 | 5.600 |
| 0 | 4.870 | 6441 | 2.667 | 123 | 7.625 | 7048 | 1.600 |
| 0 | 4.058 | 5552 | 0.864 | 13002 | 8.875 | 9724 | 2.240 |
| 0 | 6.493 | 3216 | 0.384 | 16701 | 8.625 | 3237 | 2.480 |

| CITY: DAYTON, OH | | | | CITY: DENVER, CO | | | |
|---|---|---|---|---|---|---|---|
| TRACT | DIST. | POP. | AREA | TRACT | DIST. | POP. | AREA |
| 2003 | 10.922 | 6663 | 1.094 | 101 | 3.670 | 3578 | 0.774 |
| 2005 | 10.223 | 7647 | 1.165 | 301 | 2.971 | 6407 | 0.782 |
| 2102 | 6.378 | 6168 | 4.299 | 402 | 1.660 | 7780 | 0.766 |
| 2104 | 7.339 | 5506 | 4.963 | 702 | 2.097 | 6721 | 0.610 |
| 24 | 4.107 | 3524 | 0.946 | 903 | 2.971 | 5329 | 0.821 |
| 55 | 3.844 | 6325 | 0.782 | 1301 | 3.495 | 4398 | 0.875 |
| 202 | 4.456 | 3581 | 1.094 | 1403 | 4.893 | 3372 | 1.211 |
| 206 | 6.204 | 6165 | 1.368 | 18 | 1.398 | 2905 | 0.430 |
| 210 | 4.194 | 2491 | 0.688 | 23 | 1.747 | 6944 | 0.594 |
| 214 | 6.466 | 4202 | 1.016 | 2601 | 0.786 | 3308 | 0.186 |
| 216 | 7.077 | 6673 | 1.798 | 2703 | 1.398 | 6278 | 0.195 |
| 602 | 6.029 | 2986 | 2.775 | 2901 | 3.320 | 4027 | 0.352 |
| 603 | 4.893 | 4185 | 2.345 | 3003 | 5.068 | 4305 | 0.469 |
| 703 | 4.893 | 6862 | 4.221 | 3102 | 1.660 | 4298 | 0.344 |
| 705 | 8.825 | 3756 | 2.892 | 33 | 2.883 | 4078 | 0.539 |
| 707 | 5.242 | 6079 | 1.641 | 3602 | 2.796 | 5112 | 0.899 |
| 801 | 4.543 | 7382 | 2.736 | 3703 | 2.971 | 3703 | 0.313 |
| 805 | 4.543 | 8280 | 2.892 | 4101 | 4.019 | 3971 | 1.938 |
| 902 | 4.107 | 3902 | 1.172 | 4001 | 5.854 | 8165 | 1.251 |
| 909 | 4.806 | 6058 | 1.055 | 4201 | 3.582 | 6111 | 0.774 |
| 910 | 4.194 | 4859 | 1.329 | 4303 | 4.281 | 4696 | 0.977 |
| 14 | 4.281 | 7702 | 1.329 | 4501 | 4.369 | 6591 | 0.782 |
| 213 | 5.417 | 7664 | 2.423 | 4603 | 5.679 | 6805 | 0.844 |
| 4 | 1.398 | 4871 | 0.383 | 49 | 4.893 | 2155 | 0.078 |
| 8 | 1.835 | 5062 | 0.469 | 52 | 6.291 | 4680 | 0.875 |
| 12 | 3.495 | 2764 | 0.508 | 5402 | 5.767 | 2708 | 0.969 |
| 16 | 1.660 | 4219 | 0.234 | 5601 | 8.912 | 1147 | 0.149 |
| 20 | 2.621 | 3817 | 0.313 | 6803 | 9.087 | 5577 | 2.126 |
| 28 | 2.621 | 5195 | 0.930 | 7001 | 6.990 | 2640 | 1.720 |
| 32 | 1.485 | 3878 | 0.469 | 11902 | 7.339 | 3821 | 1.016 |
| 34 | 1.573 | 2937 | 0.821 | 108 | 7.427 | 6362 | 2.032 |
| 39 | 1.660 | 6209 | 1.016 | 112 | 6.640 | 5980 | 2.736 |
| 43 | 1.660 | 4483 | 0.313 | 116 | 4.631 | 7336 | 1.579 |
| 47 | 1.660 | 4856 | 0.352 | 11702 | 6.903 | 6503 | 1.165 |
| 51 | 3.058 | 6345 | 0.696 | 11704 | 8.737 | 5755 | 1.602 |
| 59 | 2.709 | 3503 | 0.539 | 11802 | 5.941 | 9053 | 1.641 |
| 60 | 2.184 | 6367 | 0.547 | 5604 | 10.048 | 10245 | 3.361 |
| 63 | 1.485 | 5761 | 0.703 | 8501 | 10.485 | 10833 | 1.798 |
| 102 | 3.233 | 7801 | 1.368 | 9304 | 9.087 | 3937 | 1.602 |
| 803 | 3.495 | 3856 | 1.000 | 9801 | 10.485 | 2756 | 10.161 |
| 905 | 3.408 | 4260 | 0.469 | 10201 | 6.640 | 12484 | 4.142 |
| 29 | 2.010 | 4057 | 0.469 | 8702 | 5.767 | 5141 | 3.283 |
| 44 | 1.223 | 4065 | 0.391 | 90 | 6.990 | 7414 | 4.846 |

| CITY: DETROIT, MI | | | | CITY: FLINT, MI | | | |
|---|---|---|---|---|---|---|---|
| TRACT | DIST. | POP. | AREA | TRACT | DIST. | POP. | AREA |
| 5 | 1.781 | 1813 | 0.315 | 1 | 3.932 | 8520 | 1.016 |
| 21 | 3.094 | 3273 | 0.225 | 2 | 3.320 | 6371 | 1.079 |
| 38 | 1.969 | 3548 | 0.450 | 42 | 3.932 | 8204 | 1.290 |
| 5702 | 7.031 | 3486 | 0.702 | 44 | 3.670 | 3548 | 1.548 |
| 75 | 7.781 | 5820 | 0.720 | 10302 | 5.679 | 7354 | 2.423 |
| 115 | 3.750 | 3120 | 0.180 | 10304 | 4.631 | 5370 | 1.180 |
| 157 | 4.406 | 3146 | 0.261 | 10802 | 3.408 | 3040 | 2.501 |
| 184 | 5.062 | 4449 | 0.180 | 10803 | 3.495 | 4497 | 2.892 |
| 570 | 3.562 | 4341 | 0.288 | 110 | 3.670 | 7647 | 2.657 |
| 654 | 6.374 | 4942 | 0.540 | 11301 | 3.670 | 5710 | 1.720 |
| 754 | 6.000 | 10592 | 0.378 | 11302 | 3.932 | 5186 | 1.563 |
| 769 | 4.594 | 3634 | 0.198 | 114 | 5.242 | 5708 | 8.754 |
| 172 | 7.500 | 5274 | 0.378 | 11501 | 3.757 | 3596 | 2.647 |
| 20502 | 8.250 | 3584 | 0.540 | 11502 | 4.456 | 4497 | 4.690 |
| 25601 | 9.094 | 4193 | 0.518 | 11503 | 5.679 | 4845 | 4.221 |
| 26102 | 7.781 | 9274 | 0.720 | 12001 | 5.417 | 6096 | 4.533 |
| 30102 | 8.625 | 5666 | 0.711 | 12002 | 6.729 | 7945 | 8.910 |
| 30701 | 9.750 | 2743 | 0.738 | 121 | 8.388 | 2497 | 11.021 |
| 35602 | 10.406 | 5658 | 0.702 | 12201 | 6.728 | 4931 | 5.628 |
| 405 | 12.469 | 6817 | 0.720 | 12202 | 4.806 | 4120 | 2.188 |
| 45102 | 11.719 | 4619 | 0.702 | 123 | 7.252 | 3778 | 0.938 |
| 45902 | 12.094 | 5685 | 0.702 | 34 | 3.844 | 8499 | 3.830 |
| 606 | 7.594 | 6685 | 0.819 | 43 | 3.408 | 2681 | 1.876 |
| 66801 | 8.625 | 5622 | 0.648 | 4 | 2.097 | 2794 | 0.234 |
| 706 | 8.906 | 7090 | 0.702 | 5 | 2.184 | 2838 | 0.703 |
| 784 | 6.750 | 2703 | 0.180 | 9 | 1.398 | 3032 | 0.547 |
| 875 | 9.937 | 6492 | 1.170 | 10 | 2.446 | 4307 | 0.664 |
| 10302 | 11.500 | 7397 | 1.040 | 11 | 2.971 | 8098 | 1.337 |
| 10803 | 15.000 | 4913 | 0.352 | 13 | 1.573 | 2446 | 0.313 |
| 2004 | 11.000 | 4558 | 0.496 | 15 | 0.874 | 2356 | 0.547 |
| 3403 | 17.000 | 8371 | 3.232 | 17 | 2.621 | 6308 | 2.032 |
| 2203 | 16.000 | 8648 | 0.960 | 19 | 2.796 | 6455 | 0.743 |
| 2026 | 8.500 | 10180 | 1.440 | 21 | 1.835 | 4579 | 0.328 |
| 3801 | 20.500 | 3063 | 9.280 | 23 | 1.398 | 2962 | 0.164 |
| 1002 | 12.000 | 13052 | 1.600 | 25 | 1.048 | 2776 | 0.156 |
| 1089 | 29.000 | 7611 | 1.088 | 27 | 1.048 | 3190 | 0.383 |
| 1024 | 13.500 | 14063 | 1.840 | 31 | 1.223 | 2949 | 0.860 |
| 1040 | 15.500 | 5029 | 2.880 | 33 | 1.747 | 3172 | 0.938 |
| 82105 | 8.000 | 5022 | 0.560 | 35 | 2.272 | 6036 | 1.407 |
| 82603 | 7.000 | 5306 | 0.496 | 37 | 1.922 | 7736 | 1.086 |
| 518 | 2.625 | 2599 | 0.135 | 39 | 2.359 | 4291 | 0.617 |
| 539 | 1.969 | 2419 | 0.180 | 40 | 3.058 | 9514 | 1.172 |
| 553 | 4.781 | 8149 | 0.540 | 46 | 2.796 | 3541 | 0.586 |

| CITY: | FORT WORTH, TX | | | CITY: | HOUSTON, TX | | |
|-------|-------|-------|-------|-------|-------|-------|-------|
| TRACT | DIST. | POP. | AREA | TRACT | DIST. | POP. | AREA |
| 11501 | 10.000 | 8627 | 6.080 | 201 | 2.250 | 10834 | 1.760 |
| 21601 | 10.125 | 2291 | 2.000 | 206 | 3.500 | 9231 | 1.280 |
| 21701 | 12.500 | 4878 | 1.600 | 210 | 5.750 | 11981 | 3.360 |
| 219 | 15.750 | 6082 | 2.800 | 215 | 7.250 | 16983 | 4.512 |
| 221 | 13.750 | 7039 | 1.264 | 222 | 9.000 | 6444 | 2.000 |
| 223 | 12.500 | 4316 | 0.960 | 225 | 7.750 | 15844 | 2.752 |
| 226 | 11.125 | 3635 | 0.928 | 227 | 8.750 | 5818 | 4.304 |
| 229 | 14.125 | 6601 | 0.880 | 231 | 10.250 | 6965 | 1.264 |
| 109 | 9.750 | 8169 | 11.680 | 301 | 2.625 | 10545 | 1.840 |
| 11002 | 11.625 | 4361 | 15.040 | 307 | 2.375 | 12519 | 1.248 |
| 11502 | 13.750 | 3697 | 7.840 | 313 | 4.625 | 981 | 1.920 |
| 13602 | 11.500 | 8644 | 2.720 | 316 | 3.000 | 5544 | 1.760 |
| 101 | 2.750 | 4917 | 0.784 | 320 | 6.500 | 15447 | 3.520 |
| 202 | 2.875 | 4952 | 2.240 | 327 | 6.750 | 10399 | 1.760 |
| 501 | 5.125 | 4517 | 2.160 | 332 | 8.250 | 6479 | 5.200 |
| 7 | 3.500 | 4749 | 0.992 | 339 | 7.375 | 10017 | 5.120 |
| 10 | 1.000 | 3002 | 1.440 | 347 | 11.625 | 18217 | 3.920 |
| 1202 | 1.875 | 5292 | 2.160 | 357 | 11.750 | 18931 | 3.160 |
| 1402 | 4.000 | 3312 | 0.800 | 402 | 2.000 | 11551 | 1.248 |
| 16 | 1.750 | 2913 | 0.800 | 407 | 4.500 | 10349 | 2.112 |
| 21 | 2.500 | 5677 | 1.280 | 415 | 9.750 | 14834 | 3.200 |
| 2302 | 7.625 | 5724 | 1.456 | 417 | 7.000 | 12640 | 2.240 |
| 25 | 4.875 | 6626 | 1.120 | 420 | 5.625 | 14091 | 3.360 |
| 28 | 2.000 | 2724 | 0.640 | 423 | 9.000 | 17616 | 5.600 |
| 31 | 1.000 | 2080 | 0.464 | 424 | 10.000 | 12590 | 4.448 |
| 34 | 1.750 | 2765 | 0.384 | 427 | 10.000 | 6118 | 1.472 |
| 3601 | 5.000 | 5203 | 0.832 | 431 | 10.250 | 6951 | 0.920 |
| 38 | 2.750 | 5186 | 1.264 | 441 | 8.625 | 3847 | 1.504 |
| 41 | 2.125 | 4849 | 0.640 | 442 | 6.875 | 12995 | 4.000 |
| 4202 | 3.500 | 3761 | 1.600 | 444 | 10.750 | 18175 | 4.480 |
| 4501 | 4.000 | 7460 | 2.208 | 502 | 1.625 | 3211 | 0.720 |
| 4601 | 4.500 | 4360 | 0.880 | 509 | 4.125 | 12867 | 1.760 |
| 4605 | 4.375 | 4452 | 2.080 | 515 | 4.000 | 8023 | 3.040 |
| 4801 | 4.250 | 7183 | 1.520 | 520 | 5.750 | 12975 | 2.432 |
| 5001 | 5.125 | 5503 | 2.720 | 526 | 7.250 | 16491 | 3.040 |
| 51 | 6.000 | 4194 | 1.456 | 528 | 11.750 | 2033 | 2.400 |
| 5402 | 4.875 | 7727 | 2.400 | 532 | 9.000 | 12736 | 4.400 |
| 5503 | 1200.078 | 7500053 | 0.013 | 533 | 11.625 | 10695 | 8.160 |
| 56 | 5.750 | 6049 | 1.024 | 243 | 15.750 | 1733 | 19.680 |
| 59 | 5.500 | 5081 | 2.560 | 255 | 21.250 | 1681 | 7.440 |
| 62 | 5.750 | 9977 | 1.840 | 358 | 13.500 | 4302 | 2.000 |
| 102 | 6.125 | 10401 | 4.800 | 360 | 15.500 | 12820 | 9.440 |
| 13202 | 7.375 | 8856 | 4.080 | 534 | 12.500 | 1734 | 6.240 |

| CITY: JACKSONVILLE, FL | | | | CITY: KANSAS CITY, KS | | | |
|---|---|---|---|---|---|---|---|
| TRACT | DIST. | POP. | AREA | TRACT | DIST. | POP. | AREA |
| 1 | 3.857 | 6979 | 2.740 | 506 | 7.875 | 7228 | 1.600 |
| 3 | 2.375 | 4215 | 1.600 | 51803 | 10.750 | 5037 | 1.104 |
| 5 | 1.875 | 3708 | 1.760 | 51902 | 11.000 | 8869 | 1.088 |
| 7 | 2.125 | 4650 | 2.000 | 510 | 7.875 | 5418 | 0.944 |
| 10 | 0.750 | 3789 | 0.768 | 517 | 11.625 | 3701 | 2.080 |
| 12 | 1.500 | 4234 | 0.496 | 52002 | 9.250 | 9094 | 2.240 |
| 14 | 3.375 | 6590 | 2.160 | 52301 | 9.375 | 3496 | 5.840 |
| 16 | 1.250 | 2766 | 0.320 | 44102 | 7.625 | 4692 | 0.880 |
| 18 | 0.625 | 3090 | 0.512 | 44202 | 6.625 | 4278 | 1.200 |
| 20 | 1.875 | 6061 | 1.440 | 203 | 6.125 | 6115 | 2.080 |
| 22 | 3.500 | 5661 | 2.080 | 20601 | 7.000 | 9395 | 3.520 |
| 24 | 4.250 | 1558 | 1.280 | 211 | 8.500 | 13942 | 4.880 |
| 25 | 3.375 | 9170 | 1.472 | 110 | 7.125 | 7054 | 1.760 |
| 27 | 3.000 | 10093 | 2.480 | 11401 | 11.875 | 5503 | 6.240 |
| 29 | 2.250 | 14562 | 1.360 | 120 | 7.500 | 4659 | 1.440 |
| 104 | 6.125 | 7137 | 4.320 | 105 | 7.125 | 6483 | 2.560 |
| 107 | 6.375 | 6911 | 2.880 | 111 | 8.000 | 4007 | 1.760 |
| 109 | 6.125 | 3545 | 2.480 | 133 | 14.750 | 12349 | 6.880 |
| 111 | 4.625 | 4090 | 1.520 | 137 | 1.700 | 11940 | 8.640 |
| 115 | 3.750 | 6844 | 1.680 | 432 | 4.806 | 4335 | 0.625 |
| 118 | 4.875 | 4672 | 4.160 | 434 | 4.718 | 3004 | 1.876 |
| 122 | 5.000 | 6472 | 1.920 | 436 | 5.941 | 6550 | 2.032 |
| 126 | 6.250 | 9772 | 2.800 | 445 | 4.369 | 3050 | 2.970 |
| 134 | 6.500 | 6860 | 3.680 | 74 | 4.806 | 5606 | 1.172 |
| 149 | 5.750 | 7465 | 2.640 | 79 | 6.116 | 6488 | 1.094 |
| 158 | 5.500 | 8210 | 3.920 | 84 | 5.767 | 3621 | 0.821 |
| 161 | 4.000 | 7223 | 2.080 | 402 | 1.835 | 3260 | 0.508 |
| 164 | 3.500 | 6274 | 1.680 | 405 | 3.320 | 3091 | 0.938 |
| 102 | 8.500 | 7727 | 18.560 | 41201 | 0.874 | 2265 | 0.360 |
| 103 | 12.750 | 3810 | 56.960 | 416 | 1.573 | 4094 | 0.789 |
| 105 | 11.750 | 3736 | 35.200 | 421 | 1.048 | 3550 | 0.406 |
| 117 | 7.250 | 3024 | 7.040 | 426 | 2.272 | 3900 | 0.508 |
| 119 | 9.000 | 5967 | 19.840 | 42902 | 3.495 | 2483 | 1.094 |
| 127 | 8.500 | 3724 | 8.320 | 43902 | 3.844 | 2335 | 1.016 |
| 132 | 7.250 | 4833 | 9.600 | 6 | 3.844 | 5041 | 0.625 |
| 133 | 8.500 | 2191 | 4.480 | 18 | 2.097 | 5518 | 0.469 |
| 135 | 9.250 | 10502 | 13.440 | 22 | 3.495 | 4210 | 0.774 |
| 143 | 10.250 | 8452 | 3.648 | 29 | 0.786 | 2625 | 0.328 |
| 146 | 7.250 | 5190 | 12.160 | 34 | 3.582 | 4988 | 0.610 |
| 147 | 5.500 | 3914 | 7.040 | 43 | 1.660 | 4225 | 0.547 |
| 159 | 7.250 | 5364 | 11.520 | 52 | 2.621 | 4114 | 0.313 |
| 166 | 6.500 | 7996 | 6.720 | 57 | 3.670 | 4575 | 0.610 |
| 167 | 9.000 | 3199 | 18.560 | 61 | 4.194 | 6031 | 0.625 |

| CITY: | LOS ANGELES, CA | | | CITY: | LOUISVILLE, KY | | |
|---|---|---|---|---|---|---|---|
| TRACT | DIST. | POP. | AREA | TRACT | DIST. | POP. | AREA |
| 1892 | 4.893 | 5875 | 0.610 | 50301 | 5.750 | 7103 | 3.520 |
| 1899 | 6.815 | 8003 | 0.336 | 50302 | 4.875 | 6531 | 3.360 |
| 91902 | 5.767 | 3345 | 0.313 | 504 | 5.500 | 12644 | 9.920 |
| 1953 | 3.932 | 2986 | 0.297 | 702 | 6.000 | 2725 | 1.600 |
| 2091 | 0.961 | 6135 | 0.195 | 707 | 8.375 | 4006 | 2.080 |
| 2118 | 3.408 | 3785 | 0.313 | 708 | 9.250 | 6543 | 6.080 |
| 2141 | 5.592 | 4002 | 0.469 | 2 | 4.500 | 2913 | 0.800 |
| 2164 | 7.776 | 6037 | 0.274 | 4 | 6.250 | 5598 | 2.240 |
| 2182 | 5.242 | 6766 | 0.461 | 6 | 4.375 | 3501 | 1.120 |
| 2213 | 3.757 | 6801 | 0.453 | 10 | 4.500 | 4728 | 1.168 |
| 2225 | 3.932 | 3185 | 0.313 | 12 | 6.375 | 3001 | 1.248 |
| 2294 | 4.369 | 4677 | 0.594 | 14 | 5.750 | 6315 | 1.280 |
| 2325 | 5.592 | 3772 | 0.352 | 39 | 5.625 | 5417 | 1.632 |
| 36201 | 6.291 | 5968 | 0.219 | 41 | 5.125 | 3179 | 0.784 |
| 2383 | 6.640 | 7226 | 0.469 | 43 | 7.125 | 8402 | 2.240 |
| 2403 | 7.252 | 5248 | 0.336 | 45 | 8.875 | 4604 | 4.160 |
| 2652 | 11.184 | 4089 | 0.383 | 56 | 6.625 | 4548 | 1.600 |
| 2678 | 10.747 | 2559 | 0.453 | 76 | 4.750 | 8846 | 2.720 |
| 2702 | 8.038 | 2062 | 0.234 | 77 | 6.250 | 3107 | 3.360 |
| 2718 | 10.135 | 7925 | 0.547 | 79 | 4.875 | 2288 | 0.640 |
| 75301 | 11.271 | 6128 | 0.743 | 85 | 4.375 | 2528 | 0.800 |
| 2771 | 9.873 | 3737 | 0.539 | 90 | 8.875 | 8180 | 2.720 |
| 7024 | 8.213 | 4624 | 0.782 | 96 | 6.625 | 5444 | 2.400 |
| 2101 | 10.834 | 7315 | 0.594 | 10002 | 12.375 | 3144 | 7.360 |
| 6025 | 11.184 | 12285 | 1.720 | 106 | 9.625 | 4966 | 4.320 |
| 6000 | 8.825 | 4133 | 0.657 | 11001 | 10.750 | 14413 | 6.400 |
| 1811 | 7.500 | 3962 | 1.546 | 11501 | 14.250 | 14711 | 20.960 |
| 2423 | 7.000 | 2757 | 0.324 | 11702 | 16.875 | 8095 | 12.960 |
| 4809 | 7.000 | 7659 | 1.274 | 11902 | 12.625 | 7855 | 5.920 |
| 2266 | 2.500 | 2103 | 0.313 | 16 | 3.875 | 5095 | 0.720 |
| 2051 | 2.000 | 6005 | 1.034 | 19 | 3.250 | 2705 | 0.384 |
| 4501 | 1.500 | 5664 | 0.836 | 22 | 3.250 | 2739 | 1.312 |
| 2016 | 5.500 | 4874 | 0.857 | 25 | 2.375 | 1795 | 0.400 |
| 1851 | 5.000 | 4958 | 1.201 | 28 | 3.500 | 2869 | 1.152 |
| 1992 | 3.000 | 5489 | 0.836 | 35 | 3.000 | 3188 | 1.600 |
| 5426 | 10.000 | 6527 | 0.783 | 36 | 4.250 | 7052 | 1.440 |
| 5506 | 11.500 | 7923 | 1.567 | 52 | 2.000 | 5699 | 0.640 |
| 5315 | 5.000 | 9215 | 0.825 | 63 | 1.500 | 4496 | 1.120 |
| 5330 | 6.500 | 6277 | 0.574 | 66 | 1.625 | 4103 | 0.560 |
| 5302 | 7.000 | 8846 | 1.828 | 69 | 2.500 | 2898 | 1.040 |
| 7021 | 14.242 | 6289 | 0.461 | 71 | 3.375 | 4765 | 1.360 |
| 20301 | 14.766 | 7378 | 0.469 | 74000 | 4.000 | 3375 | 5.600 |
| 55420 | 14.500 | 7795 | 1.332 | 81 | 2.500 | 3604 | 1.248 |

| CITY: | MEMPHIS, TN | | | CITY: | MIAMI, FL | | |
|-------|------|------|------|-------|------|------|------|
| TRACT | DIST. | POP. | AREA | TRACT | DIST. | POP. | AREA |
| 302 | 8.563 | 7840 | 4.142 | 10003 | 12.582 | 12625 | 2.345 |
| 92 | 10.135 | 8945 | 2.423 | 75 | 6.815 | 9037 | 1.641 |
| 94 | 9.786 | 5201 | 0.821 | 502 | 10.310 | 5235 | 5.393 |
| 96 | 10.485 | 6726 | 3.048 | 602 | 9.436 | 4872 | 0.703 |
| 105 | 8.563 | 2765 | 2.501 | 702 | 8.825 | 15562 | 2.110 |
| 109 | 11.009 | 1761 | 2.970 | 9302 | 11.359 | 8343 | 2.032 |
| 221 | 9.436 | 22357 | 8.207 | 3901 | 7.689 | 8278 | 1.641 |
| 224 | 9.786 | 14714 | 12.427 | 3903 | 6.116 | 10617 | 5.784 |
| 305 | 5.941 | 3805 | 0.625 | 42 | 4.019 | 12735 | 0.977 |
| 2 | 2.097 | 4235 | 0.547 | 44 | 3.844 | 14853 | 0.719 |
| 4 | 3.408 | 5015 | 0.703 | 13 | 4.980 | 8034 | 2.736 |
| 6 | 4.456 | 5562 | 1.172 | 1802 | 3.844 | 6687 | 0.625 |
| 8 | 5.505 | 6096 | 0.641 | 1902 | 3.932 | 11336 | 0.782 |
| 11 | 7.077 | 4499 | 0.782 | 49 | 4.718 | 7931 | 1.563 |
| 13 | 6.378 | 4711 | 0.703 | 57 | 6.204 | 9156 | 1.485 |
| 15 | 4.893 | 2559 | 0.664 | 7002 | 4.631 | 5056 | 0.625 |
| 19 | 2.446 | 5030 | 0.469 | 201 | 11.883 | 5896 | 0.938 |
| 21 | 1.573 | 2889 | 0.391 | 205 | 10.310 | 5694 | 0.938 |
| 24 | 1.835 | 5465 | 0.469 | 97 | 13.194 | 11613 | 3.205 |
| 26 | 2.534 | 2754 | 0.461 | 208 | 8.475 | 6081 | 1.094 |
| 28 | 5.941 | 6106 | 0.938 | 406 | 7.951 | 6042 | 1.016 |
| 30 | 5.941 | 5893 | 1.000 | 203 | 11.446 | 9037 | 1.407 |
| 34 | 2.796 | 2803 | 0.469 | 403 | 9.961 | 7237 | 1.290 |
| 36 | 2.272 | 3668 | 0.547 | 501 | 11.533 | 5348 | 2.579 |
| 38 | 1.660 | 2025 | 0.312 | 1002 | 5.767 | 7189 | 1.094 |
| 45 | 1.311 | 3536 | 0.234 | 1201 | 7.951 | 7694 | 1.954 |
| 47 | 2.534 | 5243 | 0.743 | 1502 | 5.155 | 7884 | 0.657 |
| 49 | 1.660 | 5475 | 0.313 | 38 | 8.650 | 10353 | 4.221 |
| 53 | 3.582 | 10809 | 2.501 | 5903 | 8.126 | 3889 | 0.625 |
| 55 | 3.320 | 7411 | 1.485 | 7602 | 8.301 | 6606 | 1.766 |
| 57 | 2.796 | 6689 | 0.782 | 7703 | 10.223 | 5113 | 1.876 |
| 59 | 2.359 | 7995 | 0.563 | 6001 | 7.427 | 5292 | 1.055 |
| 63 | 3.757 | 3951 | 0.492 | 9301 | 12.495 | 4689 | 4.377 |
| 65 | 4.369 | 5531 | 1.016 | 9903 | 12.931 | 4023 | 1.641 |
| 67 | 5.155 | 8394 | 0.781 | 10001 | 14.592 | 6124 | 1.798 |
| 69 | 5.417 | 4270 | 0.938 | 2202 | 3.145 | 7133 | 0.938 |
| 71 | 5.505 | 3084 | 0.743 | 24 | 3.233 | 10415 | 1.251 |
| 74 | 7.339 | 4943 | 0.625 | 28 | 1.747 | 4209 | 0.430 |
| 78 | 4.806 | 17809 | 4.846 | 34 | 0.874 | 10623 | 0.375 |
| 80 | 7.514 | 6094 | 1.211 | 53 | 1.660 | 14541 | 0.586 |
| 82 | 7.776 | 5590 | 1.016 | 6301 | 3.844 | 6343 | 0.606 |
| 86 | 8.475 | 7308 | 2.110 | 64 | 2.621 | 10747 | 0.938 |
| 88 | 8.038 | 8715 | 1.251 | 66 | 1.398 | 10465 | 0.860 |

| CITY: MILWAUKEE, WI | | | | CITY: NASHVILLE, TN | | | |
|---|---|---|---|---|---|---|---|
| TRACT | DIST. | POP. | AREA | TRACT | DIST. | POP. | AREA |
| 3 | 10.310 | 4744 | 3.517 | 103 | 11.000 | 6168 | 6.080 |
| 7 | 9.699 | 3598 | 1.720 | 104 | 10.750 | 6428 | 5.696 |
| 11 | 7.339 | 3875 | 1.328 | 105 | 9.500 | 8892 | 10.560 |
| 13 | 8.038 | 4985 | 0.852 | 107 | 7.000 | 7259 | 2.240 |
| 14 | 8.912 | 4471 | 0.524 | 109 | 6.250 | 7285 | 5.440 |
| 17 | 7.864 | 5650 | 0.610 | 111 | 5.250 | 5158 | 1.920 |
| 24 | 5.592 | 2493 | 0.469 | 153 | 6.250 | 4886 | 7.808 |
| 30 | 6.990 | 4190 | 0.625 | 155 | 7.750 | 8699 | 4.800 |
| 36 | 5.767 | 2065 | 0.328 | 157 | 6.750 | 4320 | 7.680 |
| 51 | 5.854 | 3889 | 1.086 | 182 | 7.250 | 8258 | 7.808 |
| 55 | 7.514 | 5341 | 0.555 | 184 | 10.500 | 4640 | 17.280 |
| 195 | 7.864 | 4447 | 0.610 | 186 | 7.500 | 5834 | 9.920 |
| 196 | 6.640 | 4619 | 0.610 | 188 | 8.000 | 5943 | 7.680 |
| 197 | 6.903 | 6232 | 0.828 | 190 | 7.250 | 9375 | 3.520 |
| 215 | 6.466 | 3034 | 0.606 | 113 | 2.971 | 6320 | 1.759 |
| 702 | 5.592 | 6056 | 1.165 | 115 | 3.670 | 5097 | 1.798 |
| 904 | 8.038 | 4101 | 1.266 | 117 | 2.796 | 7603 | 1.407 |
| 1008 | 6.640 | 4161 | 1.094 | 119 | 1.747 | 2739 | 0.625 |
| 1010 | 8.425 | 4023 | 1.798 | 121 | 2.709 | 3699 | 0.563 |
| 1013 | 6.990 | 4270 | 0.610 | 123 | 1.835 | 3395 | 0.469 |
| 1302 | 10.834 | 3395 | 1.165 | 124 | 1.223 | 4362 | 0.391 |
| 42 | 4.631 | 3573 | 0.242 | 126 | 1.747 | 3091 | 0.547 |
| 47 | 4.194 | 6098 | 0.586 | 137 | 2.534 | 6588 | 3.048 |
| 61 | 4.019 | 2682 | 0.234 | 130 | 6.378 | 2244 | 6.722 |
| 66 | 3.058 | 6640 | 0.360 | 132 | 5.505 | 7024 | 2.032 |
| 70 | 2.709 | 5113 | 0.227 | 134 | 3.844 | 5355 | 1.485 |
| 75 | 2.796 | 3422 | 0.313 | 136 | 2.709 | 9689 | 1.915 |
| 80 | 2.184 | 3238 | 0.156 | 138 | 2.097 | 2686 | 0.383 |
| 85 | 2.534 | 2863 | 0.172 | 140 | 1.398 | 5032 | 1.133 |
| 90 | 3.408 | 3840 | 0.188 | 142 | 1.311 | 4378 | 0.469 |
| 94 | 4.194 | 3579 | 0.289 | 144 | 1.485 | 4374 | 0.860 |
| 99 | 2.709 | 4008 | 0.219 | 148 | 1.573 | 4799 | 0.313 |
| 125 | 3.757 | 2705 | 0.766 | 150 | 4.281 | 2648 | 3.048 |
| 179 | 2.796 | 4279 | 0.328 | 152 | 5.417 | 3702 | 1.485 |
| 184 | 3.233 | 1828 | 0.352 | 159 | 3.145 | 4085 | 2.267 |
| 190 | 4.444 | 5304 | 0.977 | 161 | 2.184 | 3313 | 1.329 |
| 192 | 5.417 | 4530 | 0.528 | 163 | 1.573 | 2949 | 0.453 |
| 200 | 4.543 | 3661 | 0.641 | 165 | 1.747 | 5336 | 0.899 |
| 203 | 4.369 | 4040 | 0.672 | 167 | 3.582 | 4625 | 1.368 |
| 206 | 4.107 | 4766 | 0.610 | 169 | 3.058 | 5847 | 1.172 |
| 210 | 5.417 | 2893 | 0.555 | 171 | 3.058 | 2787 | 0.782 |
| 801 | 4.107 | 3223 | 0.453 | 173 | 4.019 | 3918 | 0.938 |
| 803 | 4.107 | 5157 | 0.586 | 175 | 4.980 | 3295 | 1.110 |

| CITY: | NEW HAVEN, CT | | | CITY; | NEW ORLEANS, LA | | |
|---|---|---|---|---|---|---|---|
| TRACT | DIST. | POP. | AREA | TRACT | DIST. | POP. | AREA |
| 1403 | 0.601 | 4724 | 0.320 | 29 | 1.871 | 3801 | 0.183 |
| 1405 | 1.201 | 5166 | 0.434 | 265 | 4.744 | 2129 | 0.480 |
| 1407 | 0.869 | 6593 | 0.366 | 270 | 5.211 | 5420 | 1.623 |
| 1409 | 1.670 | 4421 | 0.448 | 221 | 6.280 | 5614 | 1.006 |
| 1414 | 2.004 | 5024 | 0.686 | 226 | 5.211 | 4068 | 0.617 |
| 1416 | 1.203 | 7283 | 0.457 | 248 | 4.543 | 4419 | 1.654 |
| 1418 | 1.670 | 4715 | 0.663 | 244 | 6.214 | 3848 | 0.411 |
| 1420 | 0.869 | 3736 | 0.274 | 250 | 5.078 | 8053 | 2.514 |
| 1421 | 0.869 | 2207 | 0.238 | 255 | 3.808 | 3737 | 0.457 |
| 1423 | 1.470 | 5127 | 0.571 | 260 | 3.140 | 3150 | 1.280 |
| 1425 | 2.071 | 5512 | 1.006 | 272 | 5.612 | 7022 | 0.969 |
| 1544 | 2.071 | 4469 | 1.280 | 305 | 5.078 | 5898 | 0.553 |
| 1655 | 1.250 | 4769 | 0.640 | 306 | 5.813 | 5289 | 2.331 |
| 1410 | 2.472 | 4346 | 0.823 | 2 | 1.336 | 2806 | 0.311 |
| 1412 | 3.541 | 5765 | 0.868 | 604 | 3.675 | 3542 | 0.736 |
| 1426 | 2.806 | 8545 | 3.063 | 608 | 5.545 | 7103 | 1.120 |
| 1428 | 3.274 | 6051 | 1.783 | 701 | 3.474 | 5655 | 0.526 |
| 1541 | 2.606 | 7250 | 2.971 | 902 | 4.209 | 6219 | 0.366 |
| 1542 | 3.474 | 6316 | 1.234 | 12 | 1.871 | 3657 | 0.526 |
| 1546 | 3.274 | 3889 | 1.051 | 15 | 2.405 | 2849 | 0.320 |
| 1548 | 4.744 | 6588 | 0.914 | 1704 | 3.875 | 5178 | 0.091 |
| 1550 | 2.806 | 5717 | 0.754 | 18 | 1.470 | 2899 | 0.224 |
| 1551 | 3.407 | 3924 | 0.571 | 23 | 2.806 | 5723 | 0.741 |
| 1571 | 4.750 | 2109 | 3.840 | 2503 | 4.276 | 2416 | 0.366 |
| 1572 | 6.250 | 4261 | 3.456 | 3302 | 4.076 | 6108 | 0.686 |
| 1574 | 4.500 | 4785 | 5.120 | 3306 | 3.407 | 7309 | 0.229 |
| 1601 | 5.000 | 3238 | 7.040 | 3702 | 2.272 | 5405 | 0.558 |
| 1602 | 6.000 | 4435 | 12.160 | 44 | 1.269 | 6814 | 0.338 |
| 1611 | 8.750 | 3857 | 20.480 | 49 | 1.069 | 6324 | 0.402 |
| 1651 | 3.500 | 4481 | 2.432 | 65 | 2.873 | 4461 | 0.361 |
| 1652 | 3.250 | 3317 | 1.920 | 72 | 2.539 | 4827 | 0.512 |
| 1653 | 3.750 | 2573 | 0.896 | 78 | 1.203 | 2326 | 0.128 |
| 1654 | 2.750 | 4428 | 0.768 | 81 | 1.871 | 7041 | 0.297 |
| 1656 | 3.500 | 6279 | 1.152 | 86 | 1.136 | 3587 | 0.146 |
| 1657 | 3.000 | 3943 | 1.280 | 93 | 1.470 | 7163 | 0.224 |
| 1658 | 4.750 | 7272 | 6.400 | 102 | 2.004 | 4478 | 0.187 |
| 1659 | 7.750 | 3929 | 10.880 | 108 | 3.207 | 2184 | 0.171 |
| 1660 | 7.000 | 8339 | 8.960 | 117 | 3.207 | 4016 | 0.480 |
| 1672 | 6.750 | 8941 | 8.320 | 13301 | 5.612 | 5885 | 1.143 |
| 1801 | 4.500 | 5611 | 2.560 | 124 | 2.405 | 2820 | 0.187 |
| 1802 | 3.500 | 5350 | 1.408 | 203 | 9.354 | 10064 | 2.423 |
| 1803 | 3.750 | 2915 | 1.152 | 216 | 9.220 | 5344 | 1.028 |
| 1804 | 3.250 | 1665 | 2.496 | 233 | 8.953 | 2922 | 0.338 |

| CITY: OKLAHOMA CITY, OK | | | | CITY: OMAHA, NE | | | |
|---|---|---|---|---|---|---|---|
| TRACT | DIST. | POP. | AREA | TRACT | DIST. | POP. | AREA |
| 7801 | 4.625 | 3349 | 0.992 | 301 | 5.746 | 5675 | 1.966 |
| 7804 | 5.000 | 3763 | 0.992 | 310 | 4.944 | 3399 | 0.078 |
| 7602 | 6.875 | 6443 | 1.120 | 312 | 5.946 | 2837 | 1.966 |
| 7702 | 6.625 | 4872 | 0.976 | 15000 | 5.879 | 1938 | 6.079 |
| 8002 | 8.125 | 4705 | 2.000 | 56 | 5.412 | 5374 | 1.326 |
| 8702 | 10.000 | 2501 | 4.000 | 6101 | 4.944 | 3450 | 0.686 |
| 6601 | 4.375 | 3583 | 0.800 | 6202 | 5.078 | 6130 | 1.051 |
| 6605 | 5.500 | 6730 | 1.728 | 6501 | 6.681 | 7315 | 4.342 |
| 6901 | 5.625 | 6675 | 0.992 | 66 | 6.031 | 12458 | 3.154 |
| 6904 | 6.875 | 12051 | 4.000 | 6801 | 6.280 | 6733 | 2.423 |
| 7102 | 5.000 | 5441 | 0.760 | 6902 | 8.418 | 8854 | 1.966 |
| 7203 | 4.500 | 7473 | 0.992 | 7402 | 8.352 | 11874 | 5.485 |
| 7206 | 6.125 | 3145 | 0.992 | 7406 | 10.623 | 1725 | 0.731 |
| 7301 | 4.500 | 6423 | 9.280 | 7408 | 9.888 | 4347 | 0.905 |
| 8307 | 8.125 | 3528 | 0.992 | 63 | 5.412 | 9366 | 2.834 |
| 8505 | 9.625 | 1263 | 3.200 | 30401 | 1.603 | 3390 | 1.199 |
| 8803 | 10.500 | 2028 | 4.000 | 30502 | 2.539 | 3138 | 0.526 |
| 1013 | 2.625 | 5655 | 0.640 | 307 | 4.142 | 3991 | 0.686 |
| 1021 | 3.625 | 2542 | 0.512 | 212 | 2.338 | 3268 | 2.468 |
| 1028 | 2.500 | 4631 | 0.944 | 3 | 4.209 | 3254 | 0.526 |
| 1048 | 3.000 | 3525 | 0.800 | 4 | 4.076 | 3040 | 1.531 |
| 1054 | 4.000 | 2621 | 0.800 | 7 | 3.007 | 3142 | 0.402 |
| 5901 | 4.375 | 7378 | 1.408 | 10 | 2.405 | 2177 | 0.279 |
| 5904 | 4.000 | 4094 | 1.040 | 1301 | 1.603 | 1448 | 0.155 |
| 1061 | 4.500 | 4540 | 5.920 | 15 | 1.470 | 1212 | 0.174 |
| 6303 | 6.125 | 4097 | 0.800 | 19 | 0.601 | 2408 | 0.183 |
| 6603 | 5.875 | 6227 | 1.040 | 22 | 0.935 | 2542 | 0.357 |
| 1070 | 4.250 | 9140 | 6.224 | 25 | 2.472 | 3004 | 1.508 |
| 8307 | 8.125 | 3528 | 0.992 | 28 | 4.276 | 3628 | 0.868 |
| 1002 | 3.495 | 6833 | 1.407 | 30 | 4.610 | 7581 | 1.097 |
| 1005 | 2.446 | 3601 | 1.172 | 33 | 1.470 | 3110 | 0.594 |
| 1008 | 2.796 | 3000 | 0.610 | 35 | 3.341 | 5501 | 1.303 |
| 1011 | 2.010 | 1207 | 0.305 | 38 | 1.804 | 5457 | 0.731 |
| 1015 | 1.573 | 3212 | 0.860 | 41 | 1.136 | 1326 | 0.183 |
| 1018 | 1.485 | 2224 | 0.313 | 44 | 2.606 | 2201 | 0.594 |
| 1024 | 1.573 | 3828 | 0.625 | 47 | 4.076 | 2912 | 1.234 |
| 1030 | 1.048 | 3026 | 0.360 | 50 | 2.004 | 5173 | 0.448 |
| 1032 | 0.437 | 2625 | 0.375 | 53 | 2.672 | 3197 | 0.800 |
| 1039 | 1.922 | 5030 | 1.477 | 5901 | 3.741 | 3471 | 0.548 |
| 1042 | 3.495 | 2263 | 0.953 | 6 | 3.541 | 3573 | 0.366 |
| 1045 | 2.710 | 2967 | 0.594 | 8 | 2.806 | 4004 | 0.823 |
| 1051 | 3.757 | 2002 | 2.579 | 20 | 1.336 | 3357 | 0.663 |
| 1056 | 3.844 | 5166 | 1.415 | 32 | 2.940 | 2703 | 0.754 |

| CITY: | PHILADELPHIA, PA | | | CITY; | PHOENIX, AZ | | |
|---|---|---|---|---|---|---|---|
| TRACT | DIST. | POP. | AREA | TRACT | DIST. | POP. | AREA |
| 501 | 10.834 | 5915 | 2.228 | 925 | 9.000 | 3501 | 1.040 |
| 7009 | 15.815 | 3105 | 0.844 | 928 | 8.875 | 7329 | 1.008 |
| 6061 | 7.427 | 2597 | 0.406 | 931 | 7.500 | 7109 | 2.880 |
| 6072 | 8.563 | 5359 | 1.235 | 1033 | 12.750 | 4580 | 3.040 |
| 6086 | 14.329 | 4492 | 2.110 | 36000 | 12.000 | 2957 | 9.920 |
| 4012 | 9.000 | 4638 | 0.610 | 1039 | 10.625 | 2926 | 0.992 |
| 1502 | 8.213 | 2695 | 0.625 | 1042 | 12.000 | 8373 | 18.720 |
| 4090 | 7.689 | 4439 | 0.531 | 1045 | 8.500 | 6255 | 1.104 |
| 2015 | 12.145 | 4620 | 3.517 | 1048 | 9.500 | 4000 | 3.680 |
| 1703 | 12.407 | 4162 | 0.938 | 1052 | 7.625 | 5238 | 1.680 |
| 3104 | 11.359 | 4324 | 1.798 | 1054 | 7.625 | 3762 | 1.040 |
| 3204 | 17.824 | 1592 | 3.361 | 1057 | 8.500 | 7118 | 1.040 |
| 2101 | 12.232 | 4394 | 1.188 | 1060 | 6.750 | 5665 | 1.040 |
| 215 | 7.339 | 4590 | 0.461 | 1063 | 6.625 | 3983 | 1.088 |
| 218 | 8.825 | 4005 | 0.469 | 1069 | 6.250 | 6361 | 1.040 |
| 247 | 6.640 | 7349 | 0.383 | 1071 | 6.000 | 6440 | 1.040 |
| 252 | 7.077 | 9992 | 0.328 | 1080 | 7.250 | 4222 | 1.600 |
| 263 | 8.737 | 11874 | 0.508 | 1093 | 6.125 | 3690 | 1.040 |
| 270 | 7.339 | 2796 | 0.266 | 1096 | 8.750 | 5260 | 1.040 |
| 305 | 7.602 | 12271 | 0.406 | 1099 | 6.500 | 5360 | 1.040 |
| 320 | 8.038 | 8254 | 0.313 | 1112 | 6.875 | 5098 | 4.160 |
| 331 | 9.786 | 10466 | 0.469 | 2170 | 10.500 | 7743 | 2.272 |
| 349 | 10.834 | 9595 | 0.930 | 2182 | 9.000 | 6019 | 1.040 |
| 6018 | 3.145 | 3693 | 1.266 | 1066 | 5.500 | 4047 | 1.040 |
| 6028 | 6.291 | 2523 | 0.922 | 1074 | 4.500 | 4183 | 1.040 |
| 2044 | 5.854 | 4128 | 0.954 | 1077 | 4.875 | 4072 | 1.072 |
| 19 | 0.961 | 5126 | 0.141 | 1083 | 5.500 | 7494 | 1.360 |
| 33 | 2.097 | 10328 | 0.336 | 1086 | 3.625 | 6098 | 1.040 |
| 41 | 2.097 | 17437 | 0.430 | 1089 | 3.625 | 7556 | 1.024 |
| 60 | 5.068 | 6765 | 0.531 | 1100 | 5.625 | 8414 | 1.040 |
| 67 | 4.019 | 8961 | 0.430 | 1103 | 3.250 | 5158 | 1.040 |
| 76 | 2.097 | 1355 | 0.477 | 1106 | 2.625 | 5043 | 1.040 |
| 83 | 2.184 | 13356 | 0.430 | 1109 | 4.625 | 6457 | 1.040 |
| 108 | 2.534 | 8715 | 0.227 | 1115 | 3.250 | 5860 | 1.040 |
| 115 | 5.505 | 5040 | 0.149 | 1118 | 1.500 | 5028 | 1.040 |
| 121 | 4.893 | 3306 | 0.383 | 1122 | 4.250 | 7210 | 1.040 |
| 137 | 2.446 | 9725 | 0.234 | 1126 | 4.000 | 6480 | 1.040 |
| 151 | 2.883 | 15818 | 0.305 | 1130 | 0.750 | 3694 | 0.520 |
| 169 | 3.320 | 20435 | 0.469 | 1135 | 3.000 | 5083 | 0.688 |
| 170 | 4.369 | 4921 | 0.711 | 1140 | 1.250 | 3323 | 1.040 |
| 176 | 3.582 | 13344 | 0.461 | 1145 | 3.000 | 5198 | 1.040 |
| 186 | 4.456 | 6075 | 0.313 | 1150 | 1.875 | 4816 | 1.120 |
| 195 | 4.019 | 9832 | 0.313 | 1155 | 5.375 | 3336 | 1.312 |

| CITY: PITTSBURGH, PA | | | | CITY: PORTLAND, OR | | | |
|---|---|---|---|---|---|---|---|
| TRACT | DIST. | POP. | AREA | TRACT | DIST. | POP. | AREA |
| 304 | 1.010 | 3062 | 0.112 | 201 | 7.951 | 3729 | 1.837 |
| 405 | 2.424 | 3690 | 0.209 | 203 | 7.689 | 3945 | 3.361 |
| 407 | 2.727 | 2085 | 0.124 | 210 | 5.767 | 4616 | 0.938 |
| 504 | 1.717 | 3297 | 0.183 | 215 | 7.689 | 2690 | 2.579 |
| 509 | 1.666 | 3635 | 0.196 | 220 | 10.485 | 4095 | 1.876 |
| 605 | 2.575 | 1359 | 0.157 | 225 | 12.844 | 4425 | 2.173 |
| 802 | 3.080 | 3124 | 0.154 | 305 | 6.116 | 5580 | 2.423 |
| 807 | 4.040 | 2136 | 0.125 | 310 | 7.864 | 7805 | 4.611 |
| 901 | 3.333 | 3628 | 0.339 | 307 | 7.514 | 7729 | 1.602 |
| 1001 | 4.141 | 5747 | 0.718 | 419 | 9.174 | 2263 | 0.532 |
| 1505 | 4.040 | 4618 | 0.392 | 427 | 8.563 | 1793 | 0.461 |
| 1507 | 3.939 | 7910 | 0.548 | 431 | 7.951 | 4580 | 1.329 |
| 1605 | 2.727 | 5203 | 0.535 | 602 | 6.204 | 4301 | 0.703 |
| 1803 | 2.272 | 3158 | 0.154 | 4001 | 5.505 | 5827 | 0.782 |
| 1901 | 1.464 | 3820 | 0.731 | 42 | 6.640 | 2951 | 0.727 |
| 1908 | 1.616 | 1418 | 0.164 | 83 | 5.941 | 6508 | 1.524 |
| 1908 | 2.828 | 5630 | 0.914 | 9201 | 7.514 | 5385 | 1.141 |
| 2003 | 3.888 | 2396 | 0.326 | 9802 | 10.660 | 6225 | 1.548 |
| 2007 | 2.222 | 2658 | 0.415 | 301 | 5.242 | 4622 | 3.908 |
| 2010 | 3.282 | 6235 | 1.071 | 1 | 3.670 | 6058 | 2.267 |
| 2103 | 1.767 | 2670 | 0.151 | 302 | 4.281 | 7800 | 1.391 |
| 2202 | 1.313 | 2579 | 0.117 | 501 | 4.893 | 3632 | 0.485 |
| 2401 | 1.717 | 4328 | 0.371 | 801 | 3.495 | 5031 | 0.625 |
| 2503 | 1.515 | 2932 | 0.125 | 902 | 2.883 | 3491 | 0.430 |
| 2604 | 2.020 | 3103 | 0.235 | 1201 | 1.747 | 4747 | 0.399 |
| 2608 | 3.636 | 1048 | 0.334 | 14 | 3.058 | 5283 | 0.531 |
| 2701 | 4.040 | 3853 | 0.548 | 1701 | 4.718 | 6833 | 0.938 |
| 2705 | 2.979 | 4441 | 0.300 | 1802 | 3.495 | 3180 | 0.532 |
| 2806 | 2.828 | 1908 | 0.366 | 21 | 1.136 | 2551 | 0.703 |
| 2902 | 3.232 | 6244 | 0.640 | 2301 | 1.922 | 2244 | 0.313 |
| 3001 | 2.070 | 6527 | 0.345 | 2501 | 2.621 | 5690 | 0.539 |
| 4642 | 4.040 | 3017 | 0.319 | 2801 | 4.107 | 3516 | 0.360 |
| 4690 | 3.636 | 6441 | 2.533 | 2902 | 4.806 | 6021 | 1.055 |
| 705 | 4.191 | 2389 | 0.099 | 32 | 3.058 | 4534 | 0.453 |
| 1003 | 4.949 | 1330 | 0.185 | 3401 | 2.971 | 3431 | 0.391 |
| 1104 | 4.393 | 3832 | 0.209 | 3602 | 4.019 | 6989 | 0.938 |
| 1202 | 6.312 | 3092 | 0.282 | 3702 | 3.408 | 2861 | 0.391 |
| 1207 | 5.605 | 2745 | 0.222 | 3803 | 3.495 | 3852 | 0.563 |
| 1304 | 6.413 | 4018 | 0.222 | 3901 | 4.718 | 6311 | 0.930 |
| 1404 | 4.797 | 3270 | 0.363 | 4602 | 1.398 | 2035 | 0.664 |
| 1409 | 4.848 | 5435 | 0.783 | 49 | 1.223 | 3329 | 0.313 |
| 3202 | 4.292 | 3299 | 0.444 | 52 | 0.699 | 3516 | 0.227 |
| 4263 | 7.827 | 9012 | 2.324 | 58 | 1.747 | 5640 | 1.720 |

| CITY: | PROVIDENCE, RI | | | CITY: | RICHMOND, VA | | |
|---|---|---|---|---|---|---|---|
| TRACT | DIST. | POP. | AREA | TRACT | DIST. | POP. | AREA |
| 301 | 6.375 | 4608 | 1.760 | 203 | 7.500 | 5525 | 10.240 |
| 303 | 7.375 | 4629 | 3.360 | 1005 | 15.500 | 9491 | 30.208 |
| 305 | 9.375 | 4034 | 0.640 | 801 | 7.500 | 7432 | 7.936 |
| 30602 | 10.125 | 4124 | 1.264 | 903 | 11.875 | 5308 | 1.344 |
| 308 | 13.875 | 4107 | 5.920 | 905 | 8.000 | 3764 | 7.424 |
| 30902 | 11.625 | 4766 | 10.240 | 1010 | 19.500 | 2169 | 128.000 |
| 210 | 4.250 | 8446 | 1.840 | 102 | 11.000 | 3429 | 15.360 |
| 212 | 5.000 | 4313 | 0.992 | 902 | 8.000 | 6139 | 8.704 |
| 21401 | 6.625 | 5020 | 1.120 | 1402 | 10.500 | 5239 | 28.160 |
| 21501 | 7.125 | 3511 | 2.528 | 1502 | 8.500 | 1920 | 11.776 |
| 217 | 8.750 | 4985 | 1.472 | 3007 | 6.000 | 5752 | 8.960 |
| 21901 | 10.875 | 4787 | 0.928 | 104 | 11.125 | 5781 | 4.000 |
| 201 | 11.500 | 6738 | 3.456 | 106 | 13.000 | 4243 | 2.560 |
| 20602 | 13.750 | 8882 | 4.640 | 109 | 11.375 | 2414 | 3.840 |
| 20902 | 13.750 | 5271 | 14.560 | 202 | 9.750 | 4776 | 2.880 |
| 134 | 3.500 | 5602 | 1.760 | 302 | 8.000 | 4330 | 2.224 |
| 136 | 3.125 | 3245 | 0.960 | 402 | 10.625 | 3792 | 5.840 |
| 13702 | 4.375 | 3352 | 0.360 | 501 | 7.375 | 4477 | 2.080 |
| 141 | 3.875 | 3239 | 0.800 | 503 | 10.125 | 3373 | 4.960 |
| 143 | 5.250 | 4322 | 1.104 | 2006 | 7.750 | 6173 | 1.920 |
| 145 | 2.750 | 5256 | 5.280 | 803 | 5.750 | 6987 | 8.480 |
| 147 | 3.375 | 6587 | 1.600 | 801 | 9.250 | 2235 | 4.880 |
| 10101 | 2.375 | 4027 | 1.248 | 1101 | 5.000 | 3356 | 6.160 |
| 10502 | 3.875 | 4376 | 2.880 | 1201 | 8.750 | 4688 | 10.720 |
| 10702 | 5.375 | 5029 | 0.960 | 2013 | 10.750 | 3957 | 3.040 |
| 150 | 3.670 | 4666 | 0.469 | 211 | 4.700 | 3062 | 1.280 |
| 153 | 5.155 | 3105 | 0.313 | 502 | 5.500 | 4059 | 1.600 |
| 155 | 5.592 | 4511 | 0.430 | 104 | 6.500 | 9382 | 7.840 |
| 157 | 6.553 | 4777 | 0.469 | 202 | 8.250 | 9582 | 8.160 |
| 159 | 5.242 | 3327 | 0.375 | 1002 | 4.000 | 3423 | 2.560 |
| 164 | 2.883 | 5242 | 0.528 | 102 | 5.750 | 3503 | 1.920 |
| 170 | 4.369 | 4168 | 0.860 | 104 | 4.250 | 6910 | 2.880 |
| 2 | 2.534 | 8317 | 1.016 | 107 | 3.125 | 4202 | 0.864 |
| 24 | 2.446 | 8192 | 1.329 | 109 | 2.750 | 4320 | 1.440 |
| 139 | 2.000 | 3370 | 0.976 | 111 | 2.000 | 4475 | 2.080 |
| 102 | 2.375 | 7638 | 1.280 | 202 | 3.000 | 6146 | 0.800 |
| 104 | 2.125 | 6286 | 1.680 | 204 | 1.500 | 5893 | 1.680 |
| 161 | 2.184 | 4343 | 0.391 | 207 | 2.375 | 3579 | 0.368 |
| 7 | 0.699 | 3251 | 0.641 | 209 | 3.500 | 5368 | 2.240 |
| 10 | 1.223 | 3503 | 0.234 | 402 | 2.250 | 3131 | 1.360 |
| 16 | 2.010 | 6569 | 0.461 | 404 | 1.875 | 4036 | 0.336 |
| 21 | 1.922 | 8692 | 0.703 | 407 | 4.000 | 3014 | 0.640 |
| 29 | 2.010 | 6548 | 0.899 | 413 | 1.750 | 4716 | 1.456 |

| CITY: ROCHESTER, NY | | | | CITY: SACRAMENTO, CA | | | |
|---|---|---|---|---|---|---|---|
| TRACT | DIST. | POP. | AREA | TRACT | DIST. | POP. | AREA |
| 10 | 1.136 | 4618 | 0.654 | 5602 | 5.375 | 7744 | 1.520 |
| 14 | 1.269 | 3599 | 0.187 | 4601 | 4.875 | 5720 | 0.800 |
| 17 | 1.603 | 2805 | 0.217 | 1 | 3.250 | 4498 | 0.960 |
| 22 | 2.672 | 3552 | 0.233 | 5 | 0.500 | 3106 | 0.336 |
| 27 | 1.269 | 3375 | 0.219 | 13 | 1.125 | 3005 | 0.320 |
| 34 | 1.269 | 3047 | 0.315 | 15 | 1.875 | 4818 | 0.640 |
| 37 | 1.737 | 4200 | 0.375 | 20 | 1.000 | 2734 | 0.400 |
| 40 | 2.272 | 1950 | 0.160 | 24 | 2.250 | 4927 | 1.344 |
| 42 | 2.138 | 2555 | 0.309 | 30 | 4.375 | 6576 | 0.896 |
| 48 | 3.140 | 2792 | 0.194 | 33 | 3.500 | 5478 | 0.928 |
| 49 | 1.804 | 2619 | 0.171 | 34 | 4.500 | 4949 | 0.816 |
| 55 | 1.336 | 3194 | 0.183 | 4601 | 4.875 | 5919 | 0.672 |
| 59 | 1.670 | 2886 | 0.389 | 5502 | 4.000 | 4664 | 1.200 |
| 64 | 1.737 | 5471 | 0.320 | 67 | 4.375 | 5741 | 2.560 |
| 66 | 2.004 | 3274 | 0.201 | 10201 | 1.750 | 2955 | 1.104 |
| 71 | 2.940 | 4009 | 0.309 | 3 | 2.000 | 3666 | 0.560 |
| 73 | 2.205 | 1268 | 0.128 | 18 | 2.375 | 4999 | 0.768 |
| 78 | 2.539 | 5299 | 1.326 | 22 | 1.125 | 5072 | 1.264 |
| 84 | 2.071 | 3183 | 0.331 | 28 | 3.125 | 3290 | 0.288 |
| 10901 | 3.207 | 5077 | 0.695 | 3502 | 3.750 | 3766 | 0.448 |
| 128 | 2.205 | 4868 | 1.120 | 66 | 4.125 | 5094 | 0.800 |
| 88 | 3.541 | 2783 | 0.823 | 69 | 2.625 | 4573 | 2.080 |
| 101 | 6.815 | 5209 | 1.074 | 5902 | 7.875 | 6739 | 1.120 |
| 103 | 4.410 | 4690 | 0.994 | 60 | 7.000 | 10718 | 1.760 |
| 10601 | 3.942 | 3568 | 0.969 | 79 | 11.000 | 16290 | 3.680 |
| 10902 | 4.276 | 4220 | 1.234 | 7402 | 9.500 | 8419 | 1.200 |
| 13002 | 4.410 | 5207 | 2.034 | 49 | 6.750 | 4870 | 2.592 |
| 13601 | 6.815 | 6770 | 1.143 | 8902 | 11.500 | 12034 | 2.040 |
| 13902 | 4.744 | 5586 | 0.603 | 40 | 5.875 | 11205 | 7.200 |
| 14001 | 6.815 | 2558 | 2.171 | 43 | 7.000 | 5126 | 1.440 |
| 143 | 4.810 | 8649 | 3.474 | 48 | 6.500 | 5308 | 1.200 |
| 11203 | 7.500 | 2606 | 1.320 | 52 | 6.000 | 8955 | 6.240 |
| 114 | 11.000 | 6429 | 6.864 | 61 | 6.000 | 7285 | 1.408 |
| 11603 | 5.500 | 1788 | 0.832 | 7201 | 9.875 | 2127 | 8.560 |
| 11604 | 5.000 | 3002 | 2.272 | 8002 | 13.000 | 11256 | 6.080 |
| 11701 | 12.000 | 6489 | 5.088 | 8102 | 14.500 | 4653 | 1.360 |
| 118 | 10.000 | 6474 | 1.632 | 8108 | 13.750 | 4331 | 2.440 |
| 113 | 11.500 | 6279 | 16.000 | 8204 | 15.250 | 3646 | 0.992 |
| 124 | 12.500 | 4541 | 40.960 | 91 | 7.625 | 9420 | 5.760 |
| 13204 | 8.000 | 5123 | 12.288 | 50 | 7.250 | 4127 | 2.064 |
| 13501 | 10.000 | 2841 | 14.336 | 207 | 17.000 | 6498 | 8.480 |
| 14202 | 6.500 | 4277 | 5.632 | 209 | 13.625 | 6211 | 9.920 |
| 14502 | 9.000 | 5795 | 5.632 | 211 | 20.000 | 4231 | 17.920 |

| CITY: SALT LAKE CITY, UT | | | | | CITY: SAN ANTONIO, NM | | | |
|---|---|---|---|---|---|---|---|---|
| TRACT | DIST. | POP. | AREA | | TRACT | DIST. | POP. | AREA |
| 1000 | 3.058 | 2338 | 3.830 | | 1130 | 1.125 | 6290 | 0.640 |
| 4 | 2.971 | 4804 | 0.625 | | 1106 | 1.000 | 7002 | 0.800 |
| 5 | 2.534 | 5802 | 0.860 | | 1110 | 1.500 | 3586 | 0.640 |
| 6 | 2.184 | 5013 | 1.290 | | 1205 | 6.875 | 14257 | 3.840 |
| 8 | 0.699 | 2102 | 0.328 | | 1207 | 5.500 | 8017 | 2.480 |
| 10 | 1.398 | 4204 | 0.625 | | 1210 | 7.375 | 5150 | 2.368 |
| 11 | 0.786 | 5920 | 0.469 | | 1301 | 1.500 | 5508 | 0.992 |
| 12 | 1.747 | 5305 | 0.703 | | 1305 | 2.375 | 7539 | 0.960 |
| 14000 | 3.320 | 2424 | 3.830 | | 1309 | 5.250 | 3695 | 3.680 |
| 16 | 1.922 | 3988 | 0.461 | | 1313 | 6.250 | 5955 | 2.240 |
| 18 | 1.398 | 3521 | 0.406 | | 1402 | 2.500 | 3739 | 0.800 |
| 20 | 1.048 | 3586 | 0.406 | | 1406 | 3.750 | 2337 | 0.480 |
| 26 | 1.573 | 3997 | 1.016 | | 1410 | 4.500 | 2584 | 0.640 |
| 27 | 2.272 | 5442 | 1.290 | | 1414 | 6.750 | 10097 | 4.160 |
| 28 | 2.621 | 7636 | 3.048 | | 1501 | 1.875 | 6959 | 1.040 |
| 30 | 1.398 | 3508 | 0.508 | | 1505 | 4.125 | 11251 | 1.120 |
| 32 | 2.621 | 4962 | 0.531 | | 1509 | 4.500 | 6314 | 1.088 |
| 34 | 2.446 | 5054 | 0.508 | | 1513 | 6.625 | 6446 | 2.720 |
| 36 | 2.621 | 3429 | 0.391 | | 1517 | 6.875 | 6837 | 2.608 |
| 38 | 3.408 | 2667 | 0.328 | | 1602 | 2.500 | 3375 | 0.464 |
| 40 | 3.670 | 3831 | 0.547 | | 1606 | 3.875 | 7083 | 0.960 |
| 47 | 4.194 | 5201 | 1.094 | | 1701 | 1.750 | 10133 | 0.960 |
| 49 | 3.495 | 3161 | 0.625 | | 1705 | 2.500 | 5401 | 0.976 |
| 114 | 3.500 | 5925 | 0.880 | | 1709 | 3.375 | 8354 | 0.800 |
| 42 | 4.369 | 5770 | 2.110 | | 1713 | 4.875 | 8236 | 1.280 |
| 44 | 4.893 | 2286 | 0.703 | | 1801 | 3.625 | 8261 | 1.360 |
| 102 | 6.500 | 6682 | 1.200 | | 1805 | 6.500 | 5621 | 2.720 |
| 104 | 6.000 | 6339 | 1.280 | | 1809 | 5.375 | 15137 | 2.400 |
| 106 | 7.500 | 6897 | 1.200 | | 1902 | 1.625 | 6100 | 0.960 |
| 108 | 7.500 | 4395 | 1.520 | | 1905 | 2.500 | 10432 | 1.408 |
| 110 | 10.000 | 7156 | 4.320 | | 1906 | 3.375 | 10554 | 1.600 |
| 112 | 10.000 | 5437 | 1.920 | | 1910 | 4.750 | 17287 | 2.736 |
| 117 | 6.000 | 7564 | 1.120 | | 1912 | 7.500 | 10534 | 1.840 |
| 119 | 7.000 | 7679 | 2.160 | | 1203 | 4.000 | 6933 | 2.048 |
| 121 | 8.000 | 2643 | 2.240 | | 15000 | 7.000 | 3581 | 7.520 |
| 122 | 8.500 | 6977 | 2.640 | | 1808 | 5.500 | 2504 | 0.720 |
| 124 | 11.500 | 8400 | 2.880 | | 1908 | 3.125 | 2250 | 0.720 |
| 126 | 13.500 | 14221 | 15.520 | | 1204 | 4.375 | 5225 | 1.600 |
| 127 | 13.500 | 4943 | 1.120 | | 1911 | 6.750 | 5311 | 2.240 |
| 129 | 12.000 | 5473 | 12.160 | | 1812 | 8.125 | 2390 | 1.440 |
| 13301 | 4.500 | 4529 | 3.920 | | 1213 | 9.000 | 3534 | 1.760 |
| 134 | 8.000 | 14044 | 9.920 | | 1615 | 8.875 | 10457 | 3.360 |
| 13502 | 6.000 | 5926 | 2.720 | | 1717 | 8.250 | 4944 | 4.480 |

| CITY: | SAN DIEGO, CA | | | CITY: | SAN JOSE, CA | | |
|---|---|---|---|---|---|---|---|
| TRACT | DIST. | POP. | AREA | TRACT | DIST. | POP. | AREA |
| 2 | 2.621 | 5982 | 0.875 | 5001 | 1.660 | 3766 | 0.782 |
| 5 | 3.320 | 2690 | 0.547 | 5006 | 1.311 | 3617 | 0.508 |
| 8 | 2.359 | 2826 | 0.305 | 5011 | 1.311 | 5695 | 0.852 |
| 11 | 4.019 | 2419 | 0.383 | 5016 | 0.961 | 4832 | 0.563 |
| 14 | 2.709 | 2529 | 0.313 | 5023 | 2.446 | 5556 | 0.797 |
| 17 | 3.932 | 3221 | 0.227 | 2702 | 6.291 | 5112 | 1.329 |
| 2001 | 5.330 | 3824 | 1.032 | 2904 | 5.594 | 10317 | 1.329 |
| 22 | 4.194 | 4217 | 0.313 | 3001 | 3.757 | 4579 | 0.696 |
| 2501 | 3.670 | 3360 | 0.508 | 3104 | 1.485 | 3316 | 0.703 |
| 2701 | 5.417 | 4512 | 0.477 | 3501 | 3.495 | 10272 | 1.016 |
| 2705 | 4.893 | 2872 | 0.547 | 5038 | 4.369 | 6952 | 1.720 |
| 2801 | 6.378 | 4082 | 1.172 | 4404 | 5.679 | 7520 | 1.055 |
| 2902 | 6.903 | 5022 | 0.719 | 5051 | 2.534 | 3283 | 2.657 |
| 3002 | 6.291 | 6613 | 1.798 | 6302 | 4.194 | 6928 | 0.875 |
| 3101 | 5.068 | 3933 | 0.453 | 6501 | 4.543 | 4208 | 0.391 |
| 3201 | 6.640 | 5226 | 0.703 | 5302 | 4.980 | 4180 | 0.547 |
| 33 | 4.194 | 7815 | 1.720 | 5055 | 4.194 | 4370 | 0.528 |
| 36 | 3.670 | 8061 | 0.930 | 6101 | 5.417 | 6337 | 0.625 |
| 39 | 2.446 | 5868 | 0.703 | 5015 | 1.747 | 5127 | 0.485 |
| 42 | 2.796 | 5700 | 1.055 | 2102 | 2.796 | 5241 | 0.703 |
| 45 | 1.398 | 3767 | 0.305 | 5026 | 3.757 | 6543 | 1.641 |
| 49 | 1.747 | 3762 | 0.352 | 2901 | 5.068 | 6456 | 0.844 |
| 60 | 1.485 | 3140 | 0.391 | 3003 | 4.980 | 5699 | 0.744 |
| 75 | 5.767 | 6818 | 0.782 | 3201 | 3.932 | 12695 | 4.494 |
| 66 | 3.495 | 2469 | 0.234 | 3503 | 4.980 | 1627 | 0.860 |
| 7001 | 4.107 | 4497 | 0.547 | 3701 | 3.058 | 6260 | 1.720 |
| 72 | 5.505 | 5697 | 1.016 | 5041 | 4.893 | 6847 | 1.016 |
| 74 | 4.980 | 4364 | 0.688 | 5058 | 3.058 | 4841 | 0.758 |
| 77 | 6.990 | 6284 | 0.617 | 6201 | 5.592 | 7858 | 1.329 |
| 7902 | 7.689 | 7351 | 0.703 | 6401 | 3.320 | 3257 | 0.586 |
| 8306 | 10.223 | 3634 | 1.329 | 6602 | 5.417 | 7976 | 0.954 |
| 8501 | 9.087 | 5416 | 1.172 | 8002 | 6.640 | 6700 | 0.907 |
| 8507 | 8.038 | 6602 | 0.938 | 8202 | 6.553 | 7585 | 1.158 |
| 109 | 2.272 | 1960 | 0.469 | 10201 | 5.941 | 7637 | 5.901 |
| 117 | 4.980 | 3083 | 0.606 | 6604 | 6.728 | 9429 | 1.188 |
| 120 | 5.679 | 3961 | 0.797 | 7902 | 6.990 | 9145 | 1.157 |
| 123 | 7.339 | 5168 | 1.032 | 4403 | 7.339 | 11546 | 4.924 |
| 127 | 7.514 | 3344 | 0.547 | 4801 | 8.301 | 6150 | 1.485 |
| 8101 | 11.009 | 4427 | 0.477 | 6802 | 6.815 | 6047 | 0.938 |
| 8302 | 10.834 | 6872 | 3.595 | 7302 | 10.485 | 2297 | 4.924 |
| 103 | 10.572 | 4376 | 0.516 | 7802 | 8.737 | 9360 | 1.720 |
| 13303 | 10.485 | 4414 | 0.586 | 8402 | 8.825 | 8885 | 1.251 |
| 137 | 10.398 | 4617 | 1.954 | 9101 | 10.485 | 7350 | 2.501 |

## CITY: SAN DIEGO, CA

| TRACT | DIST. | POP. | AREA |
|---|---|---|---|
| 2 | 2.621 | 5982 | 0.875 |
| 5 | 3.320 | 2690 | 0.547 |
| 8 | 2.359 | 2826 | 0.305 |
| 11 | 4.019 | 2419 | 0.383 |
| 14 | 2.709 | 2529 | 0.313 |
| 17 | 3.932 | 3221 | 0.227 |
| 2001 | 5.330 | 3824 | 1.032 |
| 22 | 4.194 | 4217 | 0.313 |
| 2501 | 3.670 | 3360 | 0.508 |
| 2701 | 5.417 | 4512 | 0.477 |
| 2705 | 4.893 | 2872 | 0.547 |
| 2801 | 6.378 | 4082 | 1.172 |
| 2902 | 6.903 | 5022 | 0.719 |
| 3002 | 6.291 | 6613 | 1.798 |
| 3101 | 5.068 | 3933 | 0.453 |
| 201 | 6.640 | 5226 | 0.703 |
| 33 | 4.194 | 7815 | 1.720 |
| 36 | 3.670 | 8061 | 0.930 |
| 39 | 2.446 | 5868 | 0.703 |
| 42 | 2.796 | 5700 | 1.055 |
| 45 | 1.398 | 3767 | 0.305 |
| 49 | 1.747 | 3762 | 0.352 |
| 50 | 1.485 | 3140 | 0.391 |
| 75 | 5.767 | 6818 | 0.782 |
| 6 | 3.495 | 2469 | 0.234 |
| 1 | 4.107 | 4497 | 0.547 |
| 2 | 5.505 | 5697 | 1.016 |
|  | 4.980 | 4364 | 0.688 |
|  | 6.990 | 6284 | 0.617 |
|  | 7.689 | 7351 | 0.703 |
|  | 10.223 | 3634 | 1.329 |
|  | 9.087 | 5416 | 1.172 |
|  | 8.038 | 6602 | 0.938 |
|  | 2.272 | 1960 | 0.469 |
|  | 4.980 | 3083 | 0.606 |
|  | 5.679 | 3961 | 0.797 |
|  | 7.339 | 5168 | 1.032 |
|  | 7.514 | 3344 | 0.547 |
|  | 11.009 | 4427 | 0.477 |
|  | 10.834 | 6872 | 3.595 |
|  | 0.572 | 4376 | 0.516 |
|  | 0.485 | 4414 | 0.586 |
|  | 0.398 | 4617 | 1.954 |

## CITY: SAN JOSE, CA

| TRACT | DIST. | POP. | AREA |
|---|---|---|---|
| 5001 | 1.660 | 3766 | 0.782 |
| 5006 | 1.311 | 3617 | 0.508 |
| 5011 | 1.311 | 5695 | 0.852 |
| 5016 | 0.961 | 4832 | 0.563 |
| 5023 | 2.446 | 5556 | 0.797 |
| 2702 | 6.291 | 5112 | 1.329 |
| 2904 | 5.594 | 10317 | 1.329 |
| 3001 | 3.757 | 4579 | 0.696 |
| 3104 | 1.485 | 3316 | 0.703 |
| 3501 | 3.495 | 10272 | 1.016 |
| 5038 | 4.369 | 6952 | 1.720 |
| 4404 | 5.679 | 7520 | 1.055 |
| 5051 | 2.534 | 3283 | 2.657 |
| 6302 | 4.194 | 6928 | 0.875 |
| 6501 | 4.543 | 4208 | 0.391 |
| 5302 | 4.980 | 4180 | 0.547 |
| 5055 | 4.194 | 4370 | 0.528 |
| 6101 | 5.417 | 6337 | 0.625 |
| 5015 | 1.747 | 5127 | 0.485 |
| 2102 | 2.796 | 5241 | 0.703 |
| 5026 | 3.757 | 6543 | 1.641 |
| 2901 | 5.068 | 6456 | 0.844 |
| 3003 | 4.980 | 5699 | 0.744 |
| 3201 | 3.932 | 12695 | 4.494 |
| 3503 | 4.980 | 1627 | 0.860 |
| 3701 | 3.058 | 6260 | 1.720 |
| 5041 | 4.893 | 6847 | 1.016 |
| 5058 | 3.058 | 4841 | 0.758 |
| 6201 | 5.592 | 7858 | 1.329 |
| 6401 | 3.320 | 3257 | 0.586 |
| 6602 | 5.417 | 7976 | 0.954 |
| 8002 | 6.640 | 6700 | 0.907 |
| 8202 | 6.553 | 7585 | 1.158 |
| 10201 | 5.941 | 7637 | 5.901 |
| 6604 | 6.728 | 9429 | 1.188 |
| 7902 | 6.990 | 9145 | 1.157 |
| 4403 | 7.339 | 11546 | 4.924 |
| 4801 | 8.301 | 6150 | 1.485 |
| 6802 | 6.815 | 6047 | 0.938 |
| 7302 | 10.485 | 2297 | 4.924 |
| 7802 | 8.737 | 9360 | 1.720 |
| 8402 | 8.825 | 8885 | 1.251 |
| 9101 | 10.485 | 7350 | 2.501 |

## CITY: PROVIDENCE, RI

| TRACT | DIST. | POP. | AREA |
|---|---|---|---|
| 301 | 6.375 | 4608 | 1.760 |
| 303 | 7.375 | 4629 | 3.360 |
| 305 | 9.375 | 4034 | 0.640 |
| 30602 | 10.125 | 4124 | 1.264 |
| 308 | 13.875 | 4107 | 5.920 |
| 30902 | 11.625 | 4766 | 10.240 |
| 210 | 4.250 | 8446 | 1.840 |
| 212 | 5.000 | 4313 | 0.992 |
| 21401 | 6.625 | 5020 | 1.120 |
| 21501 | 7.125 | 3511 | 2.528 |
| 217 | 8.750 | 4985 | 1.472 |
| 21901 | 10.875 | 4787 | 0.928 |
| 201 | 11.500 | 6738 | 3.456 |
| 20602 | 13.750 | 8882 | 4.640 |
| 20902 | 13.750 | 5271 | 14.560 |
| 134 | 3.500 | 5602 | 1.760 |
| 136 | 3.125 | 3245 | 0.960 |
| 13702 | 4.375 | 3352 | 0.360 |
| 141 | 3.875 | 3239 | 0.800 |
| 143 | 5.250 | 4322 | 1.104 |
| 145 | 2.750 | 5256 | 5.280 |
| 147 | 3.375 | 6587 | 1.600 |
| 10101 | 2.375 | 4027 | 1.248 |
| 10502 | 3.875 | 4376 | 2.880 |
| 10702 | 5.375 | 5029 | 0.960 |
| 150 | 3.670 | 4666 | 0.469 |
| 153 | 5.155 | 3105 | 0.313 |
| 155 | 5.592 | 4511 | 0.430 |
| 157 | 6.553 | 4777 | 0.469 |
| 159 | 5.242 | 3327 | 0.375 |
| 164 | 2.883 | 5242 | 0.528 |
| 170 | 4.369 | 4168 | 0.860 |
| 2 | 2.534 | 8317 | 1.016 |
| 24 | 2.446 | 8192 | 1.329 |
| 139 | 2.000 | 3370 | 0.976 |
| 102 | 2.375 | 7638 | 1.280 |
| 104 | 2.125 | 6286 | 1.680 |
| 161 | 2.184 | 4343 | 0.391 |
| 7 | 0.699 | 3251 | 0.641 |
| 10 | 1.223 | 3503 | 0.234 |
| 16 | 2.010 | 6569 | 0.461 |
| 21 | 1.922 | 8692 | 0.703 |
| 29 | 2.010 | 6548 | 0.899 |

## CITY: RICHMOND, VA

| TRACT | DIST. | POP. | AREA |
|---|---|---|---|
| 203 | 7.500 | 5525 | 10.240 |
| 1005 | 15.500 | 9491 | 30.208 |
| 801 | 7.500 | 7432 | 7.936 |
| 903 | 11.875 | 5308 | 1.344 |
| 905 | 8.000 | 3764 | 7.424 |
| 1010 | 19.500 | 2169 | 128.000 |
| 102 | 11.000 | 3429 | 15.360 |
| 902 | 8.000 | 6139 | 8.704 |
| 1402 | 10.500 | 5239 | 28.160 |
| 1502 | 8.500 | 1920 | 11.776 |
| 3007 | 6.000 | 5752 | 8.960 |
| 104 | 11.125 | 5781 | 4.000 |
| 106 | 13.000 | 4243 | 2.560 |
| 109 | 11.375 | 2414 | 3.840 |
| 202 | 9.750 | 4776 | 2.880 |
| 302 | 8.000 | 4330 | 2.224 |
| 402 | 10.625 | 3792 | 5.840 |
| 501 | 7.375 | 4477 | 2.080 |
| 503 | 10.125 | 3373 | 4.960 |
| 2006 | 7.750 | 6173 | 1.920 |
| 803 | 5.750 | 6987 | 8.480 |
| 801 | 9.250 | 2235 | 4.880 |
| 1101 | 5.000 | 3356 | 6.160 |
| 1201 | 8.750 | 4688 | 10.720 |
| 2013 | 10.750 | 3957 | 3.040 |
| 211 | 4.700 | 3062 | 1.280 |
| 502 | 5.000 | 4059 | 1.600 |
| 104 | 6.500 | 9382 | 7.840 |
| 202 | 8.250 | 9582 | 8.160 |
| 1002 | 4.000 | 3423 | 2.560 |
| 102 | 5.750 | 3503 | 1.920 |
| 104 | 4.250 | 6910 | 2.880 |
| 107 | 3.125 | 4202 | 0.864 |
| 109 | 2.750 | 4320 | 1.440 |
| 111 | 2.000 | 4475 | 2.080 |
| 202 | 3.000 | 6146 | 0.800 |
| 204 | 1.500 | 5893 | 1.680 |
| 207 | 2.375 | 3579 | 0.368 |
| 209 | 3.500 | 5368 | 2.240 |
| 402 | 2.250 | 3131 | 1.360 |
| 404 | 1.875 | 4036 | 0.336 |
| 407 | 4.000 | 3014 | 0.640 |
| 413 | 1.750 | 4716 | 1.456 |

| CITY: ROCHESTER, NY | | | | CITY: SACRAMENTO, CA | | | |
|---|---|---|---|---|---|---|---|
| TRACT | DIST. | POP. | AREA | TRACT | DIST. | POP. | AREA |
| 10 | 1.136 | 4618 | 0.654 | 5602 | 5.375 | 7744 | 1.520 |
| 14 | 1.269 | 3599 | 0.187 | 4601 | 4.875 | 5720 | 0.800 |
| 17 | 1.603 | 2805 | 0.217 | 1 | 3.250 | 4498 | 0.960 |
| 22 | 2.672 | 3552 | 0.233 | 5 | 0.500 | 3106 | 0.336 |
| 27 | 1.269 | 3375 | 0.219 | 13 | 1.125 | 3005 | 0.320 |
| 34 | 1.269 | 3047 | 0.315 | 15 | 1.875 | 4818 | 0.640 |
| 37 | 1.737 | 4200 | 0.375 | 20 | 1.000 | 2734 | 0.400 |
| 40 | 2.272 | 1950 | 0.160 | 24 | 2.250 | 4927 | 1.344 |
| 42 | 2.138 | 2555 | 0.309 | 30 | 4.375 | 6576 | 0.896 |
| 48 | 3.140 | 2792 | 0.194 | 33 | 3.500 | 5478 | 0.928 |
| 49 | 1.804 | 2619 | 0.171 | 34 | 4.500 | 4949 | 0.816 |
| 55 | 1.336 | 3194 | 0.183 | 4601 | 4.875 | 5919 | 0.672 |
| 59 | 1.670 | 2886 | 0.389 | 5502 | 4.000 | 4664 | 1.200 |
| 64 | 1.737 | 5471 | 0.320 | 67 | 4.375 | 5741 | 2.560 |
| 66 | 2.004 | 3274 | 0.201 | 10201 | 1.750 | 2955 | 1.104 |
| 71 | 2.940 | 4009 | 0.309 | 3 | 2.000 | 3666 | 0.560 |
| 73 | 2.205 | 1268 | 0.128 | 18 | 2.375 | 4999 | 0.768 |
| 78 | 2.539 | 5299 | 1.326 | 22 | 1.125 | 5072 | 1.264 |
| 84 | 2.071 | 3183 | 0.331 | 28 | 3.125 | 3290 | 0.288 |
| 10901 | 3.207 | 5077 | 0.695 | 3502 | 3.750 | 3766 | 0.448 |
| 128 | 2.205 | 4868 | 1.120 | 66 | 4.125 | 5094 | 0.800 |
| 88 | 3.541 | 2783 | 0.823 | 69 | 2.625 | 4573 | 2.080 |
| 101 | 6.815 | 5209 | 1.074 | 5902 | 7.875 | 6739 | 1.120 |
| 103 | 4.410 | 4690 | 0.994 | 60 | 7.000 | 10718 | 1.760 |
| 10601 | 3.942 | 3568 | 0.969 | 79 | 11.000 | 16290 | 3.680 |
| 10902 | 4.276 | 4220 | 1.234 | 7402 | 9.500 | 8419 | 1.200 |
| 13002 | 4.410 | 5207 | 2.034 | 49 | 6.750 | 4870 | 2.592 |
| 13601 | 6.815 | 6770 | 1.143 | 8902 | 11.500 | 12034 | 2.040 |
| 13902 | 4.744 | 5586 | 0.603 | 40 | 5.875 | 11205 | 7.200 |
| 14001 | 6.815 | 2558 | 2.171 | 43 | 7.000 | 5126 | 1.440 |
| 143 | 4.810 | 8649 | 3.474 | 48 | 6.500 | 5308 | 1.200 |
| 11203 | 7.500 | 2606 | 1.320 | 52 | 6.000 | 8955 | 6.240 |
| 114 | 11.000 | 6429 | 6.864 | 61 | 6.000 | 7285 | 1.408 |
| 11603 | 5.500 | 1788 | 0.832 | 7201 | 9.875 | 2127 | 8.560 |
| 11604 | 5.000 | 3002 | 2.272 | 8002 | 13.000 | 11256 | 6.080 |
| 11701 | 12.000 | 6489 | 5.088 | 8102 | 14.500 | 4653 | 1.360 |
| 118 | 10.000 | 6474 | 1.632 | 8108 | 13.750 | 4331 | 2.440 |
| 113 | 11.500 | 6279 | 16.000 | 8204 | 15.250 | 3646 | 0.992 |
| 124 | 12.500 | 4541 | 40.960 | 91 | 7.625 | 9420 | 5.760 |
| 13204 | 8.000 | 5123 | 12.288 | 50 | 7.250 | 4127 | 2.064 |
| 13501 | 10.000 | 2841 | 14.336 | 207 | 17.000 | 6498 | 8.480 |
| 14202 | 6.500 | 4277 | 5.632 | 209 | 13.625 | 6211 | 9.920 |
| 14502 | 9.000 | 5795 | 5.632 | 211 | 20.000 | 4231 | 17.920 |

| CITY: SALT LAKE CITY, UT | | | |
|---|---|---|---|
| TRACT | DIST. | POP. | AREA |
| 1000 | 3.058 | 2338 | 3.830 |
| 4 | 2.971 | 4804 | 0.625 |
| 5 | 2.534 | 5802 | 0.860 |
| 6 | 2.184 | 5013 | 1.290 |
| 8 | 0.699 | 2102 | 0.328 |
| 10 | 1.398 | 4204 | 0.625 |
| 11 | 0.786 | 5920 | 0.469 |
| 12 | 1.747 | 5305 | 0.703 |
| 14000 | 3.320 | 2424 | 3.830 |
| 16 | 1.922 | 3988 | 0.461 |
| 18 | 1.398 | 3521 | 0.40 |
| 20 | 1.048 | 3586 | 0.40 |
| 26 | 1.573 | 3997 | 1.0 |
| 27 | 2.272 | 5442 | 1.2 |
| 28 | 2.621 | 7636 | 3.0 |
| 30 | 1.398 | 3508 | 0. |
| 32 | 2.621 | 4962 | 0 |
| 34 | 2.446 | 5054 | 0 |
| 36 | 2.621 | 3429 | |
| 38 | 3.408 | 2667 | |
| 40 | 3.670 | 3831 | |
| 47 | 4.194 | 5201 | |
| 49 | 3.495 | 3161 | |
| 114 | 3.500 | 5925 | |
| 42 | 4.369 | 5770 | |
| 44 | 4.893 | 2286 | |
| 102 | 6.500 | 6687 | |
| 104 | 6.000 | 633 | |
| 106 | 7.500 | 689 | |
| 108 | 7.500 | 439 | |
| 110 | 10.000 | 7 | |
| 112 | 10.000 | 5 | |
| 117 | 6.000 | 7 | |
| 119 | 7.000 | 7 | |
| 121 | 8.000 | | |
| 122 | 8.500 | | |
| 124 | 11.500 | | |
| 126 | 13.500 | | |
| 127 | 13.500 | | |
| 129 | 12.000 | | |
| 13301 | 4.500 | | |
| 134 | 8.000 | | |
| 13502 | 6.000 | | |

| CITY: | SEATTLE, WA | | | CITY: | ST. LOUIS, MO | | |
|---|---|---|---|---|---|---|---|
| TRACT | DIST. | POP. | AREA | TRACT | DIST. | POP. | AREA |
| 1 | 8.737 | 3757 | 0.821 | 1011 | 6.903 | 4166 | 0.469 |
| 6 | 7.951 | 5842 | 1.524 | 1016 | 7.339 | 1345 | 0.617 |
| 11 | 7.077 | 2300 | 0.469 | 1023 | 6.815 | 2771 | 0.547 |
| 16 | 6.815 | 4264 | 0.930 | 1033 | 6.990 | 1209 | 0.406 |
| 21 | 6.466 | 3886 | 0.586 | 1037 | 5.592 | 3743 | 0.422 |
| 26 | 5.417 | 4608 | 0.610 | 1051 | 6.204 | 4538 | 0.461 |
| 31 | 6.815 | 6544 | 2.095 | 1061 | 5.767 | 9939 | 0.375 |
| 111 | 6.116 | 7006 | 1.641 | 1066 | 4.893 | 7162 | 0.375 |
| 116 | 6.466 | 7248 | 4.142 | 1074 | 5.854 | 5891 | 0.469 |
| 118 | 7.165 | 6115 | 1.798 | 1082 | 7.077 | 2876 | 0.391 |
| 121 | 8.038 | 3195 | 6.722 | 1122 | 4.543 | 6085 | 0.297 |
| 201 | 12.000 | 2954 | 2.880 | 1133 | 4.454 | 1178 | 0.430 |
| 205 | 11.000 | 6194 | 1.120 | 1141 | 6.291 | 11028 | 1.016 |
| 209 | 10.000 | 2556 | 4.320 | 1153 | 4.806 | 7177 | 0.664 |
| 213 | 9.500 | 3405 | 0.976 | 10801 | 13.000 | 9132 | 5.840 |
| 217 | 12.500 | 2926 | 2.160 | 2110 | 12.500 | 10971 | 1.600 |
| 221 | 10.000 | 4643 | 2.896 | 11303 | 14.500 | 16504 | 2.400 |
| 225 | 8.000 | 3557 | 1.520 | 2118 | 9.500 | 9866 | 1.744 |
| 228 | 9.500 | 6163 | 5.760 | 2176 | 15.000 | 9157 | 4.320 |
| 234 | 10.500 | 6470 | 5.280 | 2182 | 14.500 | 4871 | 1.888 |
| 258 | 13.500 | 12300 | 3.280 | 2190 | 6.500 | 1590 | 0.640 |
| 268 | 7.000 | 8062 | 1.408 | 2201 | 7.000 | 10476 | 2.080 |
| 273 | 9.000 | 7551 | 1.440 | 2210 | 12.500 | 4779 | 0.960 |
| 288 | 12.000 | 8752 | 3.360 | 2194 | 10.000 | 7048 | 1.440 |
| 293 | 14.000 | 8423 | 6.640 | 2102 | 9.000 | 9390 | 1.920 |
| 303 | 21.000 | 9503 | 12.640 | 10903 | 14.000 | 4881 | 1.840 |
| 309 | 22.500 | 2921 | 2.720 | 2119 | 9.500 | 3554 | 0.480 |
| 36 | 4.893 | 4330 | 0.547 | 13102 | 17.500 | 3603 | 6.720 |
| 41 | 5.068 | 8370 | 3.674 | 2142 | 7.500 | 4391 | 1.408 |
| 46 | 4.718 | 3563 | 1.016 | 15102 | 15.500 | 2299 | 1.520 |
| 51 | 3.495 | 4063 | 0.375 | 2163 | 6.000 | 5945 | 0.880 |
| 56 | 4.631 | 6907 | 0.820 | 2175 | 12.500 | 6628 | 5.120 |
| 59 | 3.320 | 6462 | 0.922 | 2184 | 16.000 | 1072 | 2.640 |
| 64 | 2.010 | 4146 | 0.430 | 2200 | 10.500 | 10503 | 1.312 |
| 68 | 2.184 | 3153 | 0.313 | 1091 | 4.019 | 6918 | 0.743 |
| 74 | 1.048 | 7343 | 0.188 | 1102 | 2.796 | 7103 | 0.320 |
| 78 | 2.796 | 6370 | 2.149 | 1112 | 3.757 | 7878 | 0.406 |
| 83 | 0.437 | 3424 | 0.117 | 1161 | 4.194 | 4083 | 0.383 |
| 88 | 1.835 | 3896 | 0.375 | 1172 | 3.233 | 10877 | 0.563 |
| 94 | 2.010 | 4918 | 0.782 | 1182 | 3.582 | 4757 | 0.625 |
| 97 | 4.893 | 11410 | 7.503 | 1192 | 3.320 | 5533 | 0.266 |
| 101 | 4.194 | 5730 | 1.798 | 1211 | 1.835 | 4235 | 0.477 |
| 106 | 5.068 | 7362 | 1.157 | 1224 | 0.874 | 7043 | 0.469 |

| CITY: SPOKANE, WA | | | | CITY: SYRACUSE, NY | | | |
|---|---|---|---|---|---|---|---|
| TRACT | DIST. | POP. | AREA | TRACT | DIST. | POP. | AREA |
| 2 | 4.476 | 4388 | 0.800 | 104 | 9.000 | 3247 | 21.760 |
| 8 | 4.944 | 6001 | 1.472 | 106 | 5.500 | 5010 | 1.536 |
| 111 | 5.479 | 856 | 1.966 | 108 | 5.500 | 6159 | 2.048 |
| 9 | 4.476 | 8407 | 2.103 | 112 | 8.500 | 4809 | 12.800 |
| 106 | 6.815 | 868 | 7.268 | 115 | 9.000 | 2457 | 10.240 |
| 108 | 6.948 | 3477 | 1.760 | 121 | 8.500 | 2239 | 20.480 |
| 122 | 4.810 | 1600 | 4.251 | 123 | 7.500 | 4946 | 5.120 |
| 115 | 6.347 | 3236 | 0.960 | 145 | 5.000 | 4922 | 5.632 |
| 119 | 8.552 | 3040 | 1.321 | 149 | 6.000 | 1734 | 6.400 |
| 121 | 6.414 | 2602 | 1.097 | 151 | 8.500 | 4677 | 5.120 |
| 123 | 4.810 | 3549 | 2.651 | 155 | 6.500 | 4403 | 5.376 |
| 125 | 7.550 | 1672 | 0.891 | 157 | 13.000 | 4536 | 68.864 |
| 127 | 9.621 | 5224 | 1.760 | 161 | 6.000 | 1277 | 7.040 |
| 128 | 8.686 | 4228 | 2.331 | 19 | 2.971 | 5591 | 0.735 |
| 112 | 6.750 | 3513 | 18.048 | 60 | 3.757 | 5015 | 1.485 |
| 114 | 10.000 | 2793 | 8.000 | 125 | 5.505 | 5176 | 0.899 |
| 117 | 8.000 | 3207 | 3.328 | 131 | 3.757 | 5372 | 1.485 |
| 124 | 8.750 | 1835 | 12.864 | 135 | 4.369 | 3614 | 2.188 |
| 129 | 9.500 | 3958 | 2.496 | 137 | 3.408 | 4864 | 1.954 |
| 130 | 11.000 | 1214 | 3.840 | 142 | 2.883 | 4964 | 1.399 |
| 131 | 12.250 | 2926 | 8.640 | 2 | 2.010 | 4400 | 0.469 |
| 134 | 5.000 | 2921 | 12.288 | 4 | 2.097 | 5030 | 0.625 |
| 105 | 9.000 | 3822 | 38.720 | 6 | 1.573 | 3575 | 0.234 |
| 4 | 3.808 | 3748 | 0.868 | 8 | 1.573 | 3171 | 0.313 |
| 6 | 3.741 | 3530 | 0.576 | 9 | 1.835 | 4543 | 0.563 |
| 10 | 3.207 | 5697 | 1.554 | 10 | 2.796 | 5066 | 0.547 |
| 12 | 2.806 | 2571 | 0.448 | 13 | 0.874 | 1785 | 0.086 |
| 14 | 2.672 | 6331 | 1.143 | 15 | 1.048 | 2939 | 0.227 |
| 16 | 3.675 | 1825 | 0.681 | 18 | 2.359 | 3617 | 0.391 |
| 18 | 2.940 | 2499 | 0.919 | 21 | 1.069 | 2545 | 0.352 |
| 20 | 1.670 | 4821 | 0.832 | 23 | 0.612 | 3056 | 0.188 |
| 23 | 1.603 | 4798 | 0.891 | 27 | 2.184 | 2530 | 0.313 |
| 24 | 0.869 | 2789 | 0.960 | 29 | 1.485 | 1452 | 0.226 |
| 25 | 1.470 | 7035 | 1.472 | 30 | 0.786 | 3242 | 0.313 |
| 27 | 2.138 | 1597 | 0.996 | 34 | 1.048 | 2043 | 0.234 |
| 29 | 3.474 | 2405 | 0.686 | 3601 | 2.097 | 2894 | 0.469 |
| 31 | 1.670 | 4484 | 1.028 | 38 | 1.747 | 3255 | 0.328 |
| 36 | 1.002 | 3184 | 0.539 | 40 | 0.786 | 3649 | 0.242 |
| 38 | 2.138 | 1520 | 1.472 | 42 | 0.699 | 3775 | 0.156 |
| 40 | 1.069 | 5347 | 0.731 | 43 | 0.961 | 10517 | 0.672 |
| 42 | 1.737 | 6154 | 1.413 | 50 | 1.835 | 3810 | 0.492 |
| 44 | 3.073 | 4853 | 0.903 | 53 | 1.223 | 4301 | 0.313 |
| 46 | 3.274 | 4851 | 1.760 | 1760 | 1.069 | 3147 | 0.313 |

| CITY: TACOMA, WA | | | | CITY; TOLEDO, OH | | | |
|---|---|---|---|---|---|---|---|
| TRACT | DIST. | POP. | AREA | TRACT | DIST. | POP. | AREA |
| 71801 | 4.744 | 8266 | 2.788 | 2 | 3.409 | 5719 | 0.411 |
| 71802 | 6.013 | 5649 | 0.800 | 6 | 2.727 | 5921 | 0.749 |
| 71901 | 5.946 | 5153 | 1.051 | 10 | 1.849 | 5312 | 0.546 |
| 71902 | 6.347 | 5636 | 1.783 | 1301 | 3.864 | 3645 | 0.447 |
| 720 | 8.485 | 4354 | 1.143 | 14 | 2.424 | 3864 | 0.400 |
| 72102 | 5.412 | 5702 | 2.148 | 17 | 1.060 | 4161 | 0.194 |
| 634 | 4.009 | 5842 | 1.074 | 20 | 1.742 | 4005 | 0.582 |
| 635 | 4.009 | 4737 | 1.051 | 21 | 1.363 | 5881 | 0.411 |
| 711 | 5.145 | 1945 | 1.600 | 2401 | 2.878 | 4658 | 0.634 |
| 715 | 6.815 | 13150 | 3.931 | 26 | 1.212 | 4422 | 0.358 |
| 717 | 5.145 | 7894 | 1.874 | 29 | 0.454 | 2546 | 0.294 |
| 72302 | 5.078 | 9654 | 5.805 | 32 | 1.969 | 3639 | 0.229 |
| 733 | 8.418 | 5047 | 1.646 | 35 | 2.424 | 3174 | 0.834 |
| 734 | 7.149 | 14529 | 5.247 | 38 | 0.833 | 2034 | 0.323 |
| 603 | 3.474 | 2845 | 2.331 | 41 | 1.136 | 3343 | 0.646 |
| 604 | 2.472 | 4891 | 0.960 | 45 | 2.727 | 4432 | 0.388 |
| 605 | 1.804 | 4594 | 0.549 | 50 | 1.894 | 2353 | 0.235 |
| 606 | 1.470 | 6129 | 1.371 | 51 | 1.288 | 6551 | 0.476 |
| 607 | 1.537 | 7721 | 0.539 | 53 | 2.197 | 3202 | 0.347 |
| 608 | 2.205 | 6427 | 0.633 | 5502 | 4.924 | 4315 | 1.866 |
| 609 | 3.140 | 11343 | 2.148 | 5802 | 4.469 | 6059 | 1.304 |
| 610 | 3.474 | 4702 | 1.554 | 61 | 4.394 | 4283 | 0.458 |
| 611 | 2.071 | 5756 | 1.143 | 67 | 3.106 | 2517 | 0.541 |
| 613 | 0.735 | 4900 | 0.375 | 69 | 4.848 | 3902 | 0.423 |
| 614 | 0.334 | 2852 | 0.229 | 56 | 4.469 | 3587 | 3.231 |
| 615 | 0.668 | 4196 | 0.297 | 10002 | 2.727 | 3260 | 0.676 |
| 617 | 1.069 | 4163 | 0.594 | 7201 | 1.136 | 1631 | 0.012 |
| 618 | 1.537 | 2659 | 0.366 | 202 | 4.000 | 3492 | 1.760 |
| 620 | 1.537 | 3912 | 0.549 | 4503 | 5.378 | 3720 | 0.499 |
| 621 | 1.871 | 2852 | 0.631 | 5801 | 5.151 | 2626 | 0.552 |
| 622 | 1.537 | 3041 | 0.434 | 74 | 5.151 | 3848 | 1.645 |
| 623 | 2.338 | 3831 | 0.571 | 78 | 5.303 | 5451 | 0.896 |
| 624 | 2.138 | 5778 | 0.549 | 7902 | 5.909 | 6085 | 0.823 |
| 625 | 2.205 | 7755 | 0.731 | 84 | 7.121 | 3164 | 1.281 |
| 626 | 2.205 | 2242 | 0.594 | 82 | 6.817 | 3027 | 2.474 |
| 628 | 3.073 | 4394 | 1.691 | 8201 | 9.393 | 4261 | 1.292 |
| 629 | 2.071 | 5771 | 0.731 | 8301 | 7.120 | 5080 | 2.321 |
| 630 | 2.205 | 3035 | 0.549 | 85 | 6.666 | 4692 | 1.234 |
| 631 | 3.007 | 4493 | 0.640 | 7102 | 8.500 | 5015 | 2.528 |
| 632 | 3.007 | 5207 | 0.603 | 204 | 8.500 | 3001 | 3.920 |
| 633 | 3.207 | 3936 | 0.823 | 205 | 8.000 | 3198 | 1.536 |
| 707 | 3.140 | 9344 | 7.359 | 208 | 5.500 | 4120 | 8.706 |
| 710 | 3.875 | 4985 | 4.297 | 90 | 12.000 | 3340 | 25.088 |

| CITY: | TUCSON, AZ | | | CITY: | UTICA, NY | | |
|---|---|---|---|---|---|---|---|
| TRACT | DIST. | POP. | AREA | TRACT | DIST. | POP. | AREA |
| 2 | 1.048 | 2576 | 0.821 | 4502 | 6.029 | 6394 | 3.322 |
| 4 | 0.786 | 3285 | 0.860 | 4701 | 6.378 | 3572 | 15.163 |
| 5 | 1.398 | 8460 | 1.024 | 230 | 2.750 | 5093 | 2.880 |
| 6 | 2.446 | 5402 | 1.329 | 236 | 3.875 | 1012 | 0.800 |
| 7 | 2.097 | 5598 | 1.391 | 23702 | 2.625 | 3614 | 2.160 |
| 9 | 0.786 | 3965 | 0.586 | 240 | 2.375 | 4429 | 2.752 |
| 11 | 1.485 | 3805 | 0.547 | 242 | 6.125 | 3947 | 4.512 |
| 12 | 2.184 | 2825 | 1.719 | 24301 | 4.250 | 3048 | 0.208 |
| 14 | 1.835 | 4261 | 1.016 | 24303 | 4.500 | 2613 | 3.536 |
| 0 | 0.0 | 0 | 0.0 | 245 | 8.125 | 4942 | 3.360 |
| 0 | 0.0 | 0 | 0.0 | 247 | 5.000 | 6290 | 4.640 |
| 16 | 2.709 | 4072 | 0.977 | 249 | 3.875 | 4871 | 2.368 |
| 18 | 3.670 | 6947 | 1.446 | 257 | 4.125 | 3726 | 1.920 |
| 20 | 3.320 | 8188 | 1.954 | 21301 | 2.272 | 3776 | 1.600 |
| 22 | 3.145 | 3146 | 3.205 | 21601 | 2.272 | 6196 | 3.382 |
| 25 | 4.369 | 5894 | 8.285 | 21701 | 2.873 | 4505 | 0.868 |
| 26 | 3.408 | 7970 | 2.110 | 21702 | 3.073 | 3992 | 0.846 |
| 2901 | 3.844 | 5014 | 2.462 | 232 | 4.009 | 4773 | 1.166 |
| 2902 | 4.806 | 4869 | 1.251 | 233 | 2.472 | 3425 | 0.868 |
| 32 | 4.893 | 7567 | 1.798 | 231 | 6.815 | 1627 | 0.914 |
| 3302 | 4.369 | 6451 | 1.329 | 252 | 5.278 | 4920 | 5.897 |
| 37 | 4.718 | 7604 | 1.485 | 219 | 3.875 | 2869 | 1.120 |
| 4001 | 4.456 | 7630 | 1.876 | 220 | 3.750 | 4760 | 1.184 |
| 4501 | 3.932 | 8125 | 4.611 | 221 | 3.750 | 3683 | 0.800 |
| 4503 | 4.631 | 6779 | 2.647 | 223 | 3.625 | 4245 | 0.320 |
| 23 | 1.922 | 6220 | 1.251 | 224 | 3.375 | 5055 | 0.960 |
| 28 | 4.369 | 5835 | 1.407 | 225 | 3.375 | 5665 | 1.760 |
| 21 | 3.844 | 5824 | 2.501 | 22701 | 3.750 | 2195 | 1.920 |
| 4401 | 4.019 | 3161 | 13.522 | 222 | 3.750 | 2979 | 0.544 |
| 21 | 3.757 | 5824 | 2.657 | 250 | 2.250 | 9688 | 2.080 |
| 24 | 2.971 | 6546 | 1.368 | 253 | 1.250 | 7509 | 0.480 |
| 17 | 3.932 | 2771 | 0.703 | 255 | 2.250 | 4579 | 2.080 |
| 31 | 5.941 | 6491 | 3.048 | 206 | 0.935 | 1563 | 0.219 |
| 34 | 7.602 | 5664 | 1.172 | 20701 | 0.869 | 5333 | 0.320 |
| 38 | 5.767 | 8437 | 4.142 | 20702 | 1.871 | 4969 | 1.682 |
| 4001 | 7.864 | 3654 | 2.501 | 20802 | 1.470 | 4927 | 0.366 |
| 4002 | 7.776 | 9695 | 2.267 | 20803 | 0.935 | 4373 | 0.343 |
| 4005 | 9.611 | 9343 | 2.970 | 209 | 0.802 | 3972 | 0.320 |
| 4007 | 10.660 | 7152 | 6.331 | 210 | 0.534 | 2245 | 0.137 |
| 4003 | 9.174 | 8932 | 4.846 | 21102 | 1.403 | 3620 | 0.274 |
| 4004 | 8.388 | 3254 | 4.221 | 21103 | 2.071 | 2236 | 0.266 |
| 4101 | 6.116 | 3765 | 6.722 | 21201 | 0.935 | 3907 | 0.293 |
| 4301 | 6.291 | 3693 | 9.536 | 21303 | 1.804 | 4150 | 0.846 |

| TRACT | DIST. | POP. | AREA | TRACT | DIST. | POP. | AREA |
|-------|-------|------|------|-------|-------|------|------|
| CITY: WASHINGTON, D.C. | | | | CITY: WICHITA, KS | | | |
| 7 | 3.341 | 8281 | 0.402 | 1 | 3.146 | 3571 | 0.610 |
| 13 | 4.009 | 9063 | 1.874 | 2 | 2.272 | 3334 | 0.789 |
| 28 | 2.539 | 7490 | 0.178 | 4 | 1.573 | 3534 | 0.664 |
| 32 | 2.672 | 6389 | 0.187 | 6 | 2.010 | 4154 | 0.743 |
| 39 | 2.138 | 6094 | 0.146 | 7 | 2.883 | 6130 | 0.789 |
| 40 | 1.804 | 7289 | 0.233 | 8 | 2.272 | 4495 | 0.617 |
| 84 | 2.405 | 6713 | 0.183 | 11 | 2.097 | 3703 | 0.647 |
| 87 | 2.004 | 7585 | 0.366 | 14 | 1.573 | 4926 | 1.641 |
| 92 | 2.539 | 8253 | 0.663 | 15 | 1.747 | 3915 | 0.782 |
| 1017 | 2.000 | 7487 | 0.379 | 18 | 1.136 | 3567 | 0.821 |
| 1032 | 2.750 | 6696 | 0.827 | 21 | 3.670 | 4149 | 1.016 |
| 9 | 4.944 | 8729 | 2.194 | 22 | 2.796 | 2706 | 0.469 |
| 19 | 4.944 | 8609 | 0.777 | 26 | 0.349 | 2841 | 0.469 |
| 7405 | 5.011 | 10723 | 0.343 | 28 | 1.573 | 4152 | 0.703 |
| 7705 | 6.280 | 11823 | 0.539 | 29 | 2.184 | 2790 | 0.625 |
| 7805 | 5.813 | 8194 | 0.503 | 30 | 2.010 | 2816 | 0.696 |
| 1003 | 5.000 | 6842 | 2.011 | 31 | 2.010 | 2737 | 0.696 |
| 103 | 7.000 | 5723 | 0.503 | 34 | 1.747 | 2126 | 0.469 |
| 2005 | 6.250 | 5913 | 0.279 | 36 | 3.408 | 3676 | 0.610 |
| 2011 | 4.750 | 6441 | 0.640 | 38 | 2.184 | 4006 | 0.938 |
| 4007 | 12.750 | 5460 | 1.463 | 39 | 2.621 | 5485 | 1.000 |
| 4054 | 6.250 | 3074 | 1.028 | 52 | 2.883 | 5481 | 0.782 |
| 4082 | 5.000 | 2043 | 1.554 | 53 | 3.844 | 8610 | 1.329 |
| 4086 | 9.750 | 7738 | 1.737 | 60 | 3.932 | 5737 | 1.798 |
| 5002 | 7.750 | 5860 | 0.754 | 64 | 3.670 | 2360 | 0.684 |
| 905 | 12.250 | 3643 | 0.375 | 65 | 4.107 | 5307 | 0.938 |
| 1004 | 15.250 | 6556 | 1.143 | 68 | 3.932 | 5402 | 0.899 |
| 1201 | 10.000 | 6327 | 1.028 | 69 | 4.194 | 3545 | 0.578 |
| 1205 | 12.500 | 6162 | 2.834 | 70 | 4.893 | 3740 | 0.922 |
| 2602 | 7.000 | 6170 | 0.274 | 75 | 3.582 | 2434 | 0.555 |
| 3207 | 11.000 | 5108 | 1.783 | 78 | 3.844 | 4838 | 1.063 |
| 3902 | 8.750 | 6652 | 0.951 | 82 | 4.019 | 6332 | 2.110 |
| 7041 | 8.500 | 5379 | 1.737 | 84 | 3.320 | 3033 | 1.094 |
| 7046 | 8.250 | 5574 | 0.777 | 86 | 3.582 | 3830 | 0.938 |
| 7056 | 5.750 | 6385 | 0.731 | 87 | 2.621 | 3309 | 1.008 |
| 8030 | 7.000 | 4903 | 0.786 | 89 | 3.495 | 4205 | 1.647 |
| 3402 | 10.500 | 5696 | 0.658 | 90 | 2.796 | 3102 | 1.235 |
| 3603 | 11.250 | 10406 | 1.417 | 74 | 4.543 | 1141 | 0.477 |
| 8037 | 7.500 | 3831 | 0.594 | 57 | 5.767 | 4395 | 3.048 |
| 8044 | 6.000 | 2708 | 1.234 | 73 | 5.330 | 5506 | 3.595 |
| 5202 | 5.750 | 3024 | 0.434 | 93 | 5.505 | 4749 | 4.142 |
| 8055 | 6.500 | 3534 | 0.457 | 94 | 6.728 | 6602 | 2.149 |
| 8064 | 5.500 | 2926 | 0.594 | 54 | 5.941 | 4058 | 8.285 |

NOTE:

*Population data for the tracts are from the 1970 census tract statistics [U.S. Bureau of Census (1970)]. Areas in square miles were measured with a polar planimeter using tract maps. Distance in miles was measured with a ruler on the tract maps from the tract maps from the center of the CBD to the center of the tract. Density is in terms of population per square mile.

References


Achtenhagen, P., <u>An Investor-Based Marketing Plan for Sale</u>
    <u>of Real Property Investment Securities to Individuals</u>
    Unpublished doctoral dissertation, Stanford Univer-
    sity, 1974.

Ali, M. M. and Greenbaum, S. I. "A Spatial Model of the
    Banking Industry." <u>Journal of Finance</u>, 32, 1977,
    1283-1303.

Allen, R.G.D., <u>Mathematical Anlysis for Economists</u>.
    London: MacMillan, 1956.

Alonso, W. <u>Location and Land Use</u>. Cambridge, Mass:
    Harvard University Press, 1964.

Alterman, J. and Jacobs, E.E., "Estimates of Real Product
    in the United States by Industrial Sector, 1947-55."
    <u>Output, Input and Productivity Measurement</u>, National
    Bureau of Economic Research. Princeton: Princeton
    University Press, 1961.

Amano, A., "Biased Technical Progress and a Neoclassical
    Theory of Economic Growth." <u>Quarterly Journal of</u>
    <u>Economics</u>, 78, 1964, 129-138.

Anas, A. (1978), "Dynamics of Urban Residential Growth,"
    <u>Journal of Urban Economics</u>, 8, 1978, pp. 66-87.

Andrieu, M., "Derived Demand, Returns to Scale and Sta-
    bility." <u>Review of Economic Studies</u>, 41, 1974, 405-
    417.

Arnott, R. A., (1980), "A Simple Urban Growth Model with
    Durable Housing," <u>Regional Science and Urban Econo-</u>
    <u>mics</u>, No. 10, pp. 53-76.

Arrow, K. J., Cheney, H. B., Minhas, B. S., and Solow,
    R. M., "Capital-Labor Substitution and Economic
    Efficiency." <u>Review of Economics and Statistics</u>,
    43, 1961, 225-250.

Atkinson, L. C., "Empirical Estimates of the Elasticity
    of Factor Substitution:  Some Economic Considera-
    tions."  Southern Economic Journal, 41, 1975, 395-402.

Balstra, P. and Nerlove, M., "Pooling Cross Section and
    Time Series Data in the Estimation of a Dynamic Model:
    The Demand for Natural Gas."  Econometrica, 34, 1966,
    585-612.

Beckman, M., "On the Distribution of Urban Rent and Resi-
    dential Density."  Journal of Economic Theory, 1,
    1969, 60-67.

_____, "Spatial Equilibrium in the Housing
    Market."  Journal of Urban Economics, 1, 1974,
    99-107.

Beckmann, M. J. and Wallace, J. P., "Evaluation of Users
    Benefits Arising from Changes in Transportation
    Systems."  Transportation Science, 3, 1969, 344-351.

Box, G. E. P. and Cox, D. R., "An Analysis of Transforma-
    tions."  Journal of the Royal Statistical Society
    26(Series B), 1964, 211-232.

Box, G. E. P. and Tidwell, P. W., "Transformation of the
    Independent Variables."  Techometrics, 4, 1962, 531-
    550.

Bronfenbrenner, M., "Notes on the Elasticity of Derived
    Demand."  Oxford Economic Papers, 13, 1961, 254-261.

Brown, M., On the Theory and Measurement of Technological
    Changes, Cambridge, England:  Cambridge University
    Press, 1968.

Brown, M. and DeCani, J. S., "Technological Change and the
    Distribution of Income."  International Economic
    Review, 4, 1963, 289-309.

Brown, R. L., Durbin, J., and Evans, J. M. "Techniques
    for Testing the Consistency of Regression Relation-
    ships Over Time."  Journal of the Roal Statistical
    Society, 37, (Series B, #2), 1975, 149-193.

Brueckner, J. K., "A Note on Sufficient Conditions for Negative Exponential Population Densities." Journal of Regional Science, 22, 1982, 353-359.

Brueckner, J. K. "A Dynamic Model of Housing Production." Journal of Urban Economics, 10, 1981, 1-14.

_____, "Testing a Vintage Model of Urban Growth." Journal of Regional Science, 21, 1981, 23-35.

_____, "A Vintage Model of Urban Growth." Journal of Urban Economics, 8, 1980, 389-402.

Bruno, M., "Estimation of Factor Contribution to Growth Under Structural Disequalibirum." International Economic Review, 9, 1968, 49-62.

Case, F., Los Angeles Real Estate: A Study of Investment Experience (Real Estate Research Program, University of California, Los Angeles, 1960).

Christensen, L. R., Jorgenson, D. W., and Lau, L.J., "Transcendental Logarithmic Production Frontiers." Review of Economics and Statistics, 55, 1973, 28-45.

Clapp, J., "The Substitution of Urban Land For Other Inputs." Journal of Urban Economics, 6, 1979, 122-134.

_____, "The Elasticity of Substitution of Non-Land for Land: A Reconciliation of Diverse Estimates." Journal of Regional Science, 21, (1), 1981, 123-126.

Clark, C., "Urban Population Densities." Journal of the Royal Statistical Society, 114 (Series A), 1951, 490-496.

Clawson, M., Suburban Land Conversion in the United States: An Economic and Governmental Process. Baltimore: John Hopkins University Press, 1971.

Dacy, D. C., "Productivity and Price Trends in Construction Since 1967." Review of Economics and Statistics, 47, 1965, 406-411.

David, P. A. and DeKlundert, T. V., "Biased Efficiency Growth in the U.S." American Economic Review, 55, 1965, 356-394.

Davis, A., A Study of Real Estate Investment Returns to Capital and Management (Bureau of Business Research and Service: California State University, Fresno, 1973).

de Leeuw, F., "The Demand for Housing: A Review of Cross-Section Evidence." Review of Economics and Statistics, 53, 1971, 1-10.

de Leeuw, F. and Ekanem, N. F., "The Supply of Rental Housing." American Economic Review, 61, 1971, 806-817.

Denison, E. F., The Sources of Economic Growth in the United States and Alternatives Before Us. New York: CED Supp., Paper No. 13, 1962.

Diamond, Dr., Jr., Income and Residential Location in Urban Areas. Ph.D. dissertation, Department of Economics, University of Chicago, Chicago, Ill., 1978.

Domar, E. D., "On Total Productivity and All That." Journal of Political Economics, 70, 1962, 597-608.

Downing, P. B., "Estimating Land Values by Multivariate Analysis." In D. M. Holland (ed.), The Assessment of Land Values, Madison: University of Wisconsin Press, 1970.

Fales, R. and Moses, L. "Land Use Theory and the Spatial Structure of the Nineteenth-Century City." In M. Perlman, C. L. Levine, and B. Chintic (eds.), Spatial, Regional and Population Economics: Essays in Honor of Edgar M. Hoover. London: Gordon and Breach, 1973.

Fallis, G., The Technology of Production and the Location of Employment in Urban Areas, Ph.D. dissertation, Princeton University, 1975.

Fare, R. and Jansson, L., "On VES and WDI Production Functions." International Economic Review, 16, 1975, 745-750.

Farley, J. U. and Hinich, M. J., "A Test for a Shifting Slope Coefficient in a Linear Model." Journal of the American Statistical Association, 65, 1970, 1320-1329.

Farley, J. U., Hinich, M. J., and McGuire, T., "Some Comparisons of Tests for a Shift in the Slopes of a Multivariate Linear Time Series Model." Journal of Econometrics, 3, 1975, 297-318.

Ferguson, C. E., "Production, Prices, and the Theory of Jointly Derived Input Demand Functions." Economica, 33, 1966, 60-75.

_____, "Substitution, Technical Progress, and Returns to Scale." American Economic Review Papers and Proceedings, 55, 1965, 296-305.

Fisher, F. M., "Tests of Equality Between Sets of Coefficients in Two Linear Regressions: An Expository Note." Econometrica, 38, 1970, 361-366.

Friedman, H., "Real Estate Investment and Portfolio Theory." Journal of Finance and Quantitative Analysis, 6, 1971, 861-874.

Gerking, S. and Boyes, W., "The Role of Functional Form in Estimating Elasticities of Housing Expendiutures." Southern Economics Journal, 47, (2), 1980, 287-302.

Goldfeld, S. M., and Quandt, R. E., "Some Tests for Homoscedasticity." Journal of American Statistical Association, 60, 539-547.

Goldstein, G. S., and Moses, L. N., "A Survey of Urban Economics." Journal of Economic Lierature, 11, 1973, 471-515.

Golob, T. F. and Beckmann, T., "A Utility Model for Travel Forecasting." Transportation Science, 5, 1971, 79-90.

Gottlieb, M., "Influences on Value in Urban Land Market, U.S.A., 1956-61." Journal of Regional Science, 6, 1965, 1-16.

Grieson, R. E., "The Supply of Rental Housing: Comment." American Economic Review, 63, 1973, 433-436.

Griffith, D. A., "Modeling Urban Population Density in a Multi-Centered City." Journal of Urban Economics, 9, 1981, 298-310.

Griliches, Z., "The Sources of Measured Productivity Growth: United States Agriculture, 1940-1960." Journal of Political Economy, 71, 1963, 331-346.

Hallengren, E., "How Different Investment Fare During Inflationary Cycles." The Commercial and Financial Chronicle, 219, (7414), 1974, 9.

Harber, W. and Levinson, H., Labor Relations and Productivity in the Building Trades. Ann Arbor: University of Michigan Press, 1956.

Hardy, G. H., Littlewood, J. E., and Polya, G., Inequalities. Cambridge, England: Cambridge University Press, 1934.

Harrison, D., Jr. and Kain, J. F. "Cumulative Urban Growth and Urban Density Function." Journal of Urban Economics, 1, 1974, 61-98.

_____, Reply to Michelle White's Comment on "Cumulative Urban Growth and Urban Density Functions." Journal of Urban Economics, 4, 1977, 113-117.

Harvey, A. C. and Phillips, D. A., "A Comparison of the Power of Some Tests for Heteroscedasticity in the General Linear Model." Journal of Econometrics, 2, 1974, 307-316.

Heckman, J. and Polachek, S., "Empirical Evidence on the Functional Form of the Earnings-Schooling Relationship." _Journal of the American Statistical Association_, 69, 1974, 350-354.

Henderson, J. V., "The Size and Types of Cities." _American Economic Review_, 64, 1974, 640-656.

Hicks, J. R., "Marshall's Third Rule: A Further Comment." _Oxford Economic Papers_, 13, 1961, 355-60.

_____, "The Theory of Wages." (P. Smith, New York, 1948).

Hildreth, C. and Houck, J. P., "Some Estimators for a Linear Model with Random Coefficients." _Journal of the American Statistical Association_, 38, 1968, 584-593.

Hodges, J., "Computer Progress in Valuation of Income Properties." _The Appraisal Journal_, 39, 1971, 13-27.

Homer, S., _A History of Interest Rates_. New Brunswick, NJ: Rutgers University Press, 1963.

Hoyt, H., _One Hundred Years of Land Value in Chicago_. Chicago: University of Chicago Press, 1933.

Isard, W., "A Simple Rationale for Gravity Model Type Behavior." _Papers of the Regional Science Association_, 35, 1975, 25-30.

Johnston, J., _Econometric Methods_ (2nd ed). New York: McGraw-Hill, Inc., 1972.

Johnson, R. J., "Housing Technology and Housing Cost." In National Commission on Urban Problems, _Building the American City_. Washington, D.C.: U.S. Government Printing Office, 1968, 53-64.

Judge, G., Griffiths, W., Hill, R., and Lee, T., _The Theory and Practice of Econometrics_. New York: John Wiley, 1980.

Kain, J. F., "The Journey to Work as a Determinant of Residential Location." Papers and Proceedings of the Regional Science Association, 9, 1962, 137-161.

Kau, J. B., and Johnson, S., "Urban Spatial Structure: An Analysis with a Varying Coefficient Model." Journal of Urban Economics, 7, 1980, 141-154.

_____, and Lee, C. F., "Capital-Land Substitution and Urban Land Use." Journal of Regional Science, 16, 1976a, 83-92.

_____, "The Functional Form in Estimating the Density Gradient: An Empirical Investigation." Journal of the American Statistical Association, 71, 1976b, 326-327.

_____, "Functional Form, Density Gradient and the Price Elasticity of Demand for Housing." Urban Studies, 13, 1976c, 193-200.

_____, and Lee, C. F., "A Random Coefficient Model for Estimating Density Gradient." Regional Science and Urban Economics, 7, 1977, 169-177.

_____, Lee, C. F. and Chen, R. C., "The Stability of Urban Spatial Structure: An Empirical Investigation." Journal of Urban Economics, 13, 1983, 364-377.

_____, and Lee, C. F. and Sirmans, C. F., "A Variable-Elasticity-of-Substitution Production Function and Urban Land Use: A Theoretical and Empirical Investigation." In Developments in Urban and Regional Analysis, edited by M. J. Breheny, Pion, 1979.

_____, and Sirmans, C. F., "Urban Land Value Functions and the Price Elasticity of Demand for Housing." Journal of Urban Economics 6, 1976, 112-121.

_____, "The Demand for Urban Residential Land." Journal of Regional Science, 21, 1981, 519-528.

Kemper, P., and Schmenner, R., "The Density Gradient for Manufacturing Industry," "Employment Density Gradients." Journal of Urban Economics, 4, (1), 1974, 410-427.

Kendrick, J. W. and Sato, R., "Factor Prices, Productivity, and Growth." American Economic Review, 53, 1963, 974-1003.

Kmenta, J., Elements of Econometrics. New York: MacMillan, 1971.

_____, "On Estimation of the CES Production Function." International Economic Review, 8, 1967, 180-189.

Koenker, R., "An Empirical Note on the Elasticity of Substitution Between Land and Capital in a Monocentric Housing." Journal of Regional Science, 12, 1972, 299-305.

Krasher, W. S., "The Rate of Return to Storing Wines." Journal of Political Economy, 87, (6), 1979, 1363-1367.

Kravis, I. B., "Relative Income Shares in Fact and Theory." American Economic Review Paper and Proceedings, 49, 1959, 917-49.

Latham, R. F. and Yeates, M. H., "Population Density Growth in Metropolitan Toronto." Geographical Analysis, 2, 1970, 177-185.

Leamer, E. E., Specification Searcher: Ad Hoc Inference with Nonexperimental Data. New York: Wiley, 1978.

Lee, C. F. and Chen, R. C. "Further Evidence on Beta Stability and Tendency: An Application of a Variable Mean Response Regression Model." Journal of Economics and Business, 35, 1982, 201-206.

Lee, T. H., "The Stock Demand Elasticities for Non-Farm Housing." Review of Economics and Statistics, 46, 1964, 82-89.

Liu, T. C. and Hildebrand, G. H., Manufacturing Production Functions in the United States. Ithaca, NY: Cornell University Press, 1965.

Lovell, C. A., "CES and VES Production Functions in a Cross-Section Context." Journal of Political Economy, 4, 1973a, 705-720.

_____, "Estimation and Prediction with CES and VES Production Functions." International Economic Review, 14, 1973b, 676-692.

Lu, Y. C. and Fletcher, L., "A Generalization of the CES Production Function." Review of Economics and Statistics, 50, 1968, 449-452.

Marshall, A., Principles of Economics. London: MacMillan, 1920.

Mayo, S. R., "Theory and Estimation in Economics of Housing Demand," Journal of Urban Economics, 10, (1), 1981, 95-116.

McCarthy, M. D. "Approximation of the CES Production Function: A Comment." International Economic Review, 8, 1967, 190-193.

McDonald, J., "Capital-Land Substitution in Urban Housing: A Survey of Empirical Estimates." Journal of Urban Economics, 9, 1981, 190-211.

McDonald, J. and Bowman, H. W., "Land Value Functions: A Reevaluation." Journal of Urban Economics, 6, 1979, 25-41.

_____, "Some Tests of Alternative Urban Population Density Functions." Journal of Urban Economics, 3, 1976, 242-252.

Mills, E. S., "An Aggregative Model of Resource Allocation in a Metropolitan Area." American Economic Review, 58, 1967, 197-210.

_____, "The Derived Demand for Urban Residential Land." Urban Studies, 2, 1971a, 250-260.

_____, "The Value of Urban Land." In Perloff and Wingo (eds.), The Quality of the Urban Environment. Baltimore: John Hopkins, 1971b.

_____, Urban Economics, Glenview, IL: Scott, Foresman and Company, 1972a.

_____, Studies in the Structure of the Urban Economy. Baltimore: The John Hopkins University Press, 1972b.

_____, "Urban Density Functions." Urban Studies, 7, 1970, 5-20.

Mohring, H., "Land Values and the Measurement of Highway Benefits." Journal of Political Economy, 49, 1961, 236-49.

Montesano, A., "A Restatement of Beckman's Model on the Distribution of Urban Rent and Residential Density." Journal of Economic Theory, 4, 1972, 329-354.

Mundlak, Y., "Elasticities of Substitution and the Theory of Derived Demand." Review of Economic Studies, 35, 1968, 80-95.

Muth, R., Cities and Housing. Chicago: University of Chicago Press, 1969.

_____, "The Derived Demand for Urban Residential Land." Urban Studies, 8, 1971, 243-254.

_____, "The Demand for Nonfarm Housing." In Matthew Edel and Jerome Rothenberg (eds.), Readings in Urban Economics. New York: MacMillian, 1962.

_____, "The Derived Demand Curve for a Production Factor and the Industry Supply Curve." Oxford Economic Papers, 16, 1964, 221-34.

_____, "Numerical Solution of Urban Residential Land-Use Models." Journal of Urban Economics, 2, 1975, 307-332.

_____, "The Spatial Structure of the Housing Market." Papers of the Regional Science Association, Part VII, 1961, 207-220.

Nelson, R. R., Park, M. J., and Kalachak, E. D., Technology, Economic Growth and Public Policy. Washington, D.C.: The Brookings Institute, 1967.

Niedercorn, J. H. and Bechdolt, B. V., Jr., "An Economic Deviation of the 'Gravity of Law' of Spatial Intro-duction." Journal of Regional Science, 9, 1969, 273-82.

Oberhofer, W. and Kamenta, S., "A Genera Procedure for Obtaining Maximum Likelihood Estimators in Generalized Regression Models." Econometrica, 43, 1973, 579-590.

Olcott's Land Value Blue Book for Chicago. Chicago: Olcott Co., (1910-1970).

Oster, S. M. and Quigley, J. M., "Regulatory Barriers to the Diffusion of Innovation: Some Evidence From Building Codes." The Bell Journal of Economics, 8, 1977, 361-377.

Pendleton, W. C., The Value of Highway Accessibility. Ph.D. dissertation, Department of Economics, University of Chicago, 1963.

Pigou, A. C., Economics of Welfare. London: Macmillian, 1932.

Quandt, R. E., "The Estimation of the Parameters of a Linear Regression System Obeying Two Separate Regimes." Journal of the American Statistical Associations, 53, 1958, 873-880.

_____, "Tests of the Hypothesis that a Linear Regression Systems Obeys Two Separate Regimes." Journal of American Statistical Association, 55, 1960, 324-30.

_____, "A New Approach to Estimating Switching Regressions." Journal of American Statistical Association, 67, 1972, 306-310.

Reid, M. G., Housing and Income. Chicago: University of Chicago Press, 1962.

Revankar, N. S., Production Functions with Variable Elasticity of Substitution and Variable Returns to Scale. Doctoral dissertation, University of Wisconsin, 1967.

_____, "The Constant and Variable Elasticity of Substitution Production Functions: A Comparative Study in U.S. Manufacturing." Mimeographed, Systems Formulation, Methodology and Policy Workshop Paper 6603, Social Systems Research Institute, University of Wisconsin, 1966.

_____, "A Class of Variable Elasticity of Substitution Production Functions." Econometrica, 39, 1971a, 60-71.

_____, "Capital-Labor Substitution, Technological Change and Economic Growth: The U.S. Experience, 1929-1953." Metroeconomica, 23, 1971b, 154-174.

Richardson, H. W., "On the Possibility of Positive Rent Gradients." Journal of Urban Economics, 4, 1977, 60-68.

Ricks, B., Real Estate Investment: The Investment Process, Investment Performance and Federal Tax Policy (Report of the Real Estate Investment Project for the United States Treasury Department, 1968).

Rosenberg, B., "A Survey of Stochastic Parameter Regression." Annals of Economic and Social Measurement, 2, 1973a, 381-397.

Rosenberg, B. and McKibben, W., "The Prediction of Systematic and Specific Risk in Common Stocks." Journal of Financial and Quantitative Analysis, 8, 1973b, 317-333.

Rubenfeld, D., "Urban Land Prices: Empirical and Theoretical Essays." Working Paper No. 13, M.I.T. Joint Center for Urban Studies, Cambridge, Mass., 1972.

Sato, K., Production Functions and Aggregation. New York: North-Holland American Elseview, 1975.

Sato, R., "Linear Elasticity of Substitution Production Functions." Metroeconomia, 19, 1967, 33-41.

_____, "The Estimation of Biased Technical Process and Production Functions." International Economic Review, 11, 1970a, 179-208.

Sato, R. and Hoffman, R. F., "Production Functions with Variable Elasticity of Factor Substitution: Some Analysis and Testing." Review of Economics & Statistics, 50, 1968, 452-60.

Sato, Ryuzo, Koizumi, and Tetsunori, "Substitutability, Complementanity and the Theory of Derived Demand." Review of Economic Studies, 37, 1970b, 107-118.

Schuler, R. E., "The Interaction Between Local Government and Urban Residential Location." American Economic Review, 64, 1974, 682-696.

Schultz, C. L., Prices, Costs, and Output for the Post War Decade: 1947-1957. New York: C.E.D. Supp., 1962.

Singh, B., Nagar, A. L., Choudhry, N. K., and Raj, B., "On the Estimation of Structural Change: A Generalization of the Random Coefficients Regression Model." International Economic Review, 17, (2), 1976, 340-361.

Sirmans, C. F. and Redman, A. L., "Capital-Land Substitution and the Price Elasticity of Demand for Urban Residential Land." Land Economics, 55, 1979, 167-178.

_____, Kau, J. B., and Lee, C. F., "The Elasticity of Substitution in Urban Housing Production: A VES Approach." Journal of Urban Economics, 6, 1979, 407-415.

Smith, B. A., "The Supply of Urban Housing." Quarterly Journal of Economics, 65, 1976, 385-405.

Smith, A. F. M., "A General Baysian Linear Model." Journal of Royal Statistical Society, 35 (Series B), 1973, 67-75.

Smith, T. F., "An Axiomatic Theory of Spatial Discounting Behavior." Papers of the Regional Science Association, 35, 1975, 31-44.

_____, "A Choice Theory of Spatial Interaction." Discussion Paper No. 74, Regional Science Research Institute, Box 8778, Philadelphia, Pennsylvania, 1974.

Solow, R. M., "Congestion, Density and the Use of Land in Transportation." Swedish Journal of Economics, 1972, 161-173.

Stigler, G. J., The Theory of Price. New York: Macmillian, 1966.

Swamy, P.A.V.B., "Efficient Inference in a Random Coefficient Regression Mode." Econometrica, XXXVIII, 1970, 211-223.

Takayama, A., "On Biased Technological Progress." American Economic Review, 64, 1974, 631-639.

Taylor, P. J., "Distance Transformation and Distance Decay Functions." Geographical Analysis, 3, 1971, 221-38.

Theil, H., Principles of Econometrics. New York: John Wiley and Sons, Inc., 1971.

Tooze, M. J., 1976 "Regional Elasticities of Substitution in the United Kingdom in 1968." Urban Studies, 13, 1976, 35-44.

Upton, C., "An Equilibrium Model of City Size." Journal of Urban Economics, 10, (1), 1981, 15-36.

U.S. Bureau of Census, Census of Population and Housing Census Tracts, PHC 1, Washington, D.C., 1970.

U.S. Bureau of Census, Census of Population and Housing Census Tracts, PHC 1, Washington, D.C., 1970.

U.S. Department of Housing and Urban Development, Housing-FHA, Office of Management, Washington, D.C., (Selected Years).

Wallace, T. D., "Weaker Criteria and Tests for Linear Restrictions in Regression." Econometrica, 42, 1972, 689-698.

Wallace, T. D. and Ashar, V. G., "Sequential Methods in Model Construction." Review of Economics and Statistics, 54, 1972, 172-78.

Wallace, T. D. and Hassan, A., "The Use of Error Components in Combining Cross Section and Time Series Data." Econometrica, 37, 1969, 55-72.

Watkins, A., An Historical Approach to Systematizing the Process of Urbanization. Unpublished paper, Department of Government, University of Texas at Austin, 1975. Paper presented at the 1975 Regional Science Meetings in Boston.

Wendt, P. F. and Goldner, W., "Land Values and the Dynamics of Residential Location." Essays in Urban Land Economics, University of California, Los Angeles, 1966, 188-213.

Wheaton, W. C., (1982), "Urban Residential Growth Under Perfect Foresight." Journal of Urban Economics, 12, pp. 1-21.

White, K. J., "Estimation of the Liquidity Trap with a Generalized Functional Form." Econometrica, 40, 1972, 192-198.

White, M. J., "On Cumulative Urban Growth and Urban Density Functions." Journal of Urban Economics, 4, 1977, 104-112.

Wilson, A. G., Entropy in Urban and Regional Modeling. London: Pion, 1976.

_____, "A Statistical Theory of Spatial Distribution Models." Transportation Research, 1, 1967, 253-269.

_____, "Some New Forms of Spatial Interaction Models, A Review." Transportation Research, 9, (213), 1975, 167-179.

Wingo, L., Jr., Transportation and Urban Land. Washington, D.C.: Resources for the Future, Inc., 1961.

Witte, Ann D., "The Determination of Inter-Urban Residential Site Prices Differences: A Derived Demand Model with Empirical Testing." Journal of Regional Science, 15, 1975, 351-364.

_____, "An Examination of Various Elasticities for Residential Sites." Land Economics, 53, 1977, 401-409.

Yeates, M. H., "Some Factors Affecting the Spatial Distribution of Chicago Land Values, 1910-1960." Economic Geography, 19, 1969, 180-194.

Zarembka, P., "Functional Form in the Demand for Money." Journal of the American Statistical Association, 63, 1968, 502-511.

Zellner, A., "An Efficient Method of Estimating Seemingly Unrelated Regressions and Tests for Aggregation Bias." Journal of the American Statistical Association, 57, 1962, 348-368.

Zellner, A., Kmenta, J., and Drenze, J., "Specification and Estimation of Cobb-Douglas Production Function Models." Econometrica, 34, 1966, 784-795.

AUTHOR INDEX

# Research Annuals in Series in

# BUSINESS, ECONOMICS AND MANAGEMENT

**Applications of Management Science**
Edited by Randall L. Schultz, *School of Management, The University of Texas at Dallas*

**Perspectives on Local Public Finance and Public Policy**
Edited by John M. Quigley, *Graduate School of Public Policy, University of California, Berkeley*

**Public Policy and Government Organizations**
Edited by John P. Crecine, *College of Humanities and Social Sciences, Carnegie-Mellon University*

**Research in Consumer Behavior**
Edited by Jagdish N. Sheth, *School of Business, University of Southern California*

**Research in Corporate Social Performance and Policy**
Edited by Lee E. Preston, *Center for Business and Public Policy, University of Maryland*

**Research in Domestic and International Agribusiness Management**
Edited by Ray A. Goldenberg, *Graduate School of Business Administration, Harvard University*

**Research in Economic History**
Edited by Paul Uselding, *Department of Economics, University of Illinois*

**Research in Experimental Economics**
Edited by Vernon L. Smith, *Department of Economics, University of Arizona*

**Research in Finance**
Edited by Haim Levy, *School of Business, The Hebrew University and The Wharton School, University of Pennsylvania*

**Research in Governmental and Non-Profit Accounting**
Edited by James L. Chan, *Department of Accounting, University of Illinois*

**Research in Human Captial and Development**
Edited by Ismail Sirageldin, *Departments of Population Dynamics and Policital Economy, The Johns Hopkins University*

**Research in International Business and Finance**
Edited by H. Peter Grey, *Department of Economics, Rutgers University*

**Research in International Business and International Relations**
Edited by Anant R. Negandhi, *Department of Business Administration, University of Illinois*

**Research in Labor Economics**
Edited by Ronald G. Ehrenberg, *School of Industrial and Labor Relations, Cornell University*

**Research in Law and Economics**
Edited by Richard O. Zerbe, Jr., *School of Public Affairs, University of Washington*

**Research in Marketing**
Edited by Jagdish N. Sheth, *School of Business, University of Southern California*

**Research in Organizational Behavior**
Edited by Barry M. Staw, *School of Business Administration, University of California, Berkeley* and L.L. Cummings, *J.L. Kellogg Graduate School of Management, Northwestern University*

**Research in Personnel and Human Resources Management**
Edited by Kendrith M. Rowland, *Department of Business Administration, University of Illinois* and Gerald R. Ferris, *Department of Management, Texas A & M University*

**Research in Philosophy and Technology**
Edited by Paul T. Durbin, *Philosophy Department and Center for Science and Culture, University at Delaware.* Review and Bibliography Editor: Carl Mitcham, *New York Polytechnic Institute*

**Research in Political Economy**
Edited by Paul Zarembka, *Department of Economics, State University of New York at Buffalo*

**Research in Population Economics**
Edited by T. Paul Schultz, *Department of Economics, Yale University* and Kenneth I. Wolpin, *Department of Economics, Ohio State University*

**Research in Public Sector Economics**
Edited by P.M. Jackson, *Department of Economics, Leicester University*

**Research in Real Estate**
Edited by C.F. Sirmans, *Department of Finance, Louisiana State University*

**Research in the History of Economic Thought and Methodology**
Edited by Warren J. Samuels, *Department of Economics, Michigan State University*

**Research in the Sociology of Organizations**
Edited by Samuel B. Bacharach, *Department of Organizational Behavior, New York State School of Industrial and Labor Relations, Cornell University*

**Research in Transportation Economics**
Edited by Theordore E. Keeler, *Department of Economics, University of California, Berkeley*

**Research in Urban Economics**
Edited by J. Vernon Henderson, *Department of Economics, Brown University*

**Research on Technological Innovation, Management and Policy**
Edited by Richard S. Rosenbloom, *Graduate School of Business Administration, Harvard University*